How Australia Compares

How Australia Compares is a handy reference that compares Australia with 17 other developed democracies on a wide range of social, economic and political dimensions. Whenever possible, it gives not only snapshot comparisons from the present, but charts trends over recent decades or even longer.

Its scope is encyclopaedic, offering comparative data on as many aspects of social life as possible, from taxation to traffic accidents, homicide rates to health expenditure, and interest rates to internet usage.

It uses a highly accessible format, devoting a double-page spread to each topic, with tables on one page and a clear explanation and analysis on the facing page.

In each discussion the focus is to put the Australian experience into international perspective, drawing out the implications for its performance, policies and prospects.

Rodney Tiffen, Associate Professor in Government and International Relations at Sydney University, and Ross Gittins, Economics Editor of the *Sydney Morning Herald*, have gathered a fascinating array of information, and communicate the meaning of the figures in a clear and lively way.

How Australia Compares

RODNEY TIFFEN AND ROSS GITTINS

CAMBRIDGE
UNIVERSITY PRESS

PUBLISHED BY THE PRESS SYNDICATE OF THE UNIVERSITY OF CAMBRIDGE
The Pitt Building, Trumpington Street, Cambridge, United Kingdom

CAMBRIDGE UNIVERSITY PRESS
The Edinburgh Building, Cambridge CB2 2RU, UK
40 West 20th Street, New York NY 10011–4211, USA
477 Williamstown Road, Port Melbourne, VIC 3207, Australia
Ruiz de Alarcón 13, 28014 Madrid, Spain
Dock House, The Waterfront, Cape Town 8001, South Africa

http://www.cambridge.org

First published 2004

Printed in Australia by Ligare Pty Ltd

Typeface Palatino 9.5/11 pt   *System* LaTeX 2_ε [TB]

A catalogue record for this book is available from the British Library

National Library of Australia Cataloguing in Publication data

Tiffen, Rodney.
How Australia compares.
Bibliography.
ISBN 0 521 83578 X.
1. Australia – Politics and government – 2001– .   2. Australia – Economic conditions – 2001– .
3. Australia – Social life and customs – 2001– .   I. Gittins, Ross.   II. Title.
994

ISBN 0 521 83578 X

CONTENTS

READING THE TABLES

Rankings. When tables are not presented in alphabetical order, they are ordered according to one of the data columns in the table to facilitate comprehension. Most often this is according to the final column because this represents data for the most recent year. Sometimes it is the first data column. If the ordering is according to some other criterion, then the basis for the ranking is given at the bottom of the table.

Mean. All means given in the tables are unweighted arithmetic means. That is, all 18 countries contribute equally to calculating the mean, and it takes no account of the differing sizes of countries. Because our central purpose is comparison, this is the appropriate measure.

Germany. All 18 countries have had fairly stable boundaries over the last half century except for Germany. West and East Germany formally reunited on 3 October 1990. At that time West Germany's population was 62 million and East Germany's 16 million. As is the custom in most international statistics, in this book, unless otherwise indicated, figures for Germany up to 1990 are for West Germany and figures after 1990 are for the whole of Germany.

–   a dash in a table indicates missing data.

NA   indicates that data would not be applicable for that country for that category.

2000* indicates data is for 2000 or latest available year. This is a signal that many of the countries have data only from earlier years.

ACKNOWLEDGMENTS

Because the range of this book is so encyclopaedic, we have been very dependent on advice from a range of people more expert in particular areas. We would like to thank the following for kindly reading and commenting on particular sections of the book: Mark Armstrong, Deborah Brennan, David Braddock, Katrina Burgess, Mark Cooper-Stanbury, Michael de Looper, Steve Dowrick, Jon Fogarty, John Goss, Clive Hamilton, Tony Hynes, Lynelle Moon, Murray Print, Peter Saunders, Rodney Smith, Bruce Thom, Nick Wailes, Don Weatherburn, and Glenn Withers. Of course, all remaining errors of fact and interpretation are our own.

Linden Fairbairn, Ray Penn and Fiona Mackay of Sydney University's Fisher Library were enormously helpful, as also was Poonam Ramchand of Euromonitor. We would also like to thank Dominique Dalla-Pozza for assistance with the electoral data, and Peter Browne for early encouragement.

We would also like to thank Peter Debus and Karen Hildebrandt of Cambridge University Press for their forbearance during the painfully long gestation of this book. Even more we would like to thank our families, who put up with the book for a much longer period – Kathryn, Paul and Ruth and Claudia, Sandy and Katie.

ABBREVIATIONS

ABC	Australian Broadcasting Corporation	ICVS	International Crime Victims Survey
ABS	Australian Bureau of Statistics	IEA	International Energy Agency
AGPS	Australian Government Publishing Service	ILO	International Labour Organisation, Geneva
AIHW	Australian Institute of Health and Welfare	IMF	International Monetary Fund
ANU	Australian National University	IT	information technology
ATM	automatic teller machine	LAY	latest available year
BBC	British Broadcasting Corporation	LIC	low-income country
		LIS	Luxembourg Income Study
BMI	Body Mass Index	LLDC	least developed countries
BPI	Bribe Payers' Index	MFP	multi-factor productivity
CAT	computer assisted tomography	MRI	magnetic resonance imaging
CIA	Central Intelligence Agency	NAFTA	North American Free Trade Agreement
DCI	Christian Democratic Party	ODA	official development assistance
ECEC	early childhood education and care	OECD	Organisation for Economic Co-operation and Development
EFTPOS	electronic funds transfer at point of sale	OPEC	Organisation of Petroleum Exporting Countries
EIRO	European Industrial Relations Observatory	PAC	Pollution abatement and control
		PBS	Public Broadcasting Service
EU	European Union	PC	personal computer
FAO	Food and Agriculture Organisation	PISA	Programme for International Student Assessment
FDI	foreign direct investment	PPP	purchasing power parity
GATT	General Agreement on Tariffs and Trade	PR	proportional representation
		PYLL	potential years of life lost
GDI	Gender Development Index	R&D	research and development
GDP	Gross Domestic Product	SBS	Special Broadcasting Service
GEM	Gender Empowerment Measure	SIPRI	Stockholm Institute for Peace Research Incorporated
GNI	Gross National Income		
GNP	Gross National Product	SME	small and medium-sized enterprise
GST	goods and services tax		
HDI	Human Development Index	TI	Transparency International
HMSO	Her Majesty's Stationery Office	UN	United Nations
HREOC	Human Rights and Equal Opportunity Commission	UNDP	United Nations Development Programme
IALSs	International Adult Literacy Survey	UNHCR	United Nations High Commissioner for Refugees
ICT	information and communications technology	WHO	World Health Organisation
		WTO	World Trade Organisation

INTRODUCTION

'Australia is the best country in the world.' When people feel strongly about something, they often express themselves by making a comparative claim, but usually without taking the comparison seriously. Every country seems to invent myths about its own uniqueness ('Australia is the most egalitarian country in the world'), myths typically based on an ignorance of others. Mostly such casual comparisons flatter the country they are describing. More occasionally they indulge in self-flagellation ('Australia is the most over-governed country in the world, with the world's worst politicians') or express a cultural cringe ('We are always ten years behind America').

This book makes comparison its central purpose. It systematically compares Australia with 17 other countries, all affluent and stable liberal democracies, on a wide range of important social, economic and political phenomena.

Moreover, it seeks, whenever possible, not just to make snapshot comparisons from the present but to chart trends. While there is value in presenting comparisons frozen at a single point of time, it is more instructive to trace common or contrasting trajectories; whether all these countries are experiencing greater unemployment, increased health spending, rising crime rates and so on. There is an industry of politicians, journalists and market analysts devoted to intensively reporting short-term changes and sometimes exaggerating their significance. There is much less public effort devoted to analysing the medium and long term.

This book aims to go beyond the myopic preoccupation with the present that marks political controversies and most journalism to examine trends over the last decades and where possible, even longer. Such a procedure allows us more perspective on the extent (and sometimes the limits) of the change we have already experienced. More cautiously, it gives us some, though a very imperfect, basis for considering future developments. The future is rarely a simple extrapolation from the past, but charting secular trends is one tool for projecting future scenarios, and hence for planning and making policy decisions that will give societies a greater mastery of their destiny.

The 18 countries chosen all share central socio-economic characteristics. All have conquered, at least for the majority of their populations, the basic struggle for life, so that the average life expectancy in them all is at least 75 years. The bulk of their populations has access to sufficient nutrition, safe drinking water and adequate shelter. All have close to 100% basic literacy. All are among the most affluent societies in the world. All have capitalist mixed economies, with a strong public sector. All have been stable liberal democracies since at least the late 1940s, with constitutionally governed, largely non-violent political competition with different parties alternating in power while central institutions remain stable, and where the government is by some minimal criteria representative and publicly accountable. In addition a further condition of minimum size was imposed: that the countries have populations of at least 3 million. This criterion excluded Iceland (population 270 000) and Luxembourg (418 000), which otherwise would have been included.

The comparative strategy chosen for this book can be labelled bounded comparison, selecting a fairly large range of countries with sufficiently similar political, economic and social characteristics to make comparison illuminating. This of course does not mean these countries are identical with Australia. (It is a common fallacy for people to say two situations are not comparable when they mean they are not identical.) Rather it means that the similarities are sufficient to make the pattern of commonalities and contrasts interesting, and to illuminate policy choices and institutional differences.

Why compare? Comparison serves three major purposes. First, it helps us to see ourselves more clearly. As Rudyard Kipling wrote a century ago, albeit in a somewhat different spirit, what do they know of England who

1

only England know? In social science terms it allows us to delineate the individual case more precisely, to make explicit what might otherwise have remained unexamined. What we imagine to be unique may be common to many societies, while what we take for granted as the natural or only way of doing things may in fact be unusual or even unique.

Second, comparison expands our universe of possibilities. It increases our knowledge that there are alternatives – alternative policies, different institutional arrangements, contrasting cultural assumptions. Most policy discussions take place within a restricted frame of reference. Domestic contention tends to focus on our hopeless politicians, obstructive trade unions or rapacious corporations, looking only inward when looking outwards can suggest policy and social alternatives beyond the framework within which domestic politicians are casting the problem. Equally, while the focus of comparison tends to concentrate on differences and contrasts, commonalities are often just as important and interesting. When trends and problems are broadly shared among a number of countries the causes are unlikely to be solely home-grown.

Third, comparison is the social scientist's substitute for the experiment. We cannot subject whole societies to experimental testing, so disciplined comparison is our means for testing generalisations. The study of commonalities and contrasts allows us to be more disciplined in ascribing explanations and examining relationships. By charting similarities and differences, we can be more precise in our descriptions and more discriminating in our analyses.

While the potential value of comparative work is great, so unfortunately are the obstacles confronting it. One problem, common to all social science research, is particularly pronounced in comparative research: many of the most interesting and subtle aspects of socio-political life defy quantification or the construction of valid indicators to summarise in a simple manner their trends and differences. There is often truth in the charge that comparative measures are too crude to be meaningful. We do not claim that the tables in the following pages exhaust all there is to say

about the quality of social and political life in these countries, but they offer data that can set the parameters so that such qualitative discussions can proceed in a more informed way.

In terms of data quality, the two most central problems of comparative research are reliability and equivalence. Different countries often measure the same concept in different ways (or in some countries with problematic accuracy), making apparently comparable data in fact incomparable. The problem of equivalence means that comparing some isolated measure of behaviour may have very different meanings when put in its larger social context.

Although these problems are still pertinent, fortunately they have been greatly reduced over the last few decades. Care must still be taken with problems of comparability, but today's scholar has access to many more, and more extensive and harmonised, data banks than used to be the case. International bodies such as the United Nations and its member agencies, the World Bank, the IMF, the European Union, as well as commercial organisations and academics, have laboured to produce valid and reliable comparative data. In particular the many sections of the Organisation for Economic Cooperation and Development have produced a range of high-quality data on the relevant countries. Their work is the central resource for all interested in the comparative study of these advanced democracies, and we would like to think this book is testament to the importance and value of that work.

Although as will be evident we have been the beneficiaries of the competent work done by the professionals in these organisations, the frustrations have still been considerable. Discrepancies in data between different organisations often seemed inexplicable. One always had to be alert to changes or inconsistencies in the basis of measurement. Missing data for individual countries, often for no apparent reason, was another frequent irritant. As far as possible, we have only included tables where data was available for all 18 countries, to keep the basis for comparison as constant as possible. But we have often had to depart from this standard when the interest of the data outweighed its incompleteness.

This book differs from the two most common types of books calling themselves comparative, first in focusing consistently upon the same set of countries throughout and making comparison the key within each part. In academic studies, edited books calling themselves comparative are more accurately described as juxtapositions, as different authors tackle different countries in different ways, and the genuinely comparative element is minimal. Or else there may be comparative work, but the comparisons are based on convenience, without a consistent or theoretically bounded set of countries being compared.

While most academic studies focus intensively on one narrow area, our aim has been to produce an encyclopaedic source book. We have sought to provide a reference source offering comparative data on as many aspects of social life as possible, from taxation to traffic accidents, homicide rates to health expenditure, from interest rates to Internet usage. We have tracked economic indicators, but also demographic and social ones, and where possible different institutional and policy settings.

The second major source of comparative data is found in compendia of statistical information. Most are done by international agencies (sometimes constrained by diplomatic considerations to present their data in a neutral and non-controversial way), or by individuals whose primary aim is to put on record comprehensive data. These compilations often provide valuable data. But they are commonly not reader-friendly. Nor do they make any effort to explain for the non-specialist the value and limits of the measures they are reporting.

In contrast, in this book we have very deliberately exercised an editorial hand in the presentation of data. For example, we have been selective rather than comprehensive about the years for which data is presented (trying to keep tables clear, and making judgements about when added detail would add more clutter than extra meaning). Similarly, rather than invariably presenting tables with countries in alphabetical order, we have often listed them in hierarchical order according to the phenomenon being studied, so that the main ordering and differences between countries are more quickly apparent. (In such 'league tables' most people focus on rankings and differences, but as indicated earlier, what is often at least as important is how they have moved in common.)

Most importantly, this is not just a book of tables, but rather each table is accompanied by a commentary about the meaning of the data, including sometimes a discussion of its limits. In this way we have sought to provide the reader not only with reliable and pertinent data but with some discussion of its interpretation and significance. We try to probe the meaning of different measures, look at both common trends and countries which have performed quite differently from the norm, and sometimes sought to see whether there are any patterns in the differential performance of countries. In these discussions, however, as the title *How Australia Compares* indicates, we have always tried to put Australian experience into comparative perspective, invariably returning to the implications of these facts for considering Australia's performance, policies and prospects.

Table 1.1: Population

	Millions		
	1900	1950	2000
United States	76.0	152.3	282.6
Japan	43.8	83.8	126.6
Germany	56.1	68.4	82.8
United Kingdom	36.7	50.1	59.5
France	38.9	41.8	59.3
Italy	32.4	47.1	57.6
Canada	5.4	14.0	31.3
Australia	**3.8**	**8.3**	**19.2**
Netherlands	5.2	10.1	15.9
Belgium	6.7	8.6	10.2
Sweden	5.1	7.0	8.9
Austria	5.8	6.9	8.1
Switzerland	3.3	4.7	7.3
Denmark	2.4	4.3	5.3
Finland	2.7	4.0	5.2
Norway	2.2	3.3	4.5
Ireland	3.1	3.0	3.8
New Zealand	0.8	1.9	3.8

Table 1.2: Area and population density, 1998

	Population/km^2	Area (000 km^2)
Australia	**2**	**7 687**
Canada	3	9 976
Norway	14	324
New Zealand	14	269
Finland	15	338
Sweden	20	450
United States	29	9 372
Ireland	53	70
Austria	96	84
France	107	549
Denmark	123	43
Switzerland	172	41
Italy	189	301
Germany	230	357
United Kingdom	242	245
Belgium	335	31
Japan	335	378
Netherlands	385	41

Table 1.3: Population growth rates

	Population ratio 2000:1900	Annual growth rate 1900–1950 %	Annual growth rate 1950–2000 %
Canada	5.8	1.9	1.6
Australia	**5.0**	**1.6**	**1.7**
New Zealand	4.8	1.8	1.4
United States	3.7	1.4	1.2
Netherlands	3.1	1.3	0.9
Japan	2.9	1.3	0.8
Denmark	2.2	1.2	0.4
Switzerland	2.2	0.7	0.9
Norway	2.1	0.8	0.6
Finland	1.9	0.8	0.5
Italy	1.8	0.7	0.4
Sweden	1.8	0.6	0.5
United Kingdom	1.6	0.6	0.3
Belgium	1.5	0.5	0.3
France	1.5	0.1	0.7
Germany	1.5	0.4	0.4
Austria	1.4	0.4	0.3
Ireland	1.2	−0.1	0.5
Mean	2.5	0.9	0.8

Table 1.4: Population growth summary

Summary data by decades 1950–2000

	1950–60	1960–70	1970–80	1980–90	1990–2000
Mean growth rate (% pa)	1.0	1.0	0.6	0.5	0.6
Australian growth rate (% pa)	**2.3**	**2.0**	**1.4**	**1.5**	**1.2**
Fastest growing country and rate (% pa)	Canada 2.7	**Australia**	**Australia** Ireland	**Australia**	New Zealand 1.3
Slowest growing country and rate (% pa)	Ireland −0.5	Ireland 0.4	Germany Austria 0.1	Belgium Germany 0.1	Japan Italy 0.2
Australia's rank	2	1	=1	1	=2

1 PEOPLE
Population

One of the first concerns of the Australian federation was population. A Royal Commission was established to see 'whether we shall be able to people the vast areas of the continent which are capable of supporting large populations'. World War II brought a new intensity of concern with population. Australia's first Minister for Immigration, Arthur Calwell, said in 1948 that 'Additional population is Australia's greatest need. For security in wartime, for full development and prosperity in peacetime, our vital need is more Australians.'

Tables 1.1 to 1.4 both confirm and qualify Australians' traditional fears of being 'under-populated'. Table 1.2 shows that population density ranges from the sparseness of Australia's two persons/km^2 to the Netherlands' 385. On the other hand, in terms of population size, Australia is certainly not a minnow. It ranks in the top half of these countries, and 52nd among the 227 countries listed by the US Census Bureau. But it is dwarfed by the United States, the biggest European countries, and of course the most populous Asian countries: China 1.28 billion, India 1.03 billion and Indonesia 231 million.

More recently the emergence of trading blocs such as the European Union has allowed member nations to exploit economies of scale far beyond their individual size. However, no conceivable amount of population growth by Australia is going to change the crucial equations affecting either its economic or military prospects.

Neither is it likely that Australia will ever rank anywhere but near the bottom of league tables on population density. Merely to catch up with Norway and New Zealand's 14 people/km^2, Australia's population would have to increase to an improbable 107 million.

Rather, the differences in population density suggest that to some extent geography is destiny. The seven countries with the lowest population density all have substantial areas inhospitable to human settlement, with either desert or arctic wastes. At the other extreme, the area from Britain through the Low Countries into Germany has the densest population in Europe, while in Asia there is another centre of high population density running through Japan, Korea (population density 465/km^2) and some parts of China.

While these 18 countries show very different rates of population growth, and great changes in growth rates over time, socio-cultural factors and government policy seem more germane to explaining the differences than population density. The two countries with the greatest density, the Netherlands and Japan, are in the top third of countries in population growth for the whole century, though both slowed markedly over the last generation.

Population growth is most in favour among the four countries which grew out of the English New World settler colonies, and the difference was more pronounced in the second half of the century than the first. Only Australia, Canada and New Zealand more than doubled their population between 1950 and 2000. In contrast, half the countries – all European – grew by less than 50%. The cumulative impact of consistent differences in growth rates can be seen by comparing Australia and Austria, the fastest and slowest growing countries. In 1950, the difference in their populations was 1.4 million. By 2000, it was 11.1 million.

Taking the half century as a whole, Australia had the highest population growth rate, and as Table 1.4 shows, in each of the decades had either the highest or second highest growth. But as that table also shows, the population growth rate in all the countries was much slower in the last decades of the century.

Table 1.5: Life expectancy
Life expectancy at birth, years

	1900	1950	2000
Japan	44.5	63.9	80.7
Australia	**56.5**	**69.6**	**79.8**
Sweden	55.8	71.8	79.6
Switzerland	50.7	69.2	79.6
Canada	–	69.1	79.4
Italy	44.5	66.0	79.0
France	47.0	66.5	78.8
Norway	56.3	72.7	78.7
Netherlands	56.1	72.1	78.3
Belgium	47.1	67.5	77.8
New Zealand	59.4	69.6	77.8
Austria	40.1	65.7	77.7
United Kingdom	50.5	69.2	77.7
Finland	46.7	66.3	77.4
Germany	46.6	67.5	77.4
United States	49.3	69.0	77.1
Ireland	49.5	66.9	76.8
Denmark	54.6	71.0	76.5
Mean	50.3	68.5	78.3

Table 1.6: Male life expectancy
Male life expectancy at birth, years

	1960	2000
Japan	65.3	77.6
Sweden	71.2	77.4
Switzerland	68.7	76.8
Australia	**67.9**	**76.6**
Canada	68.4	76.3
Norway	71.3	76.0
New Zealand	68.7	75.7
Netherlands	71.5	75.5
Austria	65.4	75.4
Italy	67.2	75.3
France	67.0	75.0
United Kingdom	67.9	75.0
Germany	66.9	74.7
Belgium	67.7	74.4
Denmark	70.4	74.2
Ireland	68.1	73.9
United States	66.6	73.9
Finland	65.5	73.8
Mean	68.0	75.4

Table 1.7: Female life expectancy
Female life expectancy at birth, years

	1960	2000
Japan	70.2	84.6
France	73.6	82.5
Switzerland	74.5	82.5
Australia	**73.9**	**82.0**
Sweden	74.9	82.0
Canada	74.3	81.7
Italy	72.3	81.6
Norway	75.8	81.4
Austria	71.9	81.2
Finland	72.5	81.0
Belgium	73.5	80.8
New Zealand	73.9	80.8
Germany	72.4	80.7
Netherlands	75.4	80.6
United Kingdom	73.7	79.8
United States	73.1	79.4
Ireland	71.9	79.1
Denmark	74.4	79.0
Mean	73.5	81.2

Life expectancy

Politicians and social commentators are increasingly talking of the problems caused by the ageing of society. Although there are substantial policy issues posed by this demographic trend, it should be remembered that its most basic cause is good news: increased longevity. The ageing society was a problem the caveman never had to wrestle with.

The figures in Table 1.5 tell a great success story. During the course of the 20th century, average life expectancy in the advanced democracies rose by more than half: from around 50 years to nearly 80. Indeed according to James Riley, life expectancy at birth across the whole globe was only 30 in the year 1800 but had risen to 67 by the year 2000. Moreover, in both the developed and developing world life expectancy was predicted to keep on increasing in the first half of the 21st century, to produce a global mean life expectancy at birth of 76 in the year 2050.

Australia ranked second in Table 1.5, with life expectancy at birth now touching 80 years, and it was also second back in 1900. The rise was most dramatic in Japan, which went from having the lowest life expectancy in 1900 to the highest in 2000. It was particularly with its post-World War II prosperity and democracy that Japanese increases in life expectancy outpaced the other countries.

But the most notable aspect of the data is the commonality between the countries. Life expectancy in all of them increased substantially (somewhat less so in some of the already long-living north-west European countries). Now life expectancy in all 18 countries is closely grouped, all falling within a range of just over four years, and all still trending upward.

Both males and females are enjoying longer life spans, and life expectancy at birth is increasing by a similar number of years for both. Between 1960 and 2000 women's life expectancy in these countries had increased by 7.7 years and men by 7.4 years (Tables 1.6 and 1.7), so the gap between them increased marginally, with women on average expecting to live 5.8 years longer than men in the year 2000.

In every one of these countries women live longer than men. For whatever reason, the sex difference is greatest in France (7.5 years) and least in Norway and Denmark (4.6 and 4.8 years respectively). Among both males and females Australia ranks near the top, but again the outstanding feature of the tables is the close grouping and the shared trends towards greater life expectancy among both sexes and across all countries.

The OECD notes that these gains have been made possible by rising standards of living, improved working conditions, public health interventions and progress in medical care. It explains that improvements in life expectancy at birth actually reflect a decline in mortality rates at all ages, ranging from a sharp reduction in infant mortality to higher survival rates at older ages. The Australian Bureau of Statistics observed that in Australia longer life expectancy in the first half of the 20th century was because of a decline in deaths from infectious diseases, due to cleaner water and better sewerage systems, as well as initiatives like mass immunisation. Rises in life expectancy slowed in the decades after World War II largely because of increases in cardiovascular disease. In recent decades the enhanced life expectancy of older people has been a major source of increase.

It should be remembered that these figures offer the mean life expectancy for each country, and can conceal substantial differences between sub-groups of the population. Most dramatically, in Australia's case the life expectancy for indigenous people was almost 20 years lower than for whites. In 1996, the life expectancy for Aboriginal women was 61.7 years and for Aboriginal men 56.9 years.

Table 1.8: Birth rates

Live births per 1000 population

	1900	1950	2000
Ireland	23	21	15
New Zealand	26	26	14
United States	30	24	14
Australia	**27**	**23**	**13**
Norway	30	19	13
Denmark	30	19	12
France	21	21	12
Netherlands	32	23	12
United Kingdom	29	16	12
Belgium	29	17	11
Canada	29	27	11
Finland	33	25	11
Austria	35	16	10
Japan	32	28	10
Sweden	27	16	10
Switzerland	29	18	10
Germany	36	16	9
Italy	33	20	9
Mean	29	21	12

Table 1.9: Fertility rates

Average number of children born to each woman

	1900	1950	2000
United States	3.8	3.4	2.1
Ireland	–	3.3	1.9
Australia	**3.4**	**3.2**	**1.8**
New Zealand	–	3.5	1.8
Norway	4.1	2.6	1.8
Denmark	4.0	2.6	1.7
Finland	4.8	3.0	1.7
France	2.8	2.7	1.7
United Kingdom	3.4	2.2	1.7
Belgium	4.0	2.3	1.6
Canada	4.8	3.7	1.6
Netherlands	4.5	3.0	1.6
Sweden	3.9	2.2	1.5
Switzerland	3.3	2.3	1.5
Austria	4.9	2.1	1.4
Germany	4.8	2.2	1.4
Japan	5.2	3.6	1.4
Italy	4.4	2.3	1.2
Mean	4.1	2.8	1.6

Table 1.10: Age composition: young people

Proportion of population aged 15 or less

	1960	2000
New Zealand	32.9	22.9
Ireland	30.5	21.8
United States	30.8	21.3
Australia	**30.2**	**20.5**
Norway	25.9	20.0
Canada	33.7	19.1
United Kingdom	23.3	19.1
France	26.4	18.8
Netherlands	30.0	18.6
Denmark	25.2	18.5
Sweden	22.4	18.4
Finland	30.4	18.1
Belgium	23.5	17.6
Switzerland	23.5	16.8
Austria	22.0	16.7
Germany	21.3	15.3
Japan	30.2	14.6
Italy	22.4	14.5
Mean	26.9	18.5

Table 1.11: Age composition: ageing societies

	Proportion of population			
	aged 65 and over		aged 80 and over	
	1960	2000	1960	1999
Italy	9.2	17.7	–	4.0
Japan	5.7	17.3	0.7	3.6
Sweden	11.8	17.3	1.9	5.1
Germany	10.9	17.2	–	3.8
Belgium	12.0	16.6	1.8	3.6
France	11.6	16.1	2.0	3.7
Switzerland	10.2	15.8	1.5	3.8
United Kingdom	11.7	15.6	1.9	4.0
Austria	12.2	15.5	1.8	3.5
Norway	10.9	15.2	1.9	4.3
Finland	7.3	15.0	0.9	3.3
Denmark	10.6	14.8	1.6	3.9
Netherlands	9.0	13.6	1.4	3.2
United States	9.2	12.6	1.4	3.2
Canada	7.6	12.5	1.2	2.9
Australia	**8.5**	**12.3**	**1.2**	**2.8**
New Zealand	8.7	11.8	1.5	2.7
Ireland	10.9	11.2	1.9	2.6
Mean	9.9	14.9	1.5	3.6

Ranked in order of proportion aged 65+ in 2000.

Birth rates and the ageing society

Apart from increased life expectancy, the other cause of the ageing society is that people are having fewer children. Despite the glacial pace of such demographic revolutions, their long-term impact is a dramatic change in the age composition of society, as Tables 1.10 and 1.11 show.

The birth rate in the selected countries from the start of the 20th century to the end more than halved, down from 29 births per 1000 population to 12 (Table 1.8), with the reduction being more marked in the second half of the century. To some extent a reduction in the birth rate is a natural consequence of increased longevity. With a higher proportion of the population living well beyond the normal child-bearing years of 15–45, the birth rate falls for that reason alone. But this is only a small part of the explanation.

Table 1.9 shows the dramatic reduction in the number of children each woman is having: from a mean across the selected countries of 4.1 in 1900 to 1.6 in 2000. In all the countries except the United States, the fertility rate is now below the natural replacement level of 2.1 children per woman. In other words, if this rate continues, and without immigration, all these countries will eventually experience declining population size.

While the secular trend is clear and indisputable, it has not followed a smooth, linear progression. The discussion of the ageing society has become so prominent in recent years because the demographic hump of 'baby boomers' (people born in the decade and a half following World War II) is now reaching retirement age. In contrast, birth rates during the economic hardship of the 1930s depression and especially during the upheavals and suffering of the war had been reduced. For example, Chesnais' detailed figures on birth rates show that Australia's bottomed in 1934 at 16.4, in the depths of the depression. It did not reach such a low again until the mid-1970s, but has continued to decline ever since.

This is what makes the current dramatic decline in fertility historically unique. Normally falls in fertility have been associated with poverty and uncertainty, but this prolonged fall is happening amid unprecedented affluence. Clearly, however, all sorts of other factors – including the changed aspirations of women, the financial pressures of contemporary society, and the availability of reliable contraception – are also pertinent.

The inevitable result of increased longevity and reduced fertility is a change in the generational balance of society. Thus in the 40 years between 1960 and 2000, the number of children under 15 dropped as a proportion of the total populations of these countries by about a third: from 27% to 19%. Conversely the proportion 65 and over rose by a half: from 10% to 15%.

The trend is in the same direction in all 18 countries, though to varying degrees and with some differences in timing. Australia, like the other New World democracies and Ireland, remains a relatively young country in its age structure. On the whole, having children has remained somewhat more popular in these countries. While steadily increasing, Australia's proportion of older people of 12.3% in 2000 was only slightly higher than the level several European countries had already reached in 1960. Those countries with the highest proportion of older people, like Italy and Japan, combine high rates of longevity with low birth rates.

While the ageing society brings changes and challenges, there is considerable fuzziness in the framing of the issues. One concern is the increased ratio of dependent to economically productive members of society, but the proportion participating in the labour force is not simply a matter of demography but also of social institutions and attitudes. The labour force participation rate (see Table 4.1) is now at an historic peak because of the greatly increased proportion of women working.

Table 1.12: Inflow of immigrants

Net intake of immigrants

	Annual net number of immigrants 1980–94 (000s)	Net annual intake of immigrants per 1000 population 1980–94	Net number of immigrants 1950–2000 (000s)	Net intake of immigrants 1950–2000 as % of 2000 population
Australia	91.9	5.4	4 437	23.1
Canada	125.8	4.6	5 732	18.3
Germany	312.5	4.3	9 355	11.3
Switzerland	29.6	4.3	–	–
Austria	24.0	3.1	–	–
United States	622.1	2.5	30 304	10.7
Sweden	20.5	2.4	743	8.3
Netherlands	27.5	1.8	817	5.1
Norway	6.6	1.6	159	3.5
Italy	83.6	1.5	−846	−1.5
Denmark	6.4	1.2	–	–
Finland	5.1	1.0	–	–
France	59.5	1.0	4 691	7.9
Belgium	8.1	0.8	–	–
United Kingdom	40.9	0.7	408	0.7
Japan	−4.6	0.0	–	–
New Zealand	−0.3	−0.1	–	–
Ireland	−15.2	−4.3	–	–
Mean	80.2	1.8	5 580	8.8

Ranked in order of net annual intake per 1000 population, 1980–94.

Table 1.13: Scale of immigration

Foreign population as proportion of total population

Country	1980	1990	2000
Australia	20.6	22.3	23.6
Switzerland	14.3	16.3	19.3
Canada	16.1	16.1	17.4
United States	6.2	7.9	10.4
Austria	3.9	5.9	9.3
Germany	7.5	8.4	8.9
Belgium	9.0	9.1	8.8
France	6.8	6.3	5.6
Sweden	5.0	5.7	5.4
Denmark	2.0	3.1	4.8
Netherlands	3.8	4.6	4.1
Norway	2.1	3.4	4.1
United Kingdom	2.8	3.1	4.0
Ireland	2.2	2.3	3.3
Italy	0.6	1.5	2.4
Finland	0.3	0.5	1.8
Japan	–	0.9	1.3
Mean	6.1	6.9	7.9

No data on New Zealand. For Australia, the United States and Canada, figure refers to 'foreign-born'; in others to 'foreigners'.

Table 1.14: Immigrants and citizenship

Country	Mean annual number acquiring nationality 1990s (000s)	New citizens per year per 100 000 population (1990s)
Australia	118	610
Canada	146	466
Sweden	30	339
Netherlands	47	298
Belgium	27	262
Germany	208	251
Switzerland	14	195
Norway	8	176
France	102	173
Austria	14	170
United States	441	160
Denmark	6	106
United Kingdom	54	91
Finland	1	25
Italy	7	12
Japan	11	9

No data on Ireland or New Zealand.

Immigration

Tables 1.12 and 1.13 give testimony to the massive scale of Australia's postwar immigration program. Almost one in four of Australia's 2000 population was an immigrant. This is higher than for any other of these countries, and globally is second only to Israel.

The scale of immigration into the four English-speaking New World countries is much greater than for most European countries and Japan. Australia, Canada and the United States are rivalled only by Switzerland in the proportions of immigrants in their countries. The country receiving by far the largest number is the United States, with over 30 million migrants going to live there in the last half of the twentieth century.

Table 1.12 on the net intake of migrants combines figures on both immigration and emigration. Ireland and Italy have had more emigrants than immigrants over the period as a whole, though this has not been true in more recent years. The data on New Zealand is incomplete, but that country has a very distinctive pattern, marked by both high immigration and high emigration. In recent years its net intake has been positive, but for many periods the number of emigrants was greater. National estimates put New Zealand's foreign-born population at around 20%, which would make it second to Australia.

The OECD's data on immigration in Table 1.13 suffers from a lack of harmonisation, as well as irritating incompleteness. Most basically, there is a disjunction between the New World countries which report the number of foreign-born living in that country, and most European countries which report 'foreigners', that is, non-citizens living in that country. In Germany, for example, the 3 million ethnic Germans who moved to Germany from Eastern Europe from the late 1980s on are not considered foreigners, but children born in Germany to Turkish parents, who are not citizens, are considered as foreigners.

Although the extent of the difference varies between countries, generally foreign-born would be the higher figure. In the six European countries, where we have data for both, the difference is greatest in Sweden (11.3% cf 5.4%) and the Netherlands (10.1% cf 4.2%).

Another aspect confounded by the two methods of reporting data is that countries differ not only in their receptiveness to newcomers but in their willingness to allow immigrants to become citizens. Table 1.14 shows that Australia, followed by Canada, was proportionately the most welcoming in terms of numbers of immigrants acquiring citizenship.

As the natural rate of population growth has declined, 'population policy' has become a more explicit subject for consideration, and some have proposed increased immigration as a substitute for natural growth. Whatever the policy merits of this, the domestic political unpopularity of immigration is likely to dictate against it. The dominant trend has been for the developed countries to reduce their rates of immigration. In the days of labour shortages in the 1960s, Germany and some other European countries welcomed 'guest workers', but in the current environment of high unemployment, policies to encourage high immigration are not likely to be revived.

Indeed immigration has become a sensitive political issue in many democracies in the last few decades, with anti-immigration political parties and some racist violence, as well as generally more restrictive official policies and rhetoric. Sometimes there has been a direct connection with external change but generally there is only a very weak relationship between the intensity of domestic political conflict and the proportion of immigrants in a society.

In a globalised world, however, the policies of the host countries are not the only factors affecting the outcome. In 2000, at least 160 million people were living outside their country of birth or citizenship, up from 120 million in 1990. This is only a small proportion of the global population of 6 billion, but it is still indicative of a world on the move and likely to continue so.

Table 1.15: Asylum-seekers

	Total asylum-seekers 1980–89 (000s)	Total asylum-seekers 1990–99 (000s)	% of asylum-seekers accepted 1980–89	% of asylum-seekers accepted 1990–99
Germany	704.9	1 879.5	15.0	9.9
United States	395.8	897.6	26.8	43.9
United Kingdom	44.7	374.1	78.9	43.4
Netherlands	55.1	321.5	19.7	38.8
France	285.0	296.9	52.0	20.0
Switzerland	100.0	282.7	24.8	38.5
Canada	174.3	277.1	36.0	61.8
Sweden	139.1	245.5	86.5	49.7
Belgium	46.6	180.4	57.4	24.5
Austria	127.7	129.7	51.6	13.1
Australia	**1.3**	**92.7**	**19.5**	**13.1**
Italy	42.8	89.5	34.2	15.6
Norway	23.9	54.1	62.7	42.8
Denmark	35.6	25.0	96.6	73.5
Ireland	–	18.4	–	17.9
Finland	0.4	18.2	33.3	50.8
New Zealand	–	10.9	–	17.6
Japan	0.9	1.1	27.9	9.2
Total	2 178.1	5 243.2	Mean 45.2	32.5

Ranked according to total number of asylum-seekers in the 1990s.

Table 1.16: Refugees

	Total refugees accepted 1990–99 (000s)	Refugees per 100 000 population 1990s
Sweden	160	1 799
Denmark	69	1 302
Germany	976	1 188
Switzerland	82	1 127
Norway	48	1 064
Austria	83	1 019
Canada	293	935
Netherlands	139	876
Australia	**112**	**582**
United States	1 089	395
Ireland	1	324
Finland	13	246
United Kingdom	137	230
New Zealand	9	223
France	130	221
Belgium	18	176
Italy	23	40
Japan	42	33

Table 1.17: Immigrants and eligibility categories

Percentage of immigration intake in main eligibility categories, 1998

	Family	Skills	Refugee	Other
Sweden	43	1	33	23
Denmark	32	11	15	42
Canada	61	23	13	3
Australia	**27**	**34**	**11**	**28**
France	69	21	10	0
New Zealand	42	49	9	1
United States	72	12	8	8
United Kingdom	47	45	5	2
Switzerland	30	33	3	34
Mean	47	25	12	16

Ranked according to % of refugees. No data for other countries.

Refugees and asylum-seekers

In 1951 the United Nations adopted a Convention relating to the Status of Refugees, which has been further refined since. It was embraced by many countries, including Australia, in the aftermath of the Holocaust suffered by the Jews under Nazi Germany, and with huge numbers fleeing communist rule in Eastern Europe.

Since then the nature of refugees has changed: from being principally a European phenomenon to one occurring mainly in the Third World. Moreover the number of refugees is on a scale that no one envisaged in 1951. The UNHCR said there were 19.8 million people of concern to it at the start of 2002. The major categories were 12 million refugees (i.e. those deemed to meet the requirements of the 1951 Convention) and 6.3 million internally displaced people (i.e. forced from their homes but still within their own country).

The great majority of refugees flee to a neighbouring country, often in groups, and then live in camps there. By far the largest number of refugees in 2001 came from Afghanistan, with 3.8 million Afghan refugees in Pakistan and Iran. Next biggest were the half a million refugees from Burundi in Tanzania and a similar number of Iraqi refugees in Iran.

Most of the time such situations receive only passing attention in the West. From the late 1980s on there have been two new developments. The wars in the former Yugoslavia, and other political convulsions following the fall of communism, created the largest number of refugees in Europe for a generation. 'Between 1983 and 2000, some 5.7 million foreigners applied for asylum in Europe, with peak numbers between 1989 and 1993. One half of all the cases were in Germany.'

The second development has been the increasing number of asylum-seekers (numbering 940 000 globally in 2002 according to the UNHCR). The phrase strictly refers to those whose refugee status has not yet been determined, but it also points to a new phenomenon: people prepared to travel a very considerable distance, maybe half a world, beyond the country they are fleeing. Often they arrive as individuals rather than part of a group. Sometimes they enlist the aid of 'people smugglers', and so their plight becomes confounded with the quantitatively much bigger issue of illegal immigration. (In 2000, there were an estimated 8.5 million illegal immigrants in the United States.)

Asylum-seekers are then a much more confronting and impatient presence for Western governments to have to deal with than their compatriots waiting in a camp for years for their case to be adjudicated and perhaps then acted on. As a result refugee politics has become much more contentious, especially when mixed with the considerable anti-immigrant sentiment already existing, and the growing trade in illegal immigration.

The issue reached a new urgency in Australia with the arrival of asylum-seekers in the early 1990s, and then in increasing numbers in the late 1990s. In recent years there have been many claims and counter-claims about Australia's relative generosity in accepting refugees. Tables 1.15 and 1.16 show how much larger the problem was in the 1990s than the 1980s. They also show that it was much more urgent for several other countries than for Australia, and that several exceeded Australia in the numbers of refugees accepted, both proportionately and absolutely. Table 1.17 shows that refugees still constituted only about one in eight of immigrants in 1998.

Table 1.15 also points to the political plasticity of the legal determination of who constitutes a refugee. Judgements varied greatly between countries: 97% of asylum-seekers applying to Denmark in the 1980s were accepted, compared with only 9% of those applying to 1990s Japan. Judgements also became more stringent as numbers increased, with the mean acceptance rate falling by about a quarter between the 1980s and 1990s. Austria's acceptance rate, for example, dropped from 52% to 13%.

Table 1.18: Urbanisation
Percentage of population living in urban areas

	1975	2000	% urban population in cities > 750 000
Belgium	95	97	11
Australia	**86**	**91**	**69**
Netherlands	88	90	16
United Kingdom	89	90	30
Germany	81	88	51
New Zealand	83	86	31
Denmark	82	85	30
Sweden	83	83	31
Canada	76	79	54
Japan	76	79	50
United States	74	77	55
France	73	75	30
Norway	68	75	–
Austria	67	67	40
Italy	66	67	34
Switzerland	56	67	21
Finland	58	59	33
Ireland	54	59	45
Mean	75	79	37

Table 1.19: Population distribution: largest city

	Largest city	Population (millions) (2000)	City's share national population %	City's population density (000s/ sq mile) (1980s)
Japan	Tokyo	26.44	20.9	29.9
USA	New York	16.64	6.0	23.3
France	Paris	9.62	16.3	53.3
UK	London	7.64	13.0	11.1
Germany	Berlin	6.54	4.5	8.8
Canada	Toronto	4.65	14.9	2.5
Italy	Rome	4.25	4.7	4.9
Australia	**Sydney**	**3.66**	**19.4**	**2.1**
Austria	Vienna	2.07	25.2	9.6
Sweden	Stockholm	1.58	17.8	9.0
Denmark	Copenhagen	1.38	26.2	13.9
Finland	Helsinki	1.17	22.6	6.8
Belgium	Brussels	1.12	11.0	16.1
Netherlands	Amsterdam	1.11	7.0	8.6
NZ	Auckland	1.10	28.5	–
Norway	Oslo	1.00	21.9	2.7
Ireland	Dublin	0.99	26.4	2.8
Switzerland	Zurich	0.98	13.3	10.1

Urbanisation

All the selected countries are overwhelmingly urban societies, and most have been for generations, so that in the last quarter of the 20th century the proportion was still moving up but only slowly (from an overall mean of 75% to 79% – Table 1.18). As Tables 1.18 and 1.19 also show, they are all countries with one or more very big cities. All have at least one city of 1 million or more people (though Dublin and Zurich just qualify), and ranging up to the megalopolises of Tokyo and New York.

One would think that it is a simple matter to determine how many people live in urban areas and to give the size of cities, but in fact it is fraught with methodological disputes. There is no agreed operational definition of what constitutes an urban area, though in practice the different estimates are usually fairly close to each other.

There is much more difference in estimating the size of individual cities. The first source of difference concerns how to draw their boundaries, and there are two main variations. One is to follow the administrative borders, the city proper. This has the virtue of clarity, but is not valid in any sense to do with the workings of the social unit, and is normally much smaller than the 'real' city. The other measure is called the urban agglomeration. The *United Nations Statistical Yearbook* (2000: 54) defines an urban agglomeration as the city or town proper and also the suburban fringe or thickly settled territory lying outside, but adjacent to, its boundaries. This is more realistic, but more subject to variable estimates, as the functional limits of a city are more ambiguous than its legal boundaries. For this book, we have followed the UN estimates of city sizes, but readers should be aware that different sources often give substantially different city sizes.

Australia has a very distinctive pattern of population distribution. In some ways the sparseness of Australia's total population density (Table 1.2) presents a curious contrast with its high degree of urbanisation and the proportion living in big cities. Australia ranks second in the proportion living in urban areas (91%), wedged between the very high population density countries Belgium and the Netherlands. As Table 1.18 also shows, it has by far the highest proportion living in cities larger than 750 000 people: 69% compared with second placegetter, the United States, having 55%, and an 18-country mean of 37%.

Despite Australia's huge population increase over the last half century, there is little indication that its distribution is becoming less concentrated. According to the figures of Lane et al., in 1950 Sydney had 18% of Australia's population, while Table 1.19 shows that by 2000 this had increased slightly to 19.4%. Whatever else it might be doing, Australia's population increase is not filling up the outback.

Moreover Australia is unusual in having two premier cities of almost equal size, so that together Sydney and Melbourne probably occupy a larger share of Australia's population than the two largest cities in any other of these countries. Many countries have only one dominating city, with the second largest one much less significant in size and national importance. Although not close to the size of Tokyo or New York, Sydney and Melbourne are by international standards relatively large cities.

The obverse of this lopsided concentration into a few major cities is that Australia has a lot more sparsely populated areas than most of the other countries. The relative abundance of space is also evidenced by the low population density Sydney has compared with the other cities in the list (Table 1.19). According to this 1980s estimate, Paris, the most densely populated of the cities, had 25 times as many people per square mile as the relatively sprawling Sydney.

Table 1.20: Human Development Index
Possible range = from .000 (lowest) to 1.000 (highest)

	HDI 1980	HDI 2000
Norway	.877	.942
Sweden	.872	.941
Canada	.883	.940
Australia	**.861**	**.939**
Belgium	.861	.939
United States	.884	.939
Netherlands	.873	.935
Japan	.878	.933
Finland	.856	.930
Switzerland	.886	.928
France	.863	.928
United Kingdom	.848	.928
Denmark	.876	.926
Austria	.854	.926
Germany	.859	.925
Ireland	.831	.925
New Zealand	.855	.917
Italy	.846	.913
Mean	.865	.931

Human Development Index

The United Nations Development Programme has devised an index designed to create a broader view of a country's development than using income alone, which is too often equated with well-being. The Human Development Index is a simple summary measure of three dimensions of the human development concept: living a long and healthy life, being educated, and having a decent standard of living. The UNDP's rationale is that:

> Human development is a process of enlarging people's choices . . . The three essentials are for people to lead a long and healthy life, to acquire knowledge and to have access to resources needed for a decent standard of living. If these choices are not available, many other opportunities remain inaccessible.

The HDI combines the three dimensions into one index, and scores each country for each year, with a summary measure between zero and one, a higher score meaning greater human development. The idea of a composite scale is to go beyond the limits of individual measures to capture more of the integrity and complexity of the social experience. In this book we also use three others constructed by the UNDP: their human poverty scale, and their two measures of gender inequality.

An intrinsic problem of constructing composite indicators is that even if all the elements can be scored satisfactorily there is always an arbitrariness about their weightings, how the components are combined into one scale. Inevitably, such indices are surrounded by methodological disputes. They should not be viewed as more than a convenient way of encapsulating and simplifying complex realities in order to facilitate comparison and to go beyond the partiality of individual components.

Because it is a measure designed to be applied globally, the HDI is a fairly blunt instrument for distinguishing the finer aspects of social development within these rich countries, all of which score very highly on it. While Norway tops the list, only .003 points separate the first six countries, which include Australia. Overall, these 18 countries are very closely clustered, the top 16 falling between .942 and .925. Only New Zealand (because of economic performance) and Italy (because of educational performance) lag somewhat.

As is to be expected, there is a strong correlation between the economic wealth of nations and their HDIs. While the mean in 2000 for these 18 countries was .931, for the world as a whole it was .722, and in sub-Saharan Africa it was only .421.

However, when the HDI departs substantially from GDP per capita, it shows how aggregate national measures of income cannot be unthinkingly equated with human well-being. It is necessary to give due regard to distribution and to the development of social infrastructure. Two components of the HDI – longevity and educational attainment – by their nature reflect the prevalence through the whole population of these attributes. Pakistan and Vietnam, for example, have similar levels of income, both just below USPPP$2000, but Vietnam has a substantially higher HDI of .688 compared with Pakistan's .499 because it has done much more to translate that income into human development.

The HDI was originally constructed in 1990 and has been calculated retrospectively for most countries back to 1980. The improvement in the mean from .865 to .931 shows that in central respects, life is still improving for people in these 18 high-income countries, and that their relatively greater wealth is also translated into giving greater life chances to a substantial proportion of their citizens. Similarly, throughout the developing world most countries' HDIs increased steadily between 1980 and 2000. However, some poor African countries afflicted by AIDS and several of the countries that were part of the former Soviet Union suffered reversals during that 20-year period.

Table 2.1: Constitutional history

	Continuous national elections since	Date of independence	Date of current constitution
United States	1788	1776	1789
Norway	1814	1905	1814
Belgium	1831	1830	1931
United Kingdom	1832	–	–
Netherlands	1848	1814	1814
Switzerland	1848	–	1874
New Zealand	1852	1907	1852
Denmark	1855	–	1953
Sweden	1866	–	1975
Canada	1867	1867	1982
Australia	**1900**	**1901**	**1900**
Finland	1906	1917	1919
Ireland	1921	1921	1937
Austria	1945	1918	1920
France	1946	–	1958
Italy	1946	1861	1948
Japan	1946	–	1947
Germany	1949	–	1949

Table 2.2: Male suffrage

Year when male suffrage was substantially achieved

France	1848
Germany	1869
United States	1870
New Zealand	1879
Belgium	1893
Norway	1897
Australia	**1901**
Denmark	1901
Finland	1906
Austria	1907
Sweden	1909
Italy	1912
Netherlands	1917
Canada	1917
United Kingdom	1918
Ireland	1918
Switzerland	1919
Japan	1925

Table 2.3: Female suffrage

Year when female suffrage was substantially achieved

New Zealand	1893
Australia	**1902**
Finland	1906
Norway	1913
Denmark	1915
Germany	1918
Austria	1918
Canada	1918
United Kingdom	1918
Ireland	1918
Sweden	1919
Netherlands	1919
United States	1920
France	1944
Italy	1946
Japan	1947
Belgium	1948
Switzerland	1971

2   GOVERNMENT AND POLITICS
Constitutional history

These 18 countries were chosen because for the last half-century they have continuously fulfilled minimal requirements for liberal democracies. This emphatically does not mean that they are ideal democracies, or that there is not scope for further improvement towards democratic ideals. It means that for this period their governments have always changed according to constitutional processes, and that they have had to face regularly scheduled, fairly conducted, competitive elections in which (close to) all the adult population could vote. They have thus met the criteria of inclusiveness, competitiveness and constitutionality.

Australia is one of about half a dozen countries which had continuous elections throughout the 20th century. Another half-dozen or so West European countries were always democratic except for periods of foreign occupation in wartime. A third group achieved varying degrees of representative democracy but later relapsed into authoritarian rule, before again becoming liberal democracies after the end of World War II. This group includes the vanquished Axis powers, but also France (which had the most constitutionally problematic change during the contemporary period, namely the 1958 accession of de Gaulle to the presidency, and subsequent change from the Fourth to the Fifth Republic).

The tables reveal that democracy rarely emerged fully blown and did not come all at once to these countries. Rather there was often a series of struggles. In particular, many countries manifested degrees of competitiveness and pluralism before they became fully inclusive.

One aspect hidden by the neat listing of dates in the tables on suffrage is the messiness of the process. Sometimes suffrage was achieved incrementally as increasing concessions were won. Some countries moved through a series of halfway houses, such as imposing property or literacy requirements. In some federations, such as the United States, different states had different regulations for permitting voter registration. Similarly, before Federation the Australian colonies all had their own constitutional practices, and New South Wales has had continuous elections since 1855.

In the dates for Tables 2.2 and 2.3, we have followed as far as possible the consensual scholarly judgements. Our criterion has been to assign the date when the nature of the country's politics was substantially transformed in a democratic direction rather than when democratic principles were fully embraced. Sometimes, as in Australia, suffrage was achieved for the great majority of the population but in crucial ways fell short of properly embracing democratic principles. With federation in 1901, at the Commonwealth level, there was full adult suffrage for all whites, but Aboriginals did not gain those rights until 1962.

As females gained the right to vote in some countries, they were still subjected to more restrictions than men, for example having a higher minimum age. Some countries maintained a prohibition on women standing for parliament even after they achieved the vote.

The data suggests some recurring patterns. For several countries, the coming of independence also brought the coming of liberal democracy, whether independence was achieved through an evolutionary or a revolutionary process. The oldest is the most famous. The American War of Independence produced the world's oldest surviving democratic constitution, and began a process of democratic elections that has continued ever since.

A second pattern is that extensions of the franchise often followed wars. After the sacrifices suffered by societies in World Wars I and II, refusal of pressures towards greater democracy became unsustainable. The other variant of course was the imposition of democratic institutions by the Allies after World War II in the belief that bringing democracy would make the defeated countries less aggressive in future.

Some scholars have suggested that Australia and New Zealand should be judged as the first liberal democracies to achieve substantially universal suffrage for both men and women. Lijphart argues convincingly that New Zealand has the stronger claim at national level because Maoris and women had full voting rights from 1893.

Table 2.4: Heads of state and heads of government

Head of state

	Title	Executive power	Selected by
Belgium	Monarch	Weak	
Denmark	Monarch	Weak	
Japan	Monarch	Weak	
Netherlands	Monarch	Weak	
Norway	Monarch	Weak	
Sweden	Monarch	Weak	
United Kingdom	Monarch	Weak	
Australia*	**Monarch**	**Weak**	**Government**
Canada*	Monarch	Weak	Government
New Zealand*	Monarch	Weak	Government
Germany	President	Weak	Legislature – special
Italy	President	Weak	Legislature
Austria	President	Weak	Public
Ireland	President	Weak	Public
Switzerland	President	Strong	Legislature
Finland	President	Strong	Public
France	President	Strong	Public
United States	President	Strong	Public

* Australia, Canada and New Zealand have as head of state the British monarch, represented nationally by a governor-general, selected by the national government.

Heads of state and heads of government

Nearly all the liberal democracies in Table 2.4 maintain a distinction between the head of state and the executive head of government. The only outright exception is the United States of America where both are embodied in the office of the presidency. In three other cases there is a mixing or sharing of roles. The Swiss system reflects that country's peculiar traditions, with a rotating presidency (and prime ministership) investing less power in the individual leader and more in the collective, multiparty cabinet than any other country.

France and Finland have what is sometimes called a semi-presidential system or dual executive. They have a popularly elected president holding the highest office in the land, elected for a longer period than parliament and with the power to dissolve it, but also needing to rule with parliament, which is the institution where governments must be formed. Both systems arose out of problems of parliamentary instability.

In the other 14 cases, the head of state lacks substantial executive power. The most basic question then is why do these countries maintain the two separate roles: head of state and head of government. Typically there are three components of the head of state's role. The first is symbolic: to preside at ceremonial events, embodying national unity above the fray of political conflict. This may include helping celebrate national festivals and leading national mourning. It includes an international role, dealing with visiting dignitaries and representing the nation abroad.

The second common role is to certify that proper procedures are being followed in legislation and elections. The third is to have a 'reserve power' role in times of crisis. These latter two roles are infrequently exercised. They arise most often when the rules of the game – the national Constitution – do not unambiguously cover an eventuality that has arisen. In particular, they occur when the workability of the national parliament is in doubt. When heads of state do intervene in political conflicts, it is likely to involve considerable conflict, potentially threatening their capacity to fulfil the consensual parts of the role.

Perhaps the most surprising aspect of Table 2.4 is the persistence of monarchies. If the three former British colonies, whose head of state is the British monarch, represented nationally by a governor-general, are included, then a majority of countries remain monarchies. These monarchs enjoy varying degrees of prestige in their respective countries. However, their current roles and the routes to them are essentially similar. They retain their privileges and ceremonial roles, often religious as well as national, in return for renouncing all attempts to influence politics.

Sometimes this renunciation has been codified, such as in the post-World War II Japanese constitution which specified that the emperor must play no role in politics. More usually it is a matter of convention, and/or buried in constitutional double talk, which invests all power in the monarch while simultaneously withdrawing any opportunity to exercise it. The Danish constitution, for example, proclaims that 'the King shall have supreme authority in all the affairs of the Realm', but also that the signature of the King is valid only when accompanied by the signatures of his ministers.

In the four cases where there is a president with weak executive power, Ireland and Austria directly elect the president. In both cases partisan competition is less fierce than in Australia. On occasion in Ireland there was only one candidate, and in Austria nearly all presidents have been former diplomats. In Italy parliament elects the president, and both the role and selection of the president are currently a matter of some dissatisfaction. In Germany a specially convened assembly, nominated by both national and provincial parliaments, elects the president without debate. It is hard to know if any of these provides a clear model for a possible Australian republic.

Table 2.5: Federal and unitary state structures

	System	Regional governments
Australia	**Federal**	**6 states**
Austria	Federal	9 *Länder*
Belgium	Federal	10 provinces
Canada	Federal	12 provinces
Germany	Federal	16 *Länder*
Switzerland	Federal	26 cantons
United States	Federal	50 states
Denmark	Unitary	
Finland	Unitary	
France	Unitary	
Ireland	Unitary	
Italy	Unitary	
Japan	Unitary	
Netherlands	Unitary	
New Zealand	Unitary	
Norway	Unitary	
Sweden	Unitary	
United Kingdom	Unitary	

Table 2.6: Centralisation of taxation

Country	Type of state	Central government share* %
Austria	F	81
Australia	**F**	**79**
Germany	F	70
United States	F	69
Switzerland	F	65
Belgium	F	64
Canada	F	55
Ireland	U	98
Netherlands	U	97
United Kingdom	U	96
New Zealand	U	94
Italy	U	91
France	U	90
Norway	U	82
Finland	U	78
Japan	U	74
Sweden	U	69
Denmark	U	68
Federal Mean		69
Unitary Mean		85
Overall Mean		79

F = Federal; U = Unitary.
* including Social Security.

Table 2.7: Procedures for judicial review and constitutional amendment

	State system	Judicial review of government decisions	Constitutional amendment
Australia	**F**	**Y**	**Referendum/veto**
Austria	F	Y	Referendum/veto
Belgium	F	Y	Referendum/veto
Canada	F	Y	Referendum/veto
Germany	F	Y	Referendum/veto
Switzerland	F	N	Referendum/veto
United States	F	Y	Referendum/veto
Denmark	U	Y	Ref. majority
France	U	Y	Ref. majority
Ireland	U	Y	Ref. majority
Italy	U	Y	Ref. majority
Japan	U	Y	Referendum/veto
Norway	U	Y	Referendum/veto
Sweden	U	Y	Parl. majority
Finland	U	N	Referendum/veto
Netherlands	U	N	Referendum/veto
New Zealand	U	N	Parl. majority
UK	U	N	Parl. majority

F = Federal; U = Unitary; Y = Yes; N = No.

Table 2.8: National referendums

Number of national referendums, 1945–95

	Number of referendums
Switzerland	275
Italy	29
Australia	**23**
Ireland	20
Denmark	13
France	12
New Zealand	10
Sweden	3
Austria	1
Belgium	1
Canada	1
Finland	1
Norway	1
United Kingdom	1
Germany	0
Japan	0
Netherlands	0
United States	0

Federalism

All states of any size and complexity devolve some power to more local units of administration. What differentiates a federal system is that the powers of regional governments are constitutionally entrenched. The devolved powers cannot be reduced on the whim of the national government. So a federal system consists of a division of power between a national government and regional governments, each guaranteed by the constitution to be independent within defined spheres.

Federal systems tend to occur in countries which are larger in area, or where there are distinctive social interests (e.g. linguistic or ethnic) in different areas of the country. But what best explains whether a particular country has a federal or unitary system is not geography but history. In almost all the federations in Table 2.5, the current nation-state was formed by the coming together of existing more localised units of government, and in the formation of the new country some federal guarantees were enshrined. In most cases there has been no change in the regional boundaries since the original constitutions were framed (though some like the United States have added new territories). Australia, for example, had six states in 1901 when its population was less than 4 million, and still has six states as its population approaches 20 million.

The exception to this pattern is Belgium, which adopted a new fully federal constitution in 1993, following prolonged conflict between the Flemish and Walloon linguistic groups.

The arguments for federation include that it encourages greater responsiveness to local needs and variations and brings government closer to the people, that it allows diversity and experimentation in government, and that it provides a brake on the growth of centralised power. The arguments against involve issues of duplication and inefficiency, and of lack of accountability through buck-passing the responsibility for problems between different levels of government.

Some institutional characteristics follow almost automatically from federalism. One is judicial review of government decisions to ensure that one level of government is not abrogating the prerogatives of the other. (Switzerland with its unique mix of institutions is the only federation not to have such judicial review.) Of course countries have judicial review of parliamentary decisions for many reasons of constitutional protection, and, as Table 2.7 shows, most unitary systems also have this provision.

In addition, a federal constitution places some rigidity on how that constitution can be changed. Again, it is the nature of all constitutions to be relatively stable and difficult to change. Although three countries (Sweden, Britain and New Zealand) allow the possibility of change through a simple parliamentary majority, most others require a referendum. In addition, federal countries typically require not only a popular majority, but must meet 'federal' criteria as well. In Australia constitutional change needs a majority vote in a majority of states.

Referendums are rare in nearly all these countries. Table 2.8 shows that in the half-century following World War II, more than half the countries had either a single referendum or none at all. Many referendums have not been about constitutional changes but about particularly sensitive issues, for example whether to join the European Union. Only in Switzerland, with its provision for quarterly plebiscites, are referendums a normal part of a country's political life.

Finally, federalism should not be confused with decentralisation. As Table 2.6 shows, central governments tend to raise a greater share of tax in unitary systems than in federal ones, but the correlation is weak. In some federal systems, including Australia, the central government raises a higher proportion than it does in many unitary states. This is one of federalism's dilemmas. Either there is an administratively messy system with each state imposing its own taxes or there is 'vertical fiscal imbalance', where one layer of government is responsible for raising money that is spent on services provided by another, and so a potential recipe for mutual irresponsibility.

Table 2.9: Parliamentary structures

	Number of chambers	Strength of bi-cameralism	Method of election	Powers of second house
Australia	**Bi-cameral**	**Strong**	**Incongruent**	**Symmetrical**
Germany	Bi-cameral	Strong	Incongruent	Symmetrical
Switzerland	Bi-cameral	Strong	Incongruent	Symmetrical
United States	Bi-cameral	Strong	Incongruent	Symmetrical
Belgium	Bi-cameral	Weak	Congruent	Symmetrical
Italy	Bi-cameral	Weak	Congruent	Symmetrical
Netherlands	Bi-cameral	Weak	Congruent	Symmetrical
Austria	Bi-cameral	Weak	Congruent	Asymmetrical
Canada	Bi-cameral	Weak	Incongruent	Asymmetrical
France	Bi-cameral	Weak	Incongruent	Asymmetrical
Ireland	Bi-cameral	Weak	Congruent	Asymmetrical
Japan	Bi-cameral	Weak	Congruent	Asymmetrical
United Kingdom	Bi-cameral	Weak	Incongruent	Asymmetrical
Denmark	Uni-cameral			
Finland	Uni-cameral			
New Zealand	Uni-cameral			
Norway	Uni-cameral			
Sweden	Uni-cameral			

Parliamentary structures

Table 2.9 reveals a paradox. While being bi-cameral (having two parliamentary chambers) is the norm among the selected countries, having a strongly bi-cameral system is very much the exception.

Only five countries are uni-cameral. They include five of the six smallest countries in population and area. All are unitary rather than federal systems. At the other extreme only four, all federal countries, have strongly bi-cameral legislatures. The other nine countries have weakly bi-cameral systems.

To meet the criterion of strong bi-cameralism, a country must have an upper house whose composition is distinctively different from the lower house (incongruent) and where both houses have substantially the same powers (symmetrical). Even in these systems, the houses nearly always differ in their prerogatives: often the government must retain the confidence of the lower house to remain in government, the Prime Minister must be drawn from that house, and money bills must originate there. The important criterion is that all (or most) legislation must obtain a majority in both houses.

The weakly bi-cameral systems fall into two types. The first are those where the upper house lacks the powers of the lower house. They may have the power to criticise or delay legislation but not to block it. The capacity to alter the government's timing varies: the British House of Lords can delay legislation for one year; the Austrian upper house for only eight weeks, and the Japanese upper house for 60 days. The influence of these second chambers rests in moral suasion, their power to propose, disclose or embarrass. In the face of a patient and determined majority government, however, they are powerless.

In the second group, legislation must pass both houses, but because of the method of selection, the upper house tends to be an echo of the lower one. In several of these the upper house is either appointed or indirectly elected, and so tends to reproduce the partisan complexion of the government.

The source of the paradox – the prevalence of weak bi-cameralism – probably lies in the origins of parliamentary rule. Typically, upper houses were based on the suspicion and fear of popular majority rule. They were preserves of privilege to act as a check on the popularly elected lower house (and hence the vertical imagery of upper and lower). Most evolved beyond these anti-democratic origins, either by changing their method of selection or by increasingly limiting their powers.

Among the four countries with strong bi-cameralism, the situation derived from their federal origins. In each, the lower house directly reflects population size, while the upper house is based on ensuring all the regions are equally represented. Although there is no genuine sense today in which these second chambers act as states' houses, their distinctive composition can provide a check on the lower house majority.

The manner in which this happens is of course contingent on election results. For most of its history, the Australian Senate was merely a rubber stamp for the House of Representatives, but no government since 1981 has commanded a majority there. This has meant that the government must negotiate either with the opposition or with minor parties to get legislation enacted. In the United States and Switzerland, there is scope for conference committees where members from both houses seek to negotiate a solution. In both, in the absence of majority approval in both houses, the legislation lapses. In Australia there is scope to resolve such a deadlock by going to a double dissolution election, and, if needed and wanted, for a joint sitting of both houses of parliament after the election to review the legislation. The first and only such joint sitting was after the 1974 election.

Table 2.10: Governments, ministers and parliaments

	Does government depend on confidence of legislature?	Are ministers members of parliament?	Cohesion of governing parties
Australia	Y	Y	H
Ireland	Y	Y	H
Japan	Y	Y	L
New Zealand	Y	Y	H
United Kingdom	Y	Y	H
Austria	Y	M	H
Belgium	Y	M	H
Canada	Y	M	H
Denmark	Y	M	H
Germany	Y	M	H
Italy	Y	M	L
Netherlands	Y	N	H
Norway	Y	N	H
Sweden	Y	N	H
Finland	N	M	H
France	N	N	H
Switzerland	N	N	L
United States	N	N	L

Y = Yes; M = Mostly; N = No; H = High; L = Low.

Table 2.11: Government and opposition in parliament

	Government control over parliament	Opposition influence via parliamentary committees
Australia	**High**	**Low**
Canada	High	Mixed
France	High	Low
Ireland	High	Low
Japan	High	Mixed
New Zealand	High	Low
Switzerland	High	High
UK	High	Low
Austria	Medium	High
Belgium	Medium	High
Germany	Medium	High
Norway	Medium	High
Denmark	Low	High
Finland	Low	Mixed
Italy	Low	Mixed
Netherlands	Low	High
Sweden	Low	High
United States	Low	Mixed

Table 2.12: Government control over legislation

	Proportion of bills introduced by government	Proportion of government bills passed
Netherlands	99	85
Australia	**96**	**90**
New Zealand	94	98
Ireland	91	90
Norway	90	99
Switzerland	88	Most
Denmark	66	89
Japan	64	76
Germany	64	99
Austria	63	96
Finland	52	98
France	43	82
United Kingdom	36	92
Italy	29	51
Belgium	23	–
Canada	21	60
Sweden	8	Most

No data given for United States.

Parliamentary operations

Parliament is the central institution of representative democracy. It is the forum where the elected representatives are meant to express the will of the people on a continuing basis, and through which executive government is responsible to the people. However, the institutional means by which different countries seek to achieve responsible, representative government differ enormously.

Perhaps the most fundamental issue is whether the survival of the government depends on having the continuing confidence of the legislature. As Table 2.10 shows, the most common pattern among the selected countries is the British and Australian one, where governments must retain the support of parliament to stay in office.

Different liberal democracies have devised two diametrically opposed institutional solutions to achieving responsible executive government. In the British-derived Australian system, ministers must be members of parliament and continually answerable to parliament. In other systems, which emphasise the separation of powers, cabinet ministers must not be members of parliament. In the middle are a range of countries where nearly all ministers are members of parliament but which occasionally go outside parliament for some appointments.

The problem with ministers not being members of parliament is that the legislature runs the risk of lagging behind in knowing what executive government is doing. The problem with ministers being part of parliament is that in an age of tight party discipline, if the government has a secure majority, parliament simply rubber-stamps what executive government wants.

These contrasts demonstrate that summary judgements about the relative power of different legislatures can be misleading. In one sense the US Congress has less power than parliaments in the British tradition, in that except in extraordinary circumstances it cannot unseat the executive government and that government is not continually accountable to it. On the other hand it is a much less predictable institution: the executive government has less power to determine its legislative outcomes than in most parliamentary systems. In American scholar Bingham Powell's terms (Table 2.11), government control over its agenda is low, and the party not in office has more scope to influence deliberations, for example through committee processes, especially given the low level of cohesiveness and discipline in American political parties.

To a considerable extent the differences in the flavour of national parliaments and relations between executive governments and their legislatures are determined by the logic of institutional structures and partisan competition. But beyond this, countries have built their own traditions about how parliament should function. Institutionally, the relationship between executive government and the parliament in Sweden is not too different from a British-style Westminster system, but their traditions are very different. As Tables 2.11 and 2.12 suggest, the Swedish parliamentary system works much more through negotiation and deliberation in committees. Most legislation emerges in this way and then has a very high probability that parliament will approve it.

The Inter-Parliamentary Union's figures in Table 2.12 are dated, from the 1980s, and many proportions will have changed while others, such as the proportion of government bills passing, fluctuate with the partisan balance. Although the table is suggestive of institutional patterns, in other ways it is too crude to fully capture parliamentary processes. Britain, for example, has a high number of private members' bills introduced into the House, but in practice the legislative agenda is much more concerned with the government's agenda.

Neither Table 2.11 or 2.12 takes sufficient account of Australia's bi-cameral system. Table 2.12 does not allow for legislation being amended, for example. The government still has a high degree of control over the legislative agenda, and in this sense Australian parliamentary committee processes are not as developed or influential as in many other democracies, but as an avenue for scrutiny of government actions and social issues their importance is growing.

Table 2.13: Electoral systems

	Single or multi-member constituencies	Type of vote	Number of members in lower house
Plurality systems			
Canada	Single	Categorical	295
United Kingdom	Single	Categorical	651
United States	Single	Categorical	435
Majority systems			
Australia	**Single**	**Ordinal**	**150**
France	Single	Categorical/Double ballot	577
Mixed systems			
Germany	50:50 Single: Multi	Categorical	656
Italy	79:21 Single: Multi	Categorical	630
Japan	60:40 Single: Multi	Categorical	500
New Zealand	50:50 Single: Multi	Categorical	120
Proportional systems			
Austria	Multi	Categorical	183
Belgium	Multi	Categorical	150
Denmark	Multi	Categorical	179
Finland	Multi	Categorical	200
Ireland	Multi	Ordinal	166
Netherlands	Multi	Categorical	150
Norway	Multi	Categorical	165
Sweden	Multi	Categorical	349
Switzerland	Multi	Ordinal	200

In bi-cameral systems the table gives the electoral system of lower houses only.

Table 2.14: Electoral disproportionality

Index of disproportionality: 1 = completely proportional; the higher the score, the more disproportional

	Index 1971–96	Type of system
Austria	1.3	PR
Netherlands	1.3	PR
Germany	1.5	Mixed
Denmark	1.8	PR
Sweden	1.8	PR
Switzerland	3.0	PR
Belgium	3.1	PR
Finland	3.2	PR
Ireland	3.2	PR
Italy	3.8	PR
Norway	4.7	PR
Japan	5.3	SNTV
Australia	**10.2**	**Single**
Canada	12.2	Single
New Zealand	14.6	Single
United Kingdom	14.7	Single
United States	15.6	Single
France	18.7	Single

PR = proportional representation; SNTV = single non-transferable vote, now discarded Japanese system where voter casts just one vote, but several representatives are elected.

Table 2.15: Number of national elections, 1945–2002

	Number of national elections 1945–2002	Maximum interval between elections (years)	Average interval between elections (years)
Australia	**23**	**3**	**2.3**
Denmark	23	4	2.3
Japan	22	5	2.4
New Zealand	20	3	2.7
Austria	18	4	2.9
Belgium	18	4	2.9
Canada	18	5	2.9
Sweden	18	4	2.9
Ireland	17	5	3.1
Netherlands	17	4	3.1
Finland	16	4	3.3
France	16	5	3.3
United Kingdom	16	5	3.3
Germany	15	4	3.5
Italy	15	4	3.5
Norway	15	4	3.5
Switzerland	14	4	3.8
United States	14	4	3.8

Electoral systems

These countries are all representative democracies, so how they turn the wishes of the people into elected representatives is crucial. Electoral systems long fascinated scholars, who recognised that the formula by which people are elected has a large impact on who is elected. But in recent years their importance has come into popular view as well.

During the 1990s, three countries – New Zealand, Japan and Italy – changed their electoral system as part of addressing wider political discontents in their societies. Then in 2000 the world focused on the machinations in Florida as the result of the American presidency hung by ambiguous markings from the voting machines. Moreover, for the first time since 1888, the peculiar American electoral college system resulted in the candidate who got the greater popular vote losing.

Among the variety of electoral systems, the first key variable is whether each electorate chooses one member or several. If there is only one winner, it means that those who voted for another candidate will not be represented. So one difference is that multi-member systems tend to produce more proportional outcomes – the representatives elected more closely match the votes cast – as Table 2.14 shows.

Another, less commented on aspect of electoral methods is whether voters must choose only one option (categorical) or whether they can express their preferences among candidates (ordinal). In single-member systems where there are more than two candidates, under a categorical system (as in the United Kingdom and United States), the voter must make a strategic as well as a preferential decision. Which candidate do I prefer? and do they have a chance of wining? Many voters who might prefer a minority candidate decide not to 'waste' their vote on someone who has no chance of winning.

Apart from preferential voting, another solution to this problem is the one used in France. If no candidate obtains a majority in the first round, there is a run-off between the leading vote-getters. This system drew wide criticism in the 2002 presidential election, where none of the 17 candidates got more than 20% of the vote in the first round, resulting in a second round between President Chirac and the extreme right party leader, Le Pen.

Multi-member, proportional representation systems generate different problems. People can be elected with a low percentage of the vote. In the Netherlands, where the whole country is one single electorate, which elects 150 members, a candidate can be elected with less than 1% of the vote. In some variants (now largely discarded) when voters could only choose one party list or another, they had no influence over which individuals were elected. This gave the party machines, which decided the list rankings, great power. Most list systems now give voters some choice among individual candidates. Some, such as the Irish system (also used in the Australian Senate), also allow voters to express preferences across parties.

The most common criticism of PR systems is that they rarely produce clear parliamentary majorities, and that the result can therefore be weak and/or unstable government. Accidents of arithmetic can give disproportionate power to small groups holding the balance of power.

Perhaps because both systems have their drawbacks, mixed member systems, using both methods simultaneously, are becoming more popular. Witness the three countries which changed their electoral method in the 1990s.

Last but not least, only Australia and New Zealand have a maximum three-year interval between elections. The frequency of elections is also influenced by parliamentary stability and by whether the system allows governments to go to the polls early to maximise their electoral chances. Table 2.15 shows that Australia has had the equal most elections among these countries since 1945.

In sum, Australia has a distinctive and home-grown electoral mix: frequent elections, preferential, single-member voting for the House, contrasting voting systems for its two houses of parliament, and compulsory voting (Table 2.25).

Table 2.16: Election campaigns

	Are paid political ads allowed?	Is there free broadcast time to parties?	Was there a debate between leaders in the last election?
Australia	Y	Y	Y
Austria	Y	Y	Y
Canada	Y	Y	Y
Germany	Y	Y	Y
Italy	Y	Y	N
Japan	Y	Y	Y
Netherlands	Y	Y	Y
New Zealand	Y	Y	Y
Sweden	Y	Y	Y
United States	Y	N	Y
Belgium	N	Y	Y
Denmark	N	N	Y
Finland	N	N	Y
France	N	Y	Y
Ireland	N	Y	Y
Norway	N	N	Y
Switzerland	N	Y	N
United Kingdom	N	Y	N

Y = Yes; N = No. Information is for late 1990s.

Table 2.17: Election finance

	Public funding of parties' campaigns	Compulsory reporting of contributions and/or expenditures	Are parties' reports publicly audited?	Limits on contributions or expenditures?
Australia	Y	Y	Y	N
Austria	Y	Y	Y	–
Canada	Y	Y	Y	N
France	Y	–	–	Y
Germany	Y	Y	Y	N
Ireland	Y	–	–	Y
Italy	Y	Y	Y	N
Japan	Y	Y	Y	Y
Norway	Y	–	–	–
United States	Y	Y	Y	Y
Belgium	N	–	–	–
Denmark	N	–	–	Y
Finland	N	–	–	–
Netherlands	N	N	N	–
New Zealand	N	–	–	Y
Sweden	N	N	N	N
Switzerland	N	–	–	–
United Kingdom	N	Y	N	Y

Y = Yes; N = No. Information is for late 1990s. Data for columns 2–4 is very incomplete.

Election campaigns and finances

These tables capture only very partially the nature of electioneering in the different countries. While electoral systems are stable, and the rules and procedures summarised in Table 2.13 provide a good guide to actual practice, the rules governing electioneering are not so well documented, nor in some areas so rigorously enforced. Many countries including Australia require compulsory disclosure of campaign funds, for example, but such laws are typically rather ineffective. The politicians drafting them are often keener on creating than closing loopholes. Outside the practices circumscribed by law, campaign practices are constantly evolving as each party seeks to maximise its chances.

Although there are still divergent traditions and rules, as seen in the tables, the most general trend is towards what has been called an Americanisation of campaigning practices. The media-centred nature of campaigning is apparent both in advertising and as the arena in which leaders confront each other. This has reinforced the movements towards centralised control of campaigning and towards making it much more expensive. The trend towards capital-intensive campaigning has been blamed for making meaningful participation more difficult and for making political finance ever more important.

When Anthony Smith surveyed media election practices in liberal democracies around 1980, only four countries – Australia, Canada, Japan and the United States – allowed paid political television advertising. By the mid-1990s, as Table 2.16 shows, ten of the 18 countries allowed it.

Similarly, televised confrontations between the leaders were fairly rare, conducted sporadically in America (famously between Kennedy and Nixon in 1960, but then not again until Carter versus Ford in 1976) but almost nowhere else. Now they are the norm in 15 of the 18 countries. The United Kingdom does not (yet) have debates but has developed distinctive television formats for the questioning of leaders and candidates.

As campaigns have become more expensive, so there has been greater demand for public subsidies to help the parties, while the issue of political finance has become more contentious. There are two sources for the concern. One is the potential for the trading of donations for political favours. The other is that elections will be won by the richest party.

Tables 2.16 and 2.17 suggest that two trends go together. One is that public subsidies are more common in those countries which have paid political advertising. This association is not invariable, but it holds in 12 of the 18 countries. The other is that wherever there is public funding (the top ten countries in Table 2.17), there is also some compulsory reporting of campaign donations and expenditure. Despite the gaps in the data, it seems clear that political parties have chosen a trade-off: accept some scrutiny of their private finances in return for securing access to public money.

One source of the differences in campaign practices is the relative importance of privately owned versus state-owned television channels. Where television began as a state monopoly (see Chapter 13) political advertising (along with television advertising more generally) was slower to develop. The relative importance of public broadcasting also points to the contrasting importance of free broadcasting time given to the parties. In Australia, the parties only get free time on the government channels. The somewhat boring format of these telecasts means that only few are watching, compared with the many who watch paid political advertisements on the commercial channels.

Elections are the central act in democratic governance, but it would be fair to say there is widespread unease both about how electoral competition is financed, and what media formats facilitate informed choice.

Table 2.18: Party systems

	Effective number of parties 1971–96	Capsule description of system
New Zealand	2.0	Essentially two-party
Australia	**2.2**	**Essentially two-party**
United Kingdom	2.2	Essentially two-party
Canada	2.4	Essentially two-party
United States	2.4	Essentially two-party
Austria	2.7	Principally two party with signif. 3rd
Germany	2.8	Principally two party with signif. 3rd
Ireland	2.8	Principally two party with signif. 3rd
France	3.5	Moderately multi-party
Sweden	3.5	Moderately multi-party
Norway	3.6	Moderately multi-party
Japan	4.1	Moderately multi-party
Netherlands	4.7	Strongly multi-party
Denmark	5.1	Strongly multi-party
Finland	5.2	Strongly multi-party
Italy	5.2	Strongly multi-party
Belgium	5.5	Strongly multi-party
Switzerland	5.6	Strongly multi-party

Table 2.19: Electoral choice and government formation

	Identifiability of prospective governments in pre-election choice	Formation of government post-election
Australia	**High**	**Usually clear result**
Canada	High	Usually clear result
France	High	Usually clear result
Germany	High	Usually clear result
Japan	High	Usually clear result
New Zealand	High	Usually clear result
United Kingdom	High	Usually clear result
United States	High	Usually clear result
Sweden	High	Variable
Norway	Variable	Usually clear result
Austria	Variable	Variable
Ireland	Variable	Variable
Denmark	Variable	Negotiation after
Netherlands	Variable	Negotiation after
Belgium	Low	Negotiation after
Finland	Low	Negotiation after
Italy	Low	Negotiation after
Switzerland	Low	Negotiation after

Party systems and electoral choice

The most obvious difference when looking at political contests in these democracies is that some involve an essentially two-sided competition, while in others there are a larger number of competing parties. It would seem a simple matter to count the number of parties, but in fact it is a complicated exercise. To be relevant, some account has to be taken of the relative size of political parties and their role in forming government.

Political scientists have used the concept of the 'effective' number of parties to count not just their existence but their importance and support. There are continuing methodological disputes about the best way to calculate this, but Lijphart's figures in Table 2.18 provide a good guide to the party competition in the selected countries. As can be seen from the descriptions in the right-hand column, they fall into four broad groups, from essentially two-party to strongly multi-party.

In the period 1971–96 the English-speaking countries all fell at the two-party end of the spectrum. All had single-member electoral systems. The association between electoral system and party system is strong. However, parties with a strong regional basis can lead to more than two parties, and this has become more pronounced in Canada. The New Zealand party system is changing with its change of electoral system.

Next is a grouping of three countries where there is a third party whose support can influence the formation of governments. In each there has been principally a choice between two main parties for government, with some variability or uncertainty about who might join with whom in coalition. (The great Italian scholar of political parties, Giovanni Sartori, famously classified the relationship between the Liberal and National Parties in Australia as a coalescence rather than a coalition between two independent parties, given the high degree of co-operation between them.)

As we move into the multi-party systems, the patterns become ever more various. Some revolve around one dominant party. For most of the contemporary era, two countries, Japan and Italy, had dominant party systems. The Christian Democrats in Italy and the Liberal Democratic Party in Japan were far bigger than their competitors and invariably, until the early 1990s, formed the basis of the government. In Sweden most governments have either been based on the Social Democrats (often able to form government in their own right) or a coalition of much smaller conservative parties.

As the number of parties increases, the nature of the electoral choice changes. G. Bingham Powell has analysed (Table 2.19) how in half these countries the nature of the government (either single-party or coalition) they are electing is usually clear to the public before the election. But in four strongly multi-party systems, there is not such a clearly identifiable choice between competing aspirants for government.

Similarly, although no one can predict all the permutations of party balances an election might throw up, in the two-party systems it is normally clear after the election who will form the government. In other countries where many different groups are represented, there can still be considerable uncertainty about what coalition will form government. A party's own vote might go down, but because of the balance of competing powers its chance of being in government may increase. The lottery aspect of who forms government should not be exaggerated, but in some countries the post-election negotiations can be protracted.

We should conclude by noting the absence of one important type of comparative study: how similar or how different are election-night parties under the different systems? One might guess that there is drowning of sorrows and toasting of success everywhere. But in Denmark and the Netherlands, for example, unlike Australia, they rarely know for certain on election night what the composition of the new government will be, and such uncertainty might be a sobering influence.

Table 2.20: Types of government

Parliamentary situation of governments,
1945–98

	Minority government	Surplus coalition	Single party or minimal winning coalition
New Zealand	0	0	100
UK	5	0	95
Australia	**0**	**7**	**93**
Austria	5	5	90
Germany	0	19	81
Belgium	9	15	77
Canada	35	0	65
Japan	22	18	60
Ireland	45	0	55
Netherlands	0	56	44
Norway	58	0	42
Sweden	67	0	34
Finland	29	48	23
France	14	70	16
Denmark	86	0	14
Switzerland	0	89	12
Italy	38	56	6

United States not included.

Table 2.21: Duration of governments

	Number of governments 1945–98	Mean duration (days)
France	56	336
Italy	55	331
Finland	45	404
Japan	40	461
Belgium	36	511
Australia	**28**	**661**
Denmark	28	638
Germany	25	660
New Zealand	24	794
Norway	24	775
Sweden	24	752
Austria	20	917
Canada	20	947
Ireland	20	900
Netherlands	20	879
United Kingdom	19	995
Mean	30	685

Switzerland not included because governments change after one year as a constitutional requirement. United States not included because of its presidential system.

Table 2.22: Early cabinet terminations

Early cabinet terminations, 1950–99

	Internal dissent	Lack of support	Total
Italy	16	16	32
Belgium	14	5	19
Finland	14	3	17
France	8	9	17
Denmark	2	10	12
Germany	7	2	9
Netherlands	6	3	9
Ireland	2	5	7
Japan	2	4	6
Sweden	3	1	4
Norway	1	3	4
Austria	3	0	3
Canada	0	3	3
Australia	**0**	**0**	**0**
New Zealand	0	0	0
Switzerland	0	0	0
United Kingdom	0	0	0

US not included.

Table 2.23: Outcomes of elections

Proportion of national elections leading to changes in party composition of government, 1945–2002

	Major change %	Slight change %	No change %
Ireland	65	0	35
France	50	0	50
United States	50	0	50
United Kingdom	44	0	56
New Zealand	40	0	60
Norway	40	0	60
Netherlands	35	41	24
Canada	33	0	67
Denmark	32	27	41
Finland	29	41	29
Belgium	28	33	39
Australia	**22**	**0**	**78**
Sweden	22	0	78
Italy	20	53	27
Austria	17	17	67
Japan	15	0	85
Germany	14	0	86
Mean	33	12	55

Switzerland not included.

Types and duration of governments

Table 2.21 would seem to paint a picture of instability and vulnerability, with the selected countries having had an average of 30 governments in the 53 years from 1945, each lasting less than two years. But this exaggerates the degree of discontinuity. Many end for routine reasons. Governments are considered to have ended when their leader retires or dies and when they face an election (whether or not they are re-elected). Even when they are terminated early because of political problems (as shown in Table 2.22), often a government dissolves only to be replaced by a somewhat different arrangement of essentially the same parties.

Table 2.22, however, does display a stark contrast. In the bottom half of the table, it is rare, even unheard of, for national governments to be prematurely terminated for political reasons. But in Italy around 60% of their governments have ended early, either because the coalition has collapsed through internal dissent, or because the government has lost support in the wider parliament. Belgium, Finland and France have similarly manifested considerable instability because of lack of internal cohesion. The revolving door nature of Italian governments has long been a comic theme, so it may be surprising to see that France has had even more governments. This is really testament to the brevity of governments during France's fourth republic (1945–58), and since then it has had much more stability. Denmark shares with these countries a high rate of early terminations; on twelve occasions governments have been forced to the polls because of loss of parliamentary support.

Some of the explanation for the differences in Table 2.22 can be found in 2.20. The Danish experience highlights the parliamentary situation of governments. In the Australian and British systems it is common for an election to result in a government with a parliamentary majority formed by a single party, or by the minimum number of parties needed to gain that majority. Often, however, governments are formed without a parliamentary majority. Indeed more than half

the governments in Denmark, Sweden and Norway have been minority governments. Sometimes, especially in relatively consensual political systems like those countries, such governments can be fairly stable. They are by nature, however, politically vulnerable if their opponents ever unite and mobilise against them.

A third type of government is when a more inclusive coalition is formed. The attractions of such a 'surplus coalition' include insurance, so that the government will have some cushioning against the threat of a future defection, or it may be aiming to create as wide a consensus as possible. (The brief periods of surplus coalition in Australia have been when there was a Liberal–National Party coalition government, even though the Liberals could have governed alone.)

Table 2.23 further qualifies the impression of government vulnerability that Table 2.21 might have suggested. In two-thirds of national elections between 1945 and 2002 the government was either re-elected without change, or re-elected with a somewhat differing coalition make-up. Only in Ireland were governments more commonly than not voted out of office. At the other extreme lie Germany, Japan and Austria, where a government was rarely evicted by the electorate (though in Germany there were two occasions where there had been a major change of government before the election, which the election then confirmed in office). Australian governments have been relatively secure, with elections bringing a change on only five occasions since 1945.

Moreover, those most vulnerable to falling due to internal discontent in Table 2.22 are not the most electorally vulnerable in Table 2.23. In the extreme case of Italy, despite the apparent instability there was a strong, even suffocating, degree of continuity. All Italian governments from the 1940s to the early 1990s were based on the Christian Democratic Party, and it is only with the reforms of the 1990s that a more electorally responsive form of politics emerged.

Table 2.24: Partisan colour of governments, 1950–2000

Participation in office of party types, % of cabinet seats, 1950–2000

	Social Democratic	Centre	Liberal	Conservative	Other
Sweden	77	10	7	4	3
Norway	72	12	4	12	0
Austria	57	37	1	0	5
Denmark	55	4	26	14	2
Australia	**31**	**0**	**0**	**69**	**0**
United Kingdom	30	0	0	68	2
Finland	30	33	12	10	15
Belgium	30	50	17	0	3
New Zealand	26	1	0	73	0
Germany	25	53	17	0	4
Switzerland	24	30	32	15	0
Italy	22	63	7	0	8
Netherlands	21	54	23	0	2
France	19	13	18	27	23
Ireland	11	20	0	67	2
Japan	2	0	0	97	1
United States	0	45	0	55	0
Canada	0	69	0	31	0

Partisan colour of governments

Central to an understanding of any country's politics is the nature of the choices between parties, and while these countries share democratic institutions, they have had very contrasting experiences of partisan competition and of which parties have been most successful.

The most common labels, left and right, are too simplistic to apply with any precision. Parties change their positions over time. It is often asserted, for example, that contemporary labour parties in Australia, New Zealand, Britain and elsewhere have moved to the right. Likewise the British Conservative Party since Margaret Thatcher has had far more in common with the small-government views of the American Republican Party than it did under her more paternalistic predecessors.

Nor are political parties which adopt left or right views in one area compelled to be similar in all other areas. The New Zealand Labour Government of David Lange was more left-wing in its foreign policy – at least in its relations with America – but far more economic rationalist in orientation than the preceding conservative government of Piggy Muldoon.

It is the nature of political parties to be broad coalitions, to reach beyond their core base to win elections, to aggregate and balance competing interests. A successful party is thus by nature prone to flexibility, compromise and inconsistency. Nor is it easy to summarise the living and changing nature of political ideologies, or how they relate to the peculiarities of different nations' unique conflicts and challenges. No grouping of parties can then be completely satisfactory, but Manfred Schmidt's summary, shown in Table 2.24, is one of the most comprehensive and sophisticated.

The most common categorisation was built around left and right. The conservative category includes the Australian Liberal Party, the British Conservatives, and the American Republicans. The left was based on social democratic, labour and socialist parties, and was often defined by membership of the Socialist International. This included the Australian, British and New Zealand labour parties, the German and Swedish Social Democrats, and so on.

There were two major problems with this binary grouping. First, Canada and the United States were not considered to have any left-wing parties. The left-of-centre alternatives within their political spectrum – the Democrats and the Liberals – were not social democratic, and so all their governments were labelled conservative.

The other problem was that there were clear differences in orientation between, for example, the more welfare-oriented and 'big government' Christian Democratic Parties of Germany and Italy or the Austrian Conservative Party with the secular, more small-government Anglo-Saxon conservative parties. So Schmidt developed a centre category to include the American Democrats, Canadian Liberals and these Christian Democratic Parties.

Two smaller categories complete the table: an emerging European tradition of small government, secular 'liberal' parties, and a residual category, a miscellany of parties which thus far have played only small roles in government (e.g. far right, green, regionalist). No categorising can capture all the pertinent individualities, but Table 2.24 reveals contrasting patterns.

At the top are four small European countries where social democratic parties have participated in government most of the time and the political spectrum runs from left to centre. At the bottom are some countries where the pertinent political spectrum runs from centre to right.

The middle group covers wide differences in political history. Australia, Britain and New Zealand form one group which have had social democratic governments for much less than half the period alternating with conservative governments, which have been in power more often. There is another group of, for example, the Netherlands, Germany and perhaps Switzerland and Italy, where the social democratic presence in government runs at only around a quarter, but the main alternative has been centre rather than conservative parties.

To at least some extent, the very different national policy traditions, which we will see in subsequent chapters, can be traced back to these patterns in the partisan composition of governments.

Table 2.25: Electoral participation

Voting turnout as a proportion of registered voters; means for all elections 1945–2002 and for elections since 1990

	All	Since 1990
Australia	**94.5**	**95.4**
Belgium	92.5	91.5
Austria	91.3	83.8
Italy	89.8	84.5
New Zealand	88.5	84.1
Netherlands	87.0	77.0
Denmark	86.0	85.1
Sweden	85.7	84.1
Germany	85.0	79.5
Norway	80.4	76.3
Finland	76.0	67.4
United States	75.9	64.3
United Kingdom	75.2	69.6
France	74.8	65.7
Canada	73.9	66.2
Ireland	72.6	65.7
Japan	68.7	57.6
Switzerland	56.6	43.8
Mean	80.8	74.6

Table 2.26: Membership of political parties

Proportion of electorate belonging to political parties

	1970s	1980s	1990s	Change 1970s–1990s
Austria	25.9	24.2	17.1	−8.8
Finland	17.2	14.4	10.5	−6.7
Switzerland	10.4	9.1	8.7	−1.7
Norway	12.8	13.4	7.9	−4.9
Belgium	10.0	9.1	7.6	−2.4
Sweden	19.6	23.7	7.1	−12.5
Japan	1.1	2.7	4.2	+3.1
Ireland	4.6	4.5	3.4	−1.2
Germany	3.7	4.5	3.2	−0.5
Italy	12.8	7.1	3.2	−9.6
Denmark	14.0	7.5	3.1	−10.9
Netherlands	4.4	4.1	2.2	−2.2
New Zealand	14.6	7.8	2.1	−12.5
United Kingdom	6.2	3.8	1.9	−4.3
Australia	**3.7**	**2.6**	**1.5**	**−2.2**
France	1.9	3.1	1.5	−0.4
Mean	10.2	8.9	5.3	−4.9

Ranked according to 1990s membership.
Canada and the United States do not have formal party memberships as occur in the other countries.

Electoral participation

In nearly every advanced liberal democracy there is concern about increasing public alienation from politics. Considerable survey evidence suggests increasing cynicism. The figures in Tables 2.25 and 2.26 on the most institutionalised forms of electoral participation in the selected countries offer some support for this trend.

The 18-nation mean figure for voting turnout in elections since 1990 is 6 percentage points lower than for the post-World War II period as a whole, down from 80.8% of registered voters voting to 74.6%. The figures on party membership show a more precipitate decline, essentially halving as a proportion of the population between the 1970s and 1990s, from 10.2% to 5.3%.

There are large differences between the countries on these measures of electoral participation. Not surprisingly, the figures show that the best way to achieve high turnout for voting is by making it compulsory. The four countries at the top of the list – including Australia – all have some degree of compulsion about voting, though in Austria and Italy it is only weakly enforced.

It is often argued that forcing people to vote is undemocratic. The counter-argument is the undesirability of national governments being decided by minorities of citizens. Only 51% of eligible voters participated in the 2000 US presidential election. George Bush won fewer of these votes than Al Gore, meaning he was elected by roughly 25% of the American electorate.

Countries have different traditions about whether elections are held on a holiday or work day, whether there are two voting days or only one, and if the voter cannot vote in person in their own constituency how easy it is to cast an absentee or postal ballot. While modifying some procedures would probably raise the voting turnout in the more restrictive countries, voting arrangements do not correlate at all with overall levels of turnout.

The crucial variable seems to be the electorate's degree of engagement with the electoral process, and this seems to be declining. Eight of the 18 countries had less than 70% of their electorates voting at elections since 1990. The Swiss have the lowest turnout at elections, perhaps because with their capacity for quarterly referendums they feel overly blessed with opportunities to participate.

There are two ways of measuring voter turnout. One is as a proportion of registered voters (Table 2.25), the other as a proportion of the voting age population. Neither is universally satisfactory. In many countries (including Australia) registration is compulsory and so all but identical with citizenship. In countries with high numbers of immigrants who are not naturalised citizens, such as Australia, this will depress the proportion of the voting age population who can vote. In other countries, most especially the United States, registering to vote is voluntary, and sometimes – especially for minority groups – has proved difficult to achieve. So in earlier decades it was one country where the proportion of all adults voting was substantially lower than for registered voters only. In the late 1990s, however, there was a great improvement there in the proportion of adults registered.

Measuring party membership is much more problematic. Parties often inflate membership figures for their own reasons. Some organisations demand participation from their members, others are happy to have passive membership. Sometimes party membership comes from belonging to another organisation, for example a trade union.

Whatever the reservations about the precision of the figures in Table 2.26, the broad story they tell is clear. Party membership declined sharply over two decades in nearly all countries, both where it was relatively high in the 1970s (e.g. Denmark, Sweden) and where membership was already very low. Australia's share of the population belonging to a political party began in the lowest quarter of countries, and had fallen to equal last by the 1990s.

Table 2.27: Corruption Perceptions Index

Transparency International Corruption Perceptions Index, 2002. Score of 10 = least corrupt; score of 0 = most corrupt

	1996	2002
Finland	9.1	9.7
Denmark	9.3	9.5
New Zealand	9.4	9.5
Sweden	9.1	9.3
Canada	9.0	9.0
Netherlands	8.7	9.0
United Kingdom	8.4	8.7
Australia	**8.6**	**8.6**
Norway	8.9	8.5
Switzerland	8.8	8.5
Austria	7.6	7.8
United States	7.7	7.7
Germany	8.3	7.3
Belgium	6.8	7.1
Japan	7.1	7.1
Ireland	8.5	6.9
France	7.0	6.3
Italy	3.4	5.2

Table 2.28: Bribery Index

Transparency International Bribe Payers' Index, 2002. Score of 10 = least corrupt; score of 0 = most corrupt

	Bribe Payers' Index, 2002
Australia	**8.5**
Sweden	8.4
Switzerland	8.4
Austria	8.2
Canada	8.1
Belgium	7.8
Netherlands	7.8
United Kingdom	6.9
Germany	6.3
France	5.5
Japan	5.3
United States	5.3
Italy	4.1

Other countries not included.

Corruption

Corruption is corrosive of good governance and democratic accountability. However, because successful corruption often means that no offence or transgression is officially recorded or even publicly known, it is impossible to measure its extent authoritatively.

Since 1995, Transparency International, an international non-government organisation dedicated to combating corruption, has been conducting and assembling polls of business people and country analysts on their perceptions of corruption in the countries they work in. In the 2002 survey they ranked 102 countries, assigning scores from 0 (most corrupt) to 10 (least corrupt). Seven out of every ten countries globally scored less than 5.

Table 2.27 shows that our 18 countries are ranked among the less corrupt governments worldwide. The countries fall into some broad clusters. First is the cleanest group, ranking 9.0 and above, and led by Finland, Denmark and New Zealand. Australia is part of a second group, ranked fairly uncorrupt, and scoring in the mid-8 range.

Italy is scored most corrupt, and by a considerable margin. Next lowest are Ireland and France, both of which deteriorated substantially between 1996 and 2002. Japan, Belgium and Germany (which also fell by a full point in those six years) are on the next level up.

Perception of corruption is not the same as the incidence of corruption, and perceptions can be shaped by other factors beyond direct experience. Sometimes scores can be shaped by the prevalence of scandals in the news. Sometimes in surveys of expatriates about the countries they are living in, cultural distance, the opaqueness of local procedures and other frustrations can too easily become labelled as corruption. Moreover, although a convenient indicator, a score from a ten-point scale gives a somewhat spurious air of precision to the exercise. Despite these inherent problems, the Corruption Perception Index is a very useful exercise as a means of highlighting the extent of corruption in public life, and the relative ranking of countries on the scale would seem broadly accurate to most observers.

More recently TI has also constructed a Bribe Payers' Index. The 2002 BPI was conducted in 15 emerging economies in South America, Asia, Africa and Eastern Europe. It surveyed senior business people in those countries about the propensity of companies from 21 leading exporting countries (including 13 from our selected 18 countries) to engage in bribery for business purposes. The central survey question was:

In the business sectors with which you are familiar, please indicate whether companies from the following countries [list of 21 leading exporting countries] are very likely, quite likely or unlikely to pay bribes to win or retain business in this country?

Australian exporters topped the list, as being least likely to pay bribes, closely followed by Sweden, Switzerland, Austria and Canada. Italian exporters trail this list by a considerable margin, with Japan, America and France in the next group up. Among exporting nations, Russia (3.2) and China (3.5) were seen as most prone to offering bribes, but domestic companies (1.9) in these developing countries were seen as most corrupt.

We should note in conclusion that corruption, while present in various sectors of the public and business lives of the selected countries, is remote from the routine life of most of their citizens. In the International Crime Victims Survey reported in Chapter 17, fewer than 1% reported being the victim of a demand for corruption in the previous year in all countries except France (1.3%). Unfortunately Italy, the lowest-scoring country on the Corruption Perceptions Index, did not participate in that survey. In Australia (0.3%) and the United States (0.2%) very low proportions reported any direct experience of corruption, and the same was true of countries scoring relatively badly on TI's Index, such as Japan (0.0%) and Belgium (0.3%).

Table 3.1: Income per capita, 1870–1998
Per capita income in 000s of 1990 international dollars

	1870	1913	1950	1973	1998
United States	2.4	5.3	9.6	16.7	27.3
Norway	1.4	2.5	5.4	11.2	23.7
Denmark	2.0	3.9	6.9	14.0	22.1
Switzerland	2.2	4.3	9.1	18.2	21.4
Canada	1.7	4.4	7.4	13.8	20.6
Japan	0.7	1.4	1.9	11.4	20.4
Australia	**3.6**	**5.7**	**7.5**	**12.8**	**20.4**
Netherlands	2.8	4.0	6.0	13.1	20.2
France	1.9	3.5	5.3	13.1	19.6
Belgium	2.7	4.2	5.6	12.2	19.4
Austria	1.9	3.5	3.7	11.2	18.9
United Kingdom	3.2	4.9	6.9	12.0	18.7
Sweden	1.7	3.1	6.7	13.5	18.7
Finland	1.1	2.1	4.3	11.1	18.3
Ireland	–	–	3.4	6.9	18.2
Germany	1.8	3.6	3.9	12.0	17.8
Italy	1.5	2.6	3.5	10.6	17.8
New Zealand	2.7	5.2	8.5	12.5	14.8
Mean	2.1	3.8	5.9	12.6	19.9

Table 3.2: Income per capita, 2000
GDP per capita US$PPP

	US$PPP
United States	35 619
Norway	30 166
Switzerland	30 142
Ireland	29 165
Denmark	29 060
Canada	27 993
Netherlands	27 847
Austria	26 993
Australia	**26 332**
Belgium	26 188
Japan	26 056
Germany	25 876
Finland	25 240
Italy	25 160
Sweden	24 842
United Kingdom	24 455
France	24 359
New Zealand	20 277
Mean	26 987

3 ECONOMY
Income per capita

All the selected countries have experienced a huge increase in living standards over the last century. Table 3.1 shows how, overall, real living standards in these developed economies rose by a factor of more than nine over almost 130 years. It is based on the heroic efforts of the veteran scholar Angus Maddison, who has devoted his career to estimating the world's economic growth over past centuries. No doubt many of his estimates and assumptions could be argued with, but they are the best available over such a long period.

Income per person or GDP per capita is the standard way of measuring the average material standard of living of a country's population, though of course it tells us nothing about how evenly or unevenly income is distributed. Comparisons of the living standards of different countries are sometimes made by simply converting each country's GDP per capita to a common currency such as US dollars. But this fails to allow for the fact that the amount of goods or services one US dollar buys differs greatly from one country to another. For this reason, international comparisons of living standards are more accurate when the common currency used has been adjusted to ensure it has similar purchasing power in each country. In Table 3.1 Maddison has achieved this by using 'international dollars'. And because those dollars are all of the 1990 vintage, there is no need to allow for inflation when comparing amounts between years. Their increase over the periods reflects a real growth in wealth.

The table shows very well the joint phenomena of 'catch-up and convergence' between the economies of the developed world. Over the period, the gap between the richest and poorest of the selected countries narrowed from a factor of more than five to one of less than two. At one extreme, Japan's standard of living is estimated to have risen by a factor of 29; at the other, New Zealand's rose 5.5 times.

This is the appropriate context in which to view Australia's decline from being the world's richest country per capita in the second half of the 19th century to being in the middle of this league of high-income nations today. Initially, Australia was a New World country with a small population, a high proportion of which was engaged in the relatively easy exploitation of its considerable agricultural and mineral wealth. But this unusual and privileged position could not be sustained as Australia's population grew and commodity prices fell, while other countries steadily caught up. New Zealand has had a similar experience, though more recent problems have taken it to the bottom of the league.

The United States' early rise to its position as the biggest and richest economy can be seen, as can the United Kingdom's steady decline from near the top of the league to the bottom half. Japan's post-World War II ascent is evident, as is the more recent rise of oil-rich Norway.

Table 3.2 offers a contemporary ranking of the selected countries' income per capita broadly similar to Maddison's last ranking, but with some noticeable exceptions. Unsurprisingly, differing methodologies yield differing results. Table 3.2 is probably the more reliable for a present-day comparison. It uses US dollar annual amounts, painstakingly adjusted by the OECD to achieve purchasing power parity between countries. What stands out from the table is the way living standards in the developed world have converged. If you exclude the richest and poorest countries – the United States and New Zealand – you find that the remaining 16 are all within a range of about $3000 above or below the mean per-capita income of $27 000 a year. So Australians' standard of living is pretty much par for the course in the developed world.

Table 3.3: Economic growth, 1820–1998

Average per capita annual growth rates, %

	1820–70	1870–1913	1913–50	1950–73	1973–98
Ireland	–	–	–	3.04	3.97
Norway	0.52	1.30	2.13	3.19	3.02
Japan	0.19	1.48	0.89	8.05	2.34
Austria	0.85	1.45	0.18	4.94	2.10
Italy	0.59	1.26	0.85	4.95	2.07
Finland	0.76	1.44	1.91	4.25	2.03
United States	1.34	1.82	1.61	2.45	1.99
Belgium	1.44	1.05	0.70	3.55	1.89
Australia	**3.99**	**1.05**	**0.73**	**2.34**	**1.89**
Denmark	0.91	1.57	1.56	3.08	1.86
United Kingdom	1.26	1.01	0.92	2.44	1.79
Netherlands	0.83	0.90	1.07	3.45	1.76
France	0.85	1.45	1.12	4.05	1.61
Germany	1.09	1.63	0.17	5.02	1.60
Canada	1.29	2.27	1.40	2.74	1.60
Sweden	0.66	1.46	2.12	3.07	1.31
New Zealand	3.90	1.51	1.35	1.72	0.67
Switzerland	1.09	1.55	2.06	3.08	0.64
Mean	1.27	1.42	1.22	3.63	1.90

Table 3.4: Economic growth, 1889–1939

Average per capita GDP annual growth rates, %

	1889–1900	1900–10	1910–13	1913–18	1918–25	1925–29	1929–32	1932–39	Total 1889–1939
Japan	1.5	1.0	2.1	3.8	1.8	1.8	–1.1	5.3	2.2
Denmark	1.8	2.1	1.8	–2.4	3.4	3.8	0.6	2.1	1.9
Finland	1.9	1.4	3.4	–8.3	7.9	3.9	–2.1	4.2	1.9
Norway	0.9	1.5	3.5	–1.8	3.7	4.2	1.3	3.3	1.9
Sweden	2.1	1.5	1.3	–3.9	3.6	4.6	–1.8	4.6	1.8
Germany	2.1	1.2	2.8	–3.8	2.6	3.5	–9.0	7.9	1.6
Italy	0.7	2.7	3.2	5.8	–2.1	1.5	–1.6	2.6	1.6
Canada	2.0	3.4	3.0	0	–0.3	3.9	–10.2	3.8	1.5
France	1.9	0.3	5.5	–7.2	8.2	3.1	–5.6	2.8	1.5
Switzerland	–	1.4	1.1	–2.3	5.1	4.1	–3.4	1.6	1.4
United States	1.9	2.0	2.2	1.3	1.5	2.4	–10.7	4.2	1.3
Austria	1.7	1.3	1.7	–5.9	4.0	2.4	–7.4	4.9	1.1
New Zealand	1.4	2.2	–1.0	–1.0	1.1	–0.1	–6.1	5.9	1.1
Belgium	0.9	0.9	1.3	–7.5	7.2	2.0	–3.0	1.6	0.9
Netherlands	1.3	0.4	2.4	–3.7	6.0	3.1	–4.0	1.4	0.9
United Kingdom	1.1	0.3	2.2	2.1	–1.8	1.7	–2.2	2.8	0.8
Ireland	1.1	–	–	–	–	2.4	1.7	0.4	0.7
Australia	**–1.0**	**2.6**	**–0.5**	**–1.7**	**1.8**	**–2.8**	**–2.9**	**2.7**	**0.2**
Mean	1.3	1.5	2.1	–2.1	3.2	2.5	–3.7	3.5	1.4

Long-term economic growth

While Table 3.1 charted these countries' growing long-term wealth, Table 3.3 looks at this from the perspective of rates of economic growth. It does so by examining the annual growth rate of GDP per capita. The growth of economies is commonly measured simply by the increase in overall GDP, but because the population is also growing, the rise in income per capita (i.e. GDP per person) offers a better indication of whether the population is becoming wealthier.

Table 3.3 reveals that it is only since World War II that economic growth has been consistently achieved over time and across countries. Whereas, as Table 3.4 shows, there were two periods – World War I and the depression of 1929–32 – when economic disaster was almost universal, there were few periods before World War II when economic growth was universal. The postwar improvement is commonly attributed to the advent of Keynesian demand management and the greater share of the economy accounted for by the relatively more stable government spending and the services sector generally.

For all these countries the period of nearly 30 years following World War II was the golden age of rapid economic growth, unlike any period in world history before or since. The 18-nation average annual growth rate of 3.63% more than doubled that of any preceding period.

Australia's relative performance was not strong, but the same can be said of the other English-speaking countries, which together comprised the bottom third of countries. It was a period of catch-up for the non-Anglo economies, and the countries that enjoyed the fastest growth were those that lost the war and had most rebuilding to do. Moreover, despite Australia's low ranking (17th of 18 countries), this period was nevertheless Australia's time of greatest growth in the 20th century. In the last quarter of that century, Australia's rank improved to be in the middle of the field. So it needs to be stressed that although Australia's relative standing has declined since World War II, it has done so while Australia enjoyed much more material enrichment than in any period since 1870.

The golden age finished with the stagflation and oil price shock of 1973. The economic times since then have been more turbulent and the rate of growth lower. Even so, the latest period has been the second most dynamic. While there are spectacular changes in particular countries' standing – most notably the dramatic postwar rise of Japan and the later relative decline of New Zealand – the most critical feature of the contemporary era is the shared and continuing growth in wealth.

One stark fact leaps out from Table 3.4: the period from 1889 to 1939 was Australia's horror half-century. However much commentators may bemoan Australia's relatively mediocre performance after World War II, it was the previous 50 years in which it performed worst, both in absolute terms and relative to other countries.

Australia followed an idiosyncratic path with many periods of negative growth. For many countries the 1890s were a period of expansion, but Australia's standard of living in 1900 was less than it had been in 1889. Again, in the period immediately before World War I, when most of the developed world was enjoying a boom, Australia was once more in depression. From an economic perspective, World War I was much more devastating than World War II. Although Australia joined in the general postwar economic recovery, the 1920s stopped roaring in Australia before they did elsewhere. Its economy began contracting in 1925 and was well into depression before the rest of the world joined it after 1929.

So unlike the half-century after World War II, the half-century before it showed few sustained periods of shared economic growth, but rather severe boom–bust cycles and great variations between countries. Even amid this generally unimpressive picture, Australia lagged badly, its average per capita growth rate of 0.2% barely above stagnation.

Table 3.5: Economic growth, 1971–99
Average per capita GDP annual % growth rates

	1971–73	1973–79	1979–89	1989–99	1971–99
Ireland	3.5	3.3	2.7	6.1	4.1
Norway	3.9	4.3	2.3	2.7	3.0
Japan	5.3	2.4	3.1	1.4	2.6
Austria	4.8	3.0	2.0	1.8	2.4
Finland	5.0	1.9	3.2	1.2	2.4
Belgium	4.7	2.2	2.1	1.7	2.2
Italy	3.2	3.0	2.3	1.2	2.2
United States	3.6	2.0	2.0	2.0	2.2
Australia	**2.3**	**1.5**	**1.9**	**2.2**	**2.0**
France	4.0	2.3	1.8	1.3	2.0
Germany	3.5	2.5	1.9	1.3	2.0
United Kingdom	3.9	1.5	2.2	1.6	2.0
Canada	4.1	2.6	1.7	1.1	1.9
Netherlands	3.0	1.9	1.3	2.2	1.9
Denmark	2.9	1.2	1.4	1.7	1.6
Sweden	2.0	1.5	1.8	1.1	1.5
New Zealand	3.7	–0.9	1.4	1.0	1.0
Switzerland	2.5	–0.1	1.7	0.2	0.9
Mean	3.7	2.0	2.0	1.8	2.1

Contemporary economic performance

The most basic conclusion from Table 3.5 is that these economies all became steadily richer between 1970 and 2000, even if they did so at differing rates. While some outstandingly strong and weak performances over the three decades can be seen, 11 of the 18 economies – ranging from Austria and Finland on 2.4% to Canada and the Netherlands on 1.9% – had average growth rates within 0.5 percentage points of each other. This is strong evidence of the 'convergence' between the developed economies since World War II.

The high and growing amount of trade and investment between the developed economies gives them a tendency to move through the business cycle together. Even so, the timing of entry and exit from downturns can differ and particular countries are affected by idiosyncratic developments. Examining the figures for growth in real GDP per capita over a period as long as 30 years should, however, give a good guide to medium-term trends in economic performance.

Ireland's outstanding performance – winning it the title of the Celtic Tiger – was concentrated particularly in the 1990s, but has been above average since 1973. Its possession of a well-educated, English-speaking but relatively low-paid workforce has made it an ideal base for non-European corporations seeking a foothold inside the borders of the European Union. Norway's consistently strong performance is explained mainly by its wealth from North Sea oil, but also by its prudent husbanding of that windfall.

Japan offers another notable case. It would have ranked top on its performance to the end of the 1980s, but suffered a disastrous decade in the 1990s. The plethora of books saying how the West had to become more like Japan have been replaced by an equally certain set of authors writing of Japan's peculiar pathologies.

The United States' performance was very close to the mean for the period as a whole and for each sub-period. It is the largest and richest economy, with the highest level of productivity (output per unit of input). This is because it is at the frontier of technological advance. For this very reason, however, it had difficulty maintaining a high rate of productivity improvement throughout most of the period. Other countries, being back from the frontier, find it easier to achieve higher rates of productivity growth and thereby catch up somewhat.

At the other end of the spectrum, the high-taxing welfare states of Sweden and Denmark trailed just behind the main group, with growth rates of around 1.5%. Quite a bit further back were New Zealand and, perhaps surprisingly, Switzerland, with the lowest rates of growth. Switzerland is still a relatively wealthy country with the third highest GDP per capita (Table 3.2). Its low growth rate has been much less traumatic than New Zealand's, not being accompanied by alarmingly high inflation, unemployment, and trade and budget deficits. New Zealand's poor performance is explained by a succession of difficulties: its loss of a key export market when Britain joined the European Union, the constraints of an excessively regulated economy, followed by the disruption from an extensive program of deregulation.

During the 1970s, Australia was considerably below the 18-nation mean, during the 1980s just below, and during the 1990s considerably above, ranking equal third among the 18. This underlying improved rate of growth in productivity – its best since the 1960s – gave Australia a late burst of speed, which meant that it performed almost exactly on the mean for the 30-year period as a whole.

Table 3.6: Inflation

Average annual % rise in consumer price index, 1960–99

	1960–73	1973–79	1979–89	1989–99	1971–99
Germany	3.3	4.6	2.9	2.5	3.4
Switzerland	4.2	4.0	3.3	2.3	3.5
Belgium	3.6	8.4	4.9	2.1	3.9
Austria	4.2	6.2	3.8	2.4	4.0
Japan	6.2	9.9	2.5	1.1	4.1
Netherlands	4.9	7.2	2.8	2.4	4.1
United States	3.2	8.5	5.5	3.0	5.2
Canada	3.3	9.2	6.5	2.2	5.4
Denmark	6.2	10.8	6.9	2.1	6.0
France	4.6	10.7	7.3	1.9	6.0
Norway	5.1	8.7	8.3	2.4	6.2
Finland	5.7	12.6	7.1	2.2	6.6
Sweden	4.7	9.8	7.9	3.5	6.6
Australia	**3.5**	**12.2**	**8.4**	**2.5**	**6.9**
United Kingdom	5.1	15.6	7.4	3.7	7.8
Ireland	5.9	14.9	9.2	2.3	7.9
New Zealand	4.8	13.8	11.8	2.1	8.4
Italy	3.9	20.9	7.6	2.8	9.2
Mean	4.6	10.4	6.3	2.4	5.8

Inflation

Table 3.6 charts the chequered history of the developed countries' experience with inflation over the past 40 years. In the postwar period to 1973, inflation in most countries was manageable, though not negligible. The remainder of the 1970s, however, saw a dramatic acceleration in the rate of price increase, with annual inflation rates reaching double figures in almost half these countries. Although the world prices of many rural and mineral commodities rose strongly in the early 1970s, the 1973 watershed is widely attributed to the first OPEC oil price shock. This represented a sudden and massive transfer of wealth from the mainly oil-importing developed economies to the oil-exporting countries. For the developed economies, the sharp jump in petrol prices was thus both inflationary for prices and contractionary for economic activity – a rare and difficult combination for the economic managers to respond to. It was the end of the postwar golden age of trouble-free economic growth and the start of the turbulent era of 'stagflation' – the previously unknown combination of a stagnant economy with rapidly rising prices.

While the period 1960–73 found inflation within a fairly narrow band (ranging from 3.2 to 6.2%), the 1973–79 period saw not only a much higher level of inflation overall but a far greater range. Switzerland and Germany weathered the shocks best, with inflation only edging up slightly, still less than 5%. At the other extreme was Italy with an alarming 20.9% and the United Kingdom 15.6%. A further six countries including Australia experienced annual inflation rates averaging between 10 and 15%.

By the 1980s the continuing struggle to return to low inflation and restore economic stability had achieved some success, though more in some countries than others, with average inflation rates for the decade ranging from inflation-phobic Germany's 2.9% to New Zealand's 11.8%.

Australia suffered a severe recession in 1990–91, and several other countries suffered downturns to varying degrees. As the 1990s progressed, however, it became clear that the fight against inflation had been won throughout the developed world. The range between the highest and lowest inflation rates narrowed, and the overall mean inflation rate of 2.4% was actually lower than had been achieved in the halcyon 1960s. Moreover, with the notable exception of Japan, this low inflation had been accompanied by quite healthy rates of economic growth (Table 3.5).

Japan's case is instructive. Its economy dipped in and out of recession throughout the 1990s and its average inflation rate of a tiny 1.1% conceals a period in which consumer prices were actually falling. Such 'deflation' brings its own problems by discouraging spending and production. With price rises so modest in so many of the major developed economies – and the world prices of some common manufactured goods actually falling – by the early 2000s some economists were beginning to wonder whether the 20-year battle against inflation might have been replaced by a new battle to prevent deflation.

It can be seen that Australia's inflation rate was well contained during the 1960s, but it shifted to being among the worst performers after the advent of stagflation. In contrast to the United States, Japan and most of Europe, Australia's inflation rate remained above the overall mean in the 1980s. During the 1990s, however, its rate fell back into line with the rest of the developed world. Inflation was no longer a pressing problem and neither was there much sign of the dangers of deflation.

Table 3.7: Exports

Exports as % of GDP, 1970–99

	1970–73	1974–79	1980–89	1990–99
Ireland	34	44	52	72
Belgium	53	56	68	71
Netherlands	48	52	60	58
Austria	30	32	37	40
Norway	37	38	40	39
Switzerland	30	32	36	37
Sweden	25	29	33	37
Denmark	27	29	34	36
Canada	22	24	27	35
Finland	24	27	29	32
New Zealand	24	27	29	30
Germany	20	24	29	26
United Kingdom	22	28	26	26
Italy	17	22	21	24
France	16	19	21	23
Australia	**14**	**15**	**15**	**19**
United States	6	8	9	11
Japan	11	13	13	10
Mean	26	29	32	35

Table 3.8: Imports

Imports as % of GDP, 1970–99

	1970–73	1974–79	1980–89	1990–99
Belgium	50	57	68	68
Ireland	41	55	55	62
Netherlands	48	51	57	53
Austria	29	33	37	40
Switzerland	31	31	36	34
Canada	21	25	25	33
Norway	37	41	36	33
Sweden	24	29	32	32
Denmark	29	32	33	31
New Zealand	24	31	30	29
Finland	25	28	28	28
United Kingdom	22	29	26	27
Germany	18	22	26	25
France	16	20	23	22
Italy	17	22	22	21
Australia	**13**	**16**	**18**	**20**
United States	6	9	10	12
Japan	9	12	11	9
Mean	26	30	32	32

Table 3.9: Trade balance

Trade balance as % of GDP, 1970–99

	1970–73	1974–79	1980–89	1990–99
Ireland	–7.4	–11.3	–2.5	9.9
Norway	0.6	–2.7	4.1	6.3
Netherlands	0.2	1.0	3.0	5.1
Finland	–1.1	–0.9	0.4	5.0
Denmark	–1.5	–2.8	1.0	4.8
Sweden	1.4	–0.5	1.5	4.6
Switzerland	–1.2	1.4	–0.2	3.6
Belgium	2.3	–0.8	0.3	3.5
Italy	–0.1	–0.2	–0.5	2.5
Japan	1.6	0.4	1.9	1.6
New Zealand	0.2	–4.0	–1.0	1.6
Canada	1.6	–0.3	1.8	1.3
France	0.1	–0.7	–1.4	1.3
Germany	1.9	2.2	2.6	0.9
Austria	0.6	–0.8	0.2	–0.2
Australia	**0.9**	**–0.5**	**–2.2**	**–0.9**
United Kingdom	–0.1	–0.9	–0.2	–1.0
United States	0.1	–0.4	–1.8	–1.2
Mean	0.0	–1.2	0.4	2.7

Table 3.10: Current account balance

Current account balance as % of GDP, 1970–99

	1970–73	1974–79	1980–89	1990–99
Switzerland	0.1	0.4	4.0	7.2
Netherlands	1.5	1.5	3.0	5.1
Belgium	2.4	–0.8	–1.1	3.3
Norway	–1.2	–4.8	0.6	3.3
Ireland	6.1	12.4	9.6	2.6
Japan	1.4	0.3	2.1	2.3
Germany	5.5	8.0	15.6	2.1
Denmark	–2.5	–4.0	–3.6	1.1
Finland	–1.9	–2.9	–2.0	1.1
Italy	0.4	–0.2	–1.0	0.8
France	–0.3	–0.2	–2.3	0.5
Sweden	1.3	–1.6	–2.0	0.3
United Kingdom	0.3	–1.2	–0.3	–0.9
Canada	0.1	–1.9	–1.0	–1.2
Austria	0.2	–1.3	–0.3	–1.4
United States	–0.6	–0.8	–2.0	–1.7
New Zealand	1.2	–5.9	–5.1	–3.0
Australia	**0.0**	**–2.6**	**–4.9**	**–4.2**
Mean	0.8	–0.3	0.5	1.0

International trade

Tables 3.7 and 3.8 are a powerful demonstration of globalisation. Their outstanding feature is the way both exports and imports have grown steadily and strongly over the past 30 years for virtually all the selected countries. This has been brought about partly by falling transport costs, but mainly by the successive reductions in tariff barriers to trade achieved by many rounds of multilateral negotiations under the GATT (predecessor to the WTO).

In all these tables each country's exports and so forth are expressed as a percentage of that country's national income (GDP) to facilitate comparisons between countries and also over time for a particular country (because this takes account of inflation and the real growth in the country's income). It can be seen that the economies with the highest ratios of exports and imports to national income are the small European countries, many of them with contiguous borders and most of them members of the European Union. The EU's expansion and efforts to increase the economic integration of its members is another factor explaining the growth in trade over the period. Canada's jump in openness to trade during the 1990s is explained by the advent of NAFTA. The United States' and Japan's low ratios of exports and imports occur not because of high barriers to trade but because the sheer size of their economies causes them to be more self-sufficient. Even the United States, however, has become significantly more open to trade over the period. Australia's relatively low trade ratios are explained by its geographic isolation and, until the major tariff cuts of the late 1980s and early 1990s, its highly protected manufacturing sector.

Table 3.9 shows the countries' balance of trade, which is exports (Table 3.7) minus imports (Table 3.8). Because, until the 1990s, the selected countries' overall exports and imports grew at similar rates, and because this growth in trade was largely between the developed countries themselves, most of the selected countries' trade balances remained not far from zero for the first two decades of the period. During the 1990s, overall exports grew a lot faster than overall imports, causing the selected countries overall to run up a significant mean trade surplus of 2.7% of GDP. This suggests that the globalisation process progressed to significantly increased trade between the developed and developing countries, with the rich economies exporting more than they imported. Note that because of the huge size of its economy, the United States' seemingly modest average trade deficit of 1.2% of GDP during the 1990s actually meant it was 'exporting growth' to the rest of the world to a considerable extent.

Table 3.10 shows each country's current account balance, which is the country's balance of trade (Table 3.9) plus its net payments or receipts of interest on borrowings and dividends on equity investments. Thus a country that has borrowed heavily from the rest of the world and hosted much foreign investment in its businesses is likely to run a current account deficit, whereas a country that has lent to the rest of the world and invested in other countries' businesses is likely to run a current account surplus. Most of these countries were net recipients of foreign capital (and thus made net out-payments of interest and dividends), leaving four main creditor countries: Japan, Germany, the United Kingdom and Switzerland. The United States was originally a net creditor, but has since become the world's largest net debtor.

Although in the 1990s Australia's trade was not far from balance, it had the largest current account deficit. This is explained by its heavy net interest and dividend payments to foreign lenders and investors in its companies. This is often talked about in alarmist terms, but Australia has always had more potential than capital. At issue is whether the inflow of foreign capital funds growth at a greater rate than it demands the outflow of interest and dividends.

Table 3.11: Exchange rates

National currency units of $US

	1970	1980	1990	1999	Ratio 1970: 1999 value
Japan	360	227	145	114	3.16
Switzerland	4.37	1.68	1.39	1.50	2.91
Austria	26.0	12.9	11.3	12.9	2.01
Germany	3.66	1.82	1.62	1.84	1.99
Netherlands	3.62	1.99	1.82	2.07	1.75
Belgium	50.0	29.2	33.4	37.9	1.32
Denmark	7.5	5.6	6.2	7.0	1.08
Norway	7.14	4.94	6.26	7.80	0.92
France	5.55	4.23	5.45	6.16	0.90
Finland	4.20	3.73	3.82	5.58	0.75
Canada	1.05	1.17	1.17	1.49	0.71
United Kingdom	0.42	0.43	0.56	0.62	0.67
Sweden	5.17	4.23	5.92	8.26	0.63
Australia	**0.89**	**0.88**	**1.28**	**1.55**	**0.58**
Ireland	0.42	0.49	0.60	0.74	0.56
New Zealand	0.89	1.03	1.68	1.89	0.47
Italy	625	856	1 198	1 817	0.34

Table 3.12: Big Mac Index

Cost of buying a Big Mac hamburger in each country, converted to US$ and compared to US price, April 2002

	Price of Big Mac in US$	Implied relative value of currency
Australia	**1.62**	−35
New Zealand	1.77	−29
Japan	2.01	−19
Canada	2.12	−15
Euro Area	2.37	− 5
United States	2.49	−
Sweden	2.52	+ 1
United Kingdom	2.88	+16
Denmark	2.96	+19
Switzerland	3.81	+53

Exchange rates

Table 3.11 shows how each country's currency changed in value relative to the US dollar over the last 30 years of the 20th century. So, for example, whereas one US dollar was worth 360 yen in 1970, by 1999 its value had fallen to 114 yen, meaning that the yen's value had appreciated over the period by a factor of more than three. Similarly, whereas one US dollar was worth only 89 Australian cents in 1970, by 1999 its value had risen to $A1.55, meaning that the Australian dollar had depreciated by 42% (1–0.58).

It can be seen that whereas the top seven countries' currencies rose in value against the US dollar, the remaining ten fell. The single factor that should do most to explain this realignment is the selected countries' inflation rates relative to the United States' inflation rate. Economic theory suggests that if a country's inflation rate is consistently higher than another country's, its exchange rate against the second country's currency should fall over time so as to restore purchasing power parity between the two economies. And there is, in fact, a reasonably high correlation between the ranking in Table 3.11 and the ranking of inflation rates in Table 3.6. Of course, various other factors would have been at work also.

Table 3.11 has considerable potential to mislead (but it is not easy to report exchange rate movements in ways that don't). It should not be thought that the value of the US dollar stayed constant over the past 30 years while all other currencies changed around it. Clearly, the US dollar rose in value against 11 currencies, but it fell against seven (including those of the two next biggest economies, Japan and Germany). Nor is the table meant to imply that a country's exchange rate with the US dollar is the only one that matters. A country has separate exchange rates with the currencies of all the countries with which it trades, and the importance of those other exchange rates is determined by each trading partner's share of the country's trade. Finally, it should not be assumed that it is good to have an appreciating currency and bad to have one that is depreciating. Depreciation and appreciation each have (opposing) sets of advantages and disadvantages. Which direction happens to be desirable, on balance, is determined by a country's circumstances at the time and even then will be a matter of debate.

The *Economist* magazine's famous Big Mac Index (Table 3.12) is a light-hearted but enlightening exercise. We live in an era of floating exchange rates in which relativities are changing continuously. Speculative trading plays a large part in currency markets to the point where, at any particular time, it is not uncommon for markets to have 'overshot' and caused currencies to be significantly over- or undervalued. But overvalued relative to what? and to what precise extent? Economists use varying models (each based on particular theories about how exchange rates work) to attempt to answer these questions – but never with any certainty.

The theory of purchasing power parity states that exchange rates should adjust to ensure that the prices of internationally traded commodities remain the same throughout the world. The *Economist* has applied this theory to just one commodity, the Big Mac hamburger which, though not traded between countries, is produced by the McDonald's company in many countries to the same recipe. If the PPP theory held perfectly, the national-currency retail price of each country's Big Mac should, after conversion to US dollars, be identical to the hamburger's price in the United States ($US2.49 in April 2002). Hence the extent to which the hamburger's actual price in other countries exceeds or falls short of the home US price is a quick but of course imperfect measure of the extent to which those countries' currencies are over- or undervalued relative to the US dollar.

Table 3.13: Employment in agriculture

Percentage of labour force employed in agriculture

	1960–73	1974–79	1980–89	1990–99	Change 1960s–1990s
Ireland	30.8	21.4	16.4	11.8	−19.0
New Zealand	12.7	10.8	10.9	9.9	−2.8
Finland	27.0	15.1	11.6	7.7	−19.3
Italy	24.6	16.1	11.6	7.6	−17.0
Austria	17.1	11.9	9.2	7.1	−10.0
Japan	21.7	12.1	8.9	5.9	−15.8
Norway	16.5	9.3	7.4	5.3	−11.2
Australia	**9.2**	**6.6**	**6.1**	**5.1**	**−4.1**
France	16.7	9.7	7.5	4.9	−11.8
Denmark	13.8	8.4	6.6	4.6	−9.2
Switzerland	10.3	7.4	5.9	4.4	−5.9
Canada	12.5	5.9	5.0	4.1	−8.4
Netherlands	7.4	5.5	4.9	3.9	−3.5
Germany	10.4	6.2	4.6	3.3	−7.1
Sweden	10.7	6.2	4.8	3.1	−7.6
United States	5.9	3.9	3.2	2.8	−3.1
Belgium	6.1	3.6	3.0	2.4	−3.7
UK	3.8	2.8	2.5	2.0	−1.8
Mean	14.3	9.1	7.2	5.3	−9.0

Ranked according to proportion in agriculture in 1990s.

Table 3.14: Employment in manufacturing

Percentage of labour force employed in manufacturing

	1970–73	1974–79	1980–89	1990–99	Difference 1970s–1990s
Germany	36.6	34.5	32.4	26.9	−9.7
Austria	33.7	30.5	28.5	23.8	−10.0
Japan	27.1	25.4	24.6	22.9	−4.3
Italy	28.2	27.5	24.2	22.5	−5.7
Finland	22.8	22.9	21.7	20.0	−2.8
Denmark	17.7	16.5	17.8	19.8	2.1
UK	32.9	30.0	24.4	19.8	−13.1
Switzerland	36.1	33.1	31.8	19.6	−16.5
France	27.9	27.1	23.2	19.2	−8.6
Sweden	27.4	26.4	22.5	19.2	−8.2
Ireland	20.6	21.0	19.7	19.1	−1.4
Belgium	31.7	28.3	22.9	19.0	−12.6
New Zealand	26.4	24.9	22.1	17.0	−9.4
United States	25.0	23.0	19.8	16.5	−8.6
Netherlands	26.7	23.8	19.7	16.4	−10.3
Canada	22.0	20.1	17.8	15.1	−6.9
Norway	25.1	22.6	17.9	14.8	−10.2
Australia	**24.2**	**21.4**	**17.4**	**13.7**	**−10.5**
Mean	27.3	25.5	22.7	19.2	−8.2

Ranked according to proportion in manufacturing in 1990s.

Table 3.15: Employment in services

Percentage of labour force employed in services sector

	1960–73	1974–79	1980–89	1990–99	Change 1960s–1990s
Canada	58.4	64.7	68.5	72.9	14.5
Netherlands	53.0	60.7	67.0	72.9	19.9
United States	59.4	64.9	68.6	72.9	13.5
Australia	**53.5**	**60.6**	**65.9**	**71.8**	**18.3**
Norway	47.3	57.9	65.0	71.3	24.0
Belgium	50.0	58.3	66.2	70.9	20.9
Sweden	49.2	59.0	65.0	70.6	21.4
United Kingdom	50.7	57.4	63.1	69.5	18.8
Denmark	49.3	59.2	65.2	68.4	19.1
France	44.4	52.6	59.8	68.2	23.8
Switzerland	42.7	51.2	58.5	66.9	24.2
New Zealand	48.9	53.9	58.8	66.1	17.2
Finland	39.3	49.7	55.8	64.6	25.3
Japan	44.9	52.3	56.4	60.6	15.7
Italy	37.8	45.3	53.6	60.3	22.5
Ireland	41.1	47.0	54.0	60.0	18.9
Germany	41.7	48.8	54.1	59.6	17.9
Austria	41.5	46.9	52.3	59.1	17.6
Mean	47.4	55.0	61.0	67.0	19.6

Ranked according to proportion in services in 1990s.

Industrial structure

Tables 3.13, 3.14 and 3.15 show the shares of total employment accounted for by agriculture, manufacturing and services. It can be seen that the industrial structure has been changing in essentially the same direction in all the selected countries despite their differing starting points. It is important to remember that a decline in an industry's share of total employment does not necessarily imply that employment in the industry fell in absolute terms. It may have. But equally, if it has grown at a slower rate than employment generally, its share of the total will have shrunk.

The relentlessness of change means that, measured over periods as long as a decade or more, the degree of change in the structure of industry can be marked. Among the many factors changing the structure of industry the greatest is technological advance, which is relevant both because of changes in methods of production – in particular, industry's unending pursuit of labour-saving equipment – and also in the invention of new consumer products. Technological innovation drives change in consumers' spending preferences, which in turn causes change in the structure of industry. For instance, there was no demand for motor cars before they had been invented, but after they were, consumers changed their spending patterns with the effect that the motor industry (and the oil industry) expanded and industries associated with the horse and buggy contracted.

Table 3.13 shows the continuous and universal decline in agriculture's share of total employment in the last 30 to 40 years of the 20th century (though that decline began much earlier in most of these countries). The decline tended to be greatest in the countries which started with the highest levels. It does not mean that the developed world is eating less food than it did, or that the quantity of agricultural goods being produced has declined. Agriculture's ever-declining share of total employment can be explained by two factors. The lesser is that farming has progressively become more capital-intensive and less labour-intensive. That is, farmers

have increasingly used machines to do work formerly done by men, without necessarily any decline in output. The more significant factor, however, is that as spending on food has accounted for an ever-decreasing share of total consumer spending, so employment in other sectors of the economy has grown at very much faster rates than employment in agriculture.

Table 3.14 documents the much discussed process of 'deindustrialisation': the decline in the manufacturing sector's share of total production and employment, and thus of its relative importance. It shows a similar process as occurred in agriculture, though at a later time. Stylising the facts somewhat, one can envisage a progression where the process of automation begins in the agricultural sector, releasing workers and future entrants to the workforce to meet the labour requirements of the ever-expanding manufacturing sector. By the last quarter of the century, however, automation has reached manufacturing and the process is being repeated. But while these things are happening on the production side, on the consumption side the purchase of goods – whether food or manufactured articles – is accounting for a declining share of the consumer's (ever-growing) dollar, while the purchase of myriad services accounts for an ever-expanding share.

Table 3.15 serves as a reminder that the drying up of job opportunities in agriculture and manufacturing has been accompanied by a huge expansion of employment in the services sector. (Which is not to imply that workers displaced from those declining sectors could easily take up the kind of jobs being created.) The services sector's share of total employment expanded continuously during the period and universally among the countries. The sector now accounts for two-thirds to three-quarters of total employment, while covering a huge and diverse number of private and public sector industries, ranging from health and education to retailing, hospitality and recreation, communications and property and business services.

Table 3.16: Trade in agriculture

Agriculture as % of total exports or imports

	Exports 1980	Exports 1999	Imports 1980	Imports 1999
New Zealand	66	45	6	9
Australia	**43**	**26**	**5**	**5**
Denmark	31	19	12	9
Netherlands	22	16	15	10
United States	20	8	8	4
France	17	11	12	8
Ireland	36	9	13	7
Canada	11	6	8	5
Belgium	10	10	12	10
Austria	4	5	8	7
Italy	8	7	16	10
United Kingdom	8	6	15	9
Germany	5	4	14	8
Sweden	3	2	7	6
Switzerland	4	3	9	7
Finland	5	2	8	7
Norway	2	1	8	6
Japan	1	0	13	11
Mean	16	10	10	7

Ranked according to difference between 1999 export and import percentages.

Table 3.17: Support for agriculture

Gross support for agricultural producers as a % of value of production

	1986	2001
Switzerland	72	69
Norway	67	67
Japan	66	59
European Union 15	43	35
United States	25	21
Canada	33	17
Australia	**8**	**4**
New Zealand	10	1
Mean	41	34

Table 3.18: High-tech manufactured exports

High-tech exports as % of manufactured exports

	1990	2000
Ireland	41	48
Netherlands	16	35
United States	33	34
United Kingdom	24	32
Japan	24	28
Finland	8	27
France	16	24
Sweden	13	22
Denmark	15	21
Canada	14	19
Switzerland	12	19
Germany	11	18
Norway	12	17
Australia	**12**	**15**
Austria	8	14
Belgium	5	10
New Zealand	4	10
Italy	8	9
Mean	15	22

Table 3.19: Trade in services

Services as % of total exports or imports, 1990 and 1999

	Exports 1990	Exports 1999	Imports 1990	Imports 1999
United States	27.3	28.2	19.0	15.7
Switzerland	22.3	24.6	11.5	14.4
United Kingdom	23.9	27.9	19.0	21.4
France	26.4	21.9	21.3	18.8
Austria	39.9	32.1	24.2	29.1
Australia	**20.5**	**23.6**	**26.0**	**21.8**
Belgium	21.2	20.7	20.6	19.8
Netherlands	22.0	19.7	23.5	20.1
New Zealand	21.3	25.5	28.6	25.9
Italy	22.0	21.0	22.8	21.7
Denmark	–	24.2	–	26.1
Canada	12.8	12.4	19.0	15.1
Sweden	22.4	18.9	27.9	24.5
Norway	27.1	23.4	24.3	29.3
Finland	16.1	13.5	25.9	19.9
Germany	13.4	13.3	19.4	22.2
Japan	12.8	13.2	28.4	29.2
Ireland	12.4	18.0	19.1	37.9
Mean	21.4	21.2	22.4	22.9

Ranked according to difference between 1999 export and import percentages.

International trade

As Tables 3.7 and 3.8 showed, the amount of cross-border trade engaged in by the selected countries has grown continuously and significantly in the years since World War II. But not only has trade grown, its composition has changed. The share of agriculture has dropped, manufacturing exports have become increasingly 'high-tech', while services are now an important component of total trade.

Table 3.16 shows the decline in agricultural goods' share of trade – exports or imports of both goods and services – during the last 20 years of the 20th century. Advances in technology and ever-increasing affluence have caused trade in manufactured goods and in services to grow at very much faster rates than trade in agriculture. It can be seen that the highly efficient rural producers of New Zealand and Australia have the highest shares of exports devoted to agriculture. The falling share of agriculture was sharpest in Ireland and the United States, testimony to the rapid diversification of those countries' exports.

Agriculture has always been a politically sensitive area, and in many countries has remained resistant to the general pressures towards freer trade. Table 3.17 shows the gross support for farmers as a percentage of the value of their production, with support representing amounts received either from domestic consumers or taxpayers. Despite some decline, levels of assistance remain particularly high in Japan and the European Union, and could not be called low in the United States. Among all the selected countries, assistance is minor only in Australia and New Zealand. The greatest percentage falls in assistance occurred in those countries where assistance was already low. It is the protected trade within the European Union and the high degree of assistance received as part of the EU's Common Agricultural Policy that explains the high proportion of agricultural exports by some EU countries.

Table 3.18 shows how the manufactured exports of the selected countries became significantly more high-tech in the 1990s. In one decade their share of manufacturing exports in the selected countries rose by almost half, but in Australia it rose only by a quarter, from 12% to 15%. Here, high-technology exports are products that have required the application of much research and development. They include products such as aerospace, computers, pharmaceuticals, scientific instruments and electrical machinery. Despite this broad range, it is safe to conclude that what we see here is the spread of the IT revolution. But it may also be that if we were to examine the composition of the selected countries' imports of manufactures in the most recent decade, we would see more low-tech, labour-intensive goods coming from the developing countries.

Historically, it was believed that services, being intangible and non-storable, were not the sort of things that could be traded across borders. However, the boundary between what can and cannot be traded is continually being shifted by advances in technology. One innovation that has done much to increase trade in services is the advent of the jumbo jet and, with it, cheap international travel. So the rise in inbound and outbound tourism does much to account for the growth in trade in services (most of which occurred in the period before 1990). Cheap travel has also fostered trade in educational and health services, as well as facilitating cross-border consultancies. As well, advances in computing and telecommunications are permitting such services as airline ticketing, call centres and software development to be performed in other countries.

Table 3.19 reveals that exports or imports of services account for a higher proportion of the selected countries' trade – between a fifth and a quarter – than many people may expect. Services account for 28% of the United States' total exports, the highest proportion for any country bar Austria. This would do much to explain why the United States is at the forefront of efforts to use the auspices of the WTO to reduce the (mainly non-tariff) barriers to trade in services.

Table 3.20: Household saving Household saving as a % of household disposable income			
	1984	1990	2000
France	14.1	13.0	15.8
Belgium	15.7	16.9	12.8
Japan	19.4	13.9	11.3
Italy	22.8	18.4	10.2
Germany	9.5	12.0	9.8
Switzerland	–	8.7	8.8
Austria	9.9	13.8	8.2
Ireland	12.6	6.4	7.9
Netherlands	5.6	11.6	7.6
Norway	5.0	2.2	7.6
United Kingdom	10.3	8.0	5.0
Canada	16.6	12.9	3.9
Australia	**12.5**	**8.6**	**3.8**
Denmark	–	11.2	2.9
Sweden	2.9	−0.4	1.9
Finland	3.0	2.9	1.7
United States	10.6	7.8	1.0
New Zealand	6.6	3.3	0.1
Mean	11.1	9.5	6.7

Table 3.22: Household debt Household debt to income ratio, %			
	1982	1992	2002
Italy	8	31	36
France	61	80	76
Germany	–	86	112
United States	68	87	112
Sweden	–	96	112
Canada	72	96	113
New Zealand	–	67	118
Australia	**43**	**56**	**125**
United Kingdom	72	109	127
Japan	84	128	133
Norway	112	145	145
Netherlands	85	99	196
Denmark	–	–	225
Mean	67	90	125

No data for Belgium, Finland, Ireland, Switzerland or Austria.

Table 3.21: Net saving Net saving as a % of GDP, 1970–99				
	1970–73	1974–79	1980–89	1990–99
Japan	25.3	20.2	18.0	16.4
Netherlands	16.6	12.5	10.8	12.3
Switzerland	17.4	14.2	14.0	12.3
Norway	18.1	12.4	12.2	10.4
Ireland	8.7	7.7	4.3	10.3
Belgium	16.0	12.0	6.1	10.1
Austria	16.6	13.2	10.0	8.5
Germany	14.6	9.9	8.6	7.7
France	16.1	12.1	7.2	7.4
Italy	13.5	11.6	8.6	6.9
New Zealand	15.7	12.8	10.5	6.2
Denmark	27.1	13.2	0.3	4.9
United States	9.5	8.7	5.8	4.9
Canada	11.4	11.1	8.4	4.2
United Kingdom	10.3	5.5	5.0	4.0
Sweden	14.6	9.7	5.5	3.9
Finland	16.1	11.1	8.7	2.5
Australia	**12.4**	**7.4**	**4.9**	**2.2**
Mean	15.6	11.4	8.3	7.5

Saving and borrowing

Economists define saving as that part of an entity's income which is not spent on consumption. So, from the viewpoint of the individual, saving is necessarily to permit (additional) consumption in the future. From an economy-wide viewpoint, however, saving is necessary to provide the funds needed for investment spending on new housing, business plant and public infrastructure.

Table 3.20 shows the amounts households saved in particular years, expressed as a percentage of their household disposable income. A general picture of declining rates of saving can be observed over the last 16 years of the 20th century. It will be seen that almost all the English-speaking countries ended the period in the bottom half of the league. The decline is not easily explained, though some have speculated that the protections of the welfare state have reduced people's inclination to make precautionary savings to cover possible future adverse events.

Although the secular decline is clear, it is not even. Australia's saving rate fell steadily to a low of 4.1 in 1993, then rose again, being 5.5% in 1996 before trending down to 2.0% in 1999 and up to 3.8% in 2000. Similar variability is found for every country, and can partly be explained by the saving rate's tendency to move with the business cycle. Because households prefer to smooth their consumption spending over time, the usual pattern is for saving rates to rise during booms but fall during recessions. In contrast, during booms when the prices of assets such as shares and housing are rising sharply, people borrow to buy them, and the pattern may be reversed, as people respond to the asset-price bust – and thus their sudden loss of wealth – by tightening their belts and increasing their saving.

Table 3.21 shows the saving rate from an economy-wide perspective, adding to the saving of the household sector the saving by the two other parts of the domestic economy: the corporate sector and the public sector. Here, saving is shown as a percentage of GDP rather than household disposable income. 'Net' saving means that an allowance for the year's depreciation of physical assets has been deducted from the gross saving of the three sectors. Corporations save when they retain part of their after-tax income rather than paying it all out in dividends. Governments save when they spend less than all their revenue on recurrent purposes.

It can be seen that rates of national saving have been declining since the early 1970s, though there are signs of a bottoming out or reversal in some countries. The English-speaking countries are again mainly in the bottom half of the league. Australia's saving has always been well below average, though it is the United States' persistently low saving that is most noteworthy from a global perspective.

Borrowing that permits households' consumption to exceed their income is negative saving (dissaving), whereas any repayment of principal constitutes saving. Table 3.22 shows the widely quoted figures for the growth in households' outstanding debt, expressed as a percentage of annual household disposable income. This almost universally strong growth helps account for the decline in household saving. Note, however, that the great majority of household debt has been incurred to purchase homes rather than to finance consumption.

Much of the alarmist rhetoric surrounding household debt results from an inappropriate comparison. It is not unusual or of concern for home-buyers to borrow sums well in excess of their annual income. In other words, it does not make a lot of sense to compare long-term debt with annual income. It makes more sense to compare households' debt levels with the value of their assets (including their homes) and to compare their interest and principal repayments with their disposable incomes. The results from such comparisons are far less dramatic. The high levels of household indebtedness do, however, indicate a vulnerability to higher interest rates.

Table 3.23: Bank profitability

Bank profits before tax as a % of gross income

	1992	2001
Finland	−88.5	60.4
New Zealand	15.1	48.4
Australia	**−0.4**	**42.7**
Sweden	6.9	40.5
Ireland	35.4	37.4
Denmark	−38.2	34.9
United Kingdom	6.7	34.7
Norway	−4.7	29.6
Belgium	12.1	29.5
United States	22.3	29.3
France	11.9	27.5
Italy	18.6	26.8
Netherlands	22.3	22.6
Austria	12.3	22.4
Switzerland	15.6	22.1
Canada	12.0	20.3
Germany	20.8	10.6
Japan	19.8	−78.5
Mean	5.5	25.6

Table 3.24: Bank concentration

The share of total assets held by the three largest commercial banks, averaged over 1995–99, %

Netherlands	81
Sweden	78
Switzerland	77
Belgium	75
Finland	75
Denmark	71
New Zealand	70
Ireland	68
Australia	**63**
Norway	61
Canada	56
United Kingdom	47
Austria	44
France	33
Germany	32
Italy	30
Japan	27
United States	20
Mean	56

Table 3.25: Bank branches

	Branches per million population	% Change 1992–2001
Belgium	1 193	−26
Austria	561	−3
Italy	508	+48
Germany	450	−5
France	436	+2
Denmark	397	−15
Switzerland	385	−32
Netherlands	375	−21
Norway	309	−13
United States	282	−
Canada	271	−
Ireland	255	−25
Finland	247	−46
Australia	**245**	**−32**
Sweden	194	−8
United Kingdom	183	−7
Japan	103	−12
Mean	376	−13

No data on New Zealand.

Table 3.26: Automated banking

ATMs (2000) and EFTPOS machines (2002*) per million inhabitants

	ATM	EFTPOS
New Zealand	–	23 731
Australia	**616**	**20 982**
Canada	1 034	15 755
France	582	14 846
Finland	–	14 214
Belgium	669	14 047
Italy	549	12 918
United Kingdom	575	12 879
United States	991	12 771
Netherlands	435	10 333
Switzerland	675	10 174
Sweden	295	9 916
Germany	580	5 291
Japan	922	127
Mean	661	12 713

Japanese EFTPOS figure is for 1998.
No data on Austria, Denmark, Ireland, or Norway.

Banking

It is likely that bank customers around the world imagine their banks to be highly profitable businesses. Table 3.23 confirms the truth of that belief. For the selected countries in 2001, mean bank pre-tax profits accounted for 26 cents in every dollar of gross income (or 32 cents if Japan is excluded). Few industries could match such a rate of profitability.

The 1980s deregulation of banks in many countries led to a boom in lending for company takeovers and speculative property development, which left the banks with heavy bad debts when the boom turned to bust in the late 1980s and early 1990s. This accounts for the low levels of profitability in 1992. Similarly, although profits soon bounced back in most of the selected countries, and banks were markedly profitable over the course of the 1990s, 2001 was a particularly good year for them. Table 3.23 should then be interpreted as showing the sensitivity of bank profitability to the business cycle rather than as a secular trend towards ever greater profitability.

When reporting on recent banking performance, it is almost always necessary to add the caveat 'except Japan'. Japan's property bubble burst a little later, but whereas the troubled banks elsewhere were quick to recognise their losses and start rebuilding their profits, Japan's banks sought to defer the evil hour. Their weakened state does much to explain the Japanese economy's poor performance throughout the 1990s, as well as the Japanese banks' huge losses as late as 2001.

As part of financial deregulation, banks in many countries experienced increased competition from non-bank financial institutions. They sought to restore their high rates of profitability by cutting costs. As branches typically accounted for about half the banks' total costs, their closure was a common strategy. Table 3.25 shows a decline in branch numbers in 13 of the 15 countries for which figures are available. Generally speaking, countries in the top half of Table 3.25 – those with more branches relative to population – tended to be in the bottom half of the profitability league table (Table 3.23).

Perhaps because of the presence of large economies of scale, the banking industry has tended to be highly concentrated in the less populous countries, as Table 3.24 confirms. Generally speaking, countries in the top half of this table – those with more concentrated industries – were also in the top half of the profitability table. Bank takeovers and mergers continued during the 1990s, motivated partly by a desire to cut costs by closing the resulting overlapping branches.

Another part of the push to rebuild profit margins has involved encouraging retail customers to make greater use of automatic teller machines and electronic transfer of funds, thereby reducing their need for (more costly) over-the-counter transactions in bank branches. Table 3.26 provides a snapshot of the degree of ubiquity of ATMs and EFTPOS machines by 2000 and 2002. It can be added that, in the second half of the 1990s, the overall rate of ATMs per million rose by almost half, while the rate for EFTPOS terminals more than trebled.

It is clear that Australia's banking experience fits easily into the developed country pattern. Its banks' rate of profitability recovered quickly from the financial problems left by the madness of the 1980s, to the point of being third highest in profitability in 2001. Though its banks' interest-rate margins have been narrowed by competition from non-bank mortgage originators, the banks have fought back with increased charging of fees, some takeovers of regional banks by the Big Four (whose share of total bank assets had reached about 70% by 2002) and the closure of one-third (2200) of its bank branches. It has the sixth highest number of ATMs per million and, after New Zealand, the highest number of EFTPOS terminals.

Table 3.27: Inward foreign direct investment

FDI per capita, cumulated for each decade, $US

	1971–80	1981–90	1991–2000
Belgium	936	2 763	22 135
Sweden	108	1 033	16 947
Ireland	488	531	13 555
Netherlands	765	1 860	11 825
Denmark	305	690	9 503
Switzerland	–	2 047	7 657
Norway	752	986	7 050
United Kingdom	719	1 963	6 958
Finland	79	410	6 289
New Zealand	826	955	5 359
Canada	225	1 233	5 136
France	314	964	4 055
United States	247	1 474	4 020
Austria	193	426	3 637
Germany	224	244	3 605
Australia	**769**	**2 115**	**3 438**
Italy	101	433	810
Japan	12	125	731
Mean	415	1 125	7 373

Table 3.28: Outward foreign direct investment

Per capita direct investment by countries abroad, cumulated for each decade, $US

	1971–80	1981–90	1991–2000
Switzerland	–	4 882	23 832
Belgium	326	2 086	19 412
Netherlands	1 967	3 438	18 043
Sweden	553	5 659	14 718
United Kingdom	978	3 066	13 537
Finland	127	2 297	12 592
France	259	1 788	8 369
Denmark	207	1 302	8 358
Norway	264	1 488	7 953
Germany	452	1 263	5 484
Canada	461	1 564	5 181
Japan	155	2 219	3 672
United States	590	700	3 230
Austria	77	522	2 503
Australia	**171**	**1 482**	**1 549**
Italy	64	487	1 371
New Zealand	119	1 168	892
Mean	423	2 083	8 865

No data on Ireland.

Foreign direct investment

The tables on this page chart an important dimension of globalisation: the rise and rise of the transnational corporation – the company whose activities extend over a number of countries. The term 'foreign direct investment' refers to foreigners' investment in a country's business corporations where the investment in the shares of particular companies is great enough to give the foreigners a significant influence over the company's management. FDI may involve the foreigners establishing a new business, their purchase of an existing local business, or the merger of their corporation with a local one. So FDI is to be distinguished from other, more volatile forms of foreign capital inflow to a country for the purchase of small parcels of shares or lending by foreign banks.

Table 3.27 shows the total amounts of FDI flowing into the selected countries in each of the last three decades of the 20th century. Note, however, that these amounts have been given a human dimension by dividing them by each country's population to show the value of FDI inflows per person. It can be seen that, judged in this way, inward FDI plays the largest role in relatively small European economies. It plays a smaller role in the bigger, more populous economies, and also in the small but far-flung economies of New Zealand and Australia.

The point that leaps out from Table 3.27, however, is the remarkable expansion in FDI inflows over the past three decades. With the notable exceptions of Italy and Japan, all the selected countries have experienced a surge in the number of foreign companies coming to their shores to establish subsidiaries or buy up local businesses.

But this is the right moment to turn to Table 3.28, which shows each country's outflows of FDI to establish or buy businesses in other countries (again expressed on a per-person basis). It can be seen that the expansion in these outflows over the period has been even greater than that for inflows. So this table accounts for the former table – and

vice versa. While almost all countries have been experiencing increased foreign ownership of their businesses, almost all countries' businesses have been expanding their operations by buying businesses abroad. The result is that a growing proportion of the developed world's big businesses now operate across a number of countries.

The rise of the transnational corporation – one of the most salient features of globalisation – has been facilitated directly by the reduction in countries' restrictions on foreign investment and indirectly by the growth in world trade, communications and travel. The closer integration of the economies of the European Union is another important cause – as witnessed by the smaller European countries' prominence in the two league tables.

The fact that the overall means for outward FDI do not hugely exceed the means for inward FDI demonstrates another point: to date, most of the globalisation process – and most of the development in multinational companies – has occurred between the developed countries. Only fairly recently has there been significantly increased integration between the developed and the developing worlds.

It should be noted that when FDI inflows and outflows are judged as absolute amounts rather than amounts per person, the country rankings change markedly. In absolute terms, the countries with by far the largest total FDI outflows for the 1990s were (in order): United States, United Kingdom, France, Japan and Germany. Turning to FDI inflows, the US total approached three times that for the runner-up, United Kingdom, followed by Germany and France. So the United States was by far the greatest net recipient of foreign investment, while the leading net providers of FDI were the United Kingdom, Germany and France.

It can be seen that while Australia's inflow of FDI more than quadrupled over the period, its outflow grew by a factor of nine, so that, in the 1990s every $2.20 of inflow was offset by $1 of outflow.

Table 3.29: Labour productivity
Average annual % increase in output per worker

	1974–84	1985–90	1991–95	1996–2000
Ireland	4.2	4.3	3.0	4.3
Finland	2.8	3.7	4.2	3.0
Australia	**1.9**	**0.5**	**2.1**	**2.5**
Austria	2.4	2.8	2.2	2.4
Denmark	2.4	0.7	2.9	2.3
United States	1.3	1.1	1.3	2.2
Belgium	2.7	2.3	1.4	2.0
Sweden	1.5	1.6	3.6	2.0
Canada	0.8	0.9	1.5	1.7
New Zealand	0.2	0.9	0.3	1.5
France	2.6	2.6	1.6	1.4
Japan	2.7	3.7	0.7	1.2
Norway	1.9	1.2	2.7	1.2
Switzerland	0.4	0.1	−0.0	1.2
United Kingdom	2.4	1.3	2.2	1.2
Germany	2.3	2.5	2.3	1.1
Italy	2.0	2.4	2.4	1.1
Netherlands	2.1	1.2	1.4	1.0
Mean	2.0	1.9	2.0	1.9

Table 3.30: Multi-factor productivity
Average annual % increase in multi-factor productivity

	1980–90	1990–2000	1996–2000
Ireland	4.15	3.72	–
Finland	2.39	2.94	3.86
Norway	0.82	1.83	0.96
Australia	**0.35**	**1.68**	**1.94**
Netherlands	2.29	1.45	–
Denmark	1.25	1.44	0.93
Austria	2.09	1.39	–
Sweden	1.02	1.38	–
Canada	0.76	1.34	1.96
United States	1.05	1.20	1.53
Belgium	1.79	1.19	–
France	1.92	1.02	1.53
Italy	1.29	1.02	0.50
Japan	2.14	0.82	0.32
New Zealand	0.09	0.79	–
Germany	1.50	0.75	0.63
United Kingdom	2.30	0.74	–
Switzerland	–	−0.15	–
Mean	1.60	1.36	1.42

Productivity

If you want to summarise in two words the reason the developed countries got steadily richer over the last quarter of the 20th century (and, indeed, for the best part of two centuries), they are: productivity improvement. Here we take a country's wealth to be its annual production of goods and services. It can increase its output of goods and services by applying more labour and physical capital (machines and buildings etc.). But what if it were to increase its output by more than the increase in its inputs of labour or capital? This seemingly magical result is called an increase in productivity (productiveness), measured as output divided by input to give output per unit of input.

The most commonly quoted productivity measure is the productivity of labour: output per worker or, better, output per hour of work. As can be seen from Table 3.29, almost all countries achieve an improvement in the productivity of their labour almost every year. Overall, labour productivity has been increasing at a rate averaging about 2% a year for the past quarter-century, though individual countries' rates of increase vary between 1% and 4%.

The easiest and most obvious way to make workers more productive is to give them more or better machines to work with (i.e. to increase inputs of capital). This explains firms' unending quest for labour-saving equipment. But productivity is affected by various additional factors: by advances in technological know-how that aren't 'embodied' in newly developed machines (such as improvements in the way firms are managed), by economies of scale, by the removal of government-imposed policy constraints on efficiency, and by changes (for better or worse) in the composition of a country's industries and output.

All these additional causes of productivity improvement (additional to improvements caused by the use of more capital or more labour inputs) are known as 'multi-factor productivity'. MFP is the closest economists

come to being able to measure the essence of technological advance. Because labour productivity includes MFP (just as the productivity of capital also includes it), it can be seen that the rates in Table 3.29 generally exceed those in Table 3.30 and that the rankings in the two tables are strongly correlated.

Dividing a country's output of goods and services by its inputs gives its level of productivity at a point in time. The United States is the richest economy because it has the highest productivity levels in most industries. This puts it at the technological frontier and means it can achieve an increase in productivity only by coming up with inventions that push out the frontier. In consequence, it had quite low rates of annual improvement in labour productivity and MFP until the last half of the 1990s.

All other countries, by contrast, are back from the frontier and so can improve their productivity at a faster rate than the United States simply by appropriating American technology. The further back from the frontier a country is, the faster the rate at which it can catch up. This goes a fair way towards explaining Ireland's remarkably rapid productivity growth. Another part of the explanation is its greatly expanded production of IT equipment. When the computer you produce this year has twice the capacity of the one you produced last year, but sells for the same price, this is equivalent to a doubling in output.

The amazing productivity improvements achieved by IT production industries – and by one firm in particular, Nokia – explain tiny Finland's outstanding performance. But America has led the way in IT production and use and this explains much of its notably improved, so-called New Economy performance in the second half of the 1990s.

Among the larger economies, however, it is Australia that turned in the best productivity performance during the 1990s. Economists commonly attribute this to the efficiency-enhancing effects of many years of micro-economic reform.

Table 4.1: Labour force participation

Labour force as % of total population

	1960–73	1974–79	1980–89	1990–99
Switzerland	51.2	48.8	52.1	56.6
Denmark	47.6	49.9	54.0	54.7
Japan	49.1	47.9	49.4	53.1
Canada	38.4	45.3	50.4	51.0
United States	40.3	45.4	49.1	50.9
Norway	40.7	45.7	49.8	50.7
Sweden	48.7	50.6	52.6	49.9
Finland	48.1	50.2	52.5	49.8
Australia	**41.9**	**44.8**	**46.7**	**49.4**
United Kingdom	46.3	46.5	48.3	49.1
Germany	45.5	44.2	46.7	48.7
New Zealand	37.8	40.4	44.7	48.5
Netherlands	37.3	36.7	41.3	47.8
Austria	43.6	40.2	44.0	47.5
France	42.3	43.0	43.8	43.9
Belgium	39.1	40.5	41.7	42.4
Italy	40.0	38.8	41.1	41.4
Ireland	38.5	36.7	37.4	40.7
Mean	43.1	44.2	47.0	48.7

Table 4.2: Aged dependency ratio

People aged 65 and over as % of those aged 15–64

	1980	2000	2030
Switzerland	20.8	23.8	53.0
Japan	13.4	25.2	51.7
Italy	20.4	26.7	47.3
Austria	24.0	22.9	46.4
Germany	23.7	24.1	46.3
Sweden	25.4	27.1	46.0
Finland	17.7	22.3	45.7
Belgium	21.9	25.9	43.4
United Kingdom	23.5	24.1	40.4
Denmark	22.3	22.5	40.0
France	21.9	24.5	39.8
Netherlands	17.4	20.1	39.6
Norway	23.4	23.7	39.1
Canada	13.9	18.5	37.5
New Zealand	15.7	17.9	33.7
United States	16.9	18.6	32.9
Australia	**14.7**	**18.2**	**32.3**
Ireland	18.3	16.9	26.3
Mean	19.7	22.4	41.2

4   WORK AND THE LABOUR FORCE
Labour force and population ageing

The labour force 'participation rate' in Table 4.1 is the proportion of the total population that chooses to take part in the labour force. The labour force, however, includes not only those people with jobs (the workforce) but also those actively seeking work (the unemployed). The participation rate tends to move in line with the business cycle. It falls during recessions as jobseekers become discouraged and abandon the active search for jobs, thus ceasing to meet the tight definition of 'unemployed'. Then, as the cycle turns up, formerly discouraged jobseekers resume the search for work, thus returning to participation in the labour force. However, the decade-long average rates shown in Table 4.1 should iron out most of the cyclical effect, exposing the longer-term trend.

The participation rate has been increasing steadily since the 1960s almost universally throughout the developed world. The latest rates are the historical peak for almost all the selected countries. The countries show contrasting trends. Several near the top began with high participation rates and have been stable or increased only slightly. The five countries at the bottom (the most strongly Roman Catholic ones – see Table 18.1) began with a relatively low participation rate and have barely changed. Then there is a group of countries which increased their participation rates substantially: Canada, the United States, Norway, Australia, New Zealand and the Netherlands. As will be seen in Tables 4.4 and 4.5, the single most important reason for the rising participation rate is the increasing participation of women.

There seems to be little correlation between economic performance and labour force participation. Four of the five countries with the lowest participation rates are in the top half of countries in terms of economic growth (see Table 3.5), while others are spread through the table.

Much of the furore about the ageing population concerns whether societies will be able to support such a large number of people retired from the labour force. Table 4.2 addresses the demographics of this concern. It takes the number of people aged 65 and over and expresses it as a percentage of the working-age population (those aged 15 to 64). This 'aged dependency ratio' rose on average across these 18 nations by 2.7 percentage points in the last 20 years of the 20th century, increasing by far the most in Japan.

The urgency of the concern over the ageing society, however, can be seen in the last column. According to the OECD's projections, in the first 30 years of the 21st century, the 18-nation mean in the aged dependency ratio will jump from 22.4% to 41.2%. Like all projections, this rests on many problematic and changing assumptions, but the dramatic rate of change cannot be doubted. It reflects the looming progress of the bulge of 'baby boomers' into their retirement years.

Along with the other New World democracies and Ireland, Australia will remain among the 'youngest' of the developed countries, though even these countries will experience dramatically changing age ratios. At the other extreme, the aged dependency ratio in Switzerland and Japan will reach 50%.

The aged dependency ratio is an attempt to measure the economic burden of population ageing, using the assumption that those 65 and over are not working and must be 'carried' by those of working age. There are some obvious weaknesses in this simple analysis, however. First, it ignores the accompanying decline in the proportion of young people dependent on those of working age. Second, it says nothing about what may happen to the participation rate of those of working age, nor about further improvement in the productivity of their labour. Finally, it ignores the effect of the likely decline in early retirement, as well as the marked improvement that occurs in dependency when people delay their retirement beyond 65.

Table 4.3: Male labour force participation Male labour force as % of male population aged 15–64	1960–73	1974–79	1980–89	1990–99
Switzerland	104.7	96.4	95.2	98.4
Japan	89.9	89.5	87.9	90.6
Denmark	94.8	90.3	88.3	86.3
United States	87.0	84.9	84.5	85.2
Australia	**93.5**	**89.4**	**86.1**	**84.6**
United Kingdom	96.0	91.6	87.5	84.3
Norway	89.6	88.6	87.3	83.8
New Zealand	91.8	88.0	85.6	83.5
Canada	87.7	84.9	85.2	82.3
Germany	93.2	86.3	82.2	80.9
Netherlands	92.7	81.4	78.4	80.9
Austria	88.7	82.1	81.3	80.7
Sweden	91.4	88.4	85.5	80.7
Ireland	97.9	90.6	85.4	79.1
Finland	86.1	81.7	82.0	77.9
Italy	87.8	82.7	79.2	76.5
France	88.5	84.0	78.0	74.6
Belgium	84.8	80.9	75.3	72.4
Mean	91.5	86.8	84.2	82.4

Table 4.4: Female labour force participation Female labour force as % of female population aged 15–64	1960–73	1974–79	1980–89	1990–99
Sweden	56.2	69.2	77.6	76.4
Denmark	52.7	65.1	74.6	76.2
Norway	39.3	56.8	67.8	72.9
Finland	62.5	67.3	72.7	70.8
United States	46.1	55.4	63.7	70.1
Switzerland	52.3	52.4	57.3	68.6
Canada	40.0	51.6	62.2	68.0
United Kingdom	49.3	56.0	60.8	66.6
New Zealand	35.2	42.5	52.5	64.9
Australia	**46.1**	**49.9**	**55.0**	**63.2**
Japan	56.4	52.9	56.9	62.4
Germany	48.8	51.3	53.2	61.4
Austria	51.4	48.9	51.3	60.0
France	47.4	52.6	56.0	59.4
Netherlands	27.3	31.7	42.6	58.4
Belgium	38.8	44.2	49.3	55.7
Ireland	34.8	34.5	39.1	48.1
Italy	34.4	36.0	41.0	44.5
Mean	45.5	51.0	57.4	63.8

Table 4.5: Women in the labour force Females as % of total labour force	1960	1970	1980	1990	2000
Finland	40.7	43.7	46.5	47.2	48.1
Sweden	29.2	35.8	43.8	47.7	48.0
Denmark	31.7	36.1	44.0	46.1	46.4
Norway	22.7	29.2	40.5	44.9	46.4
United States	31.7	36.3	41.0	44.3	46.0
Canada	25.3	32.5	39.5	44.0	45.8
France	33.5	36.2	40.1	43.4	45.1
New Zealand	25.0	29.4	34.3	43.0	45.0
United Kingdom	32.2	35.6	38.9	42.4	44.1
Australia	**25.5**	**31.4**	**36.8**	**41.3**	**43.7**
Germany	39.1	38.6	40.1	41.8	42.3
Japan	39.0	39.0	37.9	39.8	41.4
Belgium	26.7	30.5	33.9	39.4	40.9
Netherlands	21.8	25.9	31.5	38.9	40.6
Switzerland	30.9	33.8	36.7	39.2	40.5
Austria	40.4	38.4	40.5	40.5	40.3
Italy	26.2	28.5	32.9	36.7	38.5
Ireland	25.3	26.2	28.1	31.6	34.5
Mean	30.4	33.7	38.2	41.8	43.2

Labour force participation

The labour force participation rate in Tables 4.3 and 4.4 is the percentage of the population of working age (15–64 years) that participates in the labour force either by working or actively seeking work. It makes no distinction between full-time and part-time employment. There are many reasons why the rate is likely to be well below 100%: young people still in full-time education, older people in early retirement, people who do not have paid employment because they are looking after children or other dependants, people who are disabled, and people who would like to work but have become discouraged from actively seeking it (and so no longer meet the tight definition of 'unemployed').

As was seen from Table 4.1, the overall participation rate among the selected countries has been increasing steadily since the 1960s, almost universally. However, Tables 4.3 and 4.4 reveal that this overall increase is more than fully explained by the rising participation of women and so conceals an almost universal decline in participation by men. Table 4.3 shows that the mean male participation rate fell by 9 percentage points during the period, with most of that fall coming in the 1970s. The greatest fall over the period was in Ireland (down 19 percentage points), while France, Belgium, Germany and the Netherlands all fell by 12–14 percentage points. Australia's fall was about average. It began, and also finished, in fifth position.

The decline in male participation is explained partly by the lower participation of teenagers as young people stayed longer in full-time education and partly by the trend to early retirement. One factor contributing to this has been the changing structure of the labour force. Manufacturing's relative share has been falling, while the services sector has been increasing. The labour-saving technological advances in manufacturing and (at least in Australia's case with declining tariffs) the increased international competition have meant there have been declining job opportunities in manufacturing, at least in some industries and locations. Many of the displaced older male blue-collar workers were not well suited to take advantage of emerging opportunities elsewhere, and it seems likely that some became discouraged and left the labour force, entering early retirement involuntarily.

The same structural changes help explain the remarkable rise in female participation. Women occupy many of the white-collar, indoor, services sector jobs created in the last 30 to 40 years of the 20th century. Table 4.4 shows that female participation has risen at a rapid but steady rate throughout the period and in all the selected economies. Overall, women's participation has risen by more than 18 percentage points (compared with the decline in men's participation of half that). In all countries bar Ireland and Italy, a clear majority of working-age women are now in the paid labour force. Australia's experience is about average.

The changing structure of industry accounts for an increase in employers' *demand* for female labour, but even more fundamental have been changes in women's willingness to *supply* their labour. Changing parental attitudes towards girls' entitlement to an education, increasing educational attainment, stronger career aspirations and the financial pressures of family life have all led to increasing female participation in paid employment. Intermingled with these factors – as part cause, part effect – has been a revolution in social attitudes towards women's continued involvement with paid employment after they marry or become mothers.

Table 4.5 shows how all this has increased women's share of the labour force. It is notable that in no country has women's share yet reached 50%, though the Scandinavian countries are almost at that stage. Similarly, in no country has the female participation rate exceeded the male rate. In the league table, the Scandinavians are followed by the main English-speaking countries. With some exceptions, women's employment is lowest in those countries where Roman Catholic influence has been strongest.

Table 4.6: Labour force participation among males aged 55–64

Percentage of males aged 55–64 in the labour force

	1980	1990	2000
Japan	85.4	83.3	84.1
Switzerland	88.8	87.9	79.3
Norway	79.5	72.8	74.4
Sweden	78.7	75.3	72.8
New Zealand	70.2	56.8	72.2
United States	72.1	67.8	67.3
Ireland	81.8	65.0	64.7
Denmark	76.2	69.2	64.5
United Kingdom	84.2	68.1	63.3
Australia	**68.8**	**63.2**	**61.5**
Canada	74.6	64.3	61.0
Germany	67.3	53.4	52.5
Netherlands	63.2	45.7	51.4
Finland	56.9	47.1	48.1
Austria	56.8	38.7	44.5
Italy	52.7	59.6	42.7
France	68.6	45.8	41.7
Belgium	64.7	35.4	36.3
Mean	71.7	61.1	60.1

Table 4.7: Labour force participation among females aged 55–64

Percentage of females aged 55–64 in the labour force

	1980	1990	2000
Sweden	55.3	65.8	65.9
Norway	49.8	53.9	61.6
United States	41.3	45.2	51.9
Switzerland	34.3	37.5	51.3
Japan	45.3	47.2	49.7
Denmark	41.4	45.8	48.2
New Zealand	21.8	30.7	48.0
Finland	43.8	40.8	45.2
United Kingdom	41.4	38.7	42.6
Canada	32.6	34.9	41.6
Australia	**22.0**	**24.9**	**36.3**
Germany	28.9	25.1	33.5
France	40.1	31.1	33.0
Ireland	19.2	19.9	27.8
Netherlands	14.4	16.7	26.3
Austria	23.5	14.6	18.9
Italy	13.9	15.2	16.1
Belgium	14.1	9.9	15.8
Mean	32.4	33.2	39.7

Table 4.8: Labour force participation among males aged 65+

Percentage of males aged 65 or more in the labour force

	1980	1990	1999
Japan	41.0	36.5	34.1
United States	19.0	16.3	17.5
Ireland	26.8	16.4	15.0
Switzerland	16.0	9.5	14.4
Norway	34.3	25.0	14.2
Sweden	14.2	12.4	12.8
New Zealand	12.3	10.5	10.8
Canada	13.4	10.9	9.5
Australia	**11.1**	**8.5**	**9.2**
United Kingdom	11.0	8.8	8.0
Finland	17.0	9.3	6.3
Italy	9.0	5.1	5.9
Germany	6.8	4.1	4.6
Austria	4.5	2.4	4.2
Belgium	4.6	1.9	3.4
Denmark	15.3	13.0	2.9
France	8.4	3.7	1.9
Mean	15.0	11.4	10.3

No data on Netherlands.

Table 4.9: Labour force participation among females aged 65+

Percentage of females aged 65 or more in the labour force

	1980	1990	1999
Japan	15.5	16.2	14.4
United States	8.1	8.6	9.4
Norway	12.7	12.0	8.5
Switzerland	5.2	3.3	8.2
New Zealand	2.1	3.7	4.2
United Kingdom	4.2	3.4	3.5
Canada	4.0	3.7	3.3
Australia	**2.9**	**2.3**	**2.9**
Ireland	5.9	3.4	2.8
Sweden	3.7	5.1	2.4
Austria	2.5	1.1	2.0
Finland	5.6	3.4	2.0
Germany	3.2	1.5	1.7
Italy	3.5	2.1	1.7
Denmark	5.1	3.4	1.3
Belgium	1.3	0.6	0.9
France	3.4	1.5	0.9
Mean	5.0	4.4	4.1

No data on Netherlands.

Older people in the labour force

Tables 4.6 to 4.9 continue the examination of changes in labour force participation over the last 20 years of the 20th century, this time focusing on the experience of older men and women. Three general contrasts emerge from the four tables. The first and most obvious is between the two age groups. Not surprisingly, those in the traditionally pre-retirement group of 55 to 64 have much higher participation than those aged 65 and over. At the end of the 1990s, for example, across the selected countries, 60% of males in the younger group were still in the labour force compared with only 10% of those 65 and over. For females, the corresponding figures were 40% to 4%.

Second, the tables reveal a strong contrast between the sexes. In both age groups, and in all three years, older males have a much higher participation rate than older females. However, equally interesting is the contrasting trends the sexes show over these two decades. While the male participation rate declined over the period (down on an 18-nation average by 12 percentage points for the 55 to 64-year-olds, and 5 percentage points for the over 65s), the female participation rate among the 55 to 64-year-olds has moved up by 7 percentage points. This change among females almost certainly reflects a new generation of women for whom paid employment has been a much more central part of their lives than it was for their mothers.

Third, there is a strong contrast between the 1980s and 1990s. While for males the 1980s showed declining participation rates among both the older age groups, down by 10 percentage points for 55 to 64-year-olds and 4 percentage points among the over 65s, in the 1990s the participation rates essentially remained stable.

The fall in male participation rates in the 1980s revealed by Table 4.6 was a mixture of both voluntary and involuntary retirement. Much of it was likely to have been among older, less skilled men displaced from manufacturing and other blue-collar jobs who failed to find alternative employment and eventually withdrew from the labour force. The increased rates of participation in many countries during the 1990s – and the slower rates of decline in others – may have two causes: a decline in the popularity of voluntary early retirement, and a slowing in the rate of structural change in the manufacturing sector.

Among 55 to 64-year-old women there was little change in the 1980s, but then a jump of 6 percentage points during the 1990s. The apparent movement away from earlier retirement, the increasing participation of older women, and a few tentative signs of more people staying in the labour force beyond 65 would all be music to the ears of policy-makers worrying about the burden of an ageing population.

Beyond these general trends, several differences between countries are also apparent. Although the general norm of retiring by 65 is clear, certain countries have stronger traditions of working beyond that age – in descending order: Japan, Norway, Ireland and the United States. This is particularly true for men, but these countries also had, and still have, relatively high participation by elderly women. In contrast, several European countries have had a much stronger trend towards males retiring early. In six of them less than half 55 to 64-year-old men are still in the labour force, and in Belgium the figure is nearly down to one-third.

Australia was generally close to the average in all these areas, except for the participation rate of women aged 55 to 64, which began significantly below average but is climbing substantially.

Table 4.10: Male youth participation in education and the labour force
Percentage of 15 to 19-year-old males in work and/or school, 1984 and 1994

		In work only	Both work and school	In school only	In neither work nor school
Australia	**1984**	**28.5**	**20.8**	**39.1**	**11.6**
	1994	**18.2**	**24.1**	**47.4**	**10.3**
Belgium	1984	10.0	3.2	79.0	7.9
	1994	4.2	2.1	82.4	11.4
Canada	1984	14.4	22.2	51.6	11.7
	1994	10.7	24.6	55.8	9.0
Denmark	1984	17.7	43.1	34.1	5.1
	1994	9.5	54.1	34.5	1.9
France	1984	12.7	7.5	64.0	15.8
	1994	2.3	6.0	86.4	5.2
Germany	1984	11.1	28.6	57.4	3.0
	1994	4.8	28.7	64.2	2.4
Ireland	1984	18.7	9.2	58.9	13.3
	1994	11.0	6.0	74.0	8.9
Italy	1984	22.2	1.4	61.8	14.7
	1994	14.7	0.8	70.6	13.8
Japan	1984	15.3	2.9	78.7	3.2
	1994	13.8	4.4	76.6	5.2
Netherlands	1984	7.8	25.3	64.1	2.8
	1994	7.0	30.2	58.8	4.0
Switzerland	1984	15.8	40.6	42.7	0.9
	1994	10.6	44.8	43.4	1.1
United Kingdom	1984	21.9	19.9	43.8	14.3
	1994	17.5	22.3	44.8	15.4
United States	1984	20.0	16.9	51.5	11.7
	1994	20.0	18.5	52.2	9.4
Mean	1984	16.6	18.6	55.9	8.9
	1994	11.1	20.5	60.8	7.5

No data for Austria, Finland, New Zealand, Norway or Sweden.

Table 4.11: Female youth participation in education and the labour force
Percentage of 15 to 19-year-old females in work and/or school, 1984 and 1994

		At work only	Both work and school	In school only	In neither work nor school
Australia	**1984**	**30.9**	**16.8**	**38.7**	**13.6**
	1994	**15.4**	**27.3**	**47.0**	**10.3**
Belgium	1984	7.0	1.7	82.3	9.0
	1994	3.2	0.7	82.8	13.3
Canada	1984	14.9	24.5	49.0	11.6
	1994	8.7	27.6	53.6	10.1
Denmark	1984	16.5	36.6	40.6	6.3
	1994	10.7	47.6	37.8	3.9
France	1984	9.9	2.7	68.3	21.0
	1994	2.2	2.8	89.8	5.2
Germany	1984	11.5	22.4	61.4	4.8
	1994	4.5	23.1	69.7	2.7
Ireland	1984	18.6	5.3	65.5	10.7
	1994	7.4	4.7	80.4	7.5
Italy	1984	14.4	0.6	60.7	24.3
	1994	9.0	0.9	71.5	18.5
Japan	1984	15.5	2.7	78.7	3.2
	1994	12.0	5.3	79.4	3.4
Netherlands	1984	10.4	20.0	64.9	4.7
	1994	7.7	26.7	61.6	4.0
Switzerland	1984	24.7	25.8	47.3	2.2
	1994	14.8	33.5	49.7	1.9
United Kingdom	1984	25.4	14.6	43.7	16.2
	1994	20.1	19.5	44.4	15.8
United States	1984	19.1	16.8	49.1	15.0
	1994	17.8	18.6	50.0	13.6
Mean	1984	16.8	14.7	57.7	10.8
	1994	10.3	18.3	62.9	8.5

No data for Austria, Finland, New Zealand, Norway or Sweden.

Teenagers in the labour force

Tables 4.10 and 4.11 continue the exploration of changes in the labour force, this time by looking at patterns of entry rather than of exits. The last 20 or so years of the 20th century were a period of significant change in the relationship of teenagers to the labour force. One change was that more teenagers stayed on to complete their high school education – a rise in the school 'retention rate' – and more went on to university. The second was a decline in employers' willingness to offer full-time jobs to school-leavers, particularly early school-leavers. Employers became more inclined to hire university graduates for full-time jobs. At the same time, however, many employers – particularly those in retailing and entertainment – became more inclined to offer part-time jobs. It is likely that many formerly full-time jobs in retailing and elsewhere were divided into several part-time jobs, with the advantage to employers of more closely matching their staff levels with their busiest times of the week. It is also likely that the decline in young people's supply of full-time labour and the decline in employers' demand for young people's full-time labour were inter-related.

Tables 4.10 and 4.11 from the OECD have data for only 13 of the selected countries, but they offer a more discriminating approach than usual by allowing for four possibilities. The last column would approximate the rate of unemployment among the entire age group (rather than, as conventional, comparing the number of unemployed just with those in the age group who were actually in the labour force). It is slightly higher for females than males, and is lower for both in 1994 than in 1984.

For both males and females the decline over the decade was sharpest for the percentage of teenagers 'At work only' in all countries. It can be seen that the fall in the percentage of teenagers 'At work only' tended to be greatest in those countries where its level in 1984 was highest. If we then combine the two 'out of school' columns (i.e. data columns 1 and 4), we find that the 13-nation mean dropped from 25% to 18% for males and from 28% to 19% for females. The two countries with the smallest proportion of these late adolescents out of school in 1994 were France and Germany – both 7% for both sexes. At the other extreme was Britain with 33% of males and 36% of females out of school, with Italy having the second highest percentage of school-leavers and Australia the third. Strangely, in 1994, the country with the biggest sex difference was America: 20% of males but 31% of females no longer in school.

Australia showed the biggest decline in youths no longer in school over this decade: down from 45% to 26% for young females and 40% to 29% for young males. This still puts it above the mean in both groups, but showing rapid change, especially for young women.

The other two columns – In school only and in Both work and school – both increased slightly over the decade for both sexes. The combined increase of these two at-school (or university) categories produces a combined rise that offers strong support for the contention that young people are tending to go further in the education system. Overall, the sex differences in both columns combined were negligible by 1994 – a sign of changing parental attitudes towards girls' entitlement to an education and of girls' increasing aspirations.

There was a slight trend for more males than females to be combining work and school. These people are likely to have had part-time jobs. For both males and females, Australia had above-average rises in the proportion of young people with jobs while at school. For many, this combination of school and work will be a positive choice; for others it will reflect the financial pressures of keeping adolescents longer in education.

Table 4.12: Unemployment

Unemployed as proportion of the labour force

	1970–73	1974–79	1980–89	1990–99	2000–02
Switzerland	0.4	0.4	0.6	3.1	2.0
Netherlands	1.7	4.9	9.8	6.1	2.6
Norway	1.2	1.8	2.8	4.8	3.5
Sweden	2.3	1.9	2.5	6.5	4.4
Ireland	6.1	7.9	14.0	12.1	4.6
Denmark	0.9	6.1	8.1	7.6	4.8
Austria	1.2	1.8	3.3	3.8	4.9
United States	5.2	6.7	7.2	5.7	5.0
Japan	1.3	1.9	2.5	3.0	5.1
United Kingdom	2.6	4.2	9.7	8.1	5.3
New Zealand	0.2	0.8	4.5	7.9	5.7
Australia	**2.0**	**4.8**	**7.2**	**8.6**	**6.6**
Belgium	2.1	5.7	11.1	11.4	7.0
Canada	5.8	7.1	9.3	9.5	7.3
Germany	0.8	3.4	6.1	7.8	7.7
France	2.7	4.6	9.1	11.2	9.3
Finland	2.2	4.4	4.8	11.7	9.5
Italy	5.8	6.6	9.9	11.2	10.3
Mean	2.5	4.2	6.8	7.8	5.9

Table 4.13: Duration of unemployment one month or less

Those unemployed one month or less as % of all unemployed

	1990	2000
Norway	21.4	45.0
United States	46.3	45.0
Denmark	7.1	26.7
Canada	22.6	25.6
New Zealand	19.5	23.3
Sweden	31.3	21.4
Australia	**18.5**	**20.8**
Finland	33.5	16.2
United Kingdom	12.5	15.5
Japan	24.8	13.4
Switzerland	29.5	11.7
Belgium	4.0	8.6
Italy	2.0	6.7
Germany	6.0	6.0
France	6.1	3.8
Austria	–	2.7
Netherlands	3.5	1.8
Ireland	2.7	0.7
Mean	17.1	16.4

Table 4.14: Unemployment duration of one year or more

Those unemployed one year or more as % of all unemployed

	1990	2000
Norway	20.4	5.0
United States	5.5	6.0
Canada	7.2	11.2
New Zealand	20.9	19.2
Denmark	29.9	20.0
Japan	19.1	25.5
Sweden	12.1	26.4
Australia	**21.6**	**27.9**
United Kingdom	34.4	28.0
Austria	–	28.4
Finland	9.2	29.0
Switzerland	16.4	29.1
Netherlands	49.3	32.7
France	38.0	42.5
Germany	46.8	51.5
Ireland	66.0	55.3
Belgium	68.7	56.3
Italy	69.8	60.8
Mean	31.5	30.8

Unemployment

There could be little argument that the greatest economic and social problem plaguing the developed countries in the last 30 years of the 20th century was unemployment. It is not by chance that the other dominant economic problem was the Great Inflation of the 1970s and 1980s. In short, in the early 1970s the developed countries entered a period of economic instability and dysfunction that did not begin to lift until some time in the 1990s. Table 4.12 shows a pattern of generally worsening unemployment over the 30-year period, with each period being worse than the preceding one. The data for 2000–2002 showed an overall improvement, though it is too soon to know if this is cyclical or finally augurs a fall in the structural unemployment level.

The unemployment rate is the percentage of the total labour force that is out of work, but available for, and seeking, work. Note that someone who is seeking a full-time job, but nonetheless accepts a few hours of casual employment to earn a little cash, will not be classed as unemployed. Similarly, someone who would like to have a job, but is not actively seeking one, will not be classed as unemployed. Thus the tight definition of unemployment means that the official estimates often understate the full extent of joblessness and underemployment.

Unemployment is heavily influenced by the economy's progression through the business cycle, with the rate likely to rise sharply when the economy drops into recession, but then decline slowly as the economy enters the upswing of the cycle. However, the decade-long average rates of unemployment shown in Table 4.12 smooth away most of the cyclical effect. The steady rise in the average rates shown by the table up to the 1990s reveal a steady worsening in 'structural' unemployment: the more serious and lasting form of unemployment in which the skills, location and other characteristics of the unemployed make them unsuited to the job vacancies that arise.

Countries varied over time in the severity of their unemployment. Over the whole period, Switzerland had the best record. Until 1990 it was broadly matched by Japan, but that country's problems have steadily worsened since. Up to the 1990s Ireland had the worst record, but with its strong growth in that decade its unemployment situation has improved greatly. The United States performed worse than the mean from 1970 to 1990, and somewhat better than the mean since, though still just above the middle of the league. Australia began below the mean but has been above it in every period since 1973, though never near the worst extremes. The only country above 10% unemployment in 2000–2002 was Italy.

The greater a country's problem with structural unemployment, the more unemployed people are likely to have been without work for a year or more – to be the 'long-term unemployed'. Tables 4.13 and 4.14 show the percentages of unemployed people at the opposite ends of the duration spectrum. The tables should be interpreted with caution, however, because those percentages will shift with a country's movement through the business cycle. For example, a country may have a lower percentage of long-term unemployed simply because it has recently plunged into recession.

Even so, the data broadly show enduring differences between countries, which probably owe a lot to policy differences. The most successful countries in avoiding the unemployed becoming long-term unemployed are Norway and the United States, taking very different approaches. Norway has low rates of unemployment and has also invested most in active labour programs (Table 8.22). America also has a relatively low rate, and its more stringent approach to welfare benefits seems to provide an incentive to find employment quickly. At the other extreme, Belgium and Italy have a very large problem with long-term unemployment.

Table 4.15: Youth unemployment
Unemployment rates of 15 to 24-year-olds

	1980	1990	2000
Switzerland	0.2	0.4	4.8
Austria	–	–	6.3
Ireland	14.7	17.7	6.4
Netherlands	9.3	11.1	6.6
Denmark	–	11.5	6.7
Germany	–	5.4	8.4
Japan	3.6	4.3	9.2
United States	13.8	11.2	9.3
Norway	4.7	11.8	10.2
United Kingdom	–	10.1	11.8
Sweden	6.2	4.5	11.9
Australia	**12.2**	**13.2**	**12.3**
Canada	12.8	12.4	12.6
New Zealand	–	14.1	13.2
Belgium	–	14.5	15.2
France	15.1	19.1	20.7
Finland	8.8	9.4	21.5
Italy	25.2	28.9	29.7
Mean	10.6	11.7	12.0

Table 4.16: Youth unemployment as share of total unemployment
15 to 24-year-olds unemployed as % of total unemployed

	1980	1990	2000
Germany	–	15.1	11.2
Austria	–	–	17.5
France	41.7	25.8	18.6
Sweden	46.3	39.4	21.6
Japan	21.9	26.9	21.7
Belgium	–	25.0	24.5
Switzerland	23.1	15.9	26.2
Finland	32.5	42.7	28.3
Ireland	40.2	30.6	29.3
Canada	46.7	29.3	30.2
Denmark	–	26.5	30.2
United Kingdom	–	30.7	30.9
Italy	62.4	41.5	32.7
Netherlands	44.7	31.4	32.7
New Zealand	–	42.3	35.9
United States	45.9	35.6	37.5
Australia	**55.9**	**43.4**	**37.8**
Norway	50.0	38.2	39.5
Mean	42.6	31.8	28.1

Table 4.17: Unemployment among national and immigrant groups
Percentages unemployed, 1998

	National males	Foreign males	National females	Foreign females
Norway	3.4	5.9	4.0	6.0
United States	4.3	4.9	4.5	6.0
Australia	**8.3**	**8.6**	**6.9**	**8.2**
Switzerland	2.1	6.8	3.0	8.7
Austria	4.8	10.3	5.3	8.9
United Kingdom	6.8	10.7	5.2	9.4
Ireland	8.0	12.4	7.3	10.4
Canada	10.3	9.9	9.5	11.6
Netherlands	3.1	11.6	5.6	14.1
Germany	8.5	17.3	10.1	15.9
Denmark	3.8	7.3	6.1	16.0
Italy	9.6	5.1	16.7	17.6
Sweden	9.3	23.2	7.5	19.4
Belgium	6.5	18.9	10.9	24.1
France	9.6	22.0	13.5	26.8
Finland	12.7	36.0	13.3	43.7
Mean	6.9	13.2	8.1	15.4

Ranked according to unemployed foreign females.
No data for Japan and New Zealand.

Table 4.18: Unemployment and education
Unemployment rates among people aged 15–64 according to education level, 2000

	Less than upper secondary	Upper secondary	Tertiary
Switzerland	5.0	2.0	1.3
Austria	6.3	3.0	1.6
United States	7.9	3.6	1.8
Netherlands	3.5	2.1	1.8
Ireland	6.8	2.5	1.9
Norway	2.2	2.6	1.9
United Kingdom	8.9	4.5	2.1
Denmark	6.3	3.9	2.6
Belgium	9.8	5.3	2.7
Sweden	8.0	5.3	3.0
Japan	6.0	4.7	3.5
New Zealand	7.8	3.5	3.6
Australia	**7.5**	**4.5**	**3.6**
Canada	9.9	5.8	3.8
Germany	13.7	7.8	4.0
Finland	12.1	8.9	4.7
France	13.9	7.9	5.1
Italy	10.0	7.4	5.9
Mean	8.1	4.7	3.1

Ranked according to unemployment rates among tertiary educated.

Disadvantage in unemployment

The risk and burden of unemployment are borne far from equally among all those in the labour force. The tables on this page identify some of the groups for whom the incidence of unemployment is greatest. (Two key disadvantaged groups not shown are older workers and, for lack of comparative data, indigenous workers.)

The most basic factor accounting for the uneven distribution of unemployment within a country is that the risk of joblessness is greatest among the less skilled and less educated. As can be seen from Table 4.18, it is almost universally true that the higher one's level of educational attainment, the less one's chance of becoming or remaining unemployed. Indeed, the mean degree of unemployment among those who failed to complete secondary schooling is more than twice that for those with a tertiary education.

This is the right point to turn to the vexed question of youth unemployment, as reported in Table 4.15. Note that 'youth' is defined widely to include not just teenagers but all those aged between 15 and 24. It can be seen that, though the rate of youth unemployment fell in a third of the selected countries during the 1990s, more generally the rate rose over the last 20 years of the 20th century and seemed exceptionally high in some European countries. Australia's rate, however, fell gradually to the mean.

But Table 4.15 needs to be interpreted with care. It shows the percentage of 15 to 24-year-olds who are in the labour force and also unemployed; many people of such an age are not in the labour force, but rather in full-time education. So it should not be supposed that these figures tell us what percentage of *all* youth are unemployed. Rather, they tell us the unemployment rate among those youths who have chosen to join the labour force. But, with the exception of those in their mid-twenties who had completed their tertiary education, one would expect most of these youths to be those who had not gone on to full-time tertiary

study or who had quit secondary school prematurely. In other words, we see in these apparently high rates of youth unemployment a demonstration of the truth that unemployment is highest among the least skilled and least educated – a truth whose application is particularly harsh in the case of the young.

Table 4.16 reveals that young people account for a disproportionate share of the unemployed although, for three-quarters of the selected countries, their share has been falling. The burden of slow employment growth at times when economic growth is weak falls heavily on new entrants to the labour force. Firms cease hiring and reduce staff levels by attrition in preference to actually laying staff off, or lay workers off according to the old union rule of 'last on, first off'. In recent years, however, there has been a tendency to lay off older workers first. It may be that youth's share of unemployment is falling because more young people are learning the lesson to stay on in education. Or it may be that their share is falling because of the growing share of older unemployed workers, rejected because of their supposed inability to learn new tricks.

Table 4.17 highlights a further source of labour market disadvantage by comparing rates of unemployment for national and foreign workers. For both males and females, the mean unemployment rate is almost twice as high for foreigners, and is highest among foreign females. Recent arrivals suffer similar new-entrant problems to education-leavers and many are further disadvantaged by language difficulties. Their skills may be judged less valuable and their ability to find work may be diminished by their lack of local contacts. Table 4.17 suggests that in those countries with chronically high unemployment, foreigners have been a particularly disadvantaged group, while in high-immigration countries (the United States, Australia and Switzerland) the differences were relatively lower.

Table 4.19: Part-time employment

Persons working part-time as a proportion of total employment, 1985–2000

	1985	1990	2000
Netherlands	19.5	28.2	33.0
Australia	**20.4**	**22.6**	**27.2**
Japan	16.6	19.2	24.9
Switzerland	–	22.1	24.8
United Kingdom	19.7	20.1	23.0
New Zealand	16.5	19.6	22.7
Norway	–	21.8	20.1
Ireland	7.8	9.8	18.4
Canada	17.0	17.0	18.1
Sweden	–	14.5	17.8
Belgium	11.7	14.2	17.6
Germany	11.1	13.4	17.6
Denmark	20.3	19.2	14.5
France	11.2	12.2	13.8
United States	14.4	13.8	13.0
Austria	–	–	12.4
Italy	7.5	8.8	12.2
Finland	–	7.5	10.5
Mean	14.9	16.7	19.0

Table 4.20: Female share of part-time employment

	1990	2000
Finland	67.2	63.8
United States	68.2	68.0
Australia	**70.8**	**68.3**
Canada	70.1	69.3
Japan	70.5	69.7
Denmark	71.5	69.8
Italy	70.8	70.5
New Zealand	77.1	72.9
Sweden	81.1	72.9
Netherlands	70.4	76.2
Ireland	71.8	76.4
Norway	82.7	77.0
Belgium	79.9	79.0
United Kingdom	85.1	79.9
France	79.8	80.1
Switzerland	82.4	80.6
Germany	89.7	84.5
Austria	–	88.1
Mean	75.8	74.8

Table 4.21: Shortcomings of part-time employment

Column 1: those working part-time who would prefer to work full-time as a proportion of the whole labour force. Column 2 compares hourly earnings of full-time and part-time workers. (Full-time workers' rate = 100.)

	2000	Median hourly earnings part-time:full-time workers
New Zealand	6.0	–
Australia	**5.6**	**89**
Canada	4.3	56
Finland	3.2	–
Sweden	2.9	87
Belgium	2.8	78
France	2.6	73
Ireland	1.9	–
Italy	1.9	87
United Kingdom	1.8	58
Denmark	1.7	–
Germany	1.7	83
Japan	1.7	–
Netherlands	1.2	73
Norway	1.2	–
Austria	1.1	–
Switzerland	1.0	–
United States	–	54
Mean	2.5	74

Part-time work

In many of the selected countries, part-time work has become an increasingly important component of total employment. The term 'total employment' simply adds full-time and part-time jobs together. Similarly, the conventional figures for unemployment count those seeking part-time jobs along with those seeking full-time jobs.

Table 4.19 reveals marked differences between these countries in both the importance of part-time employment and the extent to which its share of total employment grew over the last 15 years of the 20th century. It is not a particularly important feature of employment in the United States and its significance actually declined somewhat over the period. In Australia, by contrast, its share rose from a fifth to well over a quarter in just 15 years. And in the Netherlands it now accounts for a full third of total employment. Other countries exhibiting strong growth were Japan, Ireland and Germany.

Table 4.20 reveals that, regardless of the relative importance of part-time employment – whether in the United States or Australia – it is a form of employment dominated by women. The table also reveals, however, that women's domination slipped somewhat in 14 of the selected countries during the 1990s. What the table does not reveal is that part-time jobs are predominantly in the services sector, and in many countries the rapid growth in part-time employment has accompanied the rapid growth in the services sector's share of total employment. The growth in part-time employment has also been associated with the decline in full-time job opportunities for early leavers from the education system. Thus part-time employment is dominated by two kinds of worker: students in full-time education and married women. This table is a reminder, however, that some mature-age men are now accepting part-time jobs rather than going without.

It is often assumed that part-time employment is, almost by definition, inferior to full-time employment. Such a conclusion is too sweeping and may betray a breadwinner-focused view of the labour market. The growth in part-time employment is partly a function of increased demand from employers; it suits many firms in retailing and hospitality, for instance, to have a lot of extra hands during peak periods in the week, but a lot fewer hands during slow periods. But the growth is also a product of increased willingness to supply such labour on the part of some workers. Many mothers with young families would prefer to work less than the full 35–40 hours a week, as would most full-time students.

So, though it is undoubtedly true that many people obliged to accept part-time employment would prefer to work more or even full-time hours, it is equally true that many part-time employees are perfectly happy with the amount of hours they work.

Table 4.21 sheds further light on the debate over the wider implications of part-time employment. The first data column shows those working part-time who would prefer to be working full-time and expresses this as a proportion of the entire labour force. So this is actually a measure of 'underemployment' and it can be seen that the rates of underemployment are particularly high in such English-speaking countries as New Zealand, Australia and Canada. An ABS survey in 2003 found that four in five part-time workers in Australia would prefer to be working more hours.

The second data column in Table 4.21 takes the median hourly rate of earnings for all part-time employees and expresses it as a proportion of the median hourly rate for all full-time employees. Not surprisingly, this ratio falls well below parity. It is saying that those who are more advanced in their careers and thus are paid more highly tend to be full-time, not part-time. Only in countries where the ratio is particularly low – Canada, the United Kingdom and the United States – is it reasonable to interpret this as a sign that part-time employment is particularly badly paid.

Table 4.22: Temporary employment

Temporary employment as % of all employment

	1983	1994
Australia	15.6	23.5
Finland	11.3	13.5
Sweden	12.0	13.5
Denmark	12.5	12.0
France	3.3	11.0
Netherlands	5.8	10.9
Japan	10.3	10.4
Germany	10.0	10.3
Ireland	6.1	9.4
Canada	7.5	8.8
Italy	6.6	7.3
United Kingdom	5.5	6.5
Belgium	5.4	5.1
United States	–	2.2
Mean	8.6	10.3

No data on Austria, New Zealand, Norway and Switzerland.

Table 4.23: Duration of employment

	Median duration of employment, all adults (years)	Mean duration of employment, all adults (years)	Mean duration of employment, those aged 45+ (years)
Germany	10.7	9.7	16.2
Italy	8.9	11.6	19.2
Belgium	8.4	11.2	19.4
Japan	8.3	11.3	18.0
Finland	7.8	10.5	16.6
Sweden	7.8	10.5	15.9
France	7.7	10.7	17.5
Austria	6.9	10.0	17.8
Switzerland	6.0	9.0	14.6
Canada	5.9	7.9	13.8
Netherlands	5.5	8.7	16.0
Ireland	5.3	8.7	15.4
United Kingdom	5.0	7.8	12.2
Denmark	4.4	7.9	14.5
United States	4.2	7.4	12.4
Australia	3.4	6.4	11.1
Mean	6.6	9.3	15.7

Figures given are for 1995.
No data for New Zealand and Norway.

Table 4.24: Employment protection legislation

Higher score represents greater legislative protection for employees.
Data is for regular employees in 1990s.

	Overall protection score	Procedural stringency	Compensation no-fault dismissal	Difficulty of dismissal
Netherlands	3.1	5.0	1.0	3.3
Germany	2.8	3.5	1.3	3.5
Italy	2.8	1.5	2.9	4.0
Sweden	2.8	3.0	1.6	3.8
Japan	2.7	2.0	1.8	4.3
Austria	2.6	2.5	2.0	3.3
Norway	2.4	1.5	1.1	4.5
France	2.3	2.8	1.5	2.8
Finland	2.1	2.8	1.4	2.3
New Zealand	1.7	1.3	1.4	2.3
Denmark	1.6	0.5	1.9	2.3
Ireland	1.6	2.0	0.8	2.0
Belgium	1.5	0.5	2.3	1.8
Switzerland	1.2	0.5	1.5	1.5
Australia	1.0	0.5	1.0	1.5
Canada	0.9	0.0	0.8	2.0
United Kingdom	0.8	1.0	1.1	0.3
United States	0.2	0.0	0.0	0.5
Mean	1.9	1.7	1.4	2.6

Overall score = mean of other three components.

Job security

For many people, having a job is nice, but a second issue quickly springs to mind: how secure is it? The tables on this page provide several indicators that help to answer that question for the selected countries.

On the face of it, Table 4.22 leads to a startling conclusion: although temporary employment seems to be increasing in almost all countries, its highest level by far, and its largest increase during the period, was in Australia. But the discrepancy is so great that we should inquire further before accepting such a conclusion. We could start with an obvious question that too often isn't asked: 'temporary' employment sounds a bad thing, but what does it mean exactly? And, speaking of exactitude, a question that should be close to our minds in all cross-country comparisons is: are we sure that what's being compared has been measured the same way in each country?

In this case the answer to the latter question is no. The term 'temporary employment' is an unfamiliar one in Australia, and the figures that appear in the table are for 'casual' (as opposed to 'permanent') employment. By contrast, the term 'temporary' is used in Europe to refer to people employed under contract for a fixed period. In Australia, people employed on a casual basis may not be in the job for long, or the job may run for many years. On the other hand, the Australian tradition of allowing for casual employment, where some rights of employment (e.g. leave entitlements) are forsaken for higher pay, is not present in many European countries. So the comparability of the figures for less regulated Australia with more regulated Europe has been a matter of dispute among scholars.

Nevertheless the picture given by Table 4.22 is consistent with that given by Table 4.23, which examines the related issue of duration of employment – how long people tend to stay with one employer before leaving, whether voluntarily or involuntarily. It can be seen from the second data column that the mean length of time is quite long, though it is shortest in Australia – shorter even than for hire-and-fire America. The first data column, however, suggests that the mean gives a somewhat exaggerated impression of the degree of job stability. The median (or dead-middle) job duration is shorter than the mean (arithmetic average) duration, suggesting that a small proportion of particularly long durations have pushed up the mean. The third data column suggests that this is because of the longer duration of older workers.

It should not be assumed, however, that the longer the duration the better. Very long job durations may be a sign of an inflexible and relatively immobile labour force, incapable of adjusting quickly and easily to changes in technology, consumer demand and other structural factors. From the employee's perspective, an immobile labour force may be one where opportunities for advancement and the challenge of a new job are limited. Clearly, some mixture of security and mobility is the ideal.

Table 4.24 offers an assessment by the OECD of the strength of legislated protections against unfair dismissal in the selected countries. Countries are ranked from strongest to weakest protection, based on a series of legislative provisions. Australia's ranking is a lot lower than could be expected judging by some of the rhetoric from employer groups and conservative politicians.

Overall, however, the ranking confirms the conventional view: the European countries have the strongest protections against dismissal and the United States has the weakest, with the other English-speaking countries (including Australia) in between. The next part of the (conservative) conventional wisdom says this is what explains why unemployment is so much higher in Europe than in the United States. But a comparison of the rankings in this table with the average rates of unemployment in the 1990s shown in Table 4.12 finds little correlation.

Table 4.25: Annual hours worked

Mean hours worked per person in employment per year

	1980	1990	2000
Australia	**1878**	**1869**	**1855**
United States	1883	1943	1835
Japan	2121	2031	1821
New Zealand	–	1820	1817
Canada	1805	1790	1767
Finland	1815	1728	1730
United Kingdom	1769	1767	1708
Ireland	1909	1728	1690
Sweden	1503	1546	1625
Italy	1790	1694	1622
France	1795	1657	1590
Switzerland	–	1606	1568
Belgium	1684	1679	1530
Denmark	–	–	1504
Germany	1724	1573	1482
Netherlands	1581	1433	1381
Norway	1512	1432	1376
Mean	1765	1708	1643

No data given for Austria.

Table 4.26: Persons working over 40 hours a week

Percentage of persons in employment working more than 40 hours/week

	1990	2000
Japan	78.3	75.9
United States	65.2	67.6
Switzerland	71.4	66.9
New Zealand	66.0	65.4
Italy	66.3	63.8
Sweden	64.0	61.5
Austria	65.9	57.6
Canada	57.5	54.7
United Kingdom	50.5	49.8
Australia	**47.1**	**48.6**
Germany	43.5	43.7
Ireland	54.5	38.4
Netherlands	31.6	36.9
Belgium	28.8	28.7
Denmark	17.1	22.1
France	26.2	21.4
Finland	12.5	16.0
Norway	18.7	15.8
Mean	48.1	46.4

Table 4.27: Annual leave and public holidays

	Public holidays each year	Statutory minimum annual leave entitlement days	Total public holidays plus statutory minimum days	Average annual leave entitlement days	Total public holidays plus average annual leave days
Australia	**10**	**20**	**30**	**–**	**–**
Austria	13	20	33	–	–
Belgium	10	20	33	–	–
Denmark	9.5	25	34.5	30	39.5
Finland	12	24	36	25	37
France	11	25	36	–	–
Germany	11	20	31	29	40
Ireland	9	20	29	20	29
Italy	12	20	32	28	40
Japan	15	10	25	18	33
Netherlands	8	20	28	31	39
New Zealand	11	–	–	–	–
Sweden	11	25	36	25	36
United Kingdom	8	20	28	25	33
United States	10	0	10	17	27

No data on Canada, Norway or Switzerland.

Working hours

There may be few matters of economic statistical fact more prone to confidently held prejudices than the question of how hard people of different nationalities work. It is widely held, for instance, that the Japanese work the longest hours, rarely taking holidays – economic ants was the cultured description of French Prime Minister Edith Cresson. The Americans would not be far behind them, whereas the Europeans are notorious for short hours and long holidays – probably with the Brits leading the way. As for the Australians, they are wonderful people in many ways, but hardly renowned for their devotion to hard work. In the land of the long weekend, the workers are so laid back the economy is down for the count.

If any of those views strike a chord, you may be in for some shocks from Table 4.25, which shows the average number of hours worked in a year by the country's workers. The first surprise is that average hours have been falling since 1980 (and probably before) in almost all the selected countries. The next surprise is that Australia's very small fall was enough to shift it up to first place – so Australians take the prize as the hardest workers in the developed world! There is a clear gap between the top four countries – Australia, Japan, the United States and New Zealand – and the rest, with several European countries averaging around 300 hours less work for each person each year.

There is a range of factors that influence the number of hours the typical worker works in a week. First would come the length of a country's standard working week – 35, 38 or 40 hours – then the extent of overtime worked, then the length of annual leave taken and the number of public holidays. Another easily forgotten factor is where a particular national economy happened to be in the business cycle. One would expect average hours to be higher when the economy was booming and lower when it was in the doldrums.

However, total annual hours worked is a crude measure that takes no account of the relative mix of full-time and part-time workers. The reminder that fully 27% of Australia's workers are part-time (Table 4.19) makes its position at the top of the league of hard workers even more remarkable.

At first blush Table 4.26 appears to offer an indicator of the degree of workaholism in the selected countries. But 40 hours is close to the standard working week in many countries, so it is nearer to being an imperfect measure of the proportion of full-time employees in the workforce. Certainly, the high proportion of part-time workers in countries such as Australia and the Netherlands does most to explain their low places in the table.

The rise in part-time work might suggest that Tables 4.25 and 4.26 would show an even greater fall in total working hours. But perhaps the totals mask trends going in opposite directions, with both more part-time workers and more full-time workers working longer. In Australia, the proportion of all employees working 35–40 hours per week dropped from 43% to 33% between 1985 and 2000. At the same time, those working more than 45 hours weekly rose from 18% to 26%.

Table 4.27 further shatters many illusions by revealing that, in the main, there is not a great deal of difference between countries in the number of public holidays per year – but with Japan, of all countries, taking the prize for the most. And while the length of annual leave differs more widely, Australia's four weeks is by no means excessive. It is noteworthy that while the United States has no statutory leave entitlement, in practice people take an average of more than three weeks. Certainly, the perception that Aussies are too laid back to take work seriously is no longer true – if it ever was.

Table 4.28: Trade union membership
Union members as % of all employees

	1970	1980	1990	2000
Sweden	68	80	84	82
Denmark	60	76	73	76
Finland	51	69	72	76
Norway	53	57	56	57
Belgium	42	53	50	53
Ireland	59	64	59	45
Austria	55	49	45	37
Italy	36	49	39	35
Canada	30	35	36	30
United Kingdom	46	52	40	29
Germany	32	35	32	26
Australia	**45**	**50**	**43**	**25**
Netherlands	32	31	25	25
Japan	35	31	25	22
New Zealand	52	60	51	22
Switzerland	30	27	24	22
United States	27	22	16	13
France	22	19	10	9
Mean	43	48	43	38

Table 4.29: Days lost in industrial disputes
Days lost per annum per 1000 employees in industrial disputes, 1970–2000

	1970–75	1976–80	1981–85	1986–90	1991–95	1996–2000
Austria	12	2	2	1	5	1
Germany	41	40	44	4	9	1
Japan	117	30	8	3	2	1
Switzerland	1	2	0	0	1	2
Netherlands	38	25	18	11	28	4
Sweden	59	220	36	120	46	8
New Zealand	164	325	339	349	41	15
Belgium	228	182	35	38	26	18
United Kingdom	512	509	384	113	20	18
France	161	148	68	31	24	20
Finland	488	487	267	336	176	45
Italy	1 027	932	491	1	131	52
Norway	37	36	48	126	53	52
United States	417	226	108	72	38	54
Ireland	386	669	358	170	83	64
Australia	**547**	**476**	**313**	**176**	**104**	**68**
Canada	719	737	447	374	141	180
Denmark	307	77	258	36	40	262
Mean	292	285	179	109	54	48

Trade unions

Tables 4.28 and 4.29 document a dramatic change in the position of trade unions in the selected countries. Between 1980 and 2000, membership of trade unions as a percentage of all employees (trade union density) fell by one-fifth from an 18-nation mean of 48% to 38%.

The movement has not been universal. The top five countries in Table 4.28 (the Scandinavian countries plus Belgium) showed an increase in trade union density over the last three decades of the 20th century, but the remaining 13 countries all showed a decline. The range from smallest to largest widened from 46 percentage points in 1970 to 73 in 2000. Some (France, the United States), where trade union membership was already small, showed even further decline. Most dramatically, in a range of countries where trade union membership was considerable (Ireland, Austria, the United Kingdom, Australia and New Zealand), density declined by a large amount. The declines were biggest in Australia (20 percentage points) and New Zealand (30).

The decline in the number of days lost through industrial disputes per 1000 employees is even more spectacular. The 18-nation mean dropped from 292 in the early 1970s to 48 in the second half of the 1990s, down to about a sixth of the earlier level. The 1970s saw a peak of union militancy because of the destabilising effects of high inflation. The change since then has been so great and so universal that Australia was ranked 16th in the early 1970s with a figure of 547, and even though that number had dropped to 68 in the late 1990s, it still ranked 16th.

The top six countries in the table all had an annual average of fewer than ten days lost per 1000 employees in the late 1990s. Switzerland and Austria have consistently been almost free of industrial stoppages, while Germany and Japan have been just behind them. Figures on industrial disputes are very volatile. The five-year average largely obliterates such blips, though Denmark's centralised system and large union membership produces large swings.

Although the substantial trends are not in doubt, there are problems of measurement in both tables. The figures on trade union density are based on both surveys and administrative data, the latter sometimes giving a higher estimate by a couple of percentage points, due to the reporting organisation inflating figures, or members (or their spouses) forgetting their memberships when polled in surveys. On the whole, these discrepancies are fairly small. Occasionally there are larger discrepancies. Normally this is because one source is using gross figures and the other net. Net membership only includes those employed, while gross union density also counts members when they are retired and unemployed. The discrepancy tends to be greatest in those countries (Denmark, Finland, Belgium and Sweden) where unions play a publicly subsidised role in welfare schemes.

The problems of gaining harmonised and consistent data for industrial disputes are much greater. In calculating the rates for time lost, there are divergences in how both the numerator and denominator are counted. Countries have different minima for number of days of labour lost before strikes are counted in their statistics. (Australia is more inclusive than many others.) Some types of strike (political and unofficial – 'wildcat') or stoppages among some groups (public sector, armed forces) are excluded in some countries. Governments also change their own methods of counting (see Italy during the 1980s for the most extreme example!). Percentages are sometimes given of all employed (as here); sometimes of civilian employees, and sometimes of some ill-defined group called workers. So these figures cannot be used to explore nice distinctions and small differences.

However, the overwhelming trends over time and the extreme differences between countries still stand, even allowing for the severe measurement problems. Tables 4.28 and 4.29 represent a significant shift in social power in many of the selected countries.

Table 4.30: Trade union and wage-setting structures

	Conflict level 1970s	Union density 2000	Wage-setting arrangements	Bargaining governability	Collective bargaining coverage 1996	Share of 3 largest affiliates of largest peak union body
Norway	Low	High	Stable centralised	High	70	74
Sweden	Low	High	More decentralised	High	92	58
Austria	Low	Medium	Stable centralised	High	99	49
Germany	Low	Medium	Stable centralised	High	84	57
Netherlands	Low	Medium	Stable centralised	High	82	63
Japan	Low	Low	Stable centralised	Low	18	33
Switzerland	Low	Low	Stable centralised	High	48	67
Belgium	Medium	High	Stable centralised	Low	96	44
Denmark	Medium	High	More decentralised	High	69	56
France	Medium	Low	More decentralised	Low	95	33
New Zealand	Medium	Low	More decentralised	High	33	41
Finland	High	High	More decentralised	High	83	46
Ireland	High	High	Stable centralised	–	–	43
Australia	**High**	**Medium**	**More decentralised**	**High**	**70**	**28**
Canada	High	Medium	Stable decentralised	High	38	63
Italy	High	Medium	More centralised	Low	82	46
United Kingdom	High	Medium	Stable decentralised	Low	37	43
United States	High	Low	Stable decentralised	Low	16	26

Patterns of industrial relations

Each country, and often each industry, has generated its own peculiar arrangements for industrial relations arising from its history. It is impossible to capture the intricacies of individual arrangements, themselves often changing with the balance of power and new threats and opportunities.

Table 4.30 very imperfectly explores the extensive differences regarding the role of trade unions in the selected countries, not only in their relative strength, but in the institutions through which industrial relations are conducted, and in the degree and nature of the conflicts surrounding industrial issues.

It is organised first according to the degree of conflict traditionally present, as revealed by their relative level of industrial disputes in the 1970s (Table 4.29), and then according to the relative strength of the unions as measured by contemporary union density (the proportion of all employees belonging to a union).

At the top are five European countries where industrial relations are relatively consensual, where union membership is high, and where industrial relations are strongly institutionalised. These countries are characterised by unions playing a prominent role, where their legitimacy is broadly accepted, and conflict is not acute or disruptive.

It has been argued that consensual relations are more likely when trade unions take a system-wide rather than sectional perspective, and this occurs when there is a fairly small number of large unions and they are broadly inclusive. A combination of their relatively high union density (second data column) and their consolidation into a relatively few large unions (last column) suggests this characterises these five countries.

Denmark and Belgium are similar to the top five, with unions an important and accepted social institution, but are characterised by rather more conflict. Switzerland and Japan are consensual systems, but where the unions are considerably weaker. In Japan's case many of the key aspects rest on informal rather than legal processes.

At the bottom are five countries which traditionally had high levels of industrial conflict. Although there are important variations between them, in at least some, unions have become more marginalised and their role has been much more contested.

Data columns 3 to 5 describe aspects of the industrialisation of industrial relations. Bargaining governability refers to whether agreements are legally enforceable and followed by a peace obligation. For the five top countries it is high, as it is for most others except for the most fragmented systems at the bottom.

The second last column describes the proportion of employees covered by a collective agreement. Again all five countries at the top of the table have a high percentage of employees who are covered. The smallest percentage covered is in the United States. Over time the percentages covered have been fairly constant in most countries, but a few have shown spectacular drops. The United Kingdom dropped from 80% in 1980 down to 37% in 1996, and New Zealand from 67% in 1990 to 33% by 1996. Australia's fall from 88% to 70% is already substantial, but does not reflect the greater changes within collective bargaining itself from award coverage to enterprise bargaining.

Centralisation of wage-setting is a complex concept, and the many permutations of national arrangements have given rise to a variety of academic measures. The most comprehensive work, by Traxler and colleagues, distinguished twelve different categories to describe the different processes. Wage-setting is most fragmented or decentralised when bargaining is confined to individual firms or plants and most centralised when it is conducted by peak organisations and/or government. Column 4 describes whether these institutions have been broadly stable or changing. Except for some change in Sweden, the top five countries have been stable in their institutional settings, which are relatively centralised. This high degree of institutionalisation gives predictability to all participants. Some countries were always fragmented in their systems, but a number, including Australia, have been moving from a more to a less centralised system.

Table 5.1: Government spending				
Total government outlays as % of GDP				
	1960–73	1974–79	1980–89	1990–99
Sweden	38.9	54.4	62.9	63.2
Denmark	33.8	46.7	56.5	57.7
Finland	30.3	38.3	43.1	55.1
Belgium	39.1	52.0	59.8	53.3
Netherlands	40.8	53.6	61.2	53.1
Austria	38.7	45.8	50.7	52.9
Italy	33.7	42.9	49.2	52.7
France	38.0	43.1	49.8	52.4
Norway	36.7	47.0	46.6	49.8
Canada	31.6	40.9	46.3	49.1
Germany	37.5	47.5	47.8	48.1
United Kingdom	36.7	44.9	45.0	42.8
Ireland	34.4	45.1	51.5	38.7
Australia	**24.4**	**34.4**	**36.9**	**36.6**
Switzerland	20.3	29.2	30.3	36.4
United States	29.1	32.2	35.3	36.2
Japan	19.5	28.4	32.7	35.1
Mean	33.1	42.7	47.4	47.8

Table 5.2: Taxation				
Total taxation as % of GDP				
	1970	1980	1990	2000
Sweden	38.7	47.5	53.6	54.2
Denmark	39.2	43.9	47.1	48.8
Finland	31.9	36.2	44.8	46.9
Belgium	34.5	42.4	43.2	45.6
France	34.1	40.6	43.0	45.3
Austria	34.6	39.8	40.4	43.7
Italy	26.1	30.4	38.9	42.0
Netherlands	35.8	43.6	43.0	41.4
Norway	34.5	42.7	41.8	40.3
Germany	32.3	37.5	35.7	37.9
United Kingdom	37.0	35.2	36.8	37.4
Canada	30.8	30.7	35.9	35.8
Switzerland	22.5	28.9	30.6	35.7
New Zealand	26.8	32.4	37.6	35.1
Australia	**22.5**	**27.4**	**29.3**	**31.5**
Ireland	28.8	31.4	33.5	31.1
United States	27.7	27.0	26.7	29.6
Japan	20.0	25.1	30.1	27.1
Mean	31.0	35.7	38.4	39.4

Table 5.3: Trends in tax levels					
Year	Mean tax level (% of GDP)	Change in 5-year period	Number of countries with increasing share in 5-year period	Number with stable share	Number with decreasing share in 5-year period
1965	28.1				
1970	31.0	+2.9	17	0	1
1975	34.2	+3.2	15	2	1
1980	35.7	+1.5	15	2	1
1985	37.4	+1.7	15	2	1
1990	38.4	+1.0	7	4	7
1995	38.6	+0.2	9	5	4
2000	39.4	+0.8	11	1	6

5 GOVERNMENT TAXES AND SPENDING
Government outlays and taxation

The tables on this page show one method of measuring the size of government: government outlays and taxation compared with the size of the economy (GDP). By this measure the size of the selected countries' governments varies considerably, with the largest roughly twice the smallest. The single factor likely to do most to explain differences in size is the comprehensiveness and generosity of countries' social welfare systems. So Sweden is at the top and Japan at the bottom. Despite the widespread belief to the contrary, Australians are not heavily taxed.

The tables reveal the quite dramatic growth in the size of government throughout the developed world over the last 30 years of the 20th century. Note that for government outlays or revenue to rise as proportion of GDP they must grow at a faster real rate than the economy overall.

It can be seen from Table 5.1 that government outlays (spending) grew particularly strongly in the 1970s in virtually all the selected countries and continued growing in the 1980s, though at a somewhat slower rate. In the 1990s, however, the rise in the overall mean was minor and, within this, outlays declined as a share of GDP in five countries and rose at a significantly slower rate in the remainder. It is notable that most of the countries where outlays failed to keep pace with the economy were countries where outlays were already particularly high. Because the outlays side of governments' budgets cannot be unrelated to the revenue side, it is possible that these countries have hit some sort of ceiling of taxpayer tolerance. Relative positions changed little, however. The countries that began the 30-year period at the bottom of the outlays league table – Australia, Switzerland, the United States and Japan – also ended it at the bottom.

Australia's government outlays share was particularly low before 1973, but jumped in the 1970s, mainly during the three-year term of the Whitlam Government. Outlays continued expanding during the 1980s – though at a

rate significantly slower than for most of the other countries – and actually fell marginally in the 1990s after many years of government concern about the size of budget deficits.

Tables 5.2 and 5.3 show that the same story of marked growth in the size of government throughout the developed world can be seen on the revenue side of government budgets. Table 5.3 makes it clear that the revenue expansion was greatest in the 1960s and 1970s, the momentum slowing in the 1980s and particularly in the 1990s. From the mid-1980s, a large minority of the countries managed to have their tax revenue grow more slowly than GDP or at least at the same rate.

It is interesting to ponder the relationship between the growth of outlays and of taxation. Did governments permit their spending to expand because their revenue was growing strongly, or did the public's demand for greater government spending oblige governments to augment their revenue? The causation is likely to have run in opposite directions at different times. Up to 1973, the steady and uneventful growth in the public's real incomes, accompanied by moderate but persistent inflation, allowed governments to expand their activities – and both sides of their budgets – with minimal complaint from voters. The high inflation of the 1970s caused rapid growth in income-tax collections as wage-earners were pushed into higher tax brackets. This allowed further expansion in government spending but seems eventually to have provoked widespread resistance to further tax increases as many people became convinced they were now overtaxed. Governments became increasingly reluctant to risk proposing overt tax increases and were under continuing pressure to limit the effects of 'bracket creep' by announcing regular (but short-lasting) 'tax cuts'. In the 1990s, almost all countries succeeded in holding down the expansion of taxation as a proportion of GDP, while a few managed to achieve slower growth in tax collections than in the economy.

Table 5.4: Components of taxation, 2000

Types of tax revenues as % of total tax

	Personal income tax	Corporate income tax	Social security employees' contributions	Social security employers' contributions	Payroll & workforce taxes	Property taxes	Goods & services taxes
Denmark	52.6	4.9	3.9	0.7	0.4	3.3	32.5
New Zealand	42.8	11.7	0	0	0.9	5.4	34.5
United States	42.4	8.5	10.2	11.9	0	10.1	15.7
Canada	36.8	11.1	5.7	8.2	2.1	9.7	24.4
Australia	**36.7**	**20.6**	**0**	**0**	**6.2**	**8.9**	**27.5**
Sweden	35.6	7.5	5.5	22.0	4.3	3.4	20.7
Belgium	31.0	8.1	9.7	18.6	0	3.3	25.4
Finland	30.8	11.8	4.7	18.8	0	2.5	29.1
Ireland	30.8	12.1	4.2	8.6	0	5.6	37.2
Switzerland	30.6	7.9	11.0	10.8	0	8.1	19.7
United Kingdom	29.2	9.8	6.7	9.4	0	11.9	32.3
Italy	25.7	7.5	5.4	19.8	0	4.3	28.4
Norway	25.6	15.2	7.7	13.3	0	2.4	34.4
Germany	25.3	4.8	17.2	19.2	0	2.3	28.1
Austria	22.1	4.7	14.0	16.4	6.2	1.3	28.4
Japan	20.6	13.5	14.2	18.6	0	10.3	18.9
France	18.0	7.0	8.9	24.9	2.3	6.8	25.8
Netherlands	14.9	10.1	19.5	11.4	0	5.4	29.0
Mean	30.6	9.8	8.3	12.9	1.2	5.8	27.3

The percentages in each row sum to less than 100% because miscellaneous 'other' taxes are omitted.

Table 5.5: Broad components of taxation, 2000

	Direct taxes on individuals	Business and property taxes	Consumption taxes
Denmark	57	9	33
United States	53	31	16
Canada	43	31	24
Germany	43	26	28
New Zealand	43	18	35
Switzerland	42	27	20
Belgium	41	30	25
Sweden	41	37	21
Australia	**37**	**36**	**28**
Austria	36	29	28
Finland	36	33	29
United Kingdom	36	31	32
Ireland	35	26	37
Japan	35	42	19
Netherlands	34	27	29
Norway	33	31	34
Italy	31	32	28
France	27	41	26
Mean 2000	39	30	27
Mean 1970	37	27	31

Direct taxes include income tax and employees' social security taxes; consumption taxes are the same as Table 5.4; the other four columns of Table 5.4 are combined under business and property taxes.
Most percentages do not sum to 100 because of rounding and because miscellaneous 'other' taxes are not included.

Components of taxation

Whereas Table 5.2 showed the levels of total taxation (as a proportion of GDP) in the selected countries, Table 5.4 shows the extent of each country's reliance on particular types of taxation. It can be seen that, overall, personal income tax – the tax of which people are most conscious – accounts for only about a third of all the tax revenue raised by all levels of government. Taxes on the purchase of goods and services account for less than a third, meaning that a host of less prominent taxes account for roughly the remaining third.

Table 5.5 reveals that, overall, the broad mix of the main tax types did not change greatly over the last 30 years of the 20th century (even though the total amount of taxes raised grew by more than 8 percentage points of GDP). Even so, they were years of almost continuous debate about the merits and demerits of particular taxes and endless adjustments and bouts of tax 'reform'. Taxes can be criticised or supported on grounds of economic efficiency (the extent to which they distort people's choices about work, consumption, saving or investment), fairness (progressive taxes take a larger proportion of high incomes than low incomes, whereas regressive taxes do the reverse) and administrative simplicity. Some taxes are more susceptible to evasion (illegal) or avoidance (the exploitation of legal loopholes) than others.

The categories in Table 5.5 are too broad to reveal some more subtle trends. One was the tendency for taxes on specific goods and services (including 'sin' taxes on alcohol, tobacco and petrol) to be outweighed by general consumption taxes. While the mean for the former fell from 18% to 10% of total tax revenue over the period, the mean for the latter rose from less than 14% to more than 16%. Most European countries have long had general consumption taxes in the form of value-added taxes, and various other countries – New Zealand, Japan, Canada and Australia – have joined them more recently with the renamed 'goods and services tax'.

Australia's reliance on the taxation of goods and services was about average even before its introduction of the GST, and has not been greatly increased by that introduction. Only the United States now has no national-level general consumption tax, which would do much to explain why it has the lowest reliance – 16% – on the taxing of goods and services.

Overall, about 20% of tax revenue is raised via compulsory social security 'contributions' from employers and employees, with the less visible employer contributions exceeding employee contributions by roughly 5:3. While its states' payroll taxes seemingly give Australia a heavy reliance on 'payroll and workforce taxes', in truth employers' social security contributions are very similar to a payroll tax.

Australia and New Zealand are exceptional in not having taxes tied directly to social security. This means that, as a matter of arithmetic, their remaining taxes account for higher proportions of total collections. But the funding of social security payments through general taxation also explains why they are among the countries most dependent on income tax.

The high proportion of revenue raised through income tax – the most visible of taxes – may explain why many Australians consider themselves to be heavily taxed, whereas Table 5.2 revealed that they are among the most lightly taxed. It is noteworthy that when personal income tax and employees' social security contributions are combined, Australia drops back to the middle of the pack.

Table 5.4 reveals that Australia is the country most heavily reliant on corporate income tax. It should be noted, however, that it also has one of the fullest dividend imputation systems, meaning that local shareholders receive an income-tax credit for the full extent of the company tax already paid on their share of company profits.

Table 5.6: Government deficits and surpluses

Government net lending as % of GDP

	1970	1975	1977	1982	1989	1993	2000
Norway	3.2	3.3	1.2	4.0	1.8	−1.4	14.8
Finland	4.3	4.9	6.2	3.0	6.7	−7.3	6.9
Ireland	−3.7	−11.1	6.5	−13.2	−2.4	−2.7	4.6
Sweden	4.4	2.8	1.7	−7.0	5.4	−11.9	4.1
Canada	0.5	−2.6	−3.1	−5.8	−3.4	−7.7	3.2
Denmark	2.1	−1.3	0.4	−8.4	0.3	−2.9	2.8
Netherlands	−1.2	−2.9	−0.8	−6.6	−4.7	−3.2	2.2
United Kingdom	2.6	−4.5	−3.3	−2.8	0.9	−8.0	1.9
United States	−1.4	−4.4	−1.3	−4.1	−2.8	−4.7	1.7
Germany	0.2	−5.6	−2.4	−3.3	0.1	−3.1	1.2
Australia	**−0.1**	**−3.9**	**−4.6**	**−5.1**	**−0.5**	**−4.9**	**0.3**
Belgium	−2.4	−5.6	−6.0	−12.6	−7.6	−7.3	0.1
Italy	−3.5	−11.7	−8.0	−11.2	−9.8	−10.0	−0.3
Austria	1.2	−2.5	−2.3	−3.4	−3.1	−4.2	−1.1
France	0.9	−2.4	−0.8	−2.9	−1.8	−6.0	−1.4
Japan	1.6	−2.8	−3.8	−3.6	2.5	−1.6	−6.6
Mean	0.5	−3.1	−2.1	−5.2	−1.1	−5.3	2.1

Countries ranked according to balance in 2000.
Data for New Zealand and Switzerland too incomplete to include.

Table 5.7: Government debt

General government debt as % of GDP

	1990	1995	2000
Norway	−42.0	−32.9	−60.0
Finland	−35.5	−13.3	−32.9
Sweden	−7.8	22.7	8.3
Australia	**10.7**	**27.3**	**12.4**
New Zealand	–	35.5	22.2
Denmark	33.0	46.2	25.9
United Kingdom	15.1	36.9	33.1
Germany	17.8	39.4	41.5
France	16.1	35.9	42.2
United States	49.9	59.2	43.4
Netherlands	35.4	–	44.8
Austria	37.5	50.5	47.5
Japan	12.4	16.9	51.1
Canada	61.2	88.0	65.0
Italy	83.7	108.7	98.7
Belgium	116.0	124.9	102.2
Mean	26.9	43.1	34.1

– sign means government has net financial assets.
No data for Switzerland or Ireland.

Table 5.8: Australian governments' comparative performance: budget balance

Mean budget surplus/deficit as % of GDP during period of each government

	McMahon 1970–72	Whitlam 1973–75	Fraser 1976–82	Hawke 1983–91	Keating 1992–95	Howard 1996–2002
17-country mean	0.4	−1.0	−3.2	−2.9	−4.7	+0.1
Australia	**−0.3**	**−2.4**	**−3.8**	**−3.1**	**−4.5**	**−0.1**
Australia's rank	**11**	**12**	**12**	**9**	**9**	**9**
Highest country	Sweden	Finland	Finland	Norway	Norway	Norway
Value	4.7	5.1	4.6	4.5	0.2	9.2
Lowest country	Italy	Italy	Ireland	Italy	Sweden	Japan
Value	−5.4	−8.6	−9.8	−10.9	−9.6	−5.8

Government deficits and debt

When governments' revenue exceeds their outlays they have a budget surplus, which is available to be lent to the private sector. More commonly over the last 30 years of the 20th century, however, outlays exceeded revenue and so governments incurred budget deficits that needed to be covered by *borrowing* from the private sector.

Unlike the pursuit of growth and lower unemployment, the budget balance is not an end in itself but a means to government's ends. Nor can it be assumed that a balanced budget is better than a budget deficit and a budget surplus better still. Because budgets are an instrument of economic management rather than an objective of that management, the desirable size and sign on the budget balance will be a function of where the economy happens to be in the business cycle at the time. The judgement will be influenced also by the degree of investment (as opposed to recurrent) spending included in the budget.

Table 5.6 first shows the modest budget balances typical before the postwar golden age ended in the early 1970s, then the ever deeper cyclical troughs reached in the world recessions of the mid-1970s, early 1980s and early 1990s, as well as the cyclical peaks reached soon before the onset of the next recession. Finally, it shows how many countries managed to achieve budget surpluses by 2000. They did so partly by the diligence of their 'fiscal consolidation' (cuts in spending), but mainly because of the length of the 1990s boom in the US and world economies.

It can be seen that notwithstanding their very high levels of government spending (Table 5.1), the Scandinavian countries have generally managed to avoid running budget deficits – though Norway's remarkable story of almost continuous surpluses is explained by its prudence in salting away for the future part of the proceeds from its exploitation of North Sea oil deposits. At the other end of the spectrum, several of the core countries of the European Union have been running large budget deficits almost continuously over the period, despite their mature economies and

relatively old populations. Japan's budgetary performance deteriorated markedly during the 1990s as it repeatedly sought to use fiscal stimulus to lift itself from its post-bubble deflation.

Australia's performance was worse than the mean until the mid-1980s, but better than the mean since then as first the Hawke Government then the Howard Government emphasised fiscal consolidation.

Clearly, when governments run budget deficits their borrowing to cover those deficits adds to the stock of their debt, whereas budget surpluses are used to repay debt. Thus the ranking of budget balances shown in Table 5.6 correlates well with the ranking of government debt shown in Table 5.7. It can be seen from the latter table that, overall, debt levels grew significantly as a result of the big budget deficits incurred during the recession of the early 1990s, but then fell back significantly as a result of the widespread budget surpluses achieved in the second half of the 1990s. Debt levels continued growing in both Germany and France, however, and despite some retrenchment remained worryingly high in Italy and Belgium. The recent explosive growth in Japan's debt is apparent. And it can be seen that the United States' low level of taxation (Table 5.2) is partly explained by its consistently above-average levels of debt. Finally, the table shows that despite Australia's preoccupation with reducing budget deficits, government debt has been particularly low.

Table 5.8 shows the general government budget balance for all levels of government, but divided into the terms of the last six Australian prime ministers. Much of the deterioration in the balance evident under Fraser was the result of increased spending commitments made by Whitlam. Keating's large deficit reflects the aftermath of the recession of the early 1990s and a lack of consolidation, whereas Howard's near-balanced budget reflects the economy's long expansion phase and absence of recession.

Table 5.9: Public ownership in different sectors

Percentage of OECD countries having at least one state-controlled company in the industry 1998. (Includes only industries where at least 50% of OECD countries had a state-controlled company.)

Communications	92
Railways	90
Financial institutions	82
Waterworks	81
Electricity	81
Support services to air transport	70
Urban passenger transport	68
Air transport	67
Gas	62
Health services	54

Table 5.10: Product market regulation

OECD regulatory indicator scale for seven industries; scale: 0–6 from least to most restrictive

	1978	1988	1998
United Kingdom	4.3	3.5	1.0
New Zealand	5.1	3.6	1.4
United States	4.0	2.5	1.4
Australia	**4.5**	**4.2**	**1.6**
Sweden	4.5	4.2	2.2
Canada	4.2	2.8	2.4
Germany	5.2	4.7	2.4
Norway	5.0	4.3	2.5
Finland	5.6	4.8	2.6
Denmark	5.6	5.5	2.9
Japan	5.2	3.9	2.9
Netherlands	5.3	5.5	3.0
Belgium	5.5	5.0	3.1
Austria	5.2	4.5	3.2
France	6.0	5.7	3.9
Switzerland	4.5	4.5	3.9
Ireland	5.7	5.1	4.0
Italy	5.8	5.8	4.3
Mean	5.1	4.5	2.7

Table 5.11: Privatisation

Proceeds from privatisation, 1990–2000

	Total $US million	$US per capita
Australia	**69 628**	**3 627**
New Zealand	9 412	2 477
Finland	11 000	2 115
Ireland	7 614	2 004
Sweden	17 295	1 943
Italy	108 586	1 885
Switzerland	10 869	1 489
Austria	10 433	1 288
France	75 489	1 273
Denmark	6 047	1 141
United Kingdom	63 130	1 061
Belgium	9 611	942
Netherlands	13 642	858
Norway	2 901	645
Canada	10 583	338
Japan	37 670	298
Germany	22 450	271
United States	6 750	24
Mean	27 395	1 315

Table 5.12: Structure of the electricity industry

	Ownership	Vertical integration	Generation and transmission
France	Public	Integrated	Integrated
Ireland	Public	Mixed	AS
Italy	Public	Integrated	Integrated
Netherlands	Public	Mixed	Integrated
New Zealand	Public	Mixed	SC
Denmark	Mostly public	Integrated	AS
Finland	Mostly public	Unbundled	SC
Norway	Mostly public	Unbundled	SC
Australia	**Mixed**	**Mixed**	**SC**
Canada	Mixed	Integrated	Integrated
Germany	Mixed	Unbundled	AS
Sweden	Mixed	Mixed	SC
Belgium	Mostly private	Integrated	Integrated
United States	Mostly private	Integrated	AS
Japan	Private	Mixed	Integrated
United Kingdom	Private	Unbundled	SC

AS = Accounting separation; SC = Separate companies.
No data on Austria or Switzerland.

Privatisation and deregulation

All our 18 countries are advanced capitalist market economies, where the major part of the economy is private enterprise. But all of them have at least some aspects which are publicly owned and some aspects where public regulation substantially constrains the conduct of the market. Traditionally state-owned (and/or state-licensed or state-controlled) enterprises operated in key areas of the economy. These included sectors where it had been judged that there was a natural monopoly with no scope for competition because of the large economies of scale arising from the infrastructure; where there was a crucial public interest and only public ownership would guarantee adequate standards; and where a crucial public service was thought not to be profitable.

How such lines were drawn was always a matter of political contestation and differed greatly between societies. Table 5.9 shows the industries where state-controlled corporations were (still) prominent in OECD countries in 1998. As can be seen, communications, transport and public utilities (water, gas and electricity) were the most prevalent areas. However public enterprise has strayed far more widely than this. Some OECD countries had state-owned motion picture companies, hotel chains and even tobacco companies.

In recent decades there has been a widespread move towards greater deregulation and privatisation. Micro-economic reform resulting in deregulation has arisen for diverse reasons. One is that what is at any time a natural monopoly is determined partly by technology, and as technology has changed competition has become more possible in some areas. A second has been ideological-cum-political. Many governments have believed that market competition would increase efficiency and consumer choice. This belief was to some degree popular on the left as well as the right as many critics believed existing regulatory regimes protected producers more than consumers.

The impetus to privatisation overlapped with the push to micro-economic reform, but differed in key respects. The selling off of public assets has been popular with governments, which obtain short-term benefits in balancing their budget or in debt reduction, and it has been popular with businesses which see new opportunities. Sometimes, however, it means that a public monopoly is simply replaced by a private one.

Tables 5.10 and 5.11 show just how widespread these movements have been. Table 5.10 is based on the OECD's scale of regulatory indicators across seven industries: gas, electricity, post, telecommunications, air transport, railways and road freight. It is based on a composite of public ownership, official barriers to entry, market structure, vertical integration and price controls. The table shows that on the six-point scale, the mean for the 18 countries reduced from 5.1 to 2.7, and reductions were greater in the 1990s than the 1980s. Four English-speaking countries, including Australia, were by a considerable margin the least restrictive. They began as somewhat less restrictive, but more importantly moved the most in the 20 years.

Table 5.11 shows that Australian and New Zealand governments engaged in privatisation on a proportionately far greater scale in the 1990s than the other countries. Differences in the amounts raised by privatisation are very marked, with Australian proceeds almost trebling the 18-country mean. Partly this was a matter of opportunity: the United States had less public ownership to begin with, while British Prime Minister Thatcher led the move to privatisation in the 1980s.

Part of the movement has been a disaggregating of what was a monolithic enterprise into component parts, some of which lend themselves more to competition than others. So the ownership of railway tracks has been separated from the services which run along them. Sometimes this has been artificial, even counter-productive judging by the criticisms of British railways since privatisation, and sometimes genuine benefits have resulted. Table 5.12 shows how this is operating in the electricity industry. In most countries electricity was once a publicly owned monopoly, but now there is a great mixture of institutional arrangements in both ownership and in disaggregating the total enterprise.

Table 5.13: Australian governments' comparative performance: economic growth

Mean per capita GDP growth rates (% per annum) during period of each government

	McMahon 1971–72	Whitlam 1973–75	Fraser 1976–82	Hawke 1983–91	Keating 1992–95	Howard 1996–2000
18-country mean	3.2	2.0	1.9	2.2	1.6	2.8
Australia	**1.6**	**1.7**	**1.1**	**1.9**	**3.1**	**3.0**
Australia's rank	**17**	**12**	**14**	**12**	**3**	**5**
Highest growth	Japan	Norway	Norway	Japan	Ireland	Ireland
Value	5.2	3.8	3.2	3.7	4.8	8.8
Lowest growth	Sweden	Switzerland	New Zealand	New Zealand	Switzerland	Japan
Value	1.1	–1.0	0.2	0.1	–0.8	1.1

Table 5.14: Australian governments' comparative performance: inflation

Mean inflation rates (CPI average annual % change) during period of each government

	McMahon 1971–72	Whitlam 1973–75	Fraser 1976–82	Hawke 1983–91	Keating 1992–95	Howard 1996–2000
18-country mean	6.1	11.5	9.6	4.8	2.4	1.6
Australia	**6.0**	**13.2**	**10.5**	**7.1**	**2.3**	**1.7**
Australia's rank	**9**	**13**	**11**	**15**	**9**	**11**
Lowest inflation	Belgium	Germany	Switzerland	Netherlands	Belgium	Japan
Value	2.7	6.6	3.4	1.7	0.5	0.2
Highest inflation	Ireland	UK	Italy	NZ	Italy	Netherlands
Value	8.8	16.5	16.6	8.7	4.8	2.6

Table 5.15: Australian governments' comparative performance: unemployment

Mean unemployment rates (% of labour force) during period of each government

	McMahon 1970–72	Whitlam 1973–75	Fraser 1976–82	Hawke 1983–91	Keating 1992–95	Howard 1996–2002
18-country mean	2.5	3.0	5.2	7.1	8.6	6.7
Australia	**2.0**	**2.9**	**5.8**	**7.8**	**9.6**	**7.3**
Australia's rank	**10**	**10**	**9**	**11**	**11**	**12**
Lowest Country	New Zealand	New Zealand	Switzerland	Switzerland	Japan	Switzerland
Value	0.3	0.2	0.4	0.9	2.7	3.2
Highest Country	Ireland	Ireland	Ireland	Ireland	Finland	Italy
Value	6.3	6.8	8.8	15.4	14.8	11.1

Performance of Australian governments

If we divide up the past 30 years or so between the terms of Australia's six prime ministers and examine them on three key criteria, what conclusions can we reach about their relative economic performance?

Table 5.13 shows that economic growth, measured as growth in GDP per person, was modest under McMahon and Whitlam, particularly weak under Fraser, picked up somewhat under Hawke and then was particularly strong under Keating and Howard. If from that you can see clear evidence of your favourite party's superiority as an economic manager – congratulations.

But there are several deeper conclusions to be drawn. The first is that (leaving aside McMahon's particularly poor performance relative to the 18-country mean) the pattern of growth rates over time in Australia bears a quite strong similarity to the average pattern for all the selected economies. This suggests that strengths and weaknesses in Australia's performance, which people tend instinctively to attribute to domestic causes, may often have causes that are beyond the control of local politicians. For most of the period, Australia's performance ranked it in the bottom third of the league table. But its performance in the 1990s did lift its ranking to the top third, suggesting that governments are by no means powerless to influence their economies' relative performance.

A second conclusion is that political leaders' terms do not fit neatly with the economy's inescapable tendency to move through cycles of boom and bust. Thus Fraser bore the brunt of Whitlam's economic miscalculations, and Hawke's record was rendered unimpressive by the aftermath of Fraser's recession of the early 1980s and by his own recession of the early 1990s, whereas Keating and Howard benefited from the economy's unusually long expansion phase – and absence of recession – during the rest of the 1990s and the early 2000s. It is also widely agreed among economists that both leaders benefited from a delayed pay-off from the many economic reforms undertaken by Hawke.

Table 5.14 shows a surprisingly poor inflation performance under McMahon, a terrible blowout under Whitlam, only modest improvement under Fraser and Hawke, but a return to low inflation under Keating and Howard. Even so, the 18-country mean exhibits a very similar pattern, leaving Australia's ranking consistently towards the top of the bottom half. The notable exception to this rule was Hawke's term. The return to low inflation began in the 1980s for most of the developed economies, but in Australia was delayed until the 1990s while Hawke concentrated on using his accord with the union movement to lower real wages and thereby increase employment.

Since the 1990–91 recession, Australia has returned to low inflation. Australian economists tend to attribute this continuing success to the side-effects of economic reform which, by heightening the degree of competition in the markets for many products, reduced the scope for excessive wage settlements ('sweetheart deals') and consequent excessive price rises. But this raises the old question: how does this purely domestic argument explain the very low inflation rates in the other developed economies?

Table 5.15 charts a dismal history of progressively worsening unemployment under successive leaders but with a modest improvement under Howard – thanks mainly to the absence of another severe recession. The 18-country mean reveals a similar experience in most of the other developed economies, though Australia's performance went from significantly better than average in the 1960s (not shown) and early 1970s to consistently worse than average for the past 30 years.

The process of averaging the unemployment rates within each leader's term flatters Whitlam (the long-term deterioration began towards the end of his watch) but maligns Hawke, who made rapid progress in reducing the 10% unemployment rate inherited from Fraser, but then presided over his own recession, which caused the rate to reach a new cyclical peak of 11% early in Keating's term.

Table 6.1: Health spending

Total spending on health as % of GDP

	1960	1970	1980	1990	2000
United States	5.1	6.9	8.7	11.9	13.1
Switzerland	4.9	5.6	7.6	8.5	10.7
Germany	4.8	6.3	8.8	8.7	10.6
France	4.2	5.8	7.4	8.8	9.3
Canada	5.4	7.0	7.2	9.0	9.2
Australia	**4.7**	**5.1**	**7.0**	**7.8**	**8.9**
Belgium	3.4	4.1	6.4	7.4	8.7
Netherlands	3.9	7.5	7.5	8.0	8.6
Sweden	4.7	6.7	9.1	8.5	8.4
Denmark	3.6	6.5	6.8	8.4	8.3
Italy	3.6	5.2	7.0	8.1	8.2
Austria	4.3	5.3	7.7	7.1	8.0
New Zealand	4.3	5.1	6.0	7.0	8.0
Norway	2.9	4.4	7.0	7.8	7.7
Japan	3.0	4.5	6.5	6.1	7.6
United Kingdom	3.9	4.5	5.7	6.0	7.3
Finland	3.9	5.7	6.4	7.9	6.7
Ireland	3.8	5.1	8.7	7.0	6.4
Mean	4.1	5.7	7.4	8.0	8.7

Table 6.2: Increases in health expenditure

Average real per person annual compound growth rate in expenditure, 1970–2000

	1970–80	1980–90	1990–2000
Ireland	8.5	1.1	6.6
Japan	7.0	2.7	3.9
United Kingdom	4.1	3.1	3.8
Belgium	8.1	3.4	3.5
United States	4.4	5.5	3.2
Australia	–	**2.7**	**3.1**
Austria	7.4	1.4	3.1
New Zealand	2.0	2.7	2.9
Norway	9.1	3.1	2.8
Switzerland	4.2	2.8	2.5
Netherlands	–	2.2	2.4
France	5.4	3.6	2.3
Germany	6.1	2.1	2.1
Canada	3.0	4.0	1.8
Denmark	–	0.8	1.7
Italy	6.3	3.6	1.4
Finland	4.5	4.8	0.1
Sweden	4.4	1.0	0.0
Mean	5.6	2.8	2.6

Table 6.3: Per capita funding of health

	Total per capita US$PPP 2000	% US spending
United States	4 631	100
Switzerland	3 222	70
Germany	2 748	59
Canada	2 535	55
Denmark	2 420	52
France	2 349	51
Belgium	2 268	49
Norway	2 268	49
Netherlands	2 246	48
Australia	**2 211**	**48**
Austria	2 162	47
Italy	2 032	44
Japan	2 011	43
Ireland	1 953	42
Sweden	1 900	41
United Kingdom	1 764	38
Finland	1 664	36
New Zealand	1 623	35
Mean 2000	2 339	50
Mean 1990	1 397	
Mean 1980	670	

6 HEALTH
Total health spending

If you wonder why arguments about the funding of health care are rarely out of the news, Table 6.1 offers a big clue. It shows total spending on health by governments, private organisations and individuals, expressed as a percentage of national income (GDP), and demonstrates how rapidly health spending grew in the selected countries over the last 40 years of the 20th century. On average, health spending's share of GDP has more than doubled. But the table shows also how much faster the growth has been in some countries than others, so that the United States' spending share is almost twice that of Finland's, with Australia close to the 18-nation mean.

It should be remembered that when spending on any item rises over time as a percentage of GDP, this means it is growing at a faster real rate than the overall economy. Thus the increases revealed by Table 6.1 are even more notable than they may at first seem. It is undoubtedly true that health spending has increased because of general inflation and because of growing populations. But those two factors do not explain the rise in health spending's share of GDP shown in Table 6.1 because the comparison with GDP effectively takes account of inflation and population growth. This conclusion is confirmed by Table 6.2, which reveals big increases in real average annual health spending per person – thus controlling explicitly for general inflation and population growth.

Many factors are driving the rise in health spending. One is the good news on greater life expectancy, reported in Table 1.5. Although there is no correlation between amounts spent on health and the age profile of these societies (Table 1.11), other OECD data suggests that on average health expenditure for those over 65 is roughly four times greater than on those less than 65. So future increases in demand are likely as the proportion of older age groups increases.

A central driver of increased expenditure is the introduction of new goods and services – new drugs and surgical procedures, for example. New technologies allow medicine to expand into areas where effective treatments were not previously possible. These typically produce better outcomes, but often also increase costs.

Health spending is what economists call a 'superior good'. That is, as people's (or nations') incomes rise, their spending on health rises disproportionately. It can be seen from Table 6.3 that the richest nation, the United States, spends twice as much per person on health as the mean of the selected countries. Even second-ranking Switzerland's spending per person is only 70% of America's. (Note that the means in Table 6.3 are not adjusted for inflation, and so give an overly dramatic impression of the increase.)

In 1960 the United States was only just above average in Table 6.1, but its growth rate was so distinctive that by 2000 it was a huge 4.4 percentage points above the mean. Considering the distinctive pattern of the United States leads to the final driver of increased spending – where health costs are going up disproportionately. America's pre-eminence in spending is partly because of its very high cost structures. For example, the ratio of physicians' income to average employee income is 5.5 in the United States, 3.4 in Germany, 3.2 in Canada, 2.2 in Australia, 1.5 in Sweden and 1.4 in the United Kingdom. American health economist Gerard Anderson and his co-authors concluded that despite their higher spending Americans had lower use of health services than many other OECD countries, and concluded 'It's the prices, stupid'.

By itself, an increase in health spending is neither a good nor a bad thing. Rather, that spending must be related to needs and outcomes. Balancing the many demands for increased health funding against optimal health outcomes will continue to be a vexed policy issue in all the selected countries.

Table 6.4: Public expenditure on health

Public health expenditure as % of GDP

	1960	1970	1980	1990	2000
Germany	3.2	4.5	6.8	6.5	7.9
France	2.4	4.3	5.8	6.6	7.1
Sweden	3.4	5.8	8.2	7.4	7.1
Denmark	–	–	8.0	7.0	6.9
Canada	2.3	4.9	5.4	6.7	6.5
Norway	2.3	4.0	5.9	6.4	6.5
Belgium	2.1	3.5	5.4	6.6	6.2
New Zealand	3.5	4.1	5.2	5.7	6.2
Australia	**2.2**	**3.1**	**4.4**	**5.2**	**6.1**
Italy	3.0	4.5	5.6	6.4	6.0
Japan	1.8	3.1	4.6	4.6	6.0
Switzerland	2.4	3.3	4.8	4.5	5.9
United Kingdom	3.3	3.9	5.0	5.0	5.9
United States	1.2	2.5	3.6	4.7	5.8
Austria	3.0	3.3	5.2	5.2	5.6
Netherlands	1.3	5.0	5.2	5.4	5.5
Finland	2.1	4.1	5.0	6.3	5.0
Ireland	2.9	4.2	6.8	4.4	4.7
Mean	2.5	4.0	5.6	5.8	6.2

Table 6.5: Private share of health funding

Percentage of health funding from private sources

	1970	1980	1990	2000
United States	64	59	60	56
Switzerland	–	–	48	44
Netherlands	–	31	33	37
Australia	**40**	**37**	**33**	**31**
Austria	37	31	27	30
Canada	30	24	26	29
Belgium	–	–	–	29
Italy	–	–	21	27
Ireland	18	18	28	27
Germany	27	21	24	25
Finland	26	21	19	25
France	–	–	23	24
New Zealand	20	12	18	22
Japan	30	29	22	22
United Kingdom	13	11	16	19
Denmark	16	12	17	18
Sweden	14	8	10	15
Norway	8	15	17	15
Mean	26	23	26	27

Table 6.6: Out-of-pocket payments and health funding

Out-of-pocket payments as % of total health spending, 2000

Switzerland	33
Italy	23
Finland	20
Australia	**19**
Austria	19
Japan	17
Canada	16
Denmark	16
New Zealand	15
Norway	15
United States	15
Ireland	14
Germany	11
United Kingdom	11
France	10
Netherlands	9
Mean	16

No data on Belgium or Sweden. UK figure is from 1990.

Table 6.7: Fairness of financial contributions to the health system

Fairness scores and ranks, 1997

	Fairness score	Global rank
Belgium	.979	3
Denmark	.979	3
Germany	.978	6
Ireland	.978	6
Finland	.977	8
Japan	.977	8
Norway	.977	8
United Kingdom	.977	8
Austria	.976	12
Sweden	.976	12
Canada	.974	17
Netherlands	.973	20
New Zealand	.972	23
Australia	**.971**	**26**
France	.971	26
Switzerland	.964	38
Italy	.961	45
United States	.954	54

Fairness score 0 = least fair; 1 = most fair.
Many tied ranks (e.g. Belgium, Denmark and one other country tied for third to fifth; number given = first of the ranks.)

Health funding

It is noteworthy that the public debate about health is dominated less by complaints about inadequate health outcomes than by complaints about perceived deficiencies in the way the nation's total spending on health is funded. This reflects the inexorably rising health costs, and also that each of the major ways of funding health has its own problems. Health can be funded publicly or privately. Private funding can be through out-of-pocket payments, where the recipient pays directly for services and goods, or through health insurance, where the individual or their employer pays a premium and particular payments are made by the insurer.

Health care can be catastrophically expensive for an individual, and much of the need for it is unpredictable. Both public funding and private insurance schemes are designed to protect people from having to choose between financial ruin and loss of health. Public funding can allow for treatment to be matched to need rather than ability to pay. But governments are often not willing to pay for all health care. Some critics argue that government provision of health care leads to over-servicing and abuse, while others argue that for budgetary reasons governments too often refuse to fund health at the needed levels.

Table 6.5 shows that in all the selected countries except the United States most health funding is from the public purse, while Table 6.4 shows what a significant expense health funding has become for the public sector. Between 1960 and 2000 the share of GDP devoted to public funding of health in the selected countries more than doubled. Other OECD data shows that health expenditure now represents an average of 14% of all government spending in the selected countries.

Table 6.5 shows that a high degree of public funding – not to mention actual public provision of services and government regulation of the whole sector – is the norm for health care systems in the selected countries. Over the last decades of the 20th century, the average proportion of funding coming from the private sector barely changed, though individual countries showed different trends. Australia's share of private funding fell during the period, but it was still in the top quarter of countries by this measure. The figures in Table 6.4 show less of a range than some of the other tables on health expenditure. All but four countries fall within 1 percentage point above or below the mean, including all the countries with the highest shares of private funding. OECD studies also suggest that in countries with higher proportions of private health funding total health expenditure commands a greater proportion of GDP (Table 6.1).

No matter to what extent they rely on public funding or on private insurance arrangements, all funding systems call on individuals to supplement this with direct payments. Out-of-pocket payments annoy the public (and add to administrative costs) but are beloved by economists, who believe they discourage overuse of services that otherwise appear to be 'free'. It can be seen from Table 6.6 that for the most part such payments account for only a small proportion of total spending. Interestingly, the rankings in Tables 6.5 and 6.6 show only a modest correlation. Countries that do not rely heavily on public funding of health care are more likely to rely on private insurance contributions than out-of-pocket payments.

Table 6.7 offers results of the WHO's necessarily crude assessment of the funding fairness of its 191 member-countries. Scores are influenced by the extent to which people's total health contributions reflect their ability to pay rather than their health or ill health. One would thus expect countries with high rates of funding from general taxation to score well. Most notably, however, 15 countries score between .979 and .971, suggesting that funding fairness receives a high priority in most of the selected countries.

Table 6.8: Number of doctors

Number of doctors per 1000 population

	1960	1970	1980	1990	2000
Italy	0.7	1.1	2.7	–	4.1
Belgium	1.3	1.5	2.3	3.3	3.9
Switzerland	1.4	1.5	2.4	3.0	3.5
Denmark	1.2	1.4	2.2	3.1	3.4
France	1.0	1.3	2.0	3.1	3.3
Germany	1.4	1.6	2.3	2.8	3.3
Netherlands	1.1	1.2	1.9	2.5	3.2
Austria	1.4	1.4	1.6	2.2	3.1
Finland	0.6	0.9	1.7	2.4	3.1
Sweden	1.0	1.3	2.2	2.9	3.0
Norway	1.2	1.4	2.0	2.6	2.9
United States	1.4	1.6	2.0	2.4	2.7
Australia	**1.1**	**1.2**	**1.8**	**2.2**	**2.4**
Ireland	1.0	1.2	1.3	1.6	2.2
New Zealand	1.1	1.1	1.6	1.9	2.2
Canada	1.2	1.5	1.8	2.1	2.1
United Kingdom	0.8	0.9	1.3	1.5	2.0
Japan	1.0	1.1	1.3	1.7	1.9
Mean	1.1	1.3	1.9	2.4	2.9

Table 6.9: Public consultations with doctors

Average number of visits per person per year

	1970	1980	1990	2000
Japan	13.6	14.4	13.8	14.4
United States	4.6	4.8	5.5	8.9
Belgium	6.0	7.1	7.7	7.9
France	3.1	4.2	5.9	6.9
Austria	5.2	5.4	5.9	6.7
Germany	10.9	11.4	5.3	6.5
Australia	**3.1**	**4.0**	**6.1**	**6.3**
Canada	4.3	5.6	6.7	6.3
Denmark	–	5.0	5.7	6.1
Italy	6.3	8.0	6.8	6.1
Netherlands	4.2	4.9	5.5	5.9
United Kingdom	5.0	5.2	6.1	4.9
New Zealand	–	3.7	–	4.4
Finland	2.4	3.2	3.9	4.3
Sweden	1.9	2.6	2.8	2.8
Ireland	5.3	5.8	–	–
Norway	4.5	5.7	3.8	–
Mean	5.0	6.0	6.2	6.6

No data on Switzerland.

Table 6.10: Expenditure on pharmaceuticals

Expenditure on pharmaceuticals as % of GDP

	1980	1990	2000
France	–	1.4	1.9
Italy	–	1.7	1.8
United States	0.8	1.1	1.6
Belgium	1.1	1.2	1.4
Canada	0.6	1.0	1.4
Germany	1.2	1.2	1.4
Japan	1.4	1.3	1.2
Sweden	0.6	0.7	1.2
Australia	**0.6**	**0.7**	**1.1**
New Zealand	0.7	1.0	1.1
Switzerland	–	0.9	1.1
United Kingdom	0.7	0.8	1.1
Finland	0.7	0.7	1.0
Netherlands	0.6	0.8	0.9
Denmark	0.6	0.6	0.7
Ireland	0.9	0.7	0.7
Norway	0.6	0.6	–
Mean	0.8	1.0	1.2

No data on Austria.

Table 6.11: Number of nurses

Nurses per 1000 population

	1980	1990	2000
Finland	8.3	10.2	14.7
Ireland	–	11.3	14.0
Netherlands	–	–	13.4
Australia	**10.3**	**11.6**	**10.7**
Switzerland	–	–	10.7
Norway	9.0	13.2	10.3
Canada	9.6	11.1	9.9
Germany	–	–	9.6
New Zealand	6.1	9.3	9.6
Denmark	6.9	8.6	9.5
Austria	5.4	7.2	9.2
Sweden	7.0	9.2	8.8
United Kingdom	–	7.8	8.8
Belgium	8.5	–	–
United States	5.6	7.2	8.1
Japan	4.2	6.0	7.8
France	4.7	5.6	6.7
Italy	–	–	5.2
Mean	7.1	9.1	9.8

Ranked in order of 2000 density of nurses, with Belgium placed according to its 1980 value.

Doctors, nurses and pharmaceuticals

Tables 6.8 and 6.9 show one strong reason for the growth in health spending and the selected societies' improved health status. On average, the number of doctors per head more than doubled between 1960 and 2000, while the average annual number of doctor visits per person also increased but much more modestly.

Table 6.8 shows that while Italy and Belgium have the highest density of doctors, all the selected countries fall within a fairly close range. All but Italy fall within 1 percentage point above or below the mean of 2.9. Japan and the English-speaking countries all come at the bottom. Australia began the period exactly on the 18-nation mean, but its number of doctors has not grown as quickly as the norm, so that by 2000 it fell 0.5 percentage points below the mean.

OECD research found that after controlling for risk factors in the population, higher doctor numbers were significantly associated with lower premature mortality. But, also according to the OECD, there is no simple relationship between the number of doctors in a country and its total spending on health. Doctor numbers are not high in the United States, for instance. Of course, the number of visits to doctors per person will be a factor affecting costs, but methods of doctor remuneration – government salary versus private fee-for-service – are a more significant influence on total spending.

Table 6.9 reveals a doubling in the annual number of visits to doctors per person in Australia between 1970 and 2000, a much sharper increase than the norm, but only bringing Australia up into the middle range of medical consultations per person. (The large jump in American consultations between 1990 and 2000 makes one suspect some change in measuring procedures.)

The very high number of consultations in Japan is partly a result of their unique system where doctors are not only the prescribers but also the dispensers of drugs. Indeed the Japanese have a unique mix: they top the longevity tables for both sexes (Tables 1.6 and 1.7), perhaps partly due to differences in their dietary intake (Tables 16.5 and 16.6) and despite the addiction of Japanese males to tobacco (Table 16.20). But in terms of commitment of GDP to health resources, Japan ranks relatively low, and Table 6.8 shows it has the lowest density of doctors. But Table 6.9 shows it has the highest number of consultations per person, suggesting either or both very brief visits or their doctors working particularly long hours. The high rate of consultations is also consistent with a Japanese propensity to hypochondria. According to other OECD data, when surveyed about their health, around 80% of the people in the other selected countries report it is good or very good, but only 42% of Japanese put themselves in these categories.

Within the fast-growing health sector, the fastest-growing area of spending is on pharmaceuticals. Table 6.10 shows that by 2000 the mean of spending on pharmaceuticals in the selected countries had risen by 50% compared to its 1980 level. In that period, the share of total health expenditure devoted to pharmaceuticals rose from 11% to 14%, according to other OECD data. France and Italy devoted the highest proportion of their incomes to the purchase of medicinal drugs, more than double the bottom-ranking countries. The data does not allow us to distinguish whether this is because they take more medicines or because the ones they take cost more.

The largest group in the health labour force is nurses, but Table 6.11 shows that their number has been growing at a slower rate than the number of doctors. It also shows the different priorities in health spending between the selected countries. The rankings in Tables 6.8 and 6.1 show little association, while the spending on pharmaceuticals and the number of nurses seem to have an almost negative relationship with each other.

Table 6.12: Acute care hospital beds

Acute care hospital beds per 1000 population

	1980	1990	2000
France	6.2	5.2	6.7
Germany	7.7	7.5	6.4
Austria	–	7.1	6.2
Belgium	5.5	4.9	4.6
Italy	7.9	6.2	4.3
Switzerland	7.1	6.5	4.1
United Kingdom	3.6	2.9	3.9
Australia	**6.4**	**4.4**	**3.8**
Netherlands	5.2	4.3	3.5
Denmark	5.3	4.1	3.3
Canada	4.6	4.0	3.2
Norway	5.2	3.8	3.1
Ireland	4.3	3.2	3.0
United States	4.4	3.8	2.9
Finland	4.9	4.3	2.4
Sweden	5.1	4.1	2.4
New Zealand	–	8.3	–
Mean	5.6	5.0	4.0

No data on Japan.

Table 6.13: Average length of stay in hospital

Mean days per patient admitted to acute care

	1980	1990	2000
Denmark	8.5	6.4	3.8
Finland	8.8	7.0	4.4
New Zealand	–	–	4.9
Sweden	8.5	6.5	5.0
United States	7.6	7.3	5.8
Norway	10.9	7.8	6.0
Australia	**7.7**	**6.5**	**6.1**
Austria	14.5	9.3	6.3
Ireland	8.5	6.7	6.4
United Kingdom	8.5	5.7	6.9
Italy	–	9.5	7.0
Canada	10.2	8.6	7.2
Belgium	10.0	8.7	8.0
France	15.9	10.6	8.5
Netherlands	14.0	11.2	9.0
Switzerland	15.5	13.4	9.3
Germany	14.5	14.1	9.6
Mean	10.9	8.7	6.7

No data on Japan.

Table 6.14: Hospital bed days: acute care

Days per person per year

	1980	1990	2000 *
Germany	2.4	2.4	1.9
Austria	2.6	2.0	1.8
Belgium	1.7	1.5	1.3
Italy	1.9	1.6	1.3
Switzerland	2.0	1.9	1.3
France	1.8	1.5	1.1
Australia	**1.6**	**1.2**	**1.0**
Canada	1.6	1.4	1.0
Denmark	1.5	1.2	1.0
Finland	–	1.1	0.9
Ireland	1.3	1.0	0.9
Norway	1.6	1.1	0.9
United Kingdom	0.9	0.9	0.9
Netherlands	1.6	1.2	0.8
Sweden	1.3	1.1	0.8
United States	1.2	0.9	0.7
New Zealand	–	–	0.3
Mean	1.7	1.4	1.1

Table 6.15: Hospital bed days: all in-patients

Hospital care bed days per person per year

	1960	1970	1980	1990	2000 *
Norway	3.1	2.8	5.3	5.0	4.5
Japan	2.1	3.0	3.4	4.1	4.0
Netherlands	–	3.8	4.1	3.7	3.4
Finland	4.2	5.0	4.9	4.1	2.8
Germany	3.6	3.6	3.6	3.3	2.7
Australia	**3.4**	**3.5**	**3.4**	**2.9**	**2.6**
Austria	3.5	3.4	3.5	3.0	2.6
France	2.6	3.4	3.6	2.9	2.4
Belgium	1.6	2.3	2.7	2.6	2.2
Switzerland	3.9	3.4	3.0	2.9	2.0
Italy	2.5	3.0	2.5	1.8	1.5
Denmark	2.6	2.6	2.3	1.7	1.4
Sweden	4.3	4.5	4.3	3.5	1.3
United Kingdom	3.4	2.9	2.4	1.8	1.2
Canada	1.8	2.0	2.1	2.0	1.1
Ireland	–	–	1.6	1.2	1.1
New Zealand	3.3	3.0	2.7	2.1	1.0
United States	2.8	2.3	1.7	1.2	0.8
Mean	3.1	3.2	3.2	2.8	2.1

Latest year available for Sweden and Norway is 1996.

Hospitals

At first glance the tables on hospitals seem to be in direct contradiction to the great changes in health spending already outlined. While the tables opposite show some of the reasons for increases in expenditure in terms of increased numbers of doctors, consultations with doctors and spending on medicines, the tables on hospital care generally indicate reductions rather than increases.

Table 6.12 shows that the number of acute care hospital beds per person declined in the selected countries between 1980 and 2000. Table 6.13 shows that in the same period the average length of stay a patient was in hospital also declined substantially, and Tables 6.14 and 6.15 show the average number of days spent in hospital per head of population also declined.

There are several possible reasons for this relative decline. One is the vigorous efforts by governments and health authorities to limit ever-spiralling health costs. The rather limited OECD data on the percentage of health expenditure devoted to in-patient care suggests that up to 1980 hospital spending was rising more rapidly than general health spending but since then has been growing less rapidly.

All the selected countries have seen substantial reductions in average length of stay in hospital, and this has been a more important reason for the reductions in Tables 6.12 and 6.14 than the percentage of the population being admitted to hospital. Average length of stay in hospital is often used as an indicator of efficiency. Like all such indicators, however, it is far from foolproof and is open to abuse. If hospital stays are too short, the comfort or recovery of patients may be compromised, and shorter stays may transfer costs to other parts of the health system or onto patients and their families. On the other hand, the reasons for shorter stays in hospital also include technological advances in anaesthetics, the development of less invasive surgical techniques, and improved pre- and post-operative treatment regimens.

Although the general trend is clear, problems in the consistency of categories make precise comparisons difficult. The figures in Tables 6.12 to 6.14 are for acute care admissions, while Table 6.15 is for all hospital admissions. Acute care covers the reasons for which most patients are admitted to hospital: childbirth, performing surgery, curing illness or providing definitive treatment of injuries, performing diagnostic or therapeutic procedures. It generally does not include long-term care, or those residing in nursing homes.

Different countries vary in their counting procedures and have changed over time. Issues of categorisation include whether acute care covers palliative care and psychiatric hospitals. One important issue is whether admissions include same-day surgery, where the treatments are performed on an out-patient basis. In nearly all countries now it does not, but in some countries in the past it did. For the medical reasons cited above, same-day procedures have become increasingly important. The Australian Institute of Health and Welfare reports that in 1996 there were 159 acute care admissions per 1000 people in Australia, but that number jumped to 288 if same-day admissions were included.

There are also counting issues of when acute care becomes long-term care. A comparison of Tables 6.14 and 6.15 shows the importance of long-term patients in boosting the relative number of hospital care bed days. There is quite a bit of variation between countries, but the average in Table 6.15 is double that for Table 6.14.

The differences in counting procedures should make us wary of being too definitive about what the differences between countries signify. Generally on most of the tables Australia is fairly close to the mean, while such European countries as France, Germany and Switzerland rank near the top. For all the selected countries, however, balancing financial pressures against the accessibility and quality of hospital care will continue to be a critical issue.

Table 6.16: Magnetic resonance imaging units

Number of units per million population

	1990	1995	2000
Japan	6.1	18.8	23.2
Switzerland	3.9	9.8	12.9
Austria	–	–	10.8
Finland	1.8	4.3	9.9
United States	3.7	6.8	8.1
Sweden	1.5	6.8	7.9
Italy	1.3	3.0	7.5
Denmark	2.5	–	6.6
Germany	1.9	4.8	6.2
Australia	**0.6**	**2.9**	**4.7**
United Kingdom	1.0	2.9	4.6
Belgium	2.0	3.2	3.2
France	0.8	2.1	2.6
New Zealand	–	–	2.6
Canada	0.7	1.3	2.5
Ireland	0.3	–	–
Netherlands	1.3	3.9	–
Norway	0.7	–	–
Mean	1.9	5.4	7.6

Table 6.17: Dialysis

Patients undergoing dialysis per 100 000 population

	1970	1980	1990	2000
Japan	0.9	31.3	83.6	162.4
United States	–	21.4	51.7	86.5
Germany	1.6	17.6	29.7	64.0
Canada	–	13.2	21.9	47.3
Denmark	2.1	10.1	19.4	38.7
Austria	1.0	10.4	25.1	37.1
France	2.2	18.4	23.6	37.0
Australia	**1.8**	**10.0**	**17.3**	**33.4**
Belgium	2.0	15.7	26.1	32.9
Italy	0.6	16.8	25.6	31.6
Netherlands	3.2	11.9	21	28.2
United Kingdom	1.7	6.8	15.5	27.4
Switzerland	3.3	16.2	24.4	26.5
Sweden	2.7	9.0	14.1	25.4
Finland	1.5	4.4	12.4	22.9
New Zealand	3.5	14.5	–	16.8
Ireland	1.6	5.2	9	9.9
Norway	0.4	3.9	5.8	6.1
Mean	1.9	13.2	25.1	40.7

Table 6.18: Kidney transplants

Kidney transplants per 100 000 population

	1970	1980	1990	2000
Austria	0.2	1.2	5.5	4.9
United States	–	2.1	3.8	4.8
Norway	0.5	2.0	4.8	4.3
Belgium	0.7	1.5	3.9	4.0
Canada	–	–	3.0	3.8
Finland	0.2	2.8	2.5	3.7
Netherlands	0.5	1.6	2.9	3.5
Switzerland	0.8	2.5	3.3	3.5
Ireland	0.2	1.2	3.9	3.4
France	0.3	0.9	3.4	3.3
Sweden	1.8	2.9	3.9	3.2
Denmark	2.5	2.0	3.6	2.9
United Kingdom	0.4	1.6	3.2	2.9
Australia	**1.5**	**2.4**	**2.6**	**2.8**
New Zealand	–	1.6	3.0	2.8
Germany	0.1	0.9	2.5	2.7
Italy	0.0	0.4	0.6	2.3
Japan	–	0.2	0.6	0.6
Mean	0.7	1.6	3.1	3.3

Table 6.19: Births by caesarean section

Number per 1000 live births

	1985	1990	1995	2000
Italy	158	208	261	333
Australia	**150**	**175**	**192**	**217**
United States	–	227	208	211
Germany	–	157	172	209
Canada	–	–	175	205
Ireland	77	105	–	204
New Zealand	–	121	151	202
Austria	–	–	124	172
France	–	139	150	171
United Kingdom	106	124	158	170
Belgium	94	105	135	159
Finland	148	142	155	157
Denmark	133	–	–	145
Sweden	121	108	120	144
Norway	120	128	126	137
Netherlands	65	74	97	129
Switzerland	198	186	–	–
Mean	125	143	159	185

Medical technology

Health care is a very technologically dynamic area, subject to continuous research and improvements in treatment. While the advances in medical procedures rightly produce widespread appreciation, there is also an ongoing debate about whether sometimes they prolong the lives of terminally ill patients at great expense and at the cost of quality of life. Are such technologies increasing the cost of health care more than the benefits they deliver? The tables on this page cannot resolve such issues, but they do offer some prime examples of the rapid take-up of life-saving and life-enhancing (but expensive) technological advances during the last part of the 20th century.

Table 6.16 shows the rapid spread of MRI machines during the 1990s. MRI machines produce anatomical images in 3-D. Unlike conventional radiography or CAT scans, they do not expose patients to ionising radiation, and at the same time they offer more functionality.

Although there are some doubts about the completeness and reliability of counting these machines in different countries, it is also clear that there are surprisingly large variations between countries in the adoption of individual technologies. In MRI, Japan's take-up rate has been far higher than any other country's, with Australia falling somewhat below the 18-nation mean.

Table 6.17 shows the marked and continuing growth in the use of kidney dialysis machines since 1970. Again, the take-up varies widely between countries, and again the Japanese are clear leaders.

Although there are several exceptions, the positions in these league tables show some relationship to relative levels of health spending in Table 6.1. Japan – a relatively low spender on health but a country of great technological innovation – is an exception. But relatively high spenders such as the United States, Switzerland and Germany are near the top of these tables, while some of the lower-spending countries rank towards the bottom.

Table 6.18 shows the strong and widespread growth in kidney transplant operations since 1970. To an extent, Japan's pre-eminence in dialysis is a result of distaste for transplant operations. Australia got an early start, but its growth has not kept up with other countries and it is now below the overall mean.

The number of kidney transplants per 100 000 population fell in almost half the 18 countries during the 1990s. The growth of transplant operations has not been as rapid or continuous as some of the other procedures, perhaps due to a lack of donors. Heart transplants – perhaps the epitome of the modern medical miracle – have never become a widespread procedure, and OECD data shows that rates fell in the 1990s. Again the reason may be partly the availability of donors, but perhaps also doubts about its cost-effectiveness.

Table 6.19 reports yet another remarkable change in health procedures: the large growth in rates of birth by caesarean section in the short time since 1985. Across the selected countries the growth has been continuous and almost universal. But the countries' rates have diverged rather than converged. It may also be noteworthy that the rate seems to have reached a plateau in the richest and almost top-ranking United States.

The obvious question is what is driving this remarkable growth? It is good if the extra cost (and risks) of the operation has resulted in significantly reduced risks for babies and their mothers. It is good if countries' higher incomes have allowed them to afford to satisfy genuine need that formerly went unsatisfied.

On the other hand, it is a bad development if the rapid growth has occurred because of over-servicing by doctors, or to suit the convenience of hospitals. Consider the case of Italy, where the rate has doubled in just 15 years to be almost twice the average rate for the other countries. It is hard to believe that this increase is explained solely by a need to improve the safety of mothers and babies.

Table 6.20: Infant mortality

Deaths per 1000 live births

	1900	1925	1950	1975	2000
Japan	155	142	60	10	3.2
Sweden	99	56	21	9	3.4
Finland	153	85	44	10	3.8
Norway	91	50	28	11	3.8
Germany	229	105	60	19	4.4
Italy	174	119	64	21	4.5
France	162	89	52	14	4.6
Austria	231	119	66	21	4.8
Belgium	172	100	53	15	4.8
Switzerland	150	58	31	11	4.9
Netherlands	155	58	25	11	5.1
Australia	**83**	**53**	**25**	**14**	**5.2**
Canada	–	102	41	16	5.3
Denmark	128	80	31	10	5.3
United Kingdom	148	79	31	16	5.6
New Zealand	62	40	28	16	5.8
Ireland	109	68	45	17	6.2
United States	142	72	29	16	6.9
Mean	144	82	41	14	4.8

Table 6.21: Maternal mortality

Deaths per 100 000 live births

	1960	1970	1980	1990	2000
Ireland	–	31.1	6.8	3.8	1.8
Austria	87.3	25.8	7.7	6.6	2.6
Italy	–	54.5	12.8	8.6	2.7
Canada	45.0	20.0	8.0	2.5	3.4
Norway	–	10.8	11.8	3.3	3.4
Switzerland	–	25.2	5.4	6.0	3.8
Sweden	–	10.0	8.2	3.2	4.4
Finland	71.8	12.4	1.6	6.1	5.3
Belgium	–	20.4	5.6	3.2	5.6
Germany	106.3	51.8	20.6	9.1	5.6
Australia	**52.5**	**25.6**	**9.8**	**6.1**	**6.0**
Japan	130.6	52.1	20.5	8.6	6.6
New Zealand	–	–	13.8	6.6	7.0
United Kingdom	47.0	24.0	11.0	8.0	7.0
Denmark	–	8.5	1.8	1.6	7.4
France	–	28.2	12.9	10.4	7.4
Netherlands	38.9	13.4	8.8	7.6	8.7
United States	37.1	21.5	9.2	8.2	9.8
Mean	63.7	25.6	9.8	6.1	5.6

Table 6.22: Probability of surviving to age 60

Percentage of people expected to die before reaching 60 years of age

Sweden	8.0
Japan	8.2
Australia	**9.1**
Italy	9.1
Norway	9.1
Netherlands	9.2
Canada	9.5
Switzerland	9.6
United Kingdom	9.9
Ireland	10.4
Belgium	10.5
Austria	10.6
Germany	10.6
New Zealand	10.7
Finland	11.3
France	11.4
Denmark	12.0
United States	12.8
Mean	10.1

Table 6.23: Years of good and ill health

Mean expected number of years of good and ill health, 2001

	Females expected good health	Males expected good health	Females expected ill health	Males expected ill health
Japan	75.8	71.4	8.9	6.5
Switzerland	74.4	71.1	8.4	6.2
France	73.5	69.0	9.5	6.6
Australia	**73.2**	**70.1**	**9.5**	**7.3**
Sweden	73.2	70.5	9.1	7.2
Austria	73.0	68.9	8.8	7.0
Italy	72.9	69.2	9.3	7.0
Finland	72.5	67.7	8.8	6.8
Germany	72.2	68.3	8.9	6.8
Norway	72.2	69.3	9.3	6.8
Belgium	71.8	67.7	9.4	7.1
Canada	71.6	68.2	10.4	8.4
New Zealand	71.5	69.1	9.4	6.9
Netherlands	71.1	68.7	9.6	7.1
United Kingdom	70.9	68.4	9.0	6.6
Denmark	70.8	69.3	8.7	5.5
Ireland	70.4	67.6	8.9	6.1
United States	68.8	66.4	10.7	8.0
Mean	72.2	68.9	9.3	6.9

Improved life expectancy

One central reason that life expectancy has increased so dramatically is that childbirth has become much safer for both mothers and babies. Table 6.20 records, at 25-year intervals, the remarkable fall in infant mortality over the course of the 20th century. In round figures, in 1900 one in seven babies from the selected countries died before their first birthday. By 2000 the ratio was one in 200. The infant mortality rate is the number of babies who die aged less than one year per 1000 live births during the same year.

A notable feature of Table 6.20 is the process of convergence over the century. Whereas in 1900 mortality rates ranged from New Zealand's 62 to Austria's 231, by 2000 the range from best to worst was a tiny 3.2 to 6.9. The process of convergence is now virtually complete, with nine of the 18 countries clustered between 4.5 and 5.3. With the laggards catching up, however, countries such as Australia and New Zealand – which had remarkably low rates at the beginning of the century – have lost their relative advantage.

The maternal mortality rates reported in Table 6.21 are the number of maternal deaths from all causes per 100 000 live births. Note the shift from per 1000 to per 100 000. It is as though we are looking at the figures under a microscope to make minute differences easier to see. That is, death of mothers in childbirth is now very rare in all developed countries. A further implication of the numbers being so small – and the amplification so great – is that minor year-to-year variations may be mistaken for genuine improvement or deterioration.

The continuing improvement in infant and maternal mortality rates, albeit now much smaller than in the past, is a reminder that a major reason for increased life expectancy is that a smaller percentage of people die at younger ages. As noted when discussing

Table 1.5, a major reason for increasing life expectancy in the first part of the 20th century was the reduction of premature deaths due to infectious diseases. In recent decades, the more important contributor has been older people living to greater ages. However, though not as dramatic as in the past, improvements in the survival rate of younger people are still occurring (Table 17.14).

The result is that whereas in 1900 average life expectancy was only 50 years, by 2000, according to the UN figures in Table 6.22, nine out of ten people in the selected countries could expect to live to at least 60 years of age. Sweden and Japan have the highest proportion surviving. Australia is, with a group of other countries, just behind. At the other end, the greater vulnerability of Americans earlier in their life is one reason for their lower life expectancy.

In recent years, health analysts have refined the conventional measure of life expectancy to take account of the truth that extra years of life are not worth as much if they are spent in pain or with a serious disability. Table 6.23 offers estimates from the WHO of expected years of good health and ill health for males and females in 2001, though it should be noted that methods for estimating healthy life expectancy are still in their infancy.

While expected healthy lives are obviously shorter than total expected lives, allowing for ill health does not greatly change the ranking of the selected countries. It can be seen that Australia still ranks highly, with years of ill health only a fraction above the overall mean, though the countries are fairly closely clustered. The overall mean for females' ill health is more than two years longer than that for males' ill health. Women still enjoy more years of healthy life than men, but by less of a margin than the gap in total life expectancy (Tables 1.6 and 1.7).

Table 6.24: Deaths from external causes

Standardised death rates per 100 000 population

	1960	1970	1980	1990	1999
Netherlands	49	62	42	31	28
United Kingdom	50	45	40	33	28
Germany	–	–	63	42	34
Italy	51	54	53	42	34
Sweden	63	64	59	47	37
Canada	70	73	65	47	40
Australia	**72**	**77**	**58**	**44**	**41**
Norway	52	58	59	52	41
Switzerland	83	83	71	65	41
Ireland	36	49	53	43	42
New Zealand	64	76	70	58	44
Austria	93	100	83	61	46
Japan	75	67	48	41	46
Denmark	69	70	68	58	48
United States	74	82	69	58	51
Belgium	69	82	78	57	55
France	75	87	83	69	57
Finland	87	92	75	85	67
Mean	67	72	63	52	43

Table 6.25: Potential years of life lost: external causes

Number of years of life lost per 100 000 population

	1960	1970	1980	1990	1999
Netherlands	1 019	1 280	907	685	612
United Kingdom	1 087	1 049	967	867	706
Sweden	1 287	1 516	1 283	1 005	719
Italy	1 169	1 208	1 178	880	726
Germany	–	–	1 587	1 068	823
Switzerland	1 867	1 685	–	1 395	864
Japan	2 100	1 613	1 086	899	892
Denmark	1 280	1 576	1 571	1 152	904
Norway	1 193	1 421	1 336	1 100	909
Ireland	816	1 137	1 227	1 060	953
Canada	1 862	2 077	1 854	1 278	1 016
Austria	2 151	2 227	1 978	1 430	1 120
France	1 498	1 921	1 845	1 419	1 127
Australia	**1 787**	**2 004**	**1 678**	**1 250**	**1 173**
Belgium	1 446	1 770	1 738	1 391	1 370
New Zealand	1 460	1 800	1 712	1 681	1 388
Finland	2 020	2 184	1 724	1 985	1 443
United States	1 885	2 320	2 081	1 653	1 460
Mean	1 525	1 693	1 431	1 233	1 011

Table 6.26: Potential years of life lost: external causes, females

Number of years of life lost per 100 000 population

	1960	1970	1980	1990	1999 *
Italy	445	505	603	358	303
United Kingdom	558	599	527	398	327
Netherlands	492	710	516	412	336
Ireland	437	612	621	523	366
Sweden	582	850	674	578	404
Germany	799	1 054	847	506	411
Denmark	656	959	963	651	428
Norway	364	508	478	578	445
Switzerland	866	889	832	658	447
Japan	1 210	849	581	483	462
Canada	878	1 094	943	620	506
France	694	975	938	721	550
Austria	939	954	882	640	551
Australia	**845**	**1 025**	**837**	**606**	**564**
Finland	794	849	674	819	589
Belgium	681	984	964	775	710
New Zealand	700	796	969	826	714
United States	925	1 174	997	826	748
Mean	715	855	769	610	492

Table 6.27: Potential years of life lost: external causes, males

Number of years of life lost per 100 000 population

	1960	1970	1980	1990	1999 *
Netherlands	1 537	1 828	1 282	948	879
Sweden	1 978	2 157	1 870	1 475	1 023
United Kingdom	1 619	1 504	1 394	1 323	1 071
Italy	1 901	1 909	1 747	1 393	1 138
Germany	2 792	3 085	2 300	1 429	1 216
Switzerland	2 896	2 843	2 431	2 219	1 275
Japan	3 015	2 392	1 589	1 301	1 313
Norway	1 997	2 298	2 158	1 709	1 356
Denmark	1 900	2 176	2 157	1 633	1 363
Canada	2 814	3 042	2 747	1 925	1 514
Ireland	1 187	1 647	1 811	1 581	1 533
Austria	3 429	3 540	3 071	2 200	1 676
France	2 296	2 838	2 724	2 218	1 702
Australia	**2 676**	**2 937**	**2 488**	**1 878**	**1 774**
Belgium	2 209	2 541	2 487	1 987	2 011
New Zealand	2 192	2 768	2 436	2 727	2 071
United States	2 871	3 507	3 174	2 626	2 167
Finland	3 287	3 533	2 759	3 184	2 271
Mean	2 366	2 586	2 257	1 875	1 520

Deaths from external causes

The three most important causes of death in the selected countries, in order of their prevalence, are circulatory diseases (heart disease and stroke), cancer, and death from external causes. Deaths in general, and deaths from particular causes, are conventionally measured as age-standardised death rates per 100 000, which takes into account the differences in age structure of populations. This allows comparisons over time and between countries.

However, death rates may be measured from a different perspective, one that takes account not just of death itself but also of the number of years of life the deaths cost. Clearly, a death that strikes early exacts a heavier toll than one that strikes late in life. This explains the construction of the measure Potential Years of Life Lost, which weights a particular death by subtracting the person's age at death from 70 years. The total number of years lost by all those dying from a particular cause in a given year is then expressed as the number of years of life lost per 100 000 of population.

Deaths from external causes – external to the body – include a variety of causes, some of which are also examined separately in other sections, including deaths from suicide (Table 17.10), homicide (Table 17.3) and traffic accidents (Table 17.16). The category further includes deaths from other accidents, such as falls, accidental poisoning or drowning.

As a cause of death, the external category is much smaller than cancer or heart disease and is comparable with relatively lesser causes, such as deaths from diseases of the respiratory and digestive systems. However, whereas most deaths from illness are more prevalent among older people, death from external causes is no respecter of age. External causes of death are so important because they are strongly associated with premature or untimely death, and so in terms of total potential years of life lost they rank with cancer and heart disease as a major cause of mortality.

Table 6.24 shows the conventional death rate from external causes rising between 1960 and 1970 in most countries, but then falling almost universally and continually in the last 30 years of the 20th century. It is also apparent that the dispersion in death rates between the selected countries has narrowed over the period. Australia's performance, however, has gone from worse than the overall mean to slightly better.

The PYLL rates reported in Table 6.25 tell a similar story to the conventional death rates, implying that although the total number of deaths from external causes has fallen they are still concentrated among younger age groups. Thus both the overall annual death rate and the overall annual PYLL rate have declined by about 40% since 1970, a notable achievement. The single factor most responsible, at least in Australia, is probably the fall in the road toll (Table 17.2). As with the conventional death rates, the dispersion of countries' PYLL rates has narrowed. Australia's PYLL rate, however, has remained worse than the overall average, showing only a marginal improvement relative to the other countries.

For most causes of death, the PYLL measure shows somewhat higher rates for males, but for deaths from external causes, the difference is pronounced. As can be deduced by comparing Tables 6.26 and 6.27, the overall mean for males is three times that for females. This remained true throughout the period since 1960 and it is also true for Australia.

Another conclusion to be drawn from the measures of PYLL is that the United States is the most dangerous of the selected countries, with a PYLL rate 44% higher than the overall mean, and more than double the safest countries, the Netherlands and the United Kingdom. As Table 6.25 shows, because it has improved less than the norm, the United States has become relatively more dangerous than the other countries since 1960.

Table 6.28: Deaths from circulatory diseases

Standardised death rates per 100 000 population

	1960	1970	1980	1990	1999
Japan	473	468	339	215	151
France	372	332	283	195	168
Australia	**624**	**637**	**444**	**310**	**214**
Switzerland	517	435	366	274	218
Canada	584	488	379	261	219
Netherlands	429	426	345	279	230
Italy	520	465	409	289	243
Belgium	474	478	399	274	246
New Zealand	564	555	487	338	247
Denmark	512	457	402	347	251
Norway	448	446	373	332	258
Sweden	516	443	416	326	260
United Kingdom	583	533	461	350	265
United States	632	557	414	311	265
Finland	662	658	488	397	284
Germany	–	–	450	350	292
Austria	537	540	497	371	297
Ireland	586	584	544	403	324
Mean	531	500	416	312	246

Table 6.29: Potential years of life lost: circulatory diseases

Number of years of life lost per 100 000 population

	1960	1970	1980	1990	1999 *
Switzerland	1 176	935	795	589	422
France	1 083	949	780	528	447
Australia	**2 036**	**1 980**	**1 292**	**735**	**471**
Japan	1 738	1 305	882	625	485
Norway	1 059	1 183	993	797	515
Italy	1 454	1 199	994	651	520
Sweden	1 085	975	962	689	521
Canada	1 811	1 514	1 162	692	548
Denmark	1 133	1 108	1 049	834	557
Netherlands	945	1 169	982	726	595
Germany	–	–	1 097	907	666
New Zealand	1 831	1 878	1 499	989	678
United Kingdom	1 677	1 664	1 474	996	710
Belgium	1 472	1 392	1 107	715	715
Austria	1 428	1 357	1 227	869	726
Finland	2 072	2 194	1 522	1 154	746
Ireland	1 843	1 758	1 554	1 068	765
United States	2 289	2 031	1 438	1 047	880
Mean	1 537	1 447	1 156	812	609

Table 6.30: Potential years of life lost: circulatory diseases, females

Number of years of life lost per 100 000 population

	1960	1970	1980	1990	1999 *
France	764	597	423	269	230
Switzerland	772	546	435	308	239
Norway	668	569	445	365	264
Australia	**1 364**	**1 251**	**718**	**393**	**270**
Japan	1 476	970	591	396	282
Sweden	759	547	462	361	296
Italy	1 183	853	590	373	299
Finland	1 286	1 147	647	489	320
Canada	1 079	831	625	378	323
Denmark	724	642	566	492	331
Belgium	980	848	652	431	367
Germany	892	772	615	507	372
Netherlands	638	628	504	375	386
New Zealand	1 277	1 192	1 004	623	400
Ireland	1 549	1 187	916	609	423
United Kingdom	1 132	990	825	557	430
Austria	998	863	743	491	444
United States	1 452	1 237	860	652	578
Mean	1 055	871	646	448	347

Table 6.31: Potential years of life lost: circulatory diseases, males

Number of years of life lost per 100 000 population

	1960	1970	1980	1990	1999 *
Switzerland	1 625	1 357	1 184	886	608
Australia	**2 707**	**2 711**	**1 866**	**1 071**	**671**
France	1 436	1 324	1 152	797	671
Japan	2 016	1 680	1 199	861	692
Sweden	1 423	1 410	1 475	1 025	745
Italy	1 755	1 578	1 434	949	749
Norway	1 469	1 816	1 556	1 234	763
Canada	2 522	2 210	1 724	1 018	777
Denmark	1 566	1 598	1 554	1 187	785
Netherlands	1 274	1 748	1 485	1 084	804
Belgium	2 002	1 975	1 593	1 011	886
Germany	1 696	1 795	1 682	1 329	961
New Zealand	2 393	2 580	1 998	1 360	961
United Kingdom	2 285	2 386	2 159	1 448	996
Austria	1 966	1 990	1 819	1 280	1 016
Ireland	2 132	2 322	2 194	1 532	1 107
Finland	3 013	3 441	2 533	1 858	1 181
United States	3 169	2 899	2 073	1 474	1 202
Mean	2 025	2 046	1 704	1 189	865

Death from circulatory diseases

Measured in the conventional way, circulatory diseases – including heart attack and stroke – are by far the greatest single cause of death among all the categories determined by the WHO. But the tables on this page tell the remarkable story of the marked decline in death from these diseases over the last 40 years of the 20th century. Circulatory or cardiovascular disease covers all diseases and conditions involving the heart and blood vessels. The main problem is the clogging of blood vessels with fat, cholesterol and other substances that may affect the blood flow to the heart or brain.

Table 6.28 shows that, for the selected countries overall, the death rate from circulatory disease has halved since 1960. At the same time, the dispersion between the countries with the highest and lowest death rates has narrowed by 40%.

The fall of two-thirds in Japan's death rate over the period lifted its place in the league table from fourth to first, and would have contributed to its pride of place at the top of the life expectancy league. Australia and the United States began the period at similar low positions on the heart death table – 15th and 16th – but whereas Australia's improvement of almost two-thirds lifted it to third place, America's improvement of 58% was only enough to lift it to 14th position.

Table 6.29 changes the measure of mortality from the conventional death rate to the more encompassing measure of potential years of life lost through death from circulatory diseases. The PYLL rate weights each person's death by subtracting their age at death from 70 years. The total number of years lost by all those dying from a circulatory diseases in a given year is then expressed as the number of years of life lost per 100 000 of population.

Table 6.29 confirms the basic story told by Table 6.28's conventional death rate, but even more starkly. Again we see that, individually and in aggregate, the selected countries'

rates of PYLL from circulatory diseases have been falling steadily but strongly since 1960. Again we see convergence between the selected countries, with the gap between the highest and lowest countries' PYLL rates narrowing over the period by almost two-thirds.

The additional information provided by Table 6.29 is that since 1960 the overall mean PYLL rate has fallen by more than the overall mean death rate, implying that on average people are now dying from cardiovascular problems at a later age.

Australia showed one of the greatest improvements over the period. In 1960 it was third from the bottom. By 1999 it was second top, behind only France. While the 1999 PYLL mean for the 18 nations dropped to about 40% of its 1960 level, Australia's declined to about 20% of its 1960 level. At the other extreme, the United States was now firmly in bottom position, with a PYLL almost 50% above the mean.

The reasons for national differences are hard to fathom. Many analysts have focused on diet, but it is hard to think of two diets more different than the Japanese and French, though both perform near the top. Conversely the Australian and American diets may not be too dissimilar, but those countries are at opposite ends of the league table.

Comparison of Tables 6.30 and 6.31 reveals that, for circulatory diseases, the overall PYLL rate for males is 2.5 times that for women. So men are more prone to death from this cause than women, and at a younger age. Furthermore, the gap between men and women has widened noticeably since 1960, with men's PYLL rates falling more slowly than women's.

Cardiovascular disease remains Australia's largest health problem, accounting for 39% of all deaths. Nevertheless its reduction – and the success in delaying its onset until later ages – has been the single biggest reason for increasing life expectancy since 1970.

Table 6.32: Deaths from cancer

Standardised death rates per 100 000

	1960	1970	1980	1990	1999 *
Finland	202	192	180	164	147
Sweden	171	168	176	158	151
Switzerland	194	194	186	184	151
Japan	154	157	157	154	155
Australia	**159**	**176**	**178**	**179**	**163**
Austria	220	217	203	189	167
Norway	160	164	166	171	168
Italy	161	178	187	194	171
Germany	203	206	200	189	175
United States	169	176	181	188	175
Canada	177	183	186	192	177
France	182	181	192	188	178
United Kingdom	193	204	208	210	185
New Zealand	167	194	199	202	189
Netherlands	198	210	211	204	194
Ireland	166	189	199	206	195
Belgium	204	210	220	204	203
Denmark	213	202	220	220	212
Mean	183	189	192	189	175

Table 6.33: Potential years of life lost: cancer

Number of years of life lost per 100 000 population

	1960	1970	1980	1990	1999 *
Finland	1 377	1 239	1 023	852	749
Sweden	1 162	1 039	993	866	754
Switzerland	1 195	1 215	1 107	961	774
Japan	1 224	1 145	1 018	899	808
Australia	**1 130**	**1 206**	**1 133**	**1 037**	**845**
Norway	1 150	1 150	953	958	864
Italy	1 270	1 306	1 299	1 144	918
Austria	1 415	1 353	1 250	1 071	923
Canada	1 188	1 201	1 163	1 082	927
United Kingdom	1 398	1 403	1 312	1 162	944
United States	1 270	1 275	1 206	1 110	955
Germany	1 337	1 283	1 161	1 103	971
Netherlands	1 344	1 326	1 159	1 080	1 016
Ireland	1 219	1 330	1 233	1 128	1 020
New Zealand	1 225	1 365	1 332	1 219	1 047
Denmark	1 391	1 386	1 351	1 265	1 081
France	1 244	1 229	1 303	1 182	1 095
Belgium	1 382	1 332	1 282	1 150	1 116
Mean	1 273	1 266	1 182	1 071	934

Table 6.34: Potential years of life lost: cancer, females

Number of years of life lost per 100 000 population

	1960	1970	1980	1990	1999 *
Japan	1 161	1 044	876	725	674
Finland	1 159	993	851	822	677
Switzerland	1 109	1 102	943	841	702
Italy	1 157	1 126	1 027	920	761
Australia	**1 092**	**1 122**	**1 014**	**957**	**783**
Sweden	1 254	1 089	1 009	896	784
France	1 103	975	931	807	803
Austria	1 346	1 275	1 141	966	810
Germany	1 306	1 245	1 046	957	848
Norway	1 159	1 151	959	939	858
Canada	1 227	1 164	1 069	1 011	890
United States	1 238	1 192	1 106	1 033	893
United Kingdom	1 263	1 307	1 287	1 159	936
Belgium	1 243	1 174	1 086	976	956
Netherlands	1 253	1 226	1 015	1 016	983
Ireland	1 194	1 317	1 214	1 132	989
New Zealand	1 268	1 287	1 317	1 275	1 078
Denmark	1 435	1 438	1 401	1 287	1 105
Mean	1 220	1 179	1 079	984	863

Table 6.35: Potential years of life lost: cancer, males

Number of years of life lost per 100 000 population

	1960	1970	1980	1990	1999 *
Sweden	1 072	989	979	841	726
Finland	1 654	1 541	1 233	900	828
Switzerland	1 299	1 342	1 284	1 092	852
Norway	1 142	1 154	952	982	874
Australia	**1 174**	**1 295**	**1 258**	**1 119**	**905**
Japan	1 286	1 263	1 184	1 086	950
United Kingdom	1 558	1 517	1 347	1 170	954
Canada	1 149	1 240	1 265	1 160	966
New Zealand	1 185	1 446	1 353	1 164	1 014
United States	1 305	1 369	1 319	1 197	1 023
Austria	1 496	1 451	1 401	1 198	1 043
Ireland	1 245	1 342	1 257	1 130	1 051
Netherlands	1 439	1 442	1 321	1 155	1 052
Denmark	1 346	1 336	1 306	1 249	1 061
Italy	1 397	1 504	1 599	1 390	1 086
Germany	1 368	1 340	1 313	1 264	1 099
Belgium	1 535	1 507	1 499	1 337	1 287
France	1 410	1 503	1 695	1 576	1 398
Mean	1 337	1 366	1 309	1 167	1 009

Death from cancer

Cancer shows a different pattern from the previous two causes of death. The decline has been less, and the gap between the sexes is less pronounced. Cancers are a diverse group of diseases that all involve the growth and spread of abnormal cells which invade and destroy surrounding tissue. In Australia, the main types of cancer causing death among males are lung, colorectal and prostate cancers and among females are breast, colorectal and lung cancers.

In Australia in 1999, while cardiovascular diseases were a bigger cause of death overall, especially in the older age groups, cancer was a bigger killer among those under 65. Tables 6.32 and 6.33 suggest a similar pattern among the selected countries as a whole. Deaths from circulatory diseases in 1999 were higher than cancer, but in terms of potential years of life lost, cancer was the worse problem.

In the selected countries, the overall mean death rate from cardiovascular disease has been falling since 1960, and in that time has fallen by half. But Table 6.32 shows that the overall mean death rate from cancer continued rising slowly until 1980, and since then has fallen by less than 10%. Some of that increase probably reflected better diagnosis as well as increased incidence.

The table reveals little change in the dispersion of death rates between the 18 countries. Australia's rate has fallen only since 1990, by 8%. Its rate has been better than the overall mean throughout the period but is less so now than in 1960, and its ranking has dropped from equal top to fifth.

But the news on death from cancer is not all disappointing. Table 6.33 shifts the focus from the conventional death rate to the more encompassing PYLL measure. The PYLL rate weights each person's death by subtracting their age at death from 70 years, and then expressing the total number of years lost by all those dying from that cause in that year as years of life lost per 100 000 population.

The encouraging story from Table 6.33 is that when the toll from cancer deaths is measured in terms of years of life lost, rates have been falling strongly in almost all countries since 1960. Indeed, in that time the overall mean PYLL rate has fallen by almost 30%.

In other words, although most countries have had limited success in reducing the actual death rate from cancer, they have had more success in ensuring that on average it strikes at a later age. This probably reflects success in prevention, but in addition early detection and better treatment regimens now mean there is a much higher survival rate in many forms of cancer.

Australia's PYLL rate has always been better than the overall mean for the selected countries. But Australia was one of the few countries to experience a continued rise in its PYLL rate during the 1960s, before joining the rest in achieving steady improvement. This temporary setback, however, was enough to cause its place in the league table to slip from the top to fifth.

Scrutiny of Tables 6.34 and 6.35 reveals that the rates of premature death from cancer for males are only 10% or 15% higher than those for females. Furthermore, it is apparent that the progress in reducing PYLL rates since 1960 has been shared pretty much evenly between men and women.

For women, cancer is by far the greatest of the three leading causes of premature death. Its dominance has been strengthened by the greater decline in premature death from heart disease. For men, external causes, mainly accidents of all kinds, remain the greatest cause of premature death. But cancer has moved from third place to second because of the greater success in curbing the loss of years of life from heart disease.

Table 6.36: Deaths from HIV/AIDS

Deaths per 100 000 population

	1987	Peak year	Peak rate	1999 *
Japan	0.0	1996	0.1	0.0
Finland	0.0	1996	0.5	0.2
Norway	0.4	1993	1.5	0.2
New Zealand	0.5	1992	1.6	0.3
Sweden	0.2	1995	1.4	0.3
United Kingdom	–	1994	1.1	0.3
Ireland	0.2	1995	1.4	0.4
Australia	**0.7**	**1993**	**2.9**	**0.6**
Austria	0.5	1994	2.0	0.6
Denmark	–	1995	4.7	0.6
Germany	0.8	1994	2.2	0.6
Netherlands	0.6	1995	2.4	0.7
France	1.6	1994	7.7	1.5
Italy	0.8	1995	7.8	1.5
Switzerland	–	1995	7.6	1.7
Canada	1.8	1995	5.0	1.8
Belgium	0.3	1995	2.0	–
United States	5.1	1995	14.3	4.7
Mean	0.9	–	3.7	0.9

Table 6.37: Potential years of life lost: HIV/AIDS

Number of years of life lost per 100 000 population

	1990	1995	1999 *
Japan	0	1	1
Finland	0	0	6
Norway	26	35	7
New Zealand	39	41	8
Sweden	20	40	8
United Kingdom	0	34	9
Ireland	0	48	13
Denmark	–	121	15
Austria	27	54	16
Germany	44	63	16
Australia	**58**	**72**	**18**
Netherlands	46	69	18
France	139	227	41
Italy	121	269	46
Switzerland	–	249	49
Canada	94	149	50
Belgium	22	58	–
United States	277	423	129
Mean	57	109	27

Ranked according to 1999 PYLL with Belgium according to its 1995 value.

Table 6.38: Incidence of AIDS

AIDS cases per 100 000 population

	1985	1990	1993	1995	1997	2000
Finland	0.1	0.3	0.5	0.8	0.4	0.3
Japan	0.0	0.0	0.1	0.1	0.2	0.3
Ireland	0.1	1.7	2.1	1.5	0.8	0.4
Netherlands	0.5	2.8	3.1	3.5	2.2	0.6
Sweden	0.3	1.5	2.0	2.2	0.9	0.6
New Zealand	–	2.1	1.5	1.7	0.9	0.7
Germany	0.4	2.3	2.4	2.3	1.2	0.8
Norway	0.3	1.4	1.5	1.5	0.8	0.9
Austria	0.3	2.1	2.9	2.6	1.2	1.0
Denmark	0.8	3.8	4.6	4.1	2.1	1.0
Australia	**0.8**	**3.9**	**4.8**	**4.5**	**2.0**	**1.3**
Belgium	0.7	2.1	2.5	2.4	1.2	1.4
United Kingdom	0.4	2.2	3.1	3.0	1.8	1.4
Canada	1.5	5.3	6.5	6.1	2.6	2.1
Switzerland	1.3	9.7	9.5	8.5	4.7	2.5
France	1.0	7.4	9.3	8.9	3.8	2.8
Italy	0.3	5.2	8.4	9.9	5.9	3.4
United States	3.4	16.7	40.0	27.0	21.7	14.4
Mean	0.7	3.9	5.8	5.0	3.0	2.0

HIV and AIDS

In the early 1980s the most dramatic public health threat for decades confronted the selected countries. A mystery disease that struck and quickly killed apparently healthy people spread frighteningly in the United States, especially among groups deemed to be at high risk, such as male homosexuals, haemophiliacs and intravenous drug users. Eventually it was diagnosed as AIDS (Acquired Immunodeficiency Syndrome) and later it was discovered that it resulted from HIV (Human Immunodeficiency Virus).

It was also discovered that HIV is not spread by casual contact but can be contracted through exposure to blood and blood products (e.g. used hypodermic needles), semen and female genital secretions or breast milk. HIV attacks and eventually destroys the immune system. During AIDS, the last stage of HIV infection, the victim is vulnerable to being killed by a wide range of infections.

In 2002, 42 million people worldwide were living with HIV, and since 1981 more than 22 million people have died of AIDS. In 2002, 3.1 million people died of AIDS, 2.4 million of them in sub-Saharan Africa.

Despite the scale of this continuing global tragedy, Tables 6.36 to 6.38 also record the measure of success achieved by governments and community groups in the selected countries in responding to the threat. Urgent effort was put into the development of (still expensive) drugs to prevent HIV developing into AIDS, but the most important measures have been prevention, combating the spread of HIV through the promotion of safe sex, free needle-exchange programs, and better procedures when handling blood.

The tables document how the problem became rapidly more serious into the 1990s, but how its toll has been contained since then and the incidence of AIDS substantially reduced. While the scourge has by no means been eliminated, the threat reached its peak in the mid-1990s in almost all the selected countries. In the five or so years after that, its incidence fell continuously to levels typically about a third of the peak.

Among the selected countries, the disease struck first and struck most severely in the United States. The peak fatality rate there was almost twice that of the next highest countries, and in 1999 it was still four times greater than the mean of the others. The peak incidence of AIDS in America, in 1993, was ten times greater than the mean of the other countries, and in 2000 was still more than ten times greater.

The severity of the AIDS epidemic varied considerably between countries. Japan especially, but also the Scandinavian countries, the United Kingdom and Ireland, remained relatively untouched. Partly this was an accident of timing. Because AIDS hit first in the United States, it spread very rapidly there before effective strategies of prevention were known.

The data indicates that by 1987 Australia was one of the more severely affected countries, but also that its response after the initial spread was relatively effective. For example, its worst year of fatalities, 1992, was slightly earlier than many others. Australia was also relatively effective in that its peak mortality rate did not increase as greatly beyond its 1987 rate as in some other countries.

In terms of total deaths, HIV caused only a small proportion compared with cancer and heart disease. But this takes no account of its tendency to strike most severely among younger age groups, nor the early mystery and fears around its rapid spread and the then impotence of doctors to save its victims.

Although the problem has been contained in the developed countries, it became a global pandemic, and is still getting worse in much of the developing world. There are worries about its increasing incidence in such populous countries as India, China and Russia. Its impact has been most devastating in sub-Saharan Africa, where its tragic toll is still growing. In 2002, one young African adult in every 11 was living with HIV/AIDS.

Table 7.1: Educational attainment of the adult population

Highest level of education attained by 25 to 64-year-old population, 2000, % at each level

	Junior secondary	Senior secondary	Tertiary
United States	12	50	37
Switzerland	13	62	25
Norway	15	57	28
Japan	17	49	34
Germany	17	59	23
Canada	18	40	42
Sweden	19	49	32
Denmark	20	54	27
Austria	24	62	14
New Zealand	24	46	29
Finland	26	42	32
France	36	41	23
United Kingdom	37	37	26
Australia	**41**	**30**	**29**
Belgium	42	31	27
Ireland	42	22	36
Netherlands	45	32	22
Italy	57	33	10
Mean	28	44	28

Table 7.2: Secondary school completion

Percentage of each age group in 2000 who had completed at least upper secondary school

	25–34	35–44	45–54	55–64
Japan	94	94	81	63
Norway	94	91	82	71
Switzerland	92	90	85	81
Sweden	91	86	78	65
Canada	89	85	81	67
United States	88	89	89	83
Finland	87	84	70	51
Denmark	86	80	80	72
Germany	85	86	83	76
Austria	84	81	73	65
New Zealand	82	80	75	60
France	78	67	58	46
Belgium	76	64	53	39
Netherlands	75	69	61	50
Ireland	73	62	48	35
Australia	**71**	**60**	**55**	**44**
United Kingdom	68	65	61	55
Italy	57	49	39	22
Mean	82	77	70	58

Table 7.3: Tertiary qualifications among males

Percentage of males with tertiary qualifications within each age group, 2000

	25–34	35–44	45–54	55–64
Japan	46	46	32	20
Canada	45	39	38	30
Ireland	45	37	30	22
United States	36	37	41	35
Switzerland	35	37	34	33
Sweden	34	31	29	24
Belgium	33	28	23	20
France	32	21	19	16
Finland	30	32	28	25
Norway	30	28	28	23
United Kingdom	30	28	28	20
Australia	**29**	**27**	**29**	**22**
Netherlands	27	27	27	22
New Zealand	26	27	29	23
Denmark	25	24	25	21
Germany	23	30	31	28
Austria	16	19	17	15
Italy	10	11	11	8
Mean	31	29	28	23

Table 7.4: Tertiary qualifications among females

Percentage of females with tertiary qualifications in each age group, 2000

	25–34	35–44	45–54	55–64
Canada	56	46	40	30
Ireland	50	36	28	20
Japan	49	41	25	11
Finland	46	42	31	22
United States	42	38	38	27
Norway	40	30	25	18
Belgium	39	31	23	14
Sweden	39	35	34	25
Australia	**38**	**32**	**29**	**21**
France	37	24	18	13
Denmark	34	32	29	19
New Zealand	31	34	35	26
United Kingdom	29	26	24	17
Netherlands	26	22	18	13
Germany	20	21	18	12
Switzerland	17	21	15	8
Austria	14	14	10	5
Italy	13	11	10	5
Mean	34	30	25	17

7 EDUCATION
Educational attainment

A complex sophisticated economy requires an educated labour force, while the capacity of an individual to survive and prosper in such a society also depends centrally on education. So educational attainment is one measure of the extent to which countries are developing and maintaining a highly skilled labour force and are offering their populations the opportunity for personal development. The tables on this page profile the differing educational attainments of the selected countries and how they have been changing in recent generations.

Each educational system grew up with its own assumptions and methods. But international bodies have devoted considerable attention to standardising the types of institutions and qualifications in different countries. While they are broadly comparable, one should not assume that someone graduating from secondary school in one country has exactly the same skills as the same graduate from another country, or equally that a high school graduate in 1954 has the same skills as one in 2004.

Table 7.1 shows the proportion of each country's adult population (aged 25–64) and the levels of educational attainment they have achieved. Because it shows a large age range all together, it is by nature a slow-moving indicator, reflecting the legacy of past educational practice more than recent performance. Table 7.1 is testimony to just how much attitudes to education varied among these countries. Most basically, it shows how America was the first to democratise access to the upper levels of education. The North American and northern European countries and Japan gave broader access to higher levels of education earlier than did the countries near the bottom. Italy trails the other countries by a considerable distance, while the relatively low ranking of Australia and Britain may surprise many.

Completion of secondary school is often taken as the minimum desirable qualification in contemporary society. This is an oversimplification, especially if leaving school earlier is tied in to good training programs in a trade. Nevertheless, as a basic measure of educational attainment Table 7.2 shows the upward trend over 30 years. Of the cohort born between 1935 and 1945, 58% completed secondary school in the selected countries, while for those born between 1965 and 1975 the figure rises to 82%. There is a much closer grouping of countries in the younger age groups, with 11 countries between 82% and 94% completing. Among the older age group, only the United States and Switzerland had over 80% finishing secondary school. Again Italy is a distant outlier from the others, and again Australia and Britain rank low.

The same trend towards rising proportions with tertiary qualifications is evident in Tables 7.3 and 7.4. (Note that these figures represent all tertiary education, both tertiary type A programs, which broadly correspond to Australian university degrees, and tertiary type B programs, which are normally more narrowly vocational and shorter in duration.) But there are also contrasts with Table 7.2. Countries have different patterns of access to tertiary education. In the German-speaking countries, for example, only a relatively small proportion went on, and their degree programs were much longer than in the English-speaking countries. In Australia the most common university degree is three years long; in Austria, it is six. So those countries tend to have a lower proportion of tertiary graduates than their high proportion of secondary graduates would lead one to expect.

Moreover, given the great surge in Table 7.2, the rise in the percentage of male graduates is more modest than might be expected, and in recent decades male graduation rates have been only edging up. The growth of tertiary education among females has been much more dramatic, doubling between the older and younger age groups. Among the older age group, male tertiary graduates substantially outnumbered females, but among the younger age group females have the lead. Indeed it is only in the three German-speaking countries just mentioned that young male graduates still clearly outnumber female graduates.

Table 7.5: Trends in total expenditure on education

Total expenditure on education as % of GDP

	1987	1994	2000
United States	6.4	6.6	7.0
Denmark	7.6	7.0	6.7
Sweden	7.3	6.7	6.5
Canada	7.1	7.2	6.4
France	6.6	6.2	6.1
Australia	**5.6**	**5.7**	**6.0**
Norway	7.0	6.9	5.9
New Zealand	–	4.8	5.8
Austria	6.2	5.6	5.7
Switzerland	5.1	6.0	5.7
Finland	5.8	6.6	5.6
Belgium	5.4	5.8	5.5
Germany	4.4	5.8	5.3
United Kingdom	5.7	5.6	5.3
Italy	5.3	4.7	4.9
Netherlands	7.3	4.9	4.7
Ireland	6.1	5.7	4.6
Japan	6.4	4.9	4.6
Mean	6.2	6.0	5.7

Table 7.6: Trends in public expenditure on education

Public expenditure on education as % of GDP

	1975	1985	1995	2000
Denmark	6.9	6.2	6.4	6.4
Sweden	7.1	7.0	6.3	6.3
New Zealand	6.5	5.1	4.9	5.8
Norway	6.4	5.6	7.0	5.8
France	5.6	5.7	5.9	5.7
Finland	–	5.7	6.3	5.5
Austria	5.7	5.8	6.3	5.4
Switzerland	6.8	4.9	–	5.3
Canada	8.5	6.9	6.2	5.2
Belgium	–	–	–	5.1
United States	5.7	4.6	5.0	4.8
Australia	**6.2**	**5.4**	**4.5**	**4.6**
Italy	4.8	5.0	4.5	4.5
United Kingdom	6.8	4.9	4.8	4.5
Germany	5.1	4.6	4.5	4.3
Netherlands	7.4	6.6	4.6	4.3
Ireland	6.5	6.0	4.7	4.1
Japan	–	–	3.6	3.5
Mean	6.4	5.6	5.3	5.1

Table 7.7: Public share of education expenditure

Public share as % of education spending, 2000

	Total	Schools	Tertiary
Norway	99	99	96
Finland	98	100	97
Sweden	97	100	88
Denmark	96	98	98
Austria	94	96	97
Belgium	92	94	85
France	92	93	86
Switzerland	92	89	–
Ireland	91	96	79
Italy	91	98	78
Netherlands	90	95	77
United Kingdom	85	89	68
Germany	81	81	92
Canada	80	92	61
Australia	**76**	**85**	**51**
Japan	75	92	45
United States	68	90	34
Mean	88	93	77

No data on New Zealand.

Table 7.8: Enrolments in public educational institutions

Percentage of students at each level enrolled in public schools, 2000

	Primary	Senior secondary	University
Finland	99	90	90
Ireland	99	99	95
Japan	99	69	27
Norway	99	89	89
Germany	98	93	100
New Zealand	98	83	99
Sweden	97	98	95
Switzerland	97	91	92
Austria	96	91	96
United Kingdom	95	30	–
Canada	94	94	100
Italy	93	94	94
Denmark	89	98	100
United States	88	91	69
France	85	70	89
Australia	**73**	**83**	**100**
Belgium	46	40	39
Netherlands	31	8	31
Mean	88	78	82

Educational expenditure

Careless commentaries sometimes lump education and health together as two areas inexorably consuming more social resources as demand for them goes ever upward. While it is true that each generation has higher educational attainment than the one before, the trends in spending on education present a contrast to health. On average in the selected countries, education receives only two-thirds as much of GDP as health (5.7%:8.7%), and while the upward trend of resources devoted to health is clear and consistent, education shows no such direction. Indeed, as Table 7.5 shows, in the last 13 years of the 20th century educational expenditure fell very slightly as a percentage of GDP.

Recent OECD publications do not offer long-term trend tables on education expenditure, presumably because changes in definition over the years detract from precise comparability. However, Simon Marginson's research gives us systematic Australian data. Fuelled by the baby boom and greater school retention rates, Australian expenditure on education grew faster than the economy as a whole in the two and a half decades from 1950. From 1.6% of GDP in 1950, the percentage devoted to education doubled to 3.2% in 1960, and rose again to 4.6% in 1970. Then, under the Whitlam Government, there was a spurt to 6.2% in 1975. But the growth has not been sustained, and has fluctuated just below that figure ever since. Table 7.5 finds it increasing marginally from 5.6% in 1987 to 6% in 2000.

One difficulty in generating comparative data has been harmonising the private input into education spending. So Table 7.6 is able to provide data going back to 1975, but only on public education expenditure as a proportion of GDP. It shows that public education expenditure grew less quickly than the economy as a whole in the last quarter of the 20th century. In almost every country on which we have systematic data, public education expenditure's share of GDP fell. Although school retention rates were rising throughout the period, a counter-trend was that with the ageing society and the fall in the birth rate the proportion of the population in the relevant age cohorts has been falling. Australia's fall in spending was greater than average, though the demographic justification for it was less than average.

In all the selected countries, education is primarily a public responsibility, in most of the countries overwhelmingly so. Table 7.7 shows that in 11 of the 18 countries, public expenditure accounts for more than 90% of education spending. With Japan, Australia falls very much at the private end of the spectrum, with only the United States relying more on private funding.

In most countries (though Germany and Switzerland move substantially in the opposite direction) tertiary education requires a greater private contribution than does secondary education. This is particularly true of the three countries most reliant on private input – the United States, Japan and Australia. In ten of 17 countries, 80% or more of tertiary education spending is provided publicly.

Note that private support might be needed for students in public institutions, while private institutions may also receive public financial support, so Tables 7.7 and 7.8 explore different dimensions of public and private education. Table 7.8 shows that the great bulk of education in nearly all the selected countries occurs in public institutions. At school level, the major exceptions are the Netherlands and Belgium, where there is a strong (state-financed) tradition of education in church schools. The British particularly, and the Japanese to some extent, have a tendency for a great deal of senior secondary education to be completed in private schools.

Only a few of the selected countries – the Netherlands, Belgium, Japan and the United States – have a strong tradition of private universities. In most others, including Australia, their contribution is negligible.

Table 7.9: Spending per student

Annual spending US$000 PPP per student at each level, 2000

	Primary	Secondary	Tertiary
United States	7.0	8.9	20.4
Switzerland	6.6	9.8	18.5
Sweden	6.3	6.3	15.1
Canada	5.9	5.9	15.0
Norway	6.6	8.5	13.4
Australia	**5.0**	**6.9**	**12.9**
Denmark	7.1	7.7	12.0
Netherlands	4.3	5.9	11.9
Ireland	3.4	4.6	11.1
Austria	6.6	8.6	10.9
Japan	5.5	6.3	10.9
Germany	4.2	6.8	10.9
Belgium	4.3	6.9	10.8
United Kingdom	3.9	6.0	9.7
France	4.5	7.6	8.4
Finland	4.3	6.1	8.2
Italy	6.0	7.2	8.1
Mean	5.4	7.1	12.2

No data on New Zealand. Canadian figure is for primary and secondary combined.

Table 7.10: Spending per student relative to GDP

Total annual spending per student as a % of GDP per capita, 2000

	Primary	Secondary	Tertiary
Switzerland	22	33	62
United States	20	26	59
Sweden	24	24	58
Canada	21	21	53
Australia	**19**	**27**	**50**
Netherlands	16	22	44
Denmark	25	27	42
Germany	16	26	42
Japan	21	24	42
Belgium	16	26	41
Austria	23	31	39
Ireland	12	16	39
United Kingdom	16	24	39
Norway	18	23	37
Finland	17	24	33
France	18	30	33
Italy	24	29	32
Mean	19	25	44

No data on New Zealand. Canadian figure is for primary and secondary combined.

Table 7.11: Student–staff ratios

Student–staff ratios by level of education, 2000

	Primary	Secondary	Tertiary
Denmark	10.4	12.8	–
Italy	11.0	10.3	24.1
Norway	12.4	–	12.7
Sweden	12.8	14.1	–
Belgium	15.0	9.7	19.9
United States	15.8	15.2	14.8
Netherlands	16.8	17.1	–
Finland	16.9	13.8	16.1
Australia	**17.3**	**12.6**	**14.8**
Canada	18.1	18.8	9.8
France	19.8	12.5	18.6
Germany	19.8	15.2	11.7
New Zealand	20.6	16.3	15.8
Japan	20.9	15.2	12.9
United Kingdom	21.2	14.8	17.6
Ireland	21.5	–	19.4
Mean	16.9	14.2	16.0

No data on Austria or Switzerland.

Table 7.12: Teachers' salaries

Ratio of teachers' salaries at each level, after 15 years' service, to GDP per capita, 2000

	Primary	Junior secondary	Senior secondary	Senior pay per contact hour $US
Switzerland	1.53	1.83	2.18	96
Netherlands	1.18	1.26	1.77	56
Germany	1.52	1.63	1.76	64
New Zealand	1.70	1.70	1.70	35
Belgium	1.22	1.28	1.64	65
Japan	1.62	1.62	1.62	90
Canada	1.18	1.25	1.61	64
United Kingdom	1.48	1.48	1.48	–
Australia	**1.43**	**1.43**	**1.43**	**48**
Denmark	1.16	1.16	1.35	68
France	1.17	1.26	1.26	48
Ireland	1.24	1.25	1.25	49
Finland	1.03	1.18	1.23	57
Austria	1.03	1.07	1.19	49
Italy	1.03	1.13	1.16	46
Sweden	1.05	1.05	1.12	–
United States	1.12	1.12	1.12	36
Norway	0.92	0.92	0.92	53
Mean	1.27	1.32	1.43	57

Resources to education

The share of GDP is by itself a fairly crude measure of a country's commitment to education. That figure should also be related to need, in particular the number of students. This number is affected by both the number of children in the relevant age cohorts and their school retention rates. Tables 7.9 and 7.10 therefore approach the issue of education spending by looking not just at total expenditure but also at the amount spent per student. Table 7.9 does this by looking at thousands of US$ adjusted for different purchasing power in different countries and Table 7.10 by looking at the amount spent per student relative to GDP per person.

In terms of dollars spent, the richest countries, and in particular the United States, rank at the top of Table 7.9. Eight of the nine countries in the top half of Table 3.2 (income per capita) are also in the top half of Table 7.9 on annual tertiary spending per student, for example. There is more variation in spending per primary student, with six out of nine as top relative spenders on primary students. Table 7.10 refines the measure by relating the amount spent per student to a country's ability to pay. The rankings change somewhat, but most countries are in the same general area of both tables. Both tables show a large range between top and bottom, but also a large group clustering around the average. Australia is generally towards the top of this large middle cluster. (At tertiary level, countries differ in how their research activities are funded, and in some of the countries with more spent per tertiary student, tertiary educational institutions account for a greater proportion of research spending.)

As would be expected, Tables 7.9 and 7.10 show that spending per student tends to rise with the level of education, with more than double being spent annually at tertiary than at primary level. Some countries differ in their relative priority to different education levels.

In Table 7.9, Denmark tops spending per student at primary level but drops to ninth at tertiary. Italy ranks eighth at primary level and last at tertiary. Canada leaps up from below the mean at school level to third at tertiary level. Germany also ranks much lower on school spending per student than on tertiary.

The most crucial resource in education, and the area where the great bulk of spending is directed, is the teaching staff. There is less variation between different levels of education in staff ratios than there is in spending levels. The range of student–staff ratios for primary schools is quite large, with four countries having a ratio less than 12 and four others a ratio greater than 20. On average, university staff–student ratios are slightly higher than secondary school ones, but this masks considerable individual variation, especially at tertiary level. To take the two extremes, note the contrasting ratios of Canada and Italy. In terms of smaller classes, it would be better to be a secondary student in Italy and a tertiary student in Canada.

Teachers' salaries are the main component of spending at school level, and increasing their salaries or increasing staff–student ratios has major budgetary implications. On the other hand, intuitively at least, one would expect teachers' salary levels to affect the quality of people entering the profession, and also that reducing student–staff ratios would have educational benefits. The first three columns of Table 7.12 provide one measure of how relatively well rewarded teachers are in the different countries. The nature of the measure may account for the anomalously poor rewards given to teachers in Norway, whose GDP is boosted by its income from oil but which is investing a considerable sum in long-term savings for future generations. Australia is one of the few countries not to differentiate salary more according to the level of teaching.

Table 7.13: Entry rate to universities

Number entering university as % of age cohort, 2000

	2000
Finland	71
New Zealand	70
Sweden	67
Australia	**59**
Norway	59
Netherlands	51
United Kingdom	46
Italy	43
United States	43
Japan	39
France	37
Belgium	36
Austria	33
Ireland	31
Germany	30
Denmark	29
Switzerland	29
Mean	45

No data on Canada.

Table 7.14: Expenditure on tertiary education

Expenditure on tertiary education institutions as % of GDP, 1999

	Public	Private	Total
Finland	1.7	0.0	1.7
Canada	1.6	1.0	2.6
Denmark	1.5	0.0	1.6
Sweden	1.5	0.2	1.7
Austria	1.2	0.0	1.2
Belgium	1.2	0.1	1.3
Ireland	1.2	0.3	1.5
Norway	1.2	0.1	1.3
Switzerland	1.2	0.0	1.2
France	1.0	0.1	1.1
Germany	1.0	0.1	1.0
Netherlands	1.0	0.2	1.2
New Zealand	0.9	–	0.9
United States	0.9	1.8	2.7
Australia	**0.8**	**0.7**	**1.6**
Italy	0.7	0.1	0.9
United Kingdom	0.7	0.3	1.0
Japan	0.5	0.6	1.1
Mean	1.1	0.4	1.4

Numbers do not sum exactly due to rounding.

Table 7.15: Changes in tertiary funding, 1995–2000

Change in tertiary education funding, 1995–2000 (1995 level = 100)

	Public	Private	Total
Ireland	206	125	180
Canada	126	114	121
Japan	126	112	118
Switzerland	124	–	–
Italy	118	165	126
Sweden	114	225	123
France	112	101	111
Finland	110	–	113
United Kingdom	107	90	101
Denmark	106	432	108
Netherlands	104	120	107
Austria	103	96	103
Germany	102	119	104
New Zealand	98	–	–
Norway	91	53	89
Australia	**89**	**155**	**112**
Total	115	147	115

No data on Belgium or United States.
Ranked according to change in public funding.

Table 7.16: Survival rates of tertiary students

Average number of entering students who graduate, 2000, %

Japan	94
Ireland	85
United Kingdom	83
Finland	75
Germany	70
Australia	**69**
Denmark	69
Netherlands	69
United States	66
Belgium	60
Austria	59
France	59
Sweden	48
Italy	42
Mean	68

No data on Canada, New Zealand, Norway or Switzerland.

Tertiary education

With the demands of an increasingly complex economy and rising personal aspirations, tertiary education grew enormously in all the selected countries in the second half of the twentieth century. Table 7.13 reports the net entry rate to universities (i.e. tertiary type A institutions). This is the number (of any age) entering university as a proportion of the age cohort of normal university entry age. For six of the selected countries, including Australia, the net entry rate is greater than 50%, while for Germany, Denmark and Switzerland, which tend to have longer degree programs, it is only around 30%.

Table 7.14 shows the percentage of GDP devoted to tertiary education institutions in 1999. Australia is right on the mean (1.5%) in total spending, with the United States and Canada leading by a substantial margin and Italy and New Zealand trailing. But Australia is below the mean in public spending on tertiary education, lying fourth last among the selected countries.

Table 7.15 presents the growth in spending on tertiary education funding between 1995 and 1999. The apparently large growth in private spending in some countries is largely explained by the very low base from which they began. Most countries, including Australia, showed a modest rise in total spending. But Australia, Norway and New Zealand were unique in recording a decline in public spending, and Australia's public commitment declined the most. (Norway's reported total spending on education showed a marked decline between 1999 and 2000, and one suspects that a change in measuring procedures is at least partly responsible.)

Systematic, harmonised long-term comparative data on tertiary education spending is not available. However, Considine and colleagues have charted the trends within Australia. From the early 1970s until the late 1980s, Australian universities were almost 90% funded by government. Government outlays as a percentage of GDP devoted to tertiary education peaked in 1975 at 1.5%. In constant prices, government final consumption expenditure (this does not include capital outlays and personal benefits for students) peaked in 1977, when the student load was less than half its current level. The decline in spending per student in Australia has therefore been dramatic: by 1998 total government spending per student had fallen to 55% of its 1975 levels, and in final consumption expenditure to 47%. In other words, in real terms the government is now spending about half per university student of what it spent in 1975.

One rough measure of the efficiency of tertiary education systems is their drop-out rate, or its converse, in official statistics rather melodramatically labelled the survival rate. The reasons for a student leaving a degree program are varied: failure, a decision to change fields, or financial pressures. By this measure, Japan has the most efficient tertiary education system, with Ireland and the United Kingdom also recording high graduation rates (Table 7.16). In contrast, in Sweden and Italy fewer than half the entering students graduate. Again the duration of degree programs is one explanatory factor for different rates, and in Italy's case probably their large student-staff ratios (Table 7.11).

The situation in Australian universities has also changed in ways not captured in these tables. Other data shows that Australia had the second highest proportion of international students, ranking only behind Switzerland. The increase partly explains the increasing percentage of private funding. In nine of the selected countries more than 90% of university students are full-time. Australia had the second lowest proportion (after Sweden) of university students studying full-time: 62% compared with an 18-country mean of 84%. The Australian figure probably partly reflects one of the strengths of Australian higher education: the number of mature-age students. It probably also reflects increasing feelings of financial pressure in Australian families. Considine and colleagues found that the proportion of 18-year-olds who were both full-time students and working full-time or part-time rose from 35% in 1987 to 55% in 1999.

Table 7.17: Pre-school enrolments of 3-year-olds

Percentage of 3-year-olds enrolled in pre-school, 1999

Belgium	98
Italy	95
Norway	70
Denmark	67
Sweden	64
United Kingdom	52
United States	35
Finland	32
Australia	**26**
Netherlands	0
Mean	54

No data for other countries; Belgian figure is for Flanders only.

Table 7.18: Pre-school and primary enrolments of 4-year-olds

Percentage of 4-year-olds enrolled in pre-schools and primary schools, 2000

	4-year-olds at pre-school	4-year-olds at primary school
France	100	0
Netherlands	98	0
Italy	96	0
New Zealand	95	0
United Kingdom	95	0
Japan	92	0
Denmark	89	0
Germany	84	0
Norway	74	0
Austria	73	0
Sweden	67	0
United States	59	0
Canada	43	0
Australia	**40**	**2**
Finland	38	0
Switzerland	29	0
Ireland	2	51
Mean	69	3

No data given for Belgium.

Table 7.19: Pre-school and primary enrolments of 5-year-olds

Percentage of 5-year-olds attending pre-school and primary school, 2000

	5-year-olds at pre-school	5-year-olds at primary school
France	99	1
Netherlands	98	1
Japan	96	0
Denmark	94	0
Italy	94	0
Austria	91	0
Canada	86	1
Germany	86	0
Switzerland	80	1
Norway	78	0
United States	74	7
Sweden	71	0
Finland	42	0
Australia	**13**	**70**
Ireland	1	99
New Zealand	0	100
United Kingdom	0	99
Mean	65	22

No data on Belgium.

Table 7.20: Expenditure on pre-primary education

Expenditure on pre-primary institutions as % of GDP, 2000

Denmark	0.8
Norway	0.8
France	0.7
Germany	0.6
Sweden	0.6
Austria	0.5
Belgium	0.5
Finland	0.4
Italy	0.4
Netherlands	0.4
United Kingdom	0.4
United States	0.4
Canada	0.2
Japan	0.2
New Zealand	0.2
Switzerland	0.2
Australia	**0.1**
Mean	0.4

No data on Ireland.

Early childhood education and care

While the number of years of formal schooling has been increasing over the years, there has also been increasing attention to pre-school care and education. Several factors have fanned this growth: the recognition of the importance of early childhood in children's intellectual and social development; the increasing number of women in the labour force, which produces the need for institutional arrangements to better balance the demands of work and family; and the recognition that access to pre-school is an important aspect of equal educational opportunity.

Australia is out of step with the bulk of the other selected countries in early childhood education and care. As Table 7.20 shows, Australia devotes the least resources to this area. In Tables 7.17 and 7.18, Australia is in the bottom quarter of countries in the proportion of young children attending pre-school. While 12 out of 18 countries have more than two-thirds of 4-year-olds attending pre-school, only just over a third of Australian 4-year-olds do.

These bald figures understate the contrast in approach. An OECD study of early childhood education and care (ECEC – the term used to signal that care and education are inseparable and necessary parts of quality provision) found that in several countries access to ECEC is a statutory right from age 3 (occasionally even younger). The trend is toward full coverage of the 3 to 6-year-old age group, aiming to give all children at least two years of free publicly funded provision before beginning compulsory schooling. In almost all countries in the review, governments pay the largest share of costs, with parents covering about 25–30%. The two or three years of ECEC before compulsory schooling are often free.

Although categories may not be fully consistent, that OECD study also found that while pre-primary education for many countries was mainly publicly financed, in Australia it was not. The public ECEC figure for Australia dropped from the already low 0.1% in Table 7.20 to 0.03%.

There is a surprising degree of variation in the ages at which children begin primary school, ranging between 4 and 7. While more than half the 4-year-olds in Ireland and a small proportion in Australia attend primary school, in many European countries no children begin school before 6, and many not until they are 7.

As might be expected, there is more emphasis on pre-school in those countries in which formal schooling tends to begin later, but there was no wish to assimilate pre-school to a school-like model. The emphasis was not on narrow literacy and numeracy objectives, but rather on children's holistic development and well-being.

Beyond pre-school, the OECD study found that demand was high for out-of-school provision of child care, but that this had not been a high policy priority in most countries, and the norm was still for parents to pay some of the costs. It also found that when affordable child care was available there was less reliance on informal care.

Interpreted narrowly, the public provision and funding of pre-school for all children whose parents want it is an extra burden on the taxpayer. From other perspectives, however, it could also have economic benefits. On a macro-level, with the ageing society and the decline in birth rates, measures which increase the labour force participation of working-age people and which make it more affordable for people to have children may become policy objectives. The OECD found that countries with the highest female labour participation rates also had the highest fertility rates, suggesting that 'child rearing and paid work are complementary rather than alternative activities'. Similarly, a UNICEF study on educational inequality concluded: 'Educational disadvantage is born not at school but in the home. And government efforts to contain that disadvantage – in order to foster social cohesion and maximise investments in education – must also take into account what is now known about early childhood development.'

Table 7.21: Adult prose literacy

Mean of population aged 16–65 on 500-point scale, and % levels 3–5

	Mean	% Level 3+
Sweden	301	72
Finland	289	63
Norway	289	67
Netherlands	283	59
Canada	279	58
Germany	276	51
Denmark	275	54
New Zealand	275	54
Australia	**274**	**56**
United States	274	54
Belgium	272	53
United Kingdom	267	48
Ireland	266	48
Switzerland	263	45
Mean	277	56

No data on Austria, France, Italy or Japan.

Table 7.22: Adult document literacy

Mean of population aged 16–65 on 500-point scale, and % levels 3–5

	Mean	% levels 3+
Sweden	306	75
Norway	297	70
Denmark	294	68
Finland	289	63
Netherlands	286	64
Germany	285	58
Canada	279	57
Belgium	278	60
Australia	**273**	**55**
Switzerland	270	53
New Zealand	269	50
United Kingdom	268	50
United States	268	50
Ireland	259	43
Mean	280	58

No data on Austria, France, Italy or Japan.

Table 7.23: Adult quantitative literacy

Mean of population aged 16–65 on 500-point scale, and % levels 3–5

	Mean	% levels 3+
Sweden	306	75
Denmark	298	68
Norway	297	70
Germany	293	67
Netherlands	288	64
Finland	286	63
Belgium	282	60
Canada	281	57
Switzerland	279	53
Australia	**276**	**55**
United States	275	50
New Zealand	271	49
United Kingdom	267	50
Ireland	265	47
Mean	283	59

No data on Austria, France, Italy or Japan.

Table 7.24: Generational difference in prose literacy

Means of age groups on 500-point prose literacy scale

Country	Mean 26–35 years	Mean 56–65 years	Difference
Sweden	314	276	38
Finland	307	249	58
Norway	297	258	39
Netherlands	295	256	39
Canada	287	234	53
Belgium	285	234	51
Australia	**284**	**241**	**43**
Denmark	284	253	31
Germany	284	257	27
New Zealand	277	261	16
United Kingdom	275	236	39
United States	275	266	9
Switzerland	273	244	29
Ireland	272	237	35
Mean	286	250	36

No data on Austria, France, Italy or Japan.

Adult literacy levels

Comparative studies in education for a long time had a vacuum at their heart. Over the years, scholars had carefully built up data on comparative educational expenditures, and levels of attainment and participation in educational institutions. But there was nothing directly on the end product of the educational process: the skills that students took into their adult working and social life. In recent years some major projects have addressed this gap.

The first was the International Adult Literacy Survey, a large-scale cooperative endeavour designed to measure adult literacy. Sophisticated, standardised surveys were carried out in a range of countries from 1994 onwards. Many past measures assumed that everybody was either fully literate or fully illiterate. The IALS did not set a single literacy threshold but studied the skills needed to function adequately in the modern world. It examined proficiency in three literacy domains:

• Prose literacy: the knowledge and skills that are required to understand and use information from newspapers, fiction and expository text.
• Document literacy: the knowledge and skills that are required to locate and use the information contained in official forms, timetables, maps and charts.
• Quantitative literacy: the knowledge and skills required to apply arithmetic operations to numbers embedded in printed materials.

For each domain there were around 34 tasks rated at varying degrees of difficulty. The responses were used to construct a score between 0 and 500, and as well individuals were ranked into five broad levels of performance. Level 1 indicates persons with very poor skills, where the individual is able only to locate a single straightforward piece of information in simple written materials. At the other extreme, persons at level 5 are able to perform complex tasks combining several pieces of information that must be searched for in the written material. Level 3 is considered a suitable minimum for coping with the demands of everyday life and work in a complex, advanced society. It equates roughly to the skill level required for successful secondary school completion.

Tables 7.21 to 7.23 give the population mean for the three literacy domains and the proportion which performed at Levels 3, 4 and 5. It shows that Sweden topped all three tables, usually with other Scandinavian countries coming next. In all three tables, Australia is in the bottom half of the 14 selected countries that participated in the project.

Across the selected countries in each of the domains, on average more than 40% performed only at Levels 1 or 2, considered inadequate to satisfactorily meet the range of literacy demands they are likely to encounter. In addition even Sweden, the top-performing country, had around 8% of people in the lowest band, while Australia, Belgium, Canada, Ireland, New Zealand, Switzerland, the United Kingdom and the United States all had more than 15% in this band.

As one would expect, literacy levels within each country correlated broadly with levels of schooling. They also showed a strong correlation with age (as, of course, does level of schooling.) Table 7.24 shows how younger adults very substantially outperform older adults in prose literacy; very similar age differences also apply to document and quantitative literacy. The difference is essentially a generational rather than an ageing effect. In other words, it reflects the greater educational opportunities experienced by the younger generation rather than the decaying mental abilities of their elders.

Sweden, Finland and Norway still rank at the top among young adults, and Switzerland and Ireland are near the bottom. The difference between the two age groups can be taken as a very rough measure of improving educational standards. The table shows that Finland has improved most, and New Zealand and the United States the least, with Australia's improvement better than the mean. The United States ranked second among older adults, but dropped back to equal 11th (or equal third last) among younger ones.

Table 7.25: Students' reading literacy

Means of national samples of 15-year-old students on reading literacy scale

	Mean score
Finland	546
Canada	534
New Zealand	529
Australia	**528**
Ireland	527
United Kingdom	523
Japan	522
Sweden	516
Austria	507
Belgium	507
France	505
Norway	505
United States	504
Denmark	497
Switzerland	494
Italy	487
Germany	484
Mean	513

No data on the Netherlands.

Table 7.26: Students' mathematical literacy

Means of national samples of 15-year-old students on maths literacy scale

	Score
Japan	557
New Zealand	537
Finland	536
Australia	**533**
Canada	533
Switzerland	529
United Kingdom	529
Belgium	520
France	517
Austria	515
Denmark	514
Sweden	510
Ireland	503
Norway	499
United States	493
Germany	490
Italy	457
Mean	516

No data on the Netherlands.

Table 7.27: Students' scientific literacy

Means of national samples of 15-year-old students on scientific literacy scale

	Mean score
Japan	550
Finland	538
United Kingdom	532
Canada	529
Australia	**528**
New Zealand	528
Austria	519
Ireland	513
Sweden	512
France	500
Norway	500
United States	499
Belgium	496
Switzerland	496
Germany	487
Denmark	481
Italy	478
Mean	511

No data on the Netherlands.

Student literacy

The Programme for International Student Assessment is by far the most important and ambitious attempt so far to comparatively chart students' literacy skills. This collaborative effort surveyed 15-year-old students, beginning in 2000. At age 15, students are approaching the end of compulsory schooling but have not yet specialised too much in particular disciplines.

The PISA survey has so far been implemented in 43 countries and covered the domains of reading, mathematical and scientific literacy. Pencil and paper tests, with assessments lasting a total of two hours, are administered to large representative samples, normally between 4500 and 10 000 students in each country. The tests were constructed by educational researchers from several countries, including the Australian Council for Educational Research, and were designed to produce an overall mean of 500 across the OECD countries. (For our 18 selected countries, the overall means were somewhat higher than 500.)

Finland topped the reading literacy scale (Table 7.25), with a fair gap back to second-placed Canada, and then New Zealand and Australia just behind in third and fourth places. On mathematical literacy (Table 7.26) Japan's mean score was the highest, 20 points ahead of anyone else. New Zealand then led the same group of four countries which had also topped reading literacy. The four, including Australia, were tightly grouped between 533 and 537. Japan also was the highest-rating country on students' scientific literacy (Table 7.27). Finland came second, with the United Kingdom, Canada, Australia and New Zealand closely grouped behind.

Australia's solid performance belies some of the alarmist claims about its educational standards, and it is clearly the fourth best performing of the selected countries. Italy and Germany were in the bottom three places on all three scales. Italy scored much worse than any other country on mathematical literacy. Denmark also scored in the bottom third on all three scales. Norway and the United States were consistently in the lower half. Switzerland was in the top third on mathematical literacy but in the bottom third on the other two.

These scores show only a modest relationship to the amount of spending on education. Finland, Japan, New Zealand and the United Kingdom all tend to be in the bottom half on educational investment measures but consistently in the top half of student literacy measures. Finland's performance on student literacy generally confirms its high standing on adult literacy measures, while New Zealand, Australia and Britain generally show an upward trend when compared with the adult measures in Tables 7.21 to 7.23.

So PISA, the most rigorous and sophisticated attempt so far to measure students' literacy levels across countries, has dispelled various myths and confirmed some expectations about national performance. It confirmed the strong educational standards in Japan, while several European countries performed lower than might have been expected. Perhaps surprisingly, it threw up two countries, Finland and New Zealand, which few would have predicted to be consistently near the top. New Zealand's performance on various measures in this chapter suggests a declining and then improving relative performance in education. It is rare for outcomes to match policy moves very directly, and no doubt other factors are involved, but as New Zealand's commitment of resources to education has belatedly improved so has the performance of its students.

Table 7.28: Gender differences in literacy

Difference of female mean from male mean in each literacy domain

	Reading	Maths	Science
New Zealand	46	3	12
Italy	38	–8	9
Japan	30	–8	7
Finland	51	–1	6
Ireland	29	–13	6
Norway	43	–11	6
United States	28	–7	5
Australia	**33**	**–12**	**3**
Canada	32	–10	2
Belgium	33	–6	2
Sweden	37	–7	1
Germany	34	–15	–2
United Kingdom	25	–8	–4
France	29	–14	–6
Switzerland	30	–14	–7
Austria	25	–27	–12
Denmark	25	–15	–12
Mean	33	–10	1

No data on the Netherlands.

Table 7.29: Social class and reading literacy

Means for first and fourth socio-economic quartile on reading literacy scale

	Bottom quartile	Top quartile	Difference
Finland	524	576	52
Canada	503	570	67
Ireland	491	570	79
Australia	**490**	**576**	**86**
New Zealand	489	574	85
Sweden	485	558	73
United Kingdom	481	579	98
Norway	477	547	70
France	469	552	83
Austria	467	547	80
United States	466	556	90
Denmark	465	543	78
Belgium	457	560	103
Italy	457	525	68
Switzerland	434	549	115
Germany	427	541	114
Mean	474	558	84

Table 7.30: Social class and mathematical literacy

Means for first and fourth socio-economic quartile on maths literacy scale

	Bottom quartile	Top quartile	Difference
Finland	513	565	52
Canada	509	563	54
New Zealand	500	584	84
Australia	**495**	**578**	**83**
Denmark	489	553	64
United Kingdom	488	578	90
France	486	560	74
Austria	479	549	70
Switzerland	478	578	100
Norway	476	537	61
Sweden	474	555	81
Belgium	473	574	101
Ireland	472	536	64
United States	452	551	99
Germany	438	541	103
Italy	433	486	53
Mean	478	556	77

No data for the Netherlands or Japan.

Table 7.31: Social class and scientific literacy

Means for first and fourth socio-economic quartile on scientific literacy scale

	Bottom quartile	Top quartile	Difference
Finland	517	565	48
Canada	501	563	62
Australia	**498**	**571**	**73**
United Kingdom	492	588	96
New Zealand	490	575	85
Sweden	485	552	67
Ireland	482	553	71
Austria	479	556	77
Norway	473	536	63
United States	464	555	91
France	460	556	96
Italy	451	514	63
Denmark	445	532	87
Belgium	444	552	108
Switzerland	442	554	112
Germany	437	539	102
Mean	473	554	81

No data on the Netherlands or Japan.

Differences in literacy

While the differences in the mean literacy scores between the selected countries (Tables 7.25 to 7.27) are substantial and interesting, it should also be remembered that the variations within each country are far greater than the differences between them. In an information age, literacy skills are crucial to many social opportunities both in work and leisure, and in an increasingly technological world all adults need to be mathematically and scientifically literate. The results of the literacy surveys among both adults and 15-year-old students in the Programme for International Student Assessment show how far away such a goal is.

Concern about gender equality has traditionally centred on the under-achievement of females. While their lower educational attainment in the past probably always owed more to different attitudes about their right to advanced education than to any difference in ability, Table 7.28 shows that contemporary sex differences in literacy are not clear cut.

In all but one country (New Zealand), girls on average perform at a lower level than boys in mathematical literacy, confirming the traditional stereotype. But the margins on mathematical literacy are generally much less than the margins in the reverse direction in reading literacy. Across the selected countries, the margin in favour of girls on reading literacy is three times as great as the margin in favour of boys on mathematical literacy. On the third scale, scientific literacy, there is almost no difference between the sexes, with the girls' mean just one point higher across the selected countries. The average scores are fairly close in nearly all countries, ranging from a margin of 12 in favour of girls in New Zealand to 12 in favour of boys in Austria and Denmark.

Now that females' participation in higher education has in many countries equalled and surpassed that of males, the issues of gender equity in education have become less intense. While there is still some work to be done to raise girls' maths performance, the greatest contemporary gender equity issue is to increase boys' reading literacy, especially because the difference often reflects a rump of under-performing boys, whose other opportunities will be adversely affected by this deficiency.

In all countries there is a very strong correlation between the socio-economic situation of students' families (based on the international socio-economic index of occupational status) and their literacy skills. In each country on each scale, the means for each socio-economic quartile progress in linear fashion, with each higher quartile recording a higher mean literacy score. As Tables 7.29 to 7.31 show, the scope of the differences is roughly the same in all three domains. The differences between the means in first and fourth quartiles across the countries are 84, 77 and 81 points respectively.

Although the pattern of substantial difference is universal, countries vary considerably in the range between more and less affluent. But there seems to be no clear relationship between the degree of inequality and the overall standard of literacy. Finland and Canada consistently have high standards and only a small gap. Italy similarly has one of the lowest ranges but is found at the bottom of the league tables on literacy standards.

At the other extreme, three countries – Switzerland, Germany and Belgium – have a range of more than 100 on all three scales. All tended to perform in the bottom half of literacy standards. The next largest inequalities were found in the United Kingdom and United States, which had contrasting literacy standards. Australia tended to have a slightly greater range than the mean range. These largely inconclusive results at least suggest that greater equality is not the enemy of excellence.

Table 7.32: Availability of computers and Internet

Number of 15-year-old students per computer in their schools and % of computers linked to the Internet, 2000

	Ratio students per computer	% linked to Internet
Australia	5	80
United States	5	39
Canada	6	80
New Zealand	6	62
Norway	6	50
Austria	7	69
Denmark	8	65
Finland	8	84
Sweden	8	74
United Kingdom	8	51
Switzerland	9	47
Netherlands	10	45
Belgium	11	45
France	11	26
Italy	12	24
Japan	12	35
Ireland	14	47
Germany	22	37
Mean	9	53

Table 7.34: Students' perceptions of teachers

Percentage of 15-year-old students who say their teachers:

	Help them with their work	Check their home work	Give students opportunity to express opinions	Continue teaching until students understand
Australia	80	49	77	72
United Kingdom	80	69	76	75
New Zealand	79	56	73	67
Canada	76	49	73	68
Denmark	74	49	76	67
Sweden	74	51	71	69
Finland	72	42	72	59
United States	70	65	66	63
Norway	69	41	62	59
Switzerland	66	56	68	66
Ireland	62	63	66	64
Japan	61	35	58	48
Austria	54	64	67	56
Germany	52	61	62	53
France	50	44	61	57
Italy	50	50	72	63
Belgium	44	60	56	58
Mean	66	53	68	63

No data on the Netherlands.

Table 7.33: Use of school resources

Percentage of 15-year-old students who say they use the following school resources at least several times a month

	Library	Computers	Laboratories
Denmark	43	79	77
Sweden	36	60	83
Australia	35	60	61
New Zealand	32	41	65
Norway	22	44	62
Canada	22	50	44
United States	20	44	34
France	20	22	33
United Kingdom	18	63	67
Japan	16	22	19
Switzerland	12	43	29
Germany	10	32	37
Ireland	7	42	59
Finland	6	64	9
Belgium	4	48	27
Austria	4	68	25
Italy	3	53	21
Mean	18	49	44

No data on the Netherlands.

Table 7.35: Students' attitudes to school

Percentage of 15-year-old students who in 2000:

	Don't want to go to school	Often feel bored at school	Report there is often noise and disorder in class
Denmark	19	41	33
Sweden	20	58	38
Norway	23	58	39
Germany	25	49	22
Japan	25	32	17
Finland	26	60	42
Switzerland	28	38	18
United Kingdom	28	54	27
Austria	29	49	19
Australia	34	60	32
Ireland	34	67	26
New Zealand	34	60	32
United States	35	61	28
Canada	37	58	33
France	37	32	42
Italy	38	54	46
Belgium	42	46	36
Mean	30	52	31

No data on the Netherlands.

Schools' learning environment

The school as a learning environment is characterised by many elements, some involving physical infrastructure and equipment; some involving teaching conditions and class sizes; some involving the relationship between teachers and students; some involving the attitudinal and behavioural traits that students bring to their learning. Some of these elements can be more easily measured than others.

The Programme for International Student Assessment gathered more systematic comparative data on schools as learning environments than had previously been available. Students doing the literacy tests also completed a half-hour background questionnaire, while school principals did likewise. Educational researchers will be able to examine the patterns of results to link learning outcomes to aspects of the educational environment. The results in Tables 7.32 to 7.35 suggest some strong differences between the selected countries.

The tables defy simple summary, but there is some tendency for English-speaking and Scandinavian countries to be more progressive in their teaching practices and the adoption of new technologies. For example, Table 7.32 shows that these countries have tended to put more computers into schools than most other European countries and Japan. Germany, despite its reputation for technological sophistication, lags considerably behind the other selected countries. Finland has the highest proportion of school computers linked to the Internet followed by Australia and Canada. France and Italy have the fewest.

With some exceptions, Table 7.33 shows a broadly similar pattern in students' reported use of school learning facilities. Whether because of lack of facilities or other factors, students in many countries seem largely unacquainted with their school libraries. They are more likely to use the school computers, while there are very big differences in use of school laboratories, ranging from Sweden's 83% to Finland's 9%. Apart from the Finns, the Scandinavian and English-speaking countries (including Australia) tend to have the highest use of school libraries and laboratories. The

Japanese and Germans are below the mean in all three categories.

In Table 7.34, students in English-speaking and Scandinavian countries are again the most likely to report that teachers help them with their work, with Australia and Britain topping the table. Students in Belgium, Italy, France and Germany rate their teachers least well on this dimension.

There is less variation between countries on students' feeling that teachers give them the opportunity to express opinions. Here Australia again tops the list. On the question about whether the teacher continues teaching until students understand, Britain tops the list, closely followed by Australia. So, perhaps unexpectedly, across these three dimensions Australian and British students rate their teachers more highly than do students in the other countries. The only area where Australian students rate their teachers below the mean is on checking homework. But before conclusions are leapt to about the impact of this on academic standards, it should be noted that by far the lowest-ranking country on homework is Japan.

Table 7.35 probes students' attitudes to school more generally, and here Australia is much more around the middle of the rankings. The Scandinavian students, as well as the Germans and Japanese, are the least likely to say they don't want to go to school, while Belgian and Italian students have the most negative attitudes to being there. Japanese and French students are the least likely to be bored at school, while Irish are the most bored. Australian, American, New Zealand and Finnish schools also draw high boredom ratings. Japanese, Swiss and Austrian students are the least likely to report noise and disorder in class, with Italian, French and Finnish students at the other extreme.

Some of the rankings on these aspects of the school environment are suggestive of countries' rankings on student literacy (Tables 7.25 to 7.27), though closer study would be needed before drawing firm conclusions. However, Australia's students generally rate their schools and teachers more favourably than do students in most of the other selected countries.

Table 8.1: Income inequality: Gini Coefficient

	Early to mid-1980s	Mid to late 1990s
Sweden	.197	.221
Norway	.223	.238
Finland	.209	.247
Belgium	.227	.250
Netherlands	.260	.253
Denmark	.254	.257
Germany	.244	.261
Japan	–	.265
Austria	.227	.277
France	.293	.288
Canada	.284	.305
Switzerland	.309	.307
Australia	**.281**	**.311**
Ireland	.328	–
Italy	.306	.342
United Kingdom	.270	.345
United States	.310	.368
Mean	.264	.286

Ranked from most to least equal, mid to late 1990s (assuming the Irish figure is the same as in the 1980s). No data on New Zealand.

Table 8.2: Inequality: ratio of rich and poor incomes

Ratio of incomes at 90th percentile to those at 10th percentile

	Early to mid-1980s	Mid to late 1990s
Sweden	2.71	2.61
Norway	2.92	2.83
Finland	2.59	2.90
Denmark	3.22	3.15
Netherlands	2.94	3.15
Germany	3.01	3.18
Belgium	2.73	3.19
France	3.92	3.54
Switzerland	3.39	3.62
Austria	2.89	3.73
Canada	4.05	4.13
Japan	–	4.17
Ireland	4.23	–
Australia	**3.97**	**4.33**
United Kingdom	3.79	4.58
Italy	4.05	4.77
United States	5.71	5.45
Mean	3.51	3.71

Ranked from most to least equal in the 1990s (assuming the Irish figure remained constant from the 1980s). No data on New Zealand.

Table 8.3: Income differences

Relative incomes of 10th percentile and 90th percentiles with median income scored as 100, mid-1990s.

	10th percentile income ratio	90th percentile income ratio	Purchasing power of 10th percentile income in each country relative to US median
Sweden	60	156	40
Finland	59	159	41
Germany	55	174	44
Netherlands	55	173	43
Norway	55	157	50
France	54	191	43
Belgium	53	173	47
Switzerland	52	188	55
Denmark	51	162	43
Ireland	49	209	–
Austria	48	179	–
Canada	46	188	41
Japan	46	192	–
United Kingdom	46	210	33
Australia	**45**	**195**	**34**
Italy	42	202	–
United States	38	214	38
Mean	50	184	43

Ranked according to relative income of those at 10th percentile. No data on New Zealand.

8   INEQUALITY AND SOCIAL WELFARE
Inequality of income

The tables on this page measure the inequality of income using different methods. Table 8.1 uses the most common measure, the Gini coefficient, which takes a value of 0 if every household has identical income and a value of 1 if one household has all the income. Thus an increase in the coefficient represents an increase in inequality. Sweden is the most equal country, followed by its Scandinavian neighbours and Belgium and the Netherlands. The United States and United Kingdom have the greatest inequality, followed by Italy. Despite its egalitarian self-image, Australia is very much towards the unequal end of the spectrum.

Table 8.2 measures income inequality over the same period but uses a different method. It compares the disposable income of those at the 90th percentile (i.e. 10% down from the top of the distribution of incomes) with the income of those at the 10th percentile (i.e. 10% up from the bottom). In this way it seeks a more representative measure of inequality, one that is unaffected by the minority of incomes that are either extremely high or extremely low.

The rankings in Tables 8.1 and 8.2 are highly correlated. The same seven countries (with some changes in order) are still the most equal, and the same five countries (again with some changes in order) the most unequal. Belgium and Japan come further down Table 8.2 than in 8.1, which suggests that although they have a relatively flat distribution through their middle incomes (captured by the Gini), the gap between their richest and poorest is still very substantial.

Table 8.3 delves deeper into the nature of income inequality. The first two data columns show how incomes at the 10th and 90th percentiles compare with the median (or dead-middle) income. So, for Sweden, people with incomes 10% up from the bottom of the distribution receive 60% as much as the middle

income, while people at the 90th percentile, at the richest 10%, had incomes 56% greater than the middle income. At the other end, America's figures showed a greater range, lower for the poor and higher for the rich. While for around two-thirds of countries people at the poorest decile received 45–55% as much as those at the median, there is a far greater range for the rich, with four countries where those at the 90th decile received twice as much (200+) as the median. In each of these the 10th percentile also received less than half (50−) what the median incomes did.

So far all the tables have compared incomes *within* the same country. The measures of national income in tables such as 3.2 take no account of the distribution of that income, while Tables 8.1 and 8.2 take no account of how rich each nation is but only of its pattern of distribution. This leads into one of the eternal arguments in social analysis: is it better to be poor in a country such as America, which is very rich but also relatively unequal? Or to be poor in a country like Sweden, which distributes its lesser riches more equally?

The last column in Table 8.3 is one very partial attempt to address this. It directly compares the living standards of people with incomes at the 10th percentile in most of the selected economies, by comparing their relative purchasing power in US$ to the US median figure. This shows that despite the difference in national income, those at the poorest 10% in Sweden are very marginally richer than the equivalent Americans. The purchasing power of incomes at the 10th percentile on those countries for which we have data turns out to be surprisingly similar. Poor people are materially best off in Switzerland and worst off in Australia and the United Kingdom, which combine being relatively unequal with being somewhat poorer than the United States.

Table 8.4: Distribution of market income

Market income shares of three broad income groups, mid-1990s

	Poorest 30%	Middle 40%	Richest 30%
Denmark	11.4	37.8	50.8
Norway	11.0	37.3	51.7
Germany	11.9	36.3	51.8
Netherlands	10.0	37.1	52.8
Sweden	9.3	36.9	53.9
Finland	10.2	35.6	54.2
Canada	9.6	35.5	54.9
France	10.9	33.5	55.6
Australia	**7.4**	**36.0**	**56.6**
United States	8.9	33.9	57.1
United Kingdom	7.8	34.9	57.4
Belgium	7.4	33.8	58.8
Italy	9.0	31.9	59.1
Ireland	5.7	33.2	61.1
Mean	9.3	35.3	55.4

No data on Austria, New Zealand, Switzerland, Japan.

Table 8.5: Redistribution by government: taxes

Proportion of taxes paid by three broad income groups, mid-1990s

	Poorest 30%	Middle 40%	Richest 30%
Denmark	14.1	37.2	48.7
Netherlands	11.7	36.1	52.2
Sweden	11.0	35.8	53.3
Germany	10.0	36.5	53.6
Norway	10.2	36.1	53.8
Finland	9.8	33.4	56.8
Canada	6.2	33.4	60.4
United Kingdom	6.0	32.0	62.0
Italy	6.7	31.0	62.3
Belgium	3.9	32.6	63.5
Australia	**3.7**	**31.1**	**65.1**
United States	6.3	28.4	65.3
Ireland	3.3	30.3	66.4
France	8.7	23.5	67.9
Mean	8.0	32.7	59.4

No data on New Zealand, Austria, Switzerland, Japan.

Table 8.6: Share of government transfers received by income groups

Proportion of general government transfers received by three broad income groups, mid-1990s

	Poorest 30%	Middle 40%	Richest 30%
Australia	**62.3**	**31.1**	**6.5**
United Kingdom	54.5	33.9	11.7
Ireland	47.1	38.1	14.8
Netherlands	45.8	36.1	18.1
Norway	45.1	36.6	18.3
Denmark	43.4	38.9	17.7
Finland	43.2	40.4	16.4
Canada	41.5	37.7	20.8
United States	41.4	35.5	23.0
Belgium	36.0	41.6	22.5
France	35.6	39.3	25.1
Sweden	33.7	40.5	25.8
Germany	31.7	37.6	30.7
Austria	26.8	40.9	32.3
Italy	20.5	45.0	34.5
Mean	40.6	38.2	21.2

No data on New Zealand, Switzerland, Japan.

Table 8.7: Market and disposable income

Gini Coefficient for market income and final disposable income, mid-1990s

	Market income	Disposable income	Difference
Sweden	.49	.23	.26
Belgium	.55	.30	.25
France	.49	.28	.21
Denmark	.42	.22	.20
Netherlands	.42	.25	.17
United Kingdom	.48	.31	.17
Italy	.51	.35	.16
Finland	.39	.23	.16
Germany	.44	.28	.16
Australia	**.46**	**.31**	**.15**
Norway	.40	.26	.14
Canada	.42	.29	.13
United States	.46	.34	.12
Japan	.34	.27	.07
Switzerland	.33	.27	.06
Mean	.44	.28	.16

Ranked according to degree of redistribution. Insufficient data for Austria, Ireland and New Zealand.

Redistribution of income

Most people earn most of their income from employment, while a minority earn from the businesses, rental properties and financial investments they own (and some people, such as the unemployed and the poor retired, earn no income). Income gained in all these ways is referred to as 'market income' and its distribution is highly unequal. Governments, however, use their budgets to redistribute income, thereby reducing the extent of inequality. Government taxes redistribute income from the rich to the poor when high-income earners lose a higher proportion of their incomes in tax than do low-income earners. Government outlays redistribute income from the rich to the poor when cash transfer payments (such as unemployment benefits and age pensions) go disproportionately to low-income earners. If you start with market income (Table 8.4), take away taxes paid (Table 8.5), then add government transfers received (Table 8.6), you end up with final disposable income. So the tables on this page examine the extent to which, and the means by which, these governments redistribute income and thereby reduce the inequality of income.

Table 8.4 shows just how unequally market income is distributed. It offers a third perspective on charting inequality, different again from Tables 8.1 and 8.2. Tables 8.4–8.6 compare the amount of income going to different income groups. Were income distributed perfectly equally, then the 'poorest' 30% of individuals would have 30% of total income and the 'richest' 30% would also have 30% of total income. Thus the extent to which each group is getting more or less than its equal share is easily determined. Overall, the poorest 30% earn only 9% of market income (partly because many of them are unemployed or retired), whereas the richest 30% account for 55% of the total. Only the middle 40% get something close to their equal share: 35%. As a generalisation, the distribution of market income is least unequal for the Scandinavian countries and most unequal for the English-speaking

countries. Australia's distribution, however, is close to the average.

Table 8.5 is based on income tax and employee social security contributions. These are 'progressive' in their redistribution of income with, overall, the richest 30% of families paying in excess of seven times more tax than the poorest 30%. Note that several of the countries with more equal market income, including the Scandinavian countries, do least to redistribute income in their tax systems. Australia has the fourth most redistributive income-taxing arrangements with France first.

Table 8.6 reveals that although the countries' cash transfer-payment systems also redistribute income from the rich to the poor, overall they do so to a significantly lesser extent than their tax systems do. This is primarily because so many countries have welfare systems involving universal payments (payments for which everyone is eligible) and even income-related unemployment and retirement benefits. In sharp contrast, Australia has by far the most redistributive transfer payments because its welfare system is so heavily means-tested. In Austria and Italy, the poorest 30% actually receive less than 30% of transfer payments, while in four other countries they receive only between 31% and 36%.

Table 8.7 compares each country's Gini coefficients for market income and final disposable income, thus giving a measure of the extent of its efforts to redistribute income in favour of the poor. Because of the different basis of measurement, it shows a rough rather than precise relationship with Tables 8.5 and 8.6. For the most part there is not a lot of correlation between redistributive effort and distributional outcome. Some countries do a lot of redistribution (e.g. difference column is above .20) and have relatively equal incomes (disposable income is less than .30). Australia's redistributive effort, as measured here, was average, but it began with above-average market inequality.

Table 8.8: Long-term trends in income distribution

	Early 1970s to early 1980s	During 1980s	Mid-1980s to late 1990s
Denmark	na	na	–
Australia	=	+	+
Belgium	=	+	+
Canada	–	=	+
Finland	–	=	+
France	–	=	+
Germany	–	+	+
Sweden	–	+	+
Switzerland	na	na	+
Austria	=	=	++
Ireland	–	=	++
Italy	—	–	++
Japan	=	+	++
Netherlands	=	+	++
Norway	=	=	++
United Kingdom	++	+++	++
United States	++	++	++
New Zealand	=	+	+++

+++ Significant rise in income inequality (>15%)
++   Rise in income inequality (7–15%)
+   Modest rise in income inequality (1–6%)
=   No change (–1 to +1% range)
–   Modest decrease in income inequality (1–6% decrease)
—   Decrease in income inequality (7–15%)

Long-term trends in income distribution

Tables 8.1 and 8.2 charted not only variations in income inequality between countries, but also changes over time. Table 8.1 found that over the 15 years or so up to the late 1990s, inequality increased in 12 of the 15 countries for which comparisons can be made. Furthermore, the gap between the least and most unequal countries widened. The increase in inequality was greatest in the United Kingdom, followed by the United States, Austria, Finland and Australia. Table 8.2 also found an increase in inequality in most of the countries. With this measure, inequality increased most in Austria, followed by the United Kingdom, Italy, Belgium and Australia.

Table 8.8, with its somewhat overlapping columns, offers a schematic view of changes in income inequality over a longer period. It can be seen from all the + signs in the table that increases in inequality were widespread, and that this was particularly the case as the 20th century approached its close. Of all 18 countries, only (the already relatively egalitarian) Denmark had a decrease in inequality. New Zealand, for which data was absent for several of our earlier tables, had the sharpest increase.

The 1980s appear to be a period of transition from an era of stable or declining inequality to a new era of rising inequality in most nations. Indeed, according to the originator of this table, Smeeding, scholars have identified a U-shaped change in the distributions of income in most countries, with inequality falling in the 1960s and early 1970s, but then rising from the late 1970s on. The turning points (the bottom of the U) and size of the U differ across countries. Many countries did not experience a rise in inequality until the 1990s. And in other countries – such as Germany, France and Canada – these increases have so far been very modest. While inequality rose rapidly in the United Kingdom and the United States during the 1980s and early 1990s, the rate of increase slowed markedly in the late 1990s.

It is important to remember that changes in inequality represent changes in the *shares* of total income enjoyed by people at the bottom, middle and top of the distribution of incomes. So a decline in any group's share doesn't necessarily imply that the people within that group now have less real income to live on than they did. With some notable exceptions (such as the United States), the general story is that people in all groups have at least maintained the real value of their incomes over the period, and more likely seen it increase.

Smeeding, who is director of the path-breaking Luxembourg Income Study, argues that the explanations for rising inequality in rich countries are many, and no single set is fully convincing. But there does not seem to be much evidence to support the common supposition that increased trade between countries has been a significant cause of greater inequality. There seems to be more support for the thesis that technological change has increased the demand for skilled labour relative to less skilled labour, accompanied by changing wage relativities.

The increase in the inequality of final disposable incomes seems to lie largely with an increase in the inequality of market incomes (incomes earned from labour, profit, interest or rent). An OECD study by Forster and Pearson suggests it is very much the ability of the top groups in many countries to further increase their share that has been the main reason for the trend to increasing inequality. That is, changes in government taxation and welfare policies do not seem to be a major cause of the increase. On the contrary, the disparate outcomes revealed by Table 8.8 suggest that to some degree at least, governments have it within their power to make tax and spending changes that moderate the effects of the widening inequality of market incomes.

Table 8.9: Relative poverty

Percentage of population with income below 50% of the country's median income

	Early to mid-1980s	Mid to late 1990s
Finland	5.4	5.4
Norway	7.2	6.4
Sweden	5.3	6.6
Germany	5.3	7.5
Belgium	4.5	8.0
France	7.3	8.0
Netherlands	3.9	8.1
Denmark	10.1	9.2
Switzerland	7.6	9.3
Austria	6.7	10.6
Ireland	11.1	–
United Kingdom	9.2	12.5
Canada	12.4	12.8
Italy	10.4	14.2
Australia	**11.3**	**14.3**
United States	15.8	17.0
Mean	8.3	10.0

Ranked according to proportion in poverty in the 1990s (assuming Irish figure remained constant). No data on Japan and New Zealand.

Table 8.10: Human Poverty Index

National scores on UN Human Poverty Index, late 1990s

	Human Poverty Index
Sweden	6.8
Norway	7.5
Netherlands	8.5
Finland	8.8
Denmark	9.1
Germany	10.5
France	11.1
Japan	11.2
Canada	12.1
Italy	12.3
Belgium	12.5
Australia	**12.9**
United Kingdom	15.1
Ireland	15.3
United States	15.8

No data for Austria, New Zealand or Switzerland.

Table 8.11: Material poverty rates

Percentage of population with income below $US11 PPP per day, 1995

Norway	4
Finland	5
Sweden	6
Netherlands	7
Germany	7
Canada	7
France	10
United States	14
United Kingdom	16
Australia	**18**

No data for other eight countries.

Poverty

Although everyone knows what poverty is, its measurement and conceptualisation are politically and intellectually contentious. In developing countries, to be poor is to have so little money as to be in danger of dying through malnutrition or exposure. This is sometimes called subsistence poverty – insufficient income to afford the most basic standards of food, clothing and shelter so that people's very survival is at stake.

Very few people in the developed countries face poverty this severe, and describing their poverty has led to two approaches. The first is an absolute material conception, using some notion of basic needs, and the second based on relative deprivation, where poverty is determined by reference to the general standard of living and social expectations. According to an originator of this approach, Peter Townsend, people are in relative poverty when their resources are so seriously below the average that they are excluded from commonly accepted living patterns and activities. The differences have political implications, with a purely absolutist approach tending to be associated with a minimalist definition and response to the problem, and a relativist approach associated with more activist and redistributive approaches.

To establish an absolute poverty line it would be necessary to determine the cost of the minimum basket of goods and services needed for survival, then raise the line over time according to the rising cost of the basket. While there is room for argument over the minimum contents of the basket, deciding where to draw the line will be less arbitrary than establishing a relative poverty line.

Table 8.9 applies the most common relative poverty line used in international comparisons: 50% of each country's median (or dead-middle) income. (Why 50% rather than 55 or 45%? It's completely arbitrary.) This means that, over time, a relative poverty line moves not according to the rise in the cost of living (inflation) but according to the rise in the standard of living (some measure of average income). This in turn means that a rise in the proportion of people falling below a relative poverty line does not necessarily mean the poor are having to get by on lower real incomes. It is more likely to mean that the incomes of the poor *have* been rising in real terms, but not as quickly as the incomes of all the other people in the community. In other words, there has been a shift in relativities. It follows that a fall in relative poverty is achieved only if the incomes of the poor grow faster than those of others, that is, there is a change in the *structure* of the distribution of income.

Table 8.10 reports the results from a broader index of poverty constructed by the UNDP, which combines the percentage of people living below a relative poverty line with several non-monetary measures of absolute deprivation: the probability of not surviving to age 60, the adult functional illiteracy rate, and the rate of long-term unemployment. Note that this data is in index points, not percentages of the population. The higher the score, the greater the problem.

Table 8.11 attempts to measure and compare absolute poverty in the selected countries. It shows the proportion in each country that cannot afford to buy each day the same basket of goods and services that in the United States would cost $US11. (In other words, it takes account of the US dollar's differing purchasing power in different countries.) It can be seen that absolute poverty is highest in the United States, the United Kingdom and Australia.

The tables for this page define poverty in terms of access to money. They thus fail to capture the qualitative experience of poverty, or how economic disadvantage compounds into other deprivation: lack of opportunity, security, status and access to health and social resources. Nor do they say anything about 'mobility' – the individual's chances of leaving (or entering) poverty over time.

Table 8.12: Social expenditure
Public social expenditure (excluding health) as % of GDP

	1980	1998
Sweden	20.5	24.4
Denmark	21.1	23.0
France	15.3	21.5
Finland	13.5	21.2
Austria	18.0	21.0
Switzerland	10.6	20.5
Norway	12.6	19.9
Italy	12.7	19.6
Netherlands	21.7	18.5
Belgium	18.8	18.4
Germany	14.3	18.2
United Kingdom	13.3	15.2
New Zealand	12.2	14.4
Australia	**6.9**	**11.8**
Canada	8.1	11.6
Ireland	10.1	11.1
Japan	5.6	9.0
United States	9.4	8.7
Mean	13.6	17.1

Table 8.14: Net social expenditure
Net social expenditure (including health) as % of GDP, 1997

	Total net	Comparison with gross public spending
Sweden	30.6	–
Germany	28.8	–
Belgium	28.5	–
Denmark	27.5	–
Finland	25.6	–
Italy	25.3	–
Norway	25.1	–
Austria	24.6	–
United Kingdom	24.6	+
Netherlands	24.0	–
United States	23.4	+
Australia	**21.9**	**+**
Canada	21.8	+
Ireland	18.4	–
New Zealand	17.5	–
Japan	15.7	+
Mean	24.0	

No data on France or Switzerland.

Table 8.13: Social security transfers
Social security transfers as % of GDP, 1970–99

	1970–73	1974–79	1980–89	1990–99
Sweden	12.0	15.9	18.3	20.9
Finland	7.5	10.4	13.1	20.3
Netherlands	18.3	23.7	26.7	20.0
Denmark	11.0	13.6	16.6	19.1
Austria	15.4	17.4	19.4	18.8
France	14.9	16.3	17.0	18.2
Italy	13.3	15.4	16.7	18.2
Germany	13.1	16.7	16.5	17.7
Belgium	12.2	15.9	18.0	16.5
Norway	13.2	12.9	12.7	15.9
United Kingdom	9.0	10.7	13.3	14.5
Canada	7.2	8.5	10.3	13.2
Japan	4.9	8.4	11.0	12.6
United States	8.3	10.2	11.0	12.6
Ireland	9.6	11.9	15.5	11.2
Switzerland	8.7	12.6	13.4	10.8
Australia	**4.2**	**6.6**	**7.1**	**8.3**
Mean	10.8	13.4	15.1	15.8

No data on New Zealand.

Social expenditure

Public social expenditure is spending by governments to provide support to individuals and households during circumstances that adversely affect their welfare. It covers cash transfer payments, but also the direct 'in-kind' provision of goods and services and tax breaks for social purposes. The label social expenditure can be used to cover different groupings of spending. The broadest is to include education, health and welfare spending. Sometimes just health and welfare are used, and sometimes, as here, only social welfare. Whereas social expenditure includes the provision of services as well as transfers (Table 8.12), a narrower and often used measure is social security transfers (Table 8.13), which covers only direct payments to recipients.

Table 8.12 shows that the growth of social expenditures in these countries significantly outpaced the general growth of economies during the last 20 years of the 20th century. The top of the table is taken by the Scandinavian and some other European countries, while the English-speaking countries and Japan are at the bottom. The data on social security transfers in Table 8.13 offers a longer historical period. It can be seen that spending grew throughout the last 30 years of the century, though by a lot more in the 1970s than in the 1980s, and by more in the 1980s than the 1990s. The rankings are broadly similar to Table 8.12, with English-speaking countries and Japan near the bottom. The slide down of Switzerland and Norway shows they invested more in providing services.

Increases in social welfare spending can result from any of three factors: an increase in the number of people who meet unchanged eligibility criteria, government decisions to widen eligibility criteria, and government decisions to increase the real value of benefits paid. All three factors would help to explain the strong growth in total spending over the period, though it is likely that the last two were more common earlier in the period and less common more recently. As the bills for earlier generosity have grown, taxpayers have become more resistant to higher taxation and governments have begun worrying about the budgetary implications of an ageing population.

Welfare spending is directed towards a number of problems, as will be examined in coming tables. In terms of funding, by far the biggest is aged pensions, which dwarfs all other categories. Coming a long way further back, but still accounting for large amounts of expenditure and involving substantial social problems, are benefits for the disabled and the unemployed, followed by pensions for 'survivors' (especially widows) and for the family (especially single mothers). Spending in some areas, such as unemployment, can vary with the business cycle, while in others – aged pensions – it is growing with a demographic inevitability.

It is notable that welfare spending is not determined by any simple notion of need. The measures of poverty in Tables 8.9–8.11 show if anything a negative correlation with levels of welfare spending. Australia's position at the bottom of Table 8.13 is explained not simply by stinginess but by its 'lean' system of flat-rate, tightly means-tested welfare benefits. Its growth over the period was also well below average.

Table 8.14 attempts to provide a more comprehensive picture than just concentrating on gross public expenditures. Net social expenditures differ from gross public social expenditures for two reasons. One is the provision of private social expenditure: highest in the United States at 30% of social expenditure, but also exceeding 10% in Australia, Canada, the Netherlands and the United Kingdom. The other is government's clawing back of cash transfers through direct taxation. This is higher in Scandinavia and the Netherlands than elsewhere. The first column shows the amounts spent (including health, where private expenditure is considerable), while the second column shows whether this is more or less than gross public social expenditure. The OECD comments that accounting for private social expenditures reduces differences in social spending but not in redistributional outcomes.

Table 8.15: Age pensions

Expenditure on age pensions as % of GDP

	1980	1998
Italy	7.4	12.8
Switzerland	5.6	11.2
France	7.6	10.6
Germany	8.7	10.5
Austria	8.5	9.9
Sweden	6.7	7.5
Belgium	6.1	7.4
Finland	4.7	7.0
Denmark	5.8	6.8
Netherlands	6.5	6.2
Norway	4.5	6.0
United Kingdom	5.1	5.9
Japan	2.9	5.7
New Zealand	7.0	5.5
United States	5.0	5.2
Canada	2.8	5.1
Australia	**3.2**	**4.3**
Ireland	4.0	2.5
Mean	5.7	7.2
% social expenditure	43.5	43.0

Table 8.16: Poverty among the elderly

Percentage of elderly people living in relative poverty

	Early to mid-1980s	Mid to late 1990s
Sweden	2.9	2.7
Netherlands	23.7	6.4
Denmark	31.5	6.6
Germany	14.4	7.0
Canada	22.0	7.8
Switzerland	19.3	8.4
Finland	11.9	8.5
France	10.3	9.8
Austria	18.5	10.3
Belgium	10.9	11.7
Italy	13.1	12.2
Norway	21.7	14.0
Ireland	14.4	–
United Kingdom	21.6	20.9
United States	27.3	24.7
Australia	**24.0**	**29.4**
Mean	18.0	12.0

Ranked in ascending order in 1990s assuming Irish rate remained constant.
No data for Japan or New Zealand.

Table 8.17: Relative income of the elderly

Income of those aged 65+ as % of those aged 18–64

	mid-1980s	mid-1990s
Canada	83	92
Switzerland	–	92
France	80	85
Sweden	76	85
United States	86	84
Austria	74	81
Germany	79	81
Netherlands	85	80
Italy	76	79
Finland	75	76
Belgium	–	75
United Kingdom	67	70
Norway	66	69
Denmark	64	67
Ireland	76	67
Australia	**65**	**60**
Mean	75	78

No data on Japan or New Zealand.

Table 8.18: Housing arrangements of the elderly

Percentage of those aged 65+ living in institutions and with their children, mid-1990s

	Living in institution	Living with children
Italy	4	39
Austria	5	25
Ireland	5	–
United Kingdom	5	16
Belgium	6	–
Finland	6	14
Japan	6	65
United States	6	15
Australia	**7**	**–**
Canada	7	–
Denmark	7	4
France	7	17
Germany	7	14
Norway	7	11
Netherlands	9	8
Sweden	9	5

No data on New Zealand or Switzerland.

Old age poverty and welfare

One of the first areas in the development of the welfare state was the desire to look after people too old to work. Growing old should not mean becoming poorer or, at least, not desperately poor. Table 8.15 shows the fairly strong growth in governments' spending on old-age pensions over the last 20 years of the 20th century, in most countries growing more rapidly than the economy as a whole. It shows only a slight tendency to be rising most rapidly in those societies with more rapidly ageing populations, such as Italy, Japan and Switzerland (Table 1.11).

It also shows the wide disparity in such spending, ranging from Italy on 12.8% of GDP to Ireland on 2.5%. Australia has the second lowest spending – and also a relatively small increase over the period – because of its 'lean' welfare system based on flat-rate, means-tested benefits. Various countries have age pension payments tied to previous income levels and many have universal eligibility for the pension for those aged 65 or more. Apart from spending a lot on age pensions, OECD data shows that Sweden, Denmark and Norway spend most on services for the old and disabled. These three countries spend roughly half the amount they do on pensions for such services, whereas the average over all the selected countries is only about one-seventh, one-fifth in Australia.

It is normal that people's incomes would go down after they retire from the paid labour force, and Table 8.17 reveals that the income of the over 65s across the selected countries is 78% of the working-age population's. In Canada and Switzerland the drop is almost imperceptible (92%), while in Ireland and especially Australia (60%), the two bottom-ranking countries in Table 8.15, the decline is more precipitous.

Table 8.16 reveals also that Australia has the highest proportion (29%) of elderly people living below the poverty line (defined simply as 50% of each country's median income for all people), again in the company of the United Kingdom and the United States. The range here is very considerable, with only 3% of elderly Swedes living in relative poverty.

The proportion of elderly people living below the poverty line fell significantly over a 15-year period in all of the selected economies bar two – one of which was Australia. This implies that the real incomes of the elderly grew faster than those of everyone else in these countries, a conclusion broadly confirmed by Table 8.17. In several countries (the Netherlands, Denmark and Canada) the reduction was quite radical. For most, the explanation for this relatively faster real growth is the maturation during the mid-1990s of the contributory public pension schemes installed in the postwar period. In Australia's case, although the age pension rose in real terms over the period, other people's incomes rose by a lot more.

Australia's position at the bottom of Tables 8.16 and 8.17 is largely explained by the frugality of its flat-rate age pension. It should be noted, however, that these figures are based entirely on income, and not related to expenses or living conditions. So in some senses this figuring might give an exaggerated impression of the privation in which Australian age pensioners actually live. For example, the rate of home ownership among Australian age pensioners is about 78%, considerably higher than in the seven other countries for which figures are available. Owning their own homes outright significantly reduces their day-to-day living expenses compared with those still paying rent to private landlords, as well as giving them a greater sense of security.

Housing is a key issue in the welfare of elderly people, and one crucial difference revealed by Table 8.18 is the different attitudes to family welfare. In Japan 65% of elderly people live with their children, ranging down to only 4% of elderly Danes.

Table 8.19: Unemployment benefits

Expenditure on unemployment benefits as % of GDP

	1980	1998
Denmark	4.9	3.4
Finland	0.7	2.6
Netherlands	1.7	2.6
Belgium	2.5	2.5
Sweden	0.4	1.9
France	–	1.8
Ireland	–	1.7
New Zealand	0.5	1.6
Germany	0.4	1.3
Australia	**0.7**	**1.1**
Canada	1.2	1.0
Switzerland	0.1	1.0
Austria	–	0.9
Italy	0.6	0.7
Japan	0.4	0.5
Norway	0.4	0.5
United Kingdom	1.1	0.3
United States	0.7	0.2
Mean	1.1	1.4
% social expenditure	7.7	8.2

Table 8.20: Level of unemployment benefits (1)

Unemployment benefits per registered unemployed person as % of GDP per capita, average 1980–99

Denmark	86.8
Netherlands	84.1
Austria	57.3
Ireland	55.1
Sweden	52.6
Germany	52.2
Belgium	52.0
Norway	43.2
New Zealand	42.7
Canada	35.6
Australia	**33.1**
Finland	33.1
France	31.6
United Kingdom	31.4
Japan	30.5
Italy	21.8
United States	16.6
Mean	44.7

No data on Switzerland.

Table 8.21: Level of unemployment benefits (2)

Net replacement rates for long-term unemployed Percentage of previous salary, average across four types of family situation, 1999

	Net replacement rate
Switzerland	83
Denmark	81
Sweden	79
Netherlands	76
Belgium	70
United Kingdom	69
Norway	69
Finland	69
Austria	66
New Zealand	66
Japan	63
Germany	63
Ireland	55
Canada	54
France	52
Australia	**49**
United States	32
Italy	13
Mean	62

Table 8.22: Active labour market programs

Active labour market program spending as % of GDP, 2000, and ratio to passive spending

	Active programs % GDP	Ratio active: passive spending
Netherlands	1.6	0.8
Denmark	1.6	0.5
France	1.3	0.8
Belgium	1.3	0.6
Germany	1.2	0.6
Sweden	1.1	0.9
Finland	1.0	0.5
Norway	0.8	1.8
Switzerland	0.7	0.7
New Zealand	0.6	0.4
Austria	0.5	0.5
Australia	**0.5**	**0.5**
Canada	0.4	0.6
United Kingdom	0.4	0.6
Japan	0.3	0.6
United States	0.2	0.5
Mean	0.8	0.7

No data on Ireland or Italy.

Unemployment benefits

Table 8.19 reveals that while spending on unemployment benefits generally accounts for a quite small proportion of GDP in the selected countries, it does range widely between Denmark's 3.4% and the United States' 0.2%. Yet again, the Scandinavian countries tend to be in the more generous half of the table and the English-speaking countries in the more frugal half. The modest growth in spending over the last 20 years of the 20th century (up from an 18-nation mean of 1.1% to 1.4%) is very roughly of the same magnitude as the increase in unemployment, which rose on average from 6.8% to 7.8% of the labour force (Table 4.12).

Table 8.19 reflects then both the number of unemployed people receiving benefits and the size of the benefits they receive. The increase over the period seems to owe more to increased numbers of beneficiaries than to more generous rates of benefit. Those countries which recorded substantial falls in spending proportions between 1980 and 1998 (Denmark, the United Kingdom and the United States) all had lower unemployment rates in the 1990s than in the 1980s.

However, the rankings in Table 8.19 show little relationship to the relative severity of the unemployment problem revealed in Table 4.12. The top three countries in the aggregate level of unemployment benefits lie in the middle of the table on unemployment rates. Sweden has the fifth lowest unemployment, but the fifth highest spending on benefits. The United States is in the middle on unemployment rates but bottom in the aggregate amount of benefits. Australia is around the middle of both tables.

Tables 8.20 and 8.21 are then more precise measures of the generosity of governments in their provision of unemployment benefits. Table 8.20 expresses expenditure on unemployment benefits as a proportion of each country's GDP per unemployed person, and finds a range from Denmark's 87% down to America's 17%.

We can speculate on the policy reasons behind these flows of resources. The countries at the top would tend to be those with unemployment insurance schemes paying income-related benefits. The United States is at the bottom because eligibility for benefits is withdrawn if people do not find work within a few months and because education-leavers who are not members of the insurance scheme are not entitled to receive a benefit. Australia is not at the bottom of the table because, even though its flat-rate, means-tested benefits are very low, eligibility continues for as long as people remain without work.

The net replacement rate (Table 8.21) compares the unemployment benefit and any family benefits currently being received with the person's previous wage, after taking account of income tax. In this case, the comparison is made for someone who has been unemployed long-term. It can be seen that the European welfare-state countries have very high replacement rates, whereas most of the English-speaking countries have much lower ones. Australia's and the United States' rates are particularly low for the reasons already discussed. Note that there are issues of equity (should different categories of unemployed receive differential benefits?) and incentive here as well as generosity. Generosity to the unemployed has to be balanced against the need to protect the interests of taxpayers by providing the jobless with sufficient monetary incentive to search hard for another job – perhaps one that pays a lot less than their previous job.

The payment of benefits to the unemployed can be thought of as a 'passive' response to the problem: it gives them money to live on without doing anything to help them find work. Table 8.22 shows countries' spending on active labour market programs, job-creation and training programs which seek to actively assist jobseekers. The countries paying least in unemployment benefits are also tending to pay least here, while the Dutch and the Danes are investing most heavily in them. Only Norway spends more on active programs than on passive payment of benefits.

Table 8.23: Child poverty

Percentage of children living in relative poverty, mid-1990s

Sweden	2.6
Norway	3.9
Finland	4.2
Denmark	5.1
Belgium	6.3
Netherlands	7.7
New Zealand	7.8
France	7.9
Switzerland	10.0
Germany	10.6
Japan	12.2
Australia	**12.6**
Ireland	13.8
Austria	15.0
Canada	15.7
United Kingdom	19.8
Italy	20.2
United States	22.4
Mean	11.0

Table 8.24: Single-mother households and poverty rates, mid-1990s

	% children in single-mother households living in poverty	% children in two-parent households living in poverty
Sweden	6.6	1.5
Finland	8.1	2.1
Belgium	10.1	7.2
Norway	13.5	2.0
Switzerland	16.0	9.3
France	25.3	6.1
Netherlands	26.4	6.6
Denmark	30.2	4.9
Italy	30.6	19.6
United Kingdom	34.0	10.0
Austria	44.0	11.4
Germany	46.2	6.1
Australia	**46.3**	**11.9**
United States	49.3	14.8
Canada	49.6	10.5
Mean		
Mid to late 1990s	29.1	8.3
Early to mid-1980s	24.2	6.0

No data on Ireland, Japan or New Zealand.

Table 8.25: Single parents working and relative poverty risk

Poverty risk > 1.0 means group has greater risk of poverty than the general population

	% single parents working, early 1990s	Poverty risk: non-working single parents	Poverty risk: working single parents
Sweden	87	3.4	0.5
Belgium	86	3.5	1.7
Finland	79	–	–
Denmark	74	9.0	2.6
United States	73	5.7	2.3
France	70	6.6	1.9
Austria	64	3.4	1.5
Canada	63	6.4	2.3
Norway	61	5.0	0.8
Italy	58	5.6	1.8
Germany	57	6.6	3.5
United Kingdom	47	5.9	2.1
Australia	**46**	**5.0**	**1.1**
Netherlands	34	5.9	2.4
Mean	64	5.5	1.9

No data on Ireland, Japan, New Zealand or Switzerland.

Child poverty

Poverty by its nature always involves deprivation and disadvantage, but among different groups each form of poverty carries its own peculiar sadness. Among the old, it seems particularly sad that after people have spent a lifetime working they cannot find material security. Among the unemployed, there are the problems of loss of respect and of self-esteem compounding their material disadvantage. Poverty among children is particularly sad if it is likely to lead to a lifetime of disadvantage. Through no fault of their own, they are growing up in a situation that could severely affect their life chances. Childhood poverty thus strikes a blow against equality of opportunity, and deprivation in childhood can adversely affect cognitive and social development.

Table 8.23 reveals that the proportions of children living in poverty (defined as those living in households with disposable income less than 50% of median income) range widely between the selected countries. They are marginally lower than the rates of poverty among the elderly (Table 8.16 – 12%:11%), but are still unacceptably high. The rankings are very broadly similar in the two tables, with the usual suspects largely in their usual places. Again the Scandinavian countries have the lowest rates of child poverty, followed by Belgium and the Netherlands, while the United States and some other English-language countries are in the bottom positions. Italy seems rather better at taking care of its elderly than its children, while Australia is the reverse, its poverty rate being 13% among children and 29% among the elderly.

The OECD argued that the most important factor affecting childhood poverty is the employment rate of parents. This becomes particularly acute when the parents are separated. Table 8.24 compares the proportions of children in single-mother and two-parent households who are living in poverty. In all countries child poverty is significantly higher in single-mother households, but the differences between countries are dramatic. While just over one in 20 children in single-mother households live in poverty in Sweden, in the United States and Canada the figure is one in two. Australia, Germany and Austria also have poverty rates among single-parent families above four in ten.

The second and third columns of Table 8.25 confirm that all children in single-parent households have a higher than usual risk of poverty (i.e. their ratios are greater than 1.0). But the risks are very different for working and non-working single parents. While being a working single parent almost doubles the risk (1.9) of being in poverty; being a non-working single parent increases it by a massive 5.5 times on average in the countries shown. In Australia for working single parents, the extra risk of poverty is all but removed (1.1). In Sweden and Norway, working single parents actually have a lower than average rate of living in poverty.

It follows from this that a policy priority in reducing child poverty should be to facilitate the employment of single parents. The first column of Table 8.25 reports the proportion of lone parents in employment drawn from Jonathan Bradshaw's research findings. Their employment rates vary from 87% to 34%. In several countries the employment rates are broadly similar or greater for single parents. But in some, including Australia to some extent and particularly the Netherlands, the employment rates for single parents are much lower. The figures in Table 8.25 are not directly comparable with Table 14.13 on mothers' employment, though overall around seven in eight lone-parent families are based on the mother rather than the father. As divorce rates show no sign of decreasing and may well further increase (Table 14.2), weakening the link between single-parent families and childhood poverty is likely to remain an area calling for constructive policy solutions.

Table 8.26: Income of disabled persons

Personal income of disabled persons aged 20–64 as % of that of non-disabled people, late 1990s

Sweden	96
Germany	93
Netherlands	88
Switzerland	88
Austria	86
Denmark	86
Canada	85
Finland	83
Belgium	82
France	80
Italy	80
Norway	79
United Kingdom	78
Ireland	70
United States	59
Australia	**44**
Mean	80

No data on Japan or New Zealand.

Table 8.27: Employment of disabled persons

Employment rate of disabled persons as % of non-disabled persons 20 to 64 years old, late 1990s
Mean income from employment for disabled persons as % of non-disabled mean, late 1990s

	Employment	Income
Switzerland	79	98
Canada	72	–
France	72	83
Norway	72	88
Sweden	69	70
Germany	67	92
Denmark	61	88
Austria	60	97
Italy	60	94
Netherlands	60	87
Finland	59	81
United States	58	71
Australia	**55**	**93**
Belgium	54	90
United Kingdom	53	84
Ireland	47	88
Mean	62	87

No data on Japan or New Zealand.
Australian income figure is proportion of median not mean.

Table 8.28: Recipients of disability benefits

Percentage of 20 to 64-year-olds receiving disability benefits

	1980	1990	1999
Norway	6.0	8.2	9.2
Netherlands	7.6	9.1	9.0
Sweden	6.2	7.3	8.2
Denmark	5.3	7.7	7.7
United Kingdom	2.6	4.2	6.6
Belgium	4.9	5.6	6.0
Italy	12.7	9.0	5.5
Switzerland	3.3	3.8	5.3
Australia	**2.7**	**3.1**	**5.2**
France	4.0	4.6	4.7
United States	3.1	3.3	4.7
Austria	2.5	4.0	4.6
Germany	3.8	3.3	4.2
Canada	–	2.5	3.9
Mean	5.0	5.4	6.0

No data on Finland, Ireland, Japan or New Zealand.

Disability

Australia may have won the most medals at the Sydney Olympics for the Disabled, but it lags badly in the relative income received by disabled people. Table 8.26 shows that disabled adults received less income than the non-disabled in all the selected countries, but whereas the 16-nation mean was to receive 80% of the non-disabled income, in Australia the figure is only 44%. This puts Australia a long way behind even the second-last placegetter the United States (59%), and more than 30 percentage points lower than nearly all the other countries.

The single greatest key to the disabled's income is whether they can gain employment. OECD figures (in which Australia unfortunately is not included) show that the income of non-employed disabled people is just over half that of their employed counterparts. Table 8.27 shows the relative employment rate of disabled to non-disabled adults. The mean for 16 nations was 62%. Other OECD data shows that the overall employment rate in these countries was around 66% for the working-age population, and for the disabled it was 42% (i.e. 62% of the total rate).

The employment ratio for the disabled in Australia was towards the bottom of the table, but in the same general range as several other countries where the disabled earn relatively much more. Switzerland has the highest employment rate, while Canada, as with its record on welfare for the elderly, departs from the other English-speaking countries to be equal second highest. Nor is the key to Australia's deviance found in how much the disabled receive at work. In nearly all countries, including Australia, the disabled earn marginally less than their non-disabled colleagues (last column). The two exceptions are the unlikely pairing of Sweden and the United States, which are both much lower at about 70%.

The term disabled covers a wide range of conditions, some that people are born with,

some that develop in later life, and some that are the result of injuries. More precise comparisons are needed to get a fully penetrating look at the welfare of the disabled. For example, in figures not shown here, the employment rate for the severely disabled is not surprisingly less than for the moderately disabled, a mean for the 16 countries of 37% compared with 70%. Nor do we have sufficient data on the generosity of benefits, but the pattern of the other data strongly implies that Australia must rank near the bottom.

Table 8.28 shows that the proportion of 20 to 64-year-olds receiving disability benefits rose somewhat between 1980 to 1999, from a mean of 5% to 6%. The exception to the general pattern is Italy, which saw the proportion of recipients more than halve, no doubt because of a change in policy rather than an increase in health. The rise probably reflects the ageing of the population, as the proportion of recipients rises steadily with age. The cross-country mean for 20 to 34-year-olds, for instance, is 15 per 1000, whereas for 55 to 59-year-olds it is 141 per 1000.

However, other factors are also at work, and one doubts that there are really twice as many disabled Norwegians as there are disabled Canadians. A country's position is influenced by many factors: by the incidence of disability in the country (which could be influenced by the diligence with which occupational health and safety laws are enforced); by the generosity or otherwise of the country's eligibility criteria for benefits; by the unemployment level (when employment is plentiful, older workers with borderline disabilities will keep working; when jobs are hard to find, they may prefer to receive disability benefits rather than unemployment benefits); and by the availability of jobs suitable for the disabled (most of whom would prefer to work than to rely on benefits).

Table 9.1: Military spending

Military spending as % of GDP

	1970	1980	1990	2000
United States	7.9	5.4	5.5	3.1
France	4.2	4.0	3.6	2.6
United Kingdom	4.8	4.9	4.0	2.5
Italy	2.7	2.1	2.1	2.1
Sweden	3.7	2.9	2.6	2.1
Norway	3.5	2.9	3.2	1.8
Australia	**3.5**	**2.6**	**2.2**	**1.7**
Netherlands	3.5	3.1	2.6	1.6
Denmark	2.7	2.4	2.1	1.5
Germany	3.3	3.3	2.8	1.5
Belgium	2.9	3.3	2.4	1.4
Finland	1.4	1.9	1.6	1.3
Canada	2.4	1.8	2.0	1.2
Switzerland	2.2	1.9	1.9	1.1
Japan	0.8	0.9	1.0	1.0
New Zealand	2.2	1.9	1.8	1.0
Austria	1.1	1.2	1.0	0.8
Ireland	1.3	1.9	1.3	0.7
Mean	3.0	2.7	2.4	1.6

Table 9.2: Size of armed forces

Total size of armed forces, 000s

	1970	2000
United States	3 188	1 366
France	577	294
Italy	557	251
Japan	–	237
Germany	499	221
United Kingdom	372	212
Canada	92	59
Sweden	–	53
Netherlands	112	52
Australia	**84**	**51**
Austria	–	40
Belgium	95	39
Finland	41	32
Switzerland	–	28
Norway	48	27
Denmark	48	22
Ireland	8	12
New Zealand	12	9
Mean	410	167

Table 9.3: Arms exports and imports

Volumes of transfers of conventional weapons aggregated for 1996–2000 (US$ billions at constant 1990 prices)

	Exports	Imports	Balance	Share world arms exports, %
United States	49.7	1.2	48.5	45.0
France	10.7	0.4	10.3	8.6
United Kingdom	7.0	1.7	5.3	6.6
Germany	5.6	0.5	5.2	5.4
Netherlands	2.0	1.1	0.9	1.8
Italy	1.7	1.1	0.6	1.7
Sweden	0.6	0.6	−0.1	1.0
Canada	0.7	0.8	−0.0	0.9
Australia	**0.6**	**0.9**	**−0.3**	**0.5**
Belgium	0.3	0.2	0.1	0.5
Switzerland	0.3	1.6	−1.3	0.3
Norway	0.1	1.0	−0.9	0.2
Austria	0.1	0.5	−0.4	0.1
Denmark	0.0	0.5	−0.5	0.0
Finland	0.0	2.8	−2.8	0.0
Ireland	0.0	0.0	−0.0	0.0
Japan	0.0	3.6	−3.5	0.0
New Zealand	0.0	0.7	−0.6	0.0

The countries with 0.0 have less than $US 100 million in exports, imports and balance, but are all greater than zero. In the balance column, −0.0 means that a country had a deficit, but less than $100 million.

9 INTERNATIONAL RELATIONS
Military spending

There are few other areas where one country so dominates. Because the GDP of the United States is larger than all others, and because it spends proportionately more on military expenditure, it dwarfs all others in absolute terms. According to the Stockholm Institute for Peace Research Incorporated, one of the two major world centres for compiling military data, in 2001 the United States' military expenditure comprised 36% of the world total, and its spending equalled the next nine countries' combined total.

Over the decades leading up to 2000, military spending as a proportion of GDP fell in all the selected countries. In some countries this meant an absolute decline in military spending. More commonly it meant that military spending grew less quickly than the economy.

The decline has not been as even as the decade intervals in the table might suggest. The United States increased its military spending greatly during the Reagan era, peaking at 6.6% of GDP in 1986. Similarly, according to SIPRI, world military expenditures reduced from 1987 to 1998, but then began climbing again. Almost certainly, since 11 September 2001 this has been at an accelerating pace. The 'peace dividend' which governments enjoyed from the reduction of military expenditures after the end of the Cold War now looks to be over.

It tends to be the larger countries that spend relatively more on their military, perhaps reflecting their own past roles as well as what they would say are their current responsibilities. Of the large countries, the least committed to military spending are Japan and to a lesser extent Germany.

The larger spending countries also tend to be those which are the biggest exporters of arms, and which are in surplus in their arms trade (Table 9.3). Again the United States dominates with 45% of the world's arms trade, and by far the biggest surplus on that trade. France comes second as an arms exporter, and these two countries along with the other major NATO allies, Britain and Germany, supply around two-thirds of the world's arms exports.

The major importers vary from year to year with the timing of major arms acquisitions. Over the period 1996–2000, the major buyers of major conventional weapons were Taiwan, Saudi Arabia, Turkey, South Korea, China, India, Greece and Egypt.

The size of the armed forces in the selected countries in 2000 was less than half the 1970 totals (Table 9.2), an absolute decline and not just the decline relative to GDP that military expenditure has shown. The much greater drop in manpower than expenditure shows that military strategies have become more technological.

Australia falls just within the top half of relative spending on the military, and has shared in the same general trends as others. Like other relatively small players, it has a deficit in its arms trade, and increases in expenditure are likely to increase that deficit.

Table 9.4: Foreign aid

Official development assistance as % of Gross National Income

	1985	2000	Change 1985–2000	Per capita ODA 2000 US$
Denmark	0.83	1.06	+0.23	337
Norway	1.02	0.80	−0.22	291
Netherlands	0.97	0.84	−0.13	210
Sweden	0.83	0.80	−0.03	203
Switzerland	0.30	0.34	+0.04	138
Japan	0.31	0.28	−0.03	112
France	0.62	0.32	−0.30	88
Belgium	0.56	0.36	−0.20	83
Finland	0.38	0.31	−0.07	81
Germany	0.46	0.27	−0.19	69
United Kingdom	0.33	0.32	−0.01	68
Ireland	0.23	0.30	+0.07	67
Austria	0.33	0.23	−0.10	62
Canada	0.50	0.25	−0.25	55
Australia	**0.47**	**0.27**	**−0.20**	**54**
New Zealand	0.25	0.25	0.00	34
United States	0.24	0.10	−0.14	34
Italy	0.27	0.13	−0.14	29
Mean	0.49	0.40	−0.09	112

Table 9.5: Targeting of foreign aid

Share of official development assistance from each donor country going to the least developed countries and to other low-income countries (%)

	Poorest countries	Other low-income countries
Ireland	65	14
Denmark	50	26
Norway	46	18
Netherlands	42	28
Sweden	42	27
Finland	41	26
Belgium	41	26
Italy	41	22
Switzerland	41	26
United Kingdom	41	28
Canada	37	36
New Zealand	36	21
Germany	31	29
United States	30	27
France	30	27
Austria	24	43
Australia	**22**	**38**
Japan	20	49
Mean	38	28

Table 9.6: Relative commitment to aid and military expenditure

Official development assistance compared with military expenditure, 1995, %

Denmark	52
Netherlands	38
Austria	36
Norway	33
Japan	29
Sweden	28
Canada	23
Belgium	23
Ireland	22
Switzerland	21
Finland	18
France	18
Germany	18
Australia	**14**
New Zealand	13
United Kingdom	9
Italy	8
United States	3
Mean	23

Foreign aid

The figures in Table 9.4 show that there are large differences in the amounts the selected countries devote to overseas aid, and that the differences are becoming greater.

In 1970 the United Nations adopted a target of rich nations giving 0.7% of their GNP to aid the poorer countries. Four donor countries surpass that target and easily exceed all others in their generosity. Denmark, Norway, the Netherlands and Sweden all give more than 0.8% of their GNI (Gross National Income, the successor concept to GNP) in overseas aid, and then there is a big gap, with the next largest giving 0.34%, and down to the United States' 0.10%.

Table 9.4 ranks the countries according to the amount each donated per head of its population in 2000. Each Dane gave the equivalent of US$337, and each Italian $US29. The Australian per capita contribution of $US54 puts it fourth bottom in the list.

In the 15 years between 1985 and 2000, 14 of the countries reduced their proportional aid commitment. Moreover, the reductions tended to be greater among those countries which already donated less. For example, the two countries at the bottom of the list, the United States and Italy, are among those who have reduced their aid the most. The biggest decline was by the former colonial power, France, down from 0.62% to about half that amount.

As a proportion of GNP/GNI, Australia's aid contribution peaked at 0.5% in 1974–75. It remained broadly stable until the mid-1980s but has been trending down ever since, somewhat more so than most other countries. While it ranked 9th in 1985, it had slid to equal 12th in 2000.

The efficacy of aid in contributing to development and alleviating poverty has long been questioned from both left and right. But the reasons for the reductions are likely to have more to do with the fiscal pressure on governments and with foreign aid being a politically painless target for spending cuts.

Although the public rationale for aid is to alleviate poverty, in practice its direction is shaped also by a variety of diplomatic, commercial and strategic factors. French aid, for example, goes disproportionately to former French colonies, while around 20% of Australian aid goes to Papua New Guinea. The biggest recipients of American aid are in the Middle East. But the scale of the consequences is still surprising. According to OECD figures, in the late 1990s poverty-stricken Bangladesh received only $US9 per head in official development assistance a year, and Ethiopia about $11, but the much more affluent Israelis received over $350 for each of their 6 million people.

The United Nations has defined a category of the poorest, least developed countries (LLDCs), those most in need on the basis of income, economic diversification and social development. There were 48 LLDCs listed in 2000, more than half of them in Africa. Other low-income countries (LICs), the next category up, are defined as those with a per capita GNP of US$760 or less. There were 24 other LICs in 2000.

Table 9.5 shows that over all 18 nations, 38% of official development assistance went to LLDCs and 28% to the LICs, again suggesting that need is not the central determinant of aid flows. Because Australian and Japanese aid goes overwhelmingly to the Asia-Pacific region, where there are few LLDCs, a relatively low proportion of their aid goes to this group, and a somewhat larger proportion to other low-income countries.

None of these countries spends nearly as much on development assistance as it does on the military. Table 9.6 shows the ratios range from Denmark, which spends half as much on foreign assistance as on their military, down to the United States, which expends only 3% as much on foreign aid as on its military budget. Australia spends 14% as much on aid as on the military.

Table 10.1: Mammals

Number of mammal species found in each country; number of endemic and threatened species

	All mammals	Endemic	Threatened
United States	432	105	35
Australia	**260**	**206**	**58**
Canada	193	7	7
Japan	188	42	29
France	93	0	13
Italy	90	3	10
Austria	83	0	7
Germany	76	0	8
Switzerland	75	0	6
Finland	60	0	4
Sweden	60	0	5
Belgium	58	0	6
Netherlands	55	0	6
Norway	54	0	4
United Kingdom	50	0	4
New Zealand	46	–	7
Denmark	43	0	3
Ireland	25	0	2

Table 10.2: Birds

Number of bird species breeding in country, number of endemic and threatened species

	All birds	Endemic	Threatened
United States	650	67	50
Australia	**649**	**350**	**45**
Canada	426	5	5
France	269	1	7
Japan	250	21	33
Sweden	249	0	4
Finland	248	0	4
Norway	243	0	3
Germany	239	0	5
Italy	234	0	7
United Kingdom	230	1	2
Austria	213	0	5
Denmark	196	0	2
Switzerland	193	0	4
Netherlands	191	0	3
Belgium	180	0	3
New Zealand	150	74	44
Ireland	142	0	1

Table 10.3: Reptiles

Number of reptile species in each country, number of endemic and threatened species

	All reptiles	Endemic	Threatened
Australia	**748**	**641**	**37**
United States	287	79	28
Austria	106	14	0
Japan	87	33	8
New Zealand	52	48	11
Canada	41	0	3
Italy	40	1	4
France	32	1	3
Switzerland	14	0	0
Germany	12	0	0
Belgium	8	0	0
United Kingdom	8	0	0
Netherlands	7	0	0
Sweden	6	0	0
Denmark	5	0	0
Finland	5	0	0
Norway	5	0	0
Ireland	1	0	0

Table 10.4: Protected areas

Protected areas for wildlife

	Area (000 hectares)	% of land area
Denmark	1 380	32.0
Austria	2 451	29.2
Germany	9 620	26.9
Switzerland	1 063	25.7
New Zealand	6 334	23.4
United Kingdom	5 000	20.4
France	7 437	13.5
United States	123 120	13.1
Canada	90 702	9.1
Sweden	3 645	8.1
Italy	2 204	7.3
Australia	**54 250**	**7.0**
Japan	2 561	6.8
Norway	2 093	6.5
Netherlands	232	5.7
Finland	1 867	5.5
Belgium	86	2.8
Ireland	65	0.9

10   ENVIRONMENT
Biodiversity

Environmental issues do not always lend themselves to comparative, quantitative summary. Every country has unique natural endowments and problems bestowed by its geographical setting. Sometimes comparative measures are merely charting these different geographic-cum-economic inheritances rather than any meaningful difference in environmental performance. Similarly, many environmental problems are primarily local: the effluent produced by a neighbourhood factory; the problems of water flow and salinity in the Murray–Darling basin; or the destruction of a particular urban heritage in the name of development. National summary measures cannot capture this local impact.

Tables 10.1 to 10.3 give a crude measure of countries' biodiversity simply by measuring the types of animals found in each. Counting species as if they are all of the same value, like a unit of currency, obviously fails to capture key dimensions of biodiversity. But the tables do show great differences among the selected countries.

Australia is recognised as one of 17 megadiverse countries whose ecosystems have exceptional variety and uniqueness. Of the selected countries, only the United States is also recognised in this way. Tables 10.1 to 10.3 give testimony to this rich biodiversity. The United States and Australia are the top two countries in all three tables, having far more mammals, birds and reptiles than any of the other selected countries. (The very large numbers in these tables are because zoologists recognise and distinguish many different types where most lay observers would see far fewer.) Australia and the United States both cover large areas, encompassing several climatic and geological zones and allowing a range of flora and fauna. Australia, for example, has 15900 native higher plants, which is more than the total for the whole of Europe (12500).

In addition, Australia's geographic isolation has given it a vast array of species not found elsewhere. The second data column in Tables 10.1 to 10.3 gives the number of endemic species, that is, species unique to that country. Here, America and Australia are still the leaders in all tables, but it is Australia which has by far the highest number. Indeed among the selected countries, Australia has more than half the endemic species of mammals listed, almost 70% of the birds, and more than 80% of the reptiles.

With economic development and population growth, wildlife has come under increasing stress. Tables 10.1 to 10.3 also summarise the numbers in each country under threat. The World Resources Institute distinguishes three levels of threatened species: critically endangered (i.e. an extremely high risk of extinction in the wild in the immediate future); endangered (a very high risk of extinction in the wild in the near future); and vulnerable (a very high risk of extinction in the wild in the medium-term future).

Because of their larger total number of species, it is not surprising that Australia and the United States are again clear leaders. In Australia's case the threat has been greatly exacerbated by ongoing programs of land clearing, and by the introduction of invasive species. Foxes and cats prey on native species, while rabbits and goats compete for their land, and degrade it. The big gap between Australia, the United States, Japan and New Zealand compared with the numbers threatened in the other countries, however, is hard to explain, and may be at least partly due to methodological differences.

A common response to the pressures on the natural habitat has been to dedicate protected areas for wildlife. Although in absolute size Australia has the third greatest area so set aside, in terms of proportion of land areas it ranks below the 18-nation mean. This is a crude measure which pays no attention to the quality of the areas, their importance for native flora and fauna, or the conflicting objectives of land use to which they might otherwise be subject. Similarly, more discriminating measures would be needed to know how well these wilderness areas redress the prospects of threatened species.

Table 10.5: Greenhouse gas emissions				Table 10.6: Carbon dioxide emissions		
Tonnes of carbon dioxide equivalents (CO_2-e) per head per year				Tonnes of carbon dioxide emissions from energy use per head per year		
	1990	1999			1990	2000
Sweden	5.8	5.2		Switzerland	6.1	5.8
Switzerland	7.4	6.9		Sweden	6.0	5.9
France	8.7	8.2		France	6.1	6.2
Norway	10.0	8.6		Italy	7.1	7.4
Austria	8.8	8.8		Norway	6.7	7.5
Italy	8.8	9.1		Austria	7.4	7.7
Japan	9.3	9.6		New Zealand	6.6	8.3
United Kingdom	13.0	10.8		United Kingdom	9.7	8.9
Germany	14.8	11.6		Japan	8.3	9.1
Finland	10.7	12.7		Denmark	9.8	9.4
Denmark	13.4	13.6		Germany	12.2	10.1
New Zealand	15.0	14.4		Finland	11.0	10.6
Netherlands	14.3	14.5		Ireland	8.6	10.9
Belgium	13.5	14.6		Netherlands	10.7	11.1
Ireland	13.8	15.6		Belgium	–	12.0
United States	20.0	20.7		Canada	15.5	17.1
Canada	19.6	22.2		**Australia**	**15.2**	**17.2**
Australia	**28.9**	**27.9**		United States	19.3	20.6
Mean	13.1	13.1		Mean	9.8	10.3

Table 10.7: Total carbon dioxide emissions

National carbon dioxide emissions from energy use (millions of tonnes of CO_2), 2000 and % of global total

	Total	World %
United States	5 665.4	24.19
Japan	1 154.8	4.93
Germany	833.0	3.56
United Kingdom	531.5	2.27
Canada	526.8	2.25
Italy	425.7	1.82
France	373.3	1.59
Australia	**329.3**	**1.41**
Netherlands	177.1	0.76
Belgium	120.3	0.51
Austria	62.8	0.27
Finland	54.8	0.23
Sweden	52.0	0.22
Denmark	50.1	0.21
Switzerland	41.7	0.18
Ireland	41.2	0.18
Norway	33.6	0.14
New Zealand	31.7	0.14
China	3 035.4	12.96
Russia	1 505.7	6.43

Greenhouse gases

Some environmental issues are purely local but others are global in scope. The issue of global warming became very prominent in the 1990s. The controversies leading up to and following the Kyoto Protocol particularly focused attention on it. As the International Energy Agency commented, 'the climate change problem is unique in at least three important ways: it is global in nature, it has an unusually long-term character, and both climate change itself and the effects of policies to mitigate it remain inadequately understood.'

While most policy issues involve reactions to already manifest problems, global warming involves the anticipation of a problem whose adverse consequences will damage future generations rather than the present one. Furthermore the measures needed to combat it have immediate and considerable costs, while their benefits are in the avoidance of future catastrophes – not the most promising scenario for decisive political action.

The weather itself is so full of extreme natural variability that it is impossible to tie any particular occurrence to the long-term trend. However, according to the United Nations Inter-Governmental Panel on Climate Change, it is likely that the 1990s were the warmest decade of the millennium in the northern hemisphere. The Panel estimates that global temperatures rose by about $0.6°$ Centigrade during the 20th century, and that if current trends continue they will further rise by between $1.4°$ and $5.8°C$ in the 21st century. This would be a bigger climate change than any experienced over the last 10 000 years. Its consequences at regional levels would be extremely varied, but some at least could be disastrous.

Global warming is attributed to the greenhouse effect, a shorthand description for the way carbon dioxide, water vapour and other gases form a blanket which stops some of the sun's heat escaping from the earth, so making the planet warmer. This effect occurs naturally but has been enhanced by the many industrial and other human activities which produce greenhouse gases.

While carbon dioxide is responsible for 60% of the enhanced greenhouse effect, mostly from burning fossil fuels, other substances also contribute. One tonne of methane, for example, has the same effect as 21 tonnes of CO_2. In order to look at the totality of their impact, the measure of carbon dioxide equivalents has been constructed (so one tonne of methane has the same warming effect as 21 CO_2-e).

Table 10.5 shows that among the selected countries, the average CO_2-e per head remained the same between 1990 and 1999. The table is couched in terms of emissions per person, to show how each country's economic patterns and lifestyle are contributing to the problem. Australia was the worst-performing country per capita, with the United States and Canada being the other two countries with figures greater than 20. At the other end of the scale, each Swede produced only about a fifth as many CO_2-e emissions as each Australian. Carbon dioxide emissions from energy (Table 10.6) produced a broadly similar ranking. Again the United States, Australia and Canada produced the greatest amount of emissions per person, and Switzerland, Sweden and France the least. The distinctive aspects which contribute to Australian pre-eminence in greenhouse gas emissions are the reliance on coal-fired power stations for electricity, the heavy reliance on road transport, and continuing land clearing.

In terms of effective action, what matters is the contribution of the biggest countries. As Table 10.7 shows, the United States by itself generates almost a quarter of global carbon dioxide emissions, while China and Russia are the next biggest contributors. Australia, with 0.3% of the world's population, generates a disproportionate 1.4% of carbon dioxide.

Although climate scientists differ with each other over the exact dimensions of future trends, the great majority believes that human-induced climate change will lead inexorably to major future problems. Whether the international political processes will be capable of meeting the challenge is yet to be seen.

Table 10.8: Energy usage per person

Total primary energy supply TOE (tonnes of oil equivalent) per person

	1973	2000
Italy	2.35	2.97
Austria	2.86	3.52
Denmark	3.95	3.64
Switzerland	3.06	3.70
Ireland	2.34	3.86
United Kingdom	3.93	3.89
Germany	4.28	4.13
Japan	2.98	4.13
France	3.31	4.25
Netherlands	4.65	4.76
New Zealand	2.78	4.86
Norway	3.82	5.70
Sweden	4.83	5.70
Australia	**4.27**	**5.71**
Belgium	4.76	5.78
Finland	4.57	6.40
Canada	7.16	8.16
United States	8.19	8.35
Mean	4.12	4.97

Table 10.9: Energy intensity

Total primary energy supply TOE per $1000 of GDP

	1973	2000
Switzerland	.08	.08
Denmark	.15	.09
Japan	.12	.09
Austria	.16	.11
Germany	.21	.13
Ireland	.27	.14
Italy	.20	.14
France	.18	.15
Netherlands	.25	.15
Norway	.22	.15
Sweden	.24	.17
United Kingdom	.29	.18
Belgium	.27	.19
Finland	.26	.20
Australia	**.29**	**.24**
United States	.43	.26
New Zealand	.19	.27
Canada	.50	.36
Mean	.24	.17

Table 10.10: Electricity prices and usage

Kilowatt hours (kWh) per $100 of GDP and electricity prices for households (US$PPP per kWh)

	kWh 2000	$ 1980	$ 2000
Switzerland	18	.050	.099
Denmark	18	.068	.192
Japan	19	.104	.149
Germany	21	.071	.139
Ireland	22	.067	.115
Netherlands	22	.081	.154
Austria	22	.084	.140
Italy	26	.080	.183
France	27	.086	.117
Belgium	27	.102	.157
United Kingdom	30	.072	.109
United States	45	.054	.082
Australia	**46**	**.036**	**.082**
Finland	49	.051	.085
Sweden	53	.035	.082
New Zealand	57	.036	.092
Norway	72	.021	.056
Canada	81	.026	–
Mean	36	.062	.120

Table 10.11: Electricity generation

Shares of fuel in electricity generation, 2000, %

	Coal	Oil	Gas	Nuclear	Hydro	Other
Australia	77	1	13	0	8	1
Germany	53	1	9	30	4	3
United States	53	3	16	20	6	2
Denmark	46	12	24	0	0	17
Ireland	36	20	39	0	4	1
United Kingdom	33	2	39	23	1	1
Netherlands	28	4	58	4	0	6
Japan	24	15	22	30	8	2
Canada	20	3	5	12	59	1
Belgium	19	1	19	58	1	2
Finland	19	1	14	32	21	13
Austria	11	3	13	0	70	3
Italy	11	32	38	0	16	3
France	6	1	2	78	13	1
New Zealand	3	0	24	0	63	11
Sweden	2	1	0	39	54	3
Norway	0	0	0	0	100	0
Switzerland	0	0	2	40	56	3
Mean	25	6	19	20	27	4

Energy usage

Energy is pivotal in all other economic activities, but energy generation can potentially have huge impacts on the environment in air pollution, in the production of greenhouse gases, and in the depletion of non-renewable resources.

Energy intensity refers to the amount of energy per unit of GDP (Table 10.9). Energy efficiency is equated with a reduction in energy intensity, but the wide differences between countries reflect variations in their geographic conditions and economic structure as well. Table 10.9 shows that energy usage per unit of GDP went down, with the 2000 mean being about 70% of its 1973 level. The reduction reflects increasing energy efficiency in the economy, but also comes from changes in the economy, notably the relative decline of manufacturing and the increasing importance of the services sector.

Moreover, while environmental awareness has been part of the reason for the changes, short-term economic calculations have been at least as important. After the 1973 oil shock, energy prices soared, and this induced many countries, especially those dependent on oil imports, to reduce energy use. The OECD noted that the energy intensity per unit of GDP dropped in many of the selected countries during the 1980s, but did not further improve in the 1990s, when energy prices fell.

Table 10.8 shows a contrasting trend to Table 10.9. The energy used per person in the selected countries rose by about 20% between 1973 and 2000, reflecting continuing growth in domestic usage and motor transport.

Table 10.10 narrows the focus from total energy consumption to electricity consumption. Nevertheless, as might be expected, the rankings of Tables 10.9 and 10.10 are broadly similar. As Table 10.10 also shows, levels of electricity use are related to the relative cheapness of electricity. The seven countries having the greatest usage, which includes Australia, are the seven with the cheapest supply.

Table 10.11 shows shares of fuels used for electricity generation in 2000. The large differences between countries are explained largely by a country's natural resource endowments, seen most obviously in their relative reliance on coal and hydro-power. For six countries, hydro is the major source of electricity, and as one would expect these tend to be mountainous countries with fast-flowing rivers. Similarly, Australia, most of all, and then Germany, the United States and Denmark, have tended to rely on their naturally occurring coal deposits as the major source of electricity.

There is great divergence between the countries in the degree to which they have embraced nuclear energy. For France and Belgium it is their major source of electricity. In contrast, seven countries, including Australia, have not developed it at all.

While the selected countries generate far more electricity than they did in 1973, the means of producing that electricity has also changed very substantially. The International Energy Agency reports that among its members (almost coterminous with the OECD) nuclear generation rose from supplying 3% of total electricity in 1973 to 17% in 2000 (though more recent indications suggest this may have reached a ceiling). Gas also showed substantial growth, from 12% to 17%. Hydro power and coal roughly kept their share, which meant that both expanded in line with the growing total. The big decrease was that oil dropped from 25% to 8%, clearly becoming uneconomic when prices rose.

The Australian *State of the Environment Report 2001* noted that cleaner renewable sources of electricity were growing at a much slower rate than the older, non-renewable sources, such as coal. Australia's liberalisation of the energy market had lowered prices without internalising the full cost of its environmental effects, and had further increased the price differential to the detriment of renewable sources of energy.

Table 10.12: Nitrogen oxide emissions

Kilograms of nitrogen oxides emissions per person per year; concentration of nitrogen dioxide in urban areas (micrograms per cubic metre), 1999

	1980	1990	1999	Concentration
Japan	14	13	13	62
Switzerland	27	23	15	42
Germany	43	43	20	40
Austria	30	26	22	40
Italy	28	34	26	124
Netherlands	41	39	26	58
United Kingdom	46	48	27	65
France	38	33	28	57
Sweden	54	41	30	30
Ireland	24	33	32	24
Belgium	45	32	36	47
Denmark	53	54	42	54
Finland	62	60	48	31
New Zealand	–	51	53	20
Norway	47	53	54	50
Canada	80	76	67	41
United States	97	88	83	61
Australia	–	**128**	**136**	**17**
Mean	46	49	42	48

Ranked according to 1999 emissions.

Table 10.13: Sulphur oxide emissions

Kilograms of sulphur oxide emissions per person per year; concentration of sulphur dioxide in urban areas (micrograms per cubic metre), 1999

	1980	1990	1999*	Concentration
Austria	51	12	5	13
Switzerland	18	6	5	11
Netherlands	35	14	6	10
Norway	34	12	6	6
Japan	11	7	7	24
Sweden	61	16	8	5
Denmark	88	35	10	7
Germany	51	84	10	13
New Zealand	–	11	12	4
Finland	122	52	16	4
France	60	22	16	14
Italy	68	30	16	16
United Kingdom	87	66	20	22
Belgium	84	33	24	21
Ireland	65	52	42	19
United States	103	86	61	15
Canada	189	119	90	13
Australia	–	**110**	**96**	**13**
	71	43	25	13

Ranked according to 1999 emissions.

Table 10.14: Petrol consumption

Annual motor gasoline consumption (litres per head)

	1987	1997
Belgium	383	334
France	443	334
Austria	438	345
Netherlands	310	353
Japan	308	422
Ireland	314	428
Italy	288	434
Finland	469	488
Germany	482	491
Denmark	398	502
Norway	559	505
United Kingdom	519	507
Sweden	649	621
Switzerland	668	703
New Zealand	695	755
Australia	**970**	**950**
Canada	1 222	1 178
United States	1 660	1 688
Mean	599	613

Table 10.15: Price of petrol

Pump price of super gasoline in US cents per litre, 2000, and tax as % of that price

	Cents	Tax %
United States	47	23
New Zealand	48	43
Australia	**57**	**51**
Canada	58	41
Switzerland	78	60
Austria	82	61
Ireland	90	59
Germany	91	69
Sweden	94	67
Belgium	96	66
Italy	97	65
France	99	70
Denmark	101	66
Netherlands	103	66
Finland	106	67
Japan	106	55
United Kingdom	117	76
Norway	119	69
Mean	88	60

Air pollution and petrol use

The problem of urban air pollution is almost as old as the industrial revolution. The word 'smog' was coined as early as the 1890s to describe the combination of smoke and fog that gave London its famous 'pea-soupers'. But the problem became far more potent in the contemporary era. In the 1950s and 1960s, on days of bad pollution in major cities, respiratory problems resulted in illness and even deaths. In the 1960s, acid rain became an international issue, especially in Europe. Its deleterious effects on buildings, crops and forests, and life in freshwater lakes were increasingly obvious. So air pollution crystallised as a political problem because of its acute short-term health impacts, the tangible damage from acid rain, plus the aesthetic assaults from urban haze and chemical smells.

The types and sources of air pollution are many and vary between countries. Its major sources are burning coal and oil in electricity generation, industrial processes, household consumption and motor vehicle emissions. Policy actions have reduced or ameliorated some problems which were previously becoming acute. For example, lead pollution and its effects on brain development was a growing problem in Australia. But with the development of lead-free petrol and removal of lead from paint, the problem has almost disappeared.

The most systematic comparative data is on oxides of sulphur and nitrogen. Both are implicated in respiratory problems and in acid rain, while nitrogen oxides are central in the formation of photochemical smog. Sulphur dioxide is emitted by vehicles, by the burning of coal, and in processes like wood pulping and paper manufacturing. Similarly, nitrogen oxide is emitted through vehicle exhausts, power plants and domestic gas stoves. As Tables 10.12 and 10.13 show, in most of the selected countries there have been concerted moves towards the reduction of these gases.

Both tables also show Australia as having the highest emissions per person, with the United States and Canada next highest.

To some extent the tables suggest that those with the lower current emissions are those with the worst concentrations of the gases. Japan, for example, ranks high in the final column of both tables but among the lowest on per person emissions. Australia has high emissions of nitrogen oxides but not in urban areas, because the power plants are outside major cities. It suggests that sustained attempts to reduce emissions follow when urban quality is recognised to be declining.

An inverse relationship between population density and air pollution – although with several exceptions – is also suggested by the tables. The importance of population density and urban density is even more pronounced in Table 10.14, which relates to one of the principal sources of pollution, travel by motor vehicles. The four English-speaking New World democracies used far more petrol per person than the European countries and Japan. In 1997 the average American used more than five times as much petrol as the average Belgian and Frenchman. Australia was not quite in the North American league, but each Australian still consumed roughly twice as much as the average European.

Petrol usage showed a strong relationship with petrol price, as recorded in Table 10.15. The four highest petrol-consuming countries had the lowest prices by a considerable margin. Ironically the only two of the selected countries which are net oil exporters, Norway and the United Kingdom, had the highest prices. Although normal market forces also operate, Table 10.15 shows that the biggest influence on petrol price is how heavily it is taxed.

As a result of changes to fuel taxes following the Howard Government's GST package, the prices of petrol and especially diesel fell for business users and heavy transport. According to the OECD the expected revenue loss from these measures is $4.4 billion per year, and they moved road taxation 'even further from a structure needed to internalise road transport externalities', including environmental costs.

Table 10.16: Pollution abatement and control spending

Expenditure as % of GDP, 1999 or latest available year

Netherlands	1.8
Austria	1.7
United States	1.6
Switzerland	1.6
Japan	1.6
Germany	1.5
France	1.4
Sweden	1.2
Norway	1.2
Finland	1.1
Canada	1.1
United Kingdom	1.0
Italy	0.9
Denmark	0.9
Belgium	0.9
Australia	**0.8**
Ireland	0.6
Mean	1.2

No data on New Zealand.

Table 10.17: Generation of waste

Kilograms of waste generated per person per year, 2000*

	Municipal	Household
New Zealand	–	380
Japan	410	270
Sweden	450	–
Finland	460	190
Italy	500	–
France	510	360
Germany	540	340
Belgium	550	450
Ireland	560	330
Austria	560	380
United Kingdom	560	480
Netherlands	610	530
Norway	620	330
Canada	640	330
Switzerland	650	450
Denmark	660	560
Australia	**690**	**400**
United States	760	460
Mean	572	390

(Australian data = 1990.)

Table 10.18: Spending on waste treatment

Annual spending on municipal waste disposal ($US000 per person) and on waste water treatment ($US per person) per year

	Municipal	Waste water
United States	18.1	105.0
Switzerland	12.4	101.8
United Kingdom	11.6	11.1
Canada	11.5	66.7
Japan	11.3	–
Australia	**10.9**	**41.9**
Austria	10.8	142.8
Italy	10.8	29.4
Germany	10.7	75.3
Belgium	10.1	38.3
France	10.0	112.8
Norway	10.0	92.1
Denmark	9.7	105.4
Ireland	9.5	–
Netherlands	9.5	109.6
New Zealand	9.0	–
Sweden	8.5	63.5
Finland	8.0	52.2
Mean	10.7	76.5

Table 10.19: Glass and paper recycling

Percentage of quantity collected for recycling to apparent total consumption

	Glass 1985	Glass 2000*	Paper 1985	Paper 2000
Switzerland	46	91	39	63
Finland	21	89	39	67
Belgium	42	87	–	52
Sweden	20	86	34	63
Norway	–	85	16	44
Austria	38	84	37	66
Germany	43	83	43	70
Japan	47	78	50	59
Netherlands	49	78	50	45
Denmark	19	65	31	48
France	26	55	35	50
New Zealand	–	42	–	65
Australia	**–**	**40**	**36**	**47**
Italy	25	40	25	37
Ireland	7	35	10	10
United Kingdom	12	26	28	41
United States	8	23	21	42
Canada	12	17	23	54
Mean	28	61	32	51

Ranked according to glass recycling in 2000.

Pollution control and waste disposal

Waste is a by-product of nearly all human activities. Even in ancient cities the hygienic and efficient disposal of waste was a major problem. With the scale of contemporary metropolises, industrial production and affluent consumer lifestyles, waste disposal and pollution control have become expensive and contentious policy issues. Who should pay for combating pollution? How are the environmental costs of goods and services to be built into prices and taxes? Where should the sites for waste disposal be situated? – not in my back yard – and are they safe?

Pollution abatement and control activities are defined as activities aimed at the prevention, reduction and elimination of pollution and other nuisances arising as a residue of production or consumption of goods and services. Tables 10.16 and 10.18 are testimony to the scale of these activities in the selected societies. Table 10.16 shows that on average these activities cost 1.2% of GDP in the late 1990s. Whether because its problems are less severe or its response has been slower, Australia is second bottom on the table, spending an amount that is only two-thirds of the mean.

Table 10.18 shows that across the selected countries, the average cost of disposing of municipal waste was over $US10 000 in 2000. Municipal waste includes waste from households, offices, shops and other commercial enterprises, but excludes sewage, construction, industrial and hazardous waste. According to the OECD, disposal of municipal waste represents more than one-third of the public sector's financial efforts to contain and control pollution.

The need for it is shown by Table 10.17. Each year in the selected countries, each person on average generates 572 kilograms of waste, which includes 390 kilograms of household waste. While Australian households are close to average in the waste they generate, Australia ranks second to the United States in total municipal waste generated per person.

The other main public sector PAC measures concern sewage and waste water treatment. Table 10.18 also shows that the cost of disposing of waste water averaged just over $US75 per person per year. It shows great variation between the countries, with the availability of suitable coastline seeming to be one factor affecting cost. It is most expensive in landlocked Austria and cheapest in the British Isles. Australia, with its preponderance of coastal cities, is also below average.

The large costs of waste disposal, plus the prospect of ever-increasing amounts of waste that will not break down naturally extending endlessly into the future, contributed to a concern with waste minimisation. One approach to waste minimisation has been the growth of recycling, defined as any re-use of material in a production process that diverts it from the waste stream.

Table 10.19 shows that the extent of paper recycling increased by over half in the selected countries between 1985 and 2000. In a majority of countries, most paper is now recycled. Australia has fallen slightly below the mean as its rate of increase has not been as great as the general trend.

Table 10.19 shows that there has been an even more dramatic increase in the extent of recycling of glass. The 18-nation mean more than doubled in the fifteen years between 1985 and 2000. Although all countries have shared the general increase, by 2000 there was a large range in their degree of glass recycling. The English-speaking countries (including Ireland) plus Italy fill the bottom seven places in the table, all recycling less than half their glass. The other European countries plus Japan all recycle more than half their glass, and nine of them recycle more than three-quarters. The OECD's Environmental Data Compendium, from which this table is drawn, gives no information on the practices (e.g. compulsory refundable deposits on bottles or taxes on plastic bags) that might account for such differences.

Table 10.20: Ecological footprint
Global hectares per person, 1999

Italy	3.8
Switzerland	4.1
Austria	4.7
Germany	4.7
Japan	4.8
Netherlands	4.8
France	5.3
Ireland	5.3
United Kingdom	5.3
Denmark	6.6
Belgium	6.7
Sweden	6.7
Australia	**7.6**
Norway	7.9
Finland	8.4
New Zealand	8.7
Canada	8.8
United States	9.7
Mean	6.3

Table 10.21: Water usage
Cubic metres of water used per person per year, 1999

Denmark	180
United Kingdom	180
Austria	280
Netherlands	280
Sweden	310
Ireland	330
Switzerland	370
Finland	480
Germany	530
New Zealand	570
Norway	600
Belgium	690
France	700
Japan	720
Australia	**840**
Italy	980
Canada	1 600
United States	1 870
Mean	639

Table 10.22: Price of water
Price of water in biggest city, 1998, US$PPP

	City	$
Italy	Rome	0.29
Canada	Toronto	0.39
Norway	Oslo	0.39
United States	New York	0.43
United Kingdom	London	0.57
New Zealand	Auckland	0.58
Sweden	Stockholm	0.62
Finland	Helsinki	0.66
Japan	Tokyo	0.74
France	Paris	0.76
Australia	**Sydney**	**0.89**
Netherlands	Amsterdam	0.99
Denmark	Copenhagen	1.32
Austria	Vienna	1.35
Switzerland	Zurich	1.37
Belgium	Brussels	1.45
Germany	Berlin	1.70
Mean		0.85

No data on Ireland.

Ecological footprint and water usage

Perhaps the most fundamental environmental issue is sustainability. Will a particular society be able to continue its practices indefinitely into the future, or are current practices exhausting resources, building up environmental problems or incurring economic and social costs so that they will have to be significantly curtailed or even end in disaster?

The concept of sustainability entered official policy discourse at a global level when governments embraced it at the UN Conference on the Environment and Development at Rio de Janeiro in 1992 (the first Earth Summit). A group called Redefining Progress has since sought to measure sustainability by constructing an Ecological Footprint.

It has drawn up Ecological Footprint Accounts, which document humanity's demands on nature and assess our ecological 'bottom line'. The accounts are based on data about the resources we consume and the wastes we generate on one hand against the corresponding land area needed to meet that demand. Its final measure is in terms of global hectares: the biologically productive space required to provide the services using current technology.

The idea of the Ecological Footprint is then a simple, comprehensible and useful indicator of sustainability. Its drawback is that the calculations needed to arrive at this bottom line are very complex, and no doubt open to question at many points.

Redefining Progress says that there are 1.9 global hectares of biologically productive space available per person on the Earth. But the world average ecological footprint is 2.3 hectares per person, which means that humanity is currently exceeding the biosphere's ecological capacity.

Table 10.20 shows that the selected countries all exceed 1.9 hectares by a considerable amount. The best-scoring (i.e. least ecologically demanding) country per person, Italy, is double that figure. The mean for the selected countries is over three times the available footprint, and 2.5 times the global average. This is not surprising. It reflects the huge differences in development between the selected countries and the Third World. The OECD, a group which includes our 18 countries but several other advanced economies as well, has one-quarter of the world's population but accounts for 80% of GDP and 80% of world trade. In the late 1990s, OECD populations consumed 45% of all meat and fish, 58% of global energy, 84% of all paper, and 87% of all cars. This huge inequity in material standards of living bedevils many global negotiations on environmental issues.

Among the selected countries, the English-speaking New World democracies and the Scandinavians generally are consuming more of the earth's resources than the others. The American standard of living demands more global hectares per person than any other country's by a large margin, while Australia also falls in the top third of the selected countries.

One aspect of the ecological footprint is water usage. Australia's semi-arid interior means that it is the driest continent, and the limited availability of water has greatly shaped Australian development. It may be surprising then that in terms of water consumption per person Australia rates fourth highest among the selected countries. Table 10.21 shows a large range, with the average Briton and Dane only consuming about a tenth of the water per year that the average American does. Before Australian readers invoke stereotypes about the washing habits of the English, it should be pointed out that the major component of water usage is in agriculture, especially irrigation. The price of water in the biggest cities shown in Table 10.22 (with local prices converted into $US and adjusted to make their purchasing power comparable) therefore has little correlation with water usage in Table 10.21.

In 1996, 70% of Australia's water use was in agriculture, and that share was increasing compared with industrial and household use. The typical Australian household used 270 litres per day, of which about half went on gardening and a quarter on flushing toilets.

Table 11.1: Investment in knowledge			
Total investment in knowledge as % of GDP, 1998 and annual growth rates 1991–98			
	Total	Growth in knowledge investment	Growth in investment structures and equipment
Sweden	6.5	7.6	−2.2
United States	6.0	3.9	6.2
Finland	5.2	6.8	−1.2
Switzerland	4.8	3.2	−2.8
Canada	4.7	2.6	3.0
Japan	4.7	2.6	−1.2
Denmark	4.6	5.9	3.5
Netherlands	4.3	3.8	2.6
Germany	4.2	2.2	−0.2
France	4.1	3.0	−1.1
Norway	4.0	5.6	5.8
Australia	**3.9**	**4.0**	**6.2**
United Kingdom	3.9	3.6	2.2
Belgium	3.7	–	1.3
Austria	3.5	6.3	1.4
Ireland	3.1	10.2	10.7
Italy	2.1	−0.6	−0.4
Mean	4.3	4.4	2.0

No data on New Zealand.

Table 11.2: Total spending on research and development			
Public and private sector R&D spending as % of GDP			
	1981	1990	1999 *
Sweden	2.21	2.84	3.80
Finland	1.17	1.88	3.19
Japan	2.13	2.85	3.04
Switzerland	2.18	2.83	2.73
United States	2.37	2.65	2.64
Germany	2.47	2.75	2.44
France	1.93	2.37	2.17
Denmark	1.06	1.57	2.00
Netherlands	1.78	2.07	1.95
United Kingdom	2.38	2.16	1.87
Belgium	1.57	1.64	1.83
Austria	1.13	1.39	1.80
Norway	1.18	1.69	1.70
Canada	1.24	1.54	1.66
Australia	**0.95**	**1.31**	**1.49**
Ireland	0.68	0.83	1.39
New Zealand	–	1.00	1.13
Italy	0.88	1.29	1.04
Mean	1.60	1.93	2.10

Table 11.3: Researchers in the labour force			
Number of researchers per 10 000 in the labour force			
	1981	1990	1999 *
Finland	37	55	99
Japan	54	75	97
Sweden	41	59	91
United States	62	71	81
Norway	38	63	78
Australia	**35**	**51**	**67**
Denmark	25	40	61
France	36	50	61
Germany	44	61	60
Canada	32	46	58
Switzerland	–	44	55
United Kingdom	47	46	55
Belgium	31	43	54
Ireland	16	35	51
Netherlands	34	44	50
New Zealand	–	30	44
Austria	21	25	34
Italy	23	32	33
Mean	36	48	63

11   SCIENCE AND TECHNOLOGY
Investment in knowledge

The ability to create, distribute and exploit knowledge is increasingly central to a country's competitive advantage and rising standard of living, as the OECD has observed. In this vein, Table 11.1 starts by introducing a new concept of 'investment in knowledge', defined as spending on higher education, research and development, and software. It covers spending by both the public and private sectors, but excludes consumer spending on software.

It can be seen that by 1998 total annual spending on knowledge averaged 4.3% of GDP across the selected countries. As the second data column shows, this level was achieved after such spending had grown in real terms at 4.4% a year since 1991. A comparison with the final column shows that over this period mean investment in knowledge grew at more than twice the rate at which conventional investment in structures and equipment (gross fixed capital formation) grew. And whereas the rate of conventional investment actually fell in many countries during the period, investment in knowledge accelerated in all countries.

The United States' high level of total investment in knowledge is not surprising – it is, after all, the country at the world's technological frontier. More surprising are the high levels and rates of growth for Sweden and tiny Finland. At the other end of the league, Ireland's low level of investment does not mean it is asleep. Its attainment of the highest rate of growth over the period suggests it is catching up rapidly. Australia's below-average level of knowledge investment is partly made up for by its seventh-highest rate of growth.

Table 11.2 narrows the focus to total public and private spending on R&D. In general, annual R&D spending rose fairly steadily as a percentage of GDP over the last two decades of the 20th century – meaning, of course, that R&D spending grew at a faster rate than economies did overall. The performances of

Sweden and Finland stand out. And again, Ireland stands out not for its high level of spending but for its rapid rate of increase. Australia's performance was well below average and over 18 years its rate of convergence on the mean has been painfully slow.

As is conventional, Table 11.2 puts each country's R&D spending into the context of that country's relative size by expressing it as a percentage of national GDP. When countries' spending is compared in absolute terms, however, a very different picture emerges. The United States accounts for 47% of the selected countries' total spending on R&D, followed by Japan (18%), Germany (9), France (6), United Kingdom (5), Italy (3), Canada (3), Sweden (1.5) and Australia (1.3).

Table 11.3 puts a more human face on the pursuit of knowledge by ranking the selected countries according to their number of researchers per 10 000 in the labour force. Here researchers are defined broadly as professionals engaged in the conception and creation of new knowledge, products, processes, methods and systems.

It can be seen that the proportion of researchers grew almost universally during the last two decades of the 20th century – meaning not merely that their ranks kept increasing, but that their numbers grew at a lot faster rate than the labour force as a whole. Indeed, the proportion of researchers increased by three-quarters over the period.

Again, Finland and Sweden stand out alongside the R&D heavyweights, the United States and Japan. Over the period, Australia's performance went from average to well into the top half of the league. So, like Norway, it ranks much higher in terms of research workers than research spending.

Even so, in absolute terms the United States accounts for 41% of all the researchers in the selected countries and Japan for 23%. Add the next three biggest economies – Germany, France and the United Kingdom – and more than 83% are covered.

Table 11.4: Business spending on research and development		
Business R&D spending as % of GDP		
	1981	1999*
Sweden	1.21	2.58
Japan	1.44	2.19
Finland	0.64	2.13
Switzerland	1.64	1.84
United States	1.16	1.76
Germany	1.40	1.57
Belgium	–	1.27
France	0.79	1.17
Denmark	0.45	1.04
Ireland	0.26	0.96
Netherlands	0.82	0.95
United Kingdom	1.00	0.92
Norway	0.47	0.87
Canada	0.51	0.74
Austria	0.57	0.71
Australia	**0.19**	**0.67**
Italy	0.44	0.46
New Zealand	–	0.34
Mean	0.81	1.23

Table 11.5: Government spending on research and development		
Government spending on R&D as% of GDP		
	1981	1999*
Finland	0.51	0.93
Sweden	0.93	0.93
France	1.03	0.81
Germany	1.03	0.81
United States	1.17	0.77
Netherlands	0.84	0.74
Switzerland	0.54	0.73
Norway	0.67	0.72
Australia	**0.69**	**0.71**
Austria	0.53	0.71
Denmark	0.57	0.70
Japan	0.53	0.59
New Zealand	–	0.59
Italy	0.42	0.53
Canada	0.63	0.52
United Kingdom	1.14	0.52
Belgium	–	0.46
Ireland	0.38	0.31
Mean	0.73	0.67

Table 11.6: Small firms and research and development	
Percentage of R&D undertaken by firms with fewer than 500 employees, 1999	
Norway	55.2
Australia	**49.9**
Denmark	39.4
Belgium	36.3
Canada	32.5
Switzerland	30.4
Finland	29.0
Netherlands	28.8
United Kingdom	25.2
Italy	24.3
France	21.1
United States	18.6
Sweden	17.8
Germany	15.0
Japan	7.2
Mean	28.7

No data on Austria, Ireland, or New Zealand.

Table 11.7: Trade balance in information and communication technology	
Balance of trade in ICT goods as % of GDP, 2001	
Ireland	11.0
Japan	6.1
Finland	5.4
Sweden	0.6
United Kingdom	–0.2
Belgium	–0.7
Netherlands	–0.7
France	–0.9
Germany	–0.9
Austria	–1.9
Denmark	–2.0
Italy	–2.0
United States	–2.1
Switzerland	–2.2
Canada	–3.5
Norway	–3.9
New Zealand	–7.1
Australia	**–8.7**

Spending on research and development

Tables 11.4 and 11.5 take Table 11.2 – total spending on research and development – and divide it between its two main components: spending by government and spending by business. Since 1981 spending by business has become the dominant source of R&D expenditure, accounting on average for almost 60% of total spending. And increased spending by business accounted for 85% of the increase in total spending during the period.

It is noteworthy that those countries where the business share of total R&D spending is below half are mainly well towards the bottom of Table 11.2's league table of total R&D spending: Austria (a business share of only 39%), Canada (45%), Australia (45%) and New Zealand (30%). In other words, in no case is government spending on R&D sufficient to give a country a high ranking on total spending.

In Australia, business's share of total R&D spending in 1981 was only 20%. It was so weak that although the country had the sixth highest level of government spending, it dropped to 15th place on total spending. By 1999 business's share had risen to 45%, involving a more than threefold increase as a proportion of GDP. Because the increase in government spending was only marginal, however, Australia remained at 15th place on total spending.

Table 11.6 shows the proportion of business R&D spending undertaken by small and medium-sized enterprises in 1999. It can be seen that, in Australia, these SMEs account for about half. Furthermore, other OECD figures show that firms with fewer than 100 employees account for more than a quarter of Australia's business R&D spending.

It is noteworthy that six of the G7 countries account for the bottom seven places in the league table. In other words, in big economies most R&D is done by big firms, whereas in the smaller economies most R&D is done by smaller firms. One reason for this may be differences in government incentives to research.

For example, in big military spenders such as the United States and France, military R&D is overwhelmingly contracted to large firms. But the difference may also point to differences in the business cultures of different countries regarding their attitude to research and their capacity to implement innovations.

Table 11.7 shifts the focus from R&D spending to a country's balance of trade in ICT goods such as computers, electronic components, telecommunications equipment and consumer electronics.

As the OECD has noted, these trade balances give a picture of countries' relative comparative advantage in ICT manufacturing. Ireland has established itself as a major producer and exporter of computers and components within the European Union. Finland and Sweden's strength is in the export of telecommmunications equipment such as mobile phones.

Not all countries with a deficit on trade in ICT goods are necessarily lacking a strong ICT industry. Many electronic components are imported (from Ireland, Japan and other parts of Asia), so that if a high proportion of the domestic industry's finished goods is sold to domestic industrial users, the country could nonetheless have greater imports than exports. This is the likely explanation of why the United States – the very home of the IT revolution, with a large and efficient ICT industry – is in deficit.

This explanation does not apply to New Zealand and Australia, however. These countries have very small ICT manufacturing industries, but heavy demand for ICT investment goods from their 'old economy' industries, thus leaving them with large import bills. Is this a bad position to be in? What matters to a country's prosperity is to extract the greatest gain in productivity from the IT revolution. The Australian authorities argue that in their case this will be achieved not by *making* ICT goods but by using them to raise the efficiency of all their other industries.

Table 12.1: Personal computers

PCs per 1000 population

	1988	1990	1995	2000	2001
United States	184	217	328	572	625
Sweden	59	105	249	507	561
Denmark	58	115	271	507	540
Switzerland	52	87	283	499	538
Australia	**103**	**150**	**276**	**470**	**516**
Norway	–	145	274	491	508
Canada	71	107	218	417	460
Netherlands	51	94	200	394	428
Finland	–	100	232	396	423
New Zealand	–	97	220	366	393
Ireland	54	86	183	359	391
Germany	67	90	178	336	382
United Kingdom	75	108	202	338	366
Japan	42	60	120	315	349
France	55	71	134	304	337
Austria	39	65	162	280	335
Belgium	51	88	178	224	233
Italy	21	36	84	180	195
Mean	65	99	211	386	421

Table 12.2: Cellular mobile telephones

Mobile phones per 1000 population

	1985	1990	1995	2000	2001
Italy	0	5	68	737	883
Austria	1	10	48	770	817
Norway	15	46	225	751	815
Finland	14	52	201	720	804
Sweden	9	54	227	717	790
Ireland	0	7	44	650	774
United Kingdom	1	19	98	727	770
Netherlands	0	5	35	673	767
Belgium	0	4	23	520	746
Denmark	9	29	158	631	738
Switzerland	0	18	63	643	728
Germany	–	4	46	586	682
France	0	5	22	493	605
New Zealand	0	16	101	408	599
Japan	1	7	93	526	588
Australia	**0**	**11**	**124**	**447**	**576**
United States	3	21	128	389	451
Canada	0	22	88	294	362
Mean	3	16	227	593	694

Table 12.3: Telecommunications revenue

Telecommunications revenue as % of GDP

	1985	2001
New Zealand	2.46	4.51
United Kingdom	2.36	3.89
Australia	**1.92**	**3.85**
Finland	1.50	3.51
United States	2.67	3.51
Sweden	1.78	3.44
Japan	1.58	3.43
Norway	1.91	3.24
Switzerland	2.15	3.19
Germany	1.60	3.10
Netherlands	1.45	3.06
Belgium	1.27	2.93
Canada	2.21	2.90
Austria	1.68	2.68
Denmark	1.49	2.61
Italy	1.48	2.48
Ireland	2.31	2.40
France	1.65	2.24
Mean	1.86	3.17

12 TELECOMMUNICATIONS AND COMPUTING
Growth in computing and telecommunications

Two of the most rapid changes in contemporary societies – the growth of personal computers and the growth of mobile phones – are documented in Tables 12.1 and 12.2.

Personal computers transformed the way people work, increasing productivity and convenience by a huge amount. They have become so much a part of everyday lives that it is almost impossible to imagine life without them. So it may be surprising to recall just how recent their invention and spread have been. They began in a small way in the early 1980s, but take-up was relatively slow. By 1988, the first year for which we have systematic data, they had established a firm foothold in offices and among some professionals. But as Table 12.1 shows, in the next 13 years their penetration rate in the selected countries increased almost sevenfold. In 1988 there was one PC for every 15 people; by 2001 there was one for every 2.5 people. That figure is depressed by two countries, Italy and Belgium, which lag a long way behind the others. In six countries, including Australia, there is one PC for every two people.

When looking at the growth recorded in Table 12.1, it should be remembered that the capacity of a personal computer in 1988 was only a fraction of what it was by 2001. It is a remarkable story of decreasing price and increasing power. The range of tasks for which people use PCs has increased, and they are the means by which most people connect to the other great popular computing innovation of recent times, the Internet (see Tables 12.4 to 12.7).

There are few more rapid social changes than the spread of personal computers, but Table 12.2 tops it. The cellular mobile telephone went from novelty to ubiquity in less than 15 years. In 1985, mobile services were only commonly used in the Scandinavian countries. By 1990 there was some mobile service in all the selected countries. In the next decade, however, their penetration rate

increased 37-fold, from one mobile phone for every 62 people to one mobile phone for every 1.4 people. Even in the year between 2000 and 2001, numbers again increased dramatically; 60% of 2001 mobile users had only been connected since 1999.

It would surprise most people that Australia is a relative laggard in this rapid diffusion, ranking third last among the selected countries, and only ahead of the two North American countries. While in Italy in 2001 there were almost nine mobile phones for every ten people, the Australian figure is only about two-thirds that.

Mobile phone technology developed first in the Scandinavian countries, and for a long time they were the world leaders in their use. It may be that the problems of keeping lines operating during the frozen winters spurred their growth. Then, in the early 1990s, the next phase of rapid adoption came in the English-speaking world. In recent years the most dramatic growth has been in some European countries – Italy, Austria and Ireland – which were relatively late adopters of the technology. Apparently this spurt owes a great deal to the introduction of pre-paid cards, which comprise over 50% of subscriptions in some countries (30% in Australia).

The growth of mobile phones and of the Internet fuelled substantial growth in the telecommunications sector. Table 12.3 shows that across these 18 countries, between 1985 and 2001 the sector's share of GDP went up by 70%. Australia was one of six countries where the share doubled. Other data shows that across the whole OECD spending on mobile phone services showed a tenfold increase in a decade, and by 2001 comprised 32% of total telecommunications revenue (26% in Australia). In sum telecommunications, with its mix of technological dynamism and very popular new services, was growing far more rapidly than the economy as a whole.

Table 12.4: Internet subscribers

Internet subscribers per 100 population

	1999	2001
Denmark	21.3	37.8
Sweden	23.0	32.0
Switzerland	12.6	30.7
Norway	15.6	27.4
United States	18.2	27.2
Netherlands	17.9	25.0
United Kingdom	12.4	22.7
Canada	20.2	22.6
Australia	**12.7**	**21.9**
Austria	6.0	20.6
Japan	8.4	18.9
Finland	10.9	18.3
Germany	17.5	18.1
New Zealand	14.0	16.7
Ireland	10.8	15.6
Italy	8.6	14.5
Belgium	10.6	13.9
France	5.1	11.8
Mean	13.7	22.0

Table 12.5: Internet hosts

Internet hosts per 1000 population

	1997	2001
United States	57	275
Canada	30	183
Finland	68	183
Sweden	35	177
Norway	41	130
Netherlands	22	119
New Zealand	30	106
Denmark	26	99
Australia	**31**	**91**
Austria	7	84
Switzerland	21	74
United Kingdom	16	70
Belgium	8	60
Germany	10	50
Japan	8	48
Italy	4	40
Ireland	13	35
France	5	27
Mean	24	103

Table 12.6: Websites

Websites per 1000 population

	2000	2002
Germany	22.0	84.7
Denmark	21.0	71.7
Norway	30.4	66.4
United Kingdom	24.2	64.2
United States	46.5	63.7
Netherlands	17.2	48.2
Canada	24.7	32.9
Sweden	19.3	28.0
Austria	10.8	22.6
Switzerland	16.9	20.5
New Zealand	10.6	15.3
Australia	**9.4**	**14.5**
Finland	7.2	13.3
Belgium	6.0	13.0
Italy	6.1	12.9
France	4.3	10.5
Ireland	3.3	5.8
Japan	1.6	2.9
Mean	15.6	32.8

Table 12.7: Secure servers

Number of secure servers per 100 000 population, July 1998 and 2002

	1998	2002
United States	5.4	37.5
New Zealand	2.4	25.5
Canada	3.1	25.0
Australia	**3.4**	**24.1**
Switzerland	2.1	21.5
United Kingdom	1.2	17.1
Ireland	1.5	15.1
Finland	1.3	14.3
Sweden	1.6	14.0
Denmark	0.8	12.3
Austria	1.2	11.7
Norway	1.2	11.7
Germany	0.6	9.7
Netherlands	0.8	8.3
Japan	0.3	5.6
Belgium	0.5	4.3
France	0.4	4.2
Italy	0.3	2.0
Mean	1.6	14.7

The Internet

The very idea of the Internet was unimaginable for most people a decade ago. Today it has transformed the way in which people seek information and entertainment. Across the OECD, in 1990 the number of Internet users was negligible; by the beginning of 2002, the number of Internet subscribers in some form or other was 250 million and the number of users was at least double that number.

Tables 12.4 to 12.7 document some of this revolution. On some aspects of online activity, we have no reliable measures. We have no reliable data, for example, on the amount of email communication (let alone any figures distinguishing wanted from unwanted emails) or of the number of hours people in different countries spend on line. The tables only give data from the late 1990s, but the recent growth they chart is still dramatic.

Table 12.4 shows that in the selected countries the number of Internet subscribers jumped by more than half between 1999 and 2001. Denmark tops the list with almost four in ten people being subscribers. At the other end is France with around one in eight. Australia is almost exactly at the mean with just over one in five being subscribers.

The number of Internet hosts is one of the most commonly used indicators of Internet development. A host includes any computer directly connected to the Internet that has an Internet address associated with it. Table 12.5 shows that in the four years between 1997 and 2001 the number of Internet hosts per 1000 population increased fourfold in the selected countries. The United States is the clear leader, followed by Canada and several Scandinavian countries. Australia is again around the middle of the field, somewhat below the mean. In Tables 12.4 to 12.6, four countries – France, Italy, Belgium and Ireland – consistently fall in the bottom third of the selected countries, reflecting their relative slowness in Internet development and usage.

While the number of Internet hosts gives an indication of the size of the Internet, the number of active websites provides information on countries' relative development of Internet content. Table 12.6 shows the number of websites per 1000 people doubled between 2000 and 2002. It also shows a huge range: the leader Germany has around 30 times the number of websites per head of population that Japan does. Japan, which in so many areas is a technological innovator, has been very slow to adopt some aspects of the Internet. Australia is above average on several other measures of Internet adoption but ranks substantially below average in the number of websites. In absolute terms, other data shows that the United States accounts for about half the websites in the OECD, with Germany providing almost another quarter.

The coming age of e-commerce has been frequently heralded in recent years. Its growth, together with increasing concerns about security, underpins the rapid recent growth in the number of secure servers. Secure servers provide a protocol for encrypted transmissions, and so protect the security of credit card transactions, a crucial step for the growth of Internet shopping. Table 12.7 shows that the number of secure servers increased eightfold in the four years between 1998 and 2002, and this growing platform suggests potential rapid growth in e-commerce. Japan, Belgium, France and Italy were again slow adopters of this technology, while the English-speaking countries, especially the United States, led the way. The five countries, including Australia, which top the table were also the leaders in 1998, but the gap between top and bottom has grown from five per 100 000 population to 35. Australia's National Office for the Information Economy reported that in 2001 Australia ranked second to the United States in readiness for e-business in a 60-country survey. Other data shows that the United States accounted for 70% of secure servers in the OECD in that year.

Table 12.8: Residential telephone charges

Cost of basket of telephone services for
residential users, August 2002
Includes international calls and calls
to mobiles

	US$PPP
Switzerland	380
Sweden	400
United Kingdom	418
Denmark	438
Norway	455
Canada	472
Netherlands	503
Ireland	511
Finland	525
Japan	525
Austria	526
Germany	541
France	555
United States	569
Belgium	572
Australia	**625**
New Zealand	677
Italy	680
Mean	521

Table 12.9: Internet charges

Cost of Internet access for 40 hours at evening
times at discounted rates, September 2002

	US$PPP
Canada	31
United Kingdom	33
France	34
United States	36
Finland	37
Australia	**39**
Germany	39
New Zealand	41
Austria	44
Sweden	44
Ireland	45
Switzerland	46
Denmark	49
Japan	49
Italy	50
Norway	52
Netherlands	53
Belgium	62
Mean	44

Table 12.10: Market share of established operators

Market share (proportion of minutes of traffic) 2001

	Long-distance	International
United States	35	32
Finland	37	50
Japan	43	53
Austria	45	45
Germany	60	50
Canada	64	59
Denmark	64	53
United Kingdom	64	47
Sweden	69	43
Australia	**71**	**51**
Switzerland	71	51
Italy	75	50
New Zealand	75	64
Netherlands	76	62
Norway	76	67
France	79	74
Belgium	85	51
Ireland	100	75
Mean	66	54

Irish figures are for 1998.

Table 12.11: Share of mobile phone market

Share of biggest and second biggest
operators in mobile market, 2001

	Biggest	Second
United States	23	17
United Kingdom	27	26
Canada	37	28
Germany	41	39
Denmark	42	24
Netherlands	42	26
Austria	43	34
Australia	**47**	**34**
France	48	34
Italy	48	32
Sweden	51	24
Belgium	54	33
Japan	57	17
New Zealand	57	43
Finland	58	29
Ireland	58	39
Switzerland	64	18
Norway	65	27
Mean	48	29

The telecommunications market

Just as telecommunications expanded its share of the total economy (Table 12.3), so with the growing use of the Internet and mobile phones households have expanded their spending. Across the OECD, the percentage of final consumption expenditure that households allocate to telecommunication increased from an average of 1.6% to 2.3% between 1991 and 2000. This was the most significant increase in any consumption area.

Because of the changing nature of services provided, it is not always easy to chart changing prices. Many technological changes should have made services much cheaper, and there is controversy over whether charges to consumers have sufficiently matched the decline in underlying costs.

While we cannot address such issues here, Table 12.8 shows very different charges among the selected countries. The OECD examined charges for a specified basket of services in August 2002 by converting national prices into $US and adjusting for their relative purchasing power. Switzerland and then Sweden have the cheapest services, and Italy the most expensive. Australia is third most expensive, with charges more than $100 greater than the average. This basket of charges includes international services (which are increasing in the volume of traffic but decreasing as a source of revenue as costs have come down) and calls from the fixed network to mobiles. The OECD also compiles a survey of charges for a basket of domestic services only. But Australia's position is the same on both.

The rank order for Internet charges in Table 12.9 is rather different, and here Australia is well within the cheaper half. Canada was the cheapest, Belgium the most expensive, with double the charges. The OECD comments that Australia, Canada, New Zealand and the United States, which have traditionally had unmetered local calls, were among the least expensive. Several other countries have moved in recent years towards unmetered access to the Internet.

It is notable that Internet costs only very weakly correlate with usage. France, for example, has relatively the lowest rate of subscribers but is second cheapest in its rates. Norway has relatively high costs but also a high rate of subscribers. On the other hand, Belgium and Italy combine high costs and low usage.

While the huge growth in telecommunications has been occurring, the sector has also been one of the areas with the most substantial deregulation. Historically, in all countries except the United States, telephone services were provided by a public monopoly. Many of these have now been at least partly privatised, while all countries have allowed some competition, sometimes highly restricted.

Some aspects of telecommunications lend themselves to competition more easily than others. The greatest obstacle has long been 'the last mile': the line connecting the customer's premises to the network, which nearly always remained a monopoly of the incumbent carrier. Efforts have been made to promote competition in services even though this infrastructure remains largely a natural monopoly.

The competition between incumbents and new entrants was also lopsided because of the former's existing infrastructure and its established customer base. It is not surprising then that incumbents have retained the dominant position in most national markets. Indeed the OECD observed that even before the dot.com bubble burst, and while profits were generally still high, taken as a whole, incumbents accounted for 100% of profits in telecommunications, with the new entrants in sum in deficit.

Table 12.10 shows that in long-distance and international calls, established operators still carry most of the traffic in the selected countries. (Their share of local traffic has remained even greater.) The mobile phone market is more suited to the development of competition, and Table 12.11 shows that there is more competition here. However, only in the United States do the two largest operators comprise less than half the mobile market. Australia rates near the middle on this measure of concentration, with the two largest operators taking 81% of the total market.

Table 12.12: Telecommunications employment

Telecommunications employment as a share (%) of national employment

	1991	2001	Change in employment 1980–2001 (1980 level = 100)
Netherlands	0.48	0.66	210
Denmark	0.69	0.83	177
Switzerland	0.53	0.62	152
Norway	0.92	0.99	126
Germany	0.61	0.66	124
Finland	0.81	1.06	120
United States	0.77	0.86	109
Canada	0.81	0.54	105
Austria	0.53	0.65	103
Belgium	0.70	0.72	99
France	0.71	0.68	98
United Kingdom	0.85	0.83	85
Ireland	1.18	0.99	83
Italy	0.49	0.43	73
Sweden	0.78	0.63	65
Australia	**1.06**	**0.85**	**64**
Japan	0.42	0.30	45
New Zealand	1.02	0.41	23
Mean	0.74	0.71	103

Table 12.13: Telecommunications revenue per employee

Revenue per employee ($US000)

	1991	2001
Japan	196	732
Switzerland	250	308
United States	169	298
Italy	173	296
New Zealand	99	283
Sweden	167	272
Canada	121	245
United Kingdom	116	241
Germany	126	236
Belgium	108	235
Norway	121	230
Netherlands	168	222
Austria	160	206
Denmark	132	188
France	131	180
Australia	**118**	**173**
Finland	112	169
Ireland	94	146
Mean	142	259

Table 12.14: Communication technology patents

Electric communication technique patents (filed in US, EU and Japan)
Total patents 1998–2000 per million population

Finland	53.5
Sweden	42.0
Japan	23.2
Netherlands	18.0
United States	13.1
Switzerland	9.2
United Kingdom	8.7
France	8.0
Belgium	7.3
Germany	5.2
Canada	4.6
Denmark	3.8
Austria	3.1
Australia	**2.3**
Ireland	1.3
Norway	1.3
Italy	1.0
New Zealand	0.8
Mean	11.5

Table 12.15: Broadband access

Broadband access per 100 population, mid-2001

Canada	6.2
Sweden	4.1
United States	3.2
Netherlands	2.7
Austria	2.4
Belgium	2.3
Denmark	2.3
Japan	1.1
Germany	1.0
Switzerland	0.8
Finland	0.7
Norway	0.7
Australia	**0.6**
France	0.6
New Zealand	0.5
Italy	0.4
United Kingdom	0.3
Ireland	0.0
Mean	1.6

Telecommunications employment and technological development

Growth in telecommunications revenue has been much greater than growth in telecommunications employment. Until the bursting of the dot.com bubble, beginning in 2000, the OECD area as a whole was recording growth in employment, but this overall trend masked great individual variations.

The last column of Table 12.12 compares employment in telecommunications in 1980 and 2001, with the 1980 level expressed as 100. It shows that half the countries increased employment in the period, and the other half decreased it. In the Netherlands, employment in telecommunications more than doubled, while in New Zealand it was reduced to a quarter of its previous level. Australia reduced employment by the third greatest extent.

The first two columns of Table 12.12 give the sector's share of total employment. Despite the radical reduction in employment in Australia, its share in the sector was still above the 18-nation mean in 2001. Finland, the home of Nokia, had the greatest share of employment in the sector, while Japan, which in 1991 already had the lowest percentage employed, further reduced that number.

This no doubt contributed to Japan topping Table 12.13 – revenue per employee – by a huge margin. In 2001, each Japanese telecommunications employee generated $US732 000 – more than double the second-ranking country, Switzerland. (The OECD makes no mention of whether the figures are adjusted for inflation or relative purchasing power.) Over the decade 1991 to 2001, measured by revenue per employee, the sector became very much more productive, almost doubly so. While Australia shared in the general trend, it remained near the bottom of the league table of revenue per employee. There was some tendency for incumbent carriers to have more revenue per employee. In Australia, for example, Telstra received $US240 000 per employee, compared with the sector as a whole of $US173 000.

One sign of the technological dynamism which has made the increasing revenue per employee possible is the number of new inventions and techniques. Table 12.14 gives the number of electric communication technique patents filed over three years per million population in each country. The OECD combines patents filed with the European Union, America and Japan. It could be argued therefore that this measure is biased against Australia and New Zealand. Nevertheless the differential pattern of inventiveness in the sector is clear. Finland and Sweden's reputation as innovators is confirmed by the data, with some distance back, Japan, the Netherlands and the United States also high on the list. Australia ranks fifth last.

This differential performance at least partly reflects differential investment. Among major telecommunications carriers, the mean amount of their expenditure devoted to research and development was 2.5%. The leader was the Japan's NTT with 3.4%. Telstra ranked equal bottom with 0.1%. In some countries, carriers are required to allocate a proportion of their revenue to research. The OECD notes that in the era of monopolies, many telecommunication carriers did significant amounts of fundamental research, while now the emphasis is much more on applying technologies.

The management of technological change is a continuing issue in the sector. In many ways it has been skilfully handled – an industry that was almost completely analogue in 1990 was almost completely digital a decade later. But there are many uncertainties. One innovation long predicted to revolutionise Internet possibilities is broadband access, though as Table 12.15 suggests this has been relatively slow to be rolled out. In 2001 only 1.6% of people in the selected countries had broadband. Canada led the way among the selected countries (though Korea leads globally). Sweden and the United States come next. Australia was one of nine countries where it was less than 1%. The best way to achieve it has been one issue, but the *Economist*, for example, has criticised conflicts of interest among the incumbents in not wanting to undercut their own profitable but slower services.

Table 13.1: Television sets
Number of television sets per 1000 people

	1970	1980	1990	2000
United States	395	562	772	854
Denmark	373	498	535	807
Australia	**216**	**381**	**522**	**738**
Japan	337	538	611	725
Canada	333	432	628	715
Finland	260	414	494	692
Norway	265	350	421	669
United Kingdom	324	401	433	653
France	236	370	539	628
Germany	362	439	525	586
Sweden	458	461	466	574
Switzerland	239	360	396	548
Belgium	285	387	446	541
Netherlands	238	399	482	538
Austria	254	391	473	536
New Zealand	280	329	443	522
Italy	223	390	420	494
Ireland	152	231	293	399
Mean	291	407	494	623

Table 13.2: Newspaper circulation
Daily newspapers sold per 1000 population

	1970	1980	1990	2000
Japan	511	567	587	577
Norway	397	463	610	573
Sweden	539	528	526	464
Finland	434	505	558	443
Switzerland	375	393	448	365
United Kingdom	453	417	388	320
Austria	312	351	351	309
Germany	–	–	305	289
Denmark	363	366	352	279
Netherlands	319	326	301	279
New Zealand	375	334	297	201
United States	296	270	245	197
Canada	197	221	209	166
Australia	**321**	**323**	**305**	**162**
Belgium	228	232	201	153
Ireland	232	229	169	151
France	238	192	208	142
Italy	144	101	105	110
Mean	337	342	343	288

Table 13.3: Concentration of newspaper ownership
Share of daily newspaper circulation of two leading corporations, 1990, %

Australia	**88**
Ireland	75
Austria	68
United Kingdom	58
Denmark	48
Norway	45
Finland	39
France	35
Netherlands	35
Belgium	34
Italy	32
Sweden	31
Germany	29
Switzerland	21
United States	16
Mean	44

No data on New Zealand, Japan or Canada.

Table 13.4: Television viewing
Mean hours of television watched by each person per week, 1990s

United Kingdom	28
United States	28
Italy	27
France	23
Germany	23
Ireland	23
Australia	**22**
Denmark	20
Netherlands	20
Belgium	19
Finland	18
Norway	18
Sweden	18
Mean	22

No data on Austria, Canada, Japan, New Zealand or Switzerland.

13 MEDIA
Television and newspapers

Television began in most of the selected countries in the decade or so after World War II, but although in many ways it is now a mature industry, the penetration of television sets continues to rise inexorably. Between 1970 and 2000 the number of television sets per 1000 people more than doubled across the 18 countries. In all except Italy and Ireland, there is at least one set for every two people.

If present trends continue, there will be more television sets than people in America before the year 2020. Australia ranked third in Table 13.1, despite the relatively high cost of purchasing a television there (Table 16.23). According to figures from the ratings company A. C. Nielsen, around 60% of Australian metropolitan households have two or more television sets, even though just over 20% comprise a single person. The increasing number of televisions seems mainly a matter of convenience because although good comparative data is lacking, it appears that the average amount of television viewing is not increasing.

While the upward trend towards purchasing more television sets is all but universal among these countries, newspaper circulation rates show much more variation, but the dominant trend is down. Fourteen of the 18 countries had lower penetration rates in 2000 than in 1970.

By far the most commonly cited source for comparisons of daily newspaper circulation is the *UNESCO Statistical Yearbook*, whose final edition appeared in 1999. At least for Australia, there was a growing discrepancy between the UNESCO figure and what one would expect using the major industry source, the Audit Bureau of Circulation. Tiffen, using Bureau figures, found that Australian metropolitan daily newspaper circulation (not all dailies, but all the biggest ones) dropped by 25% between 1987 and 1992. This is not surprising when you remember that seven of the 19 metropolitan dailies existing in 1987 closed in the late 1980s following a huge shake-up in media ownership. Metropolitan daily newspaper penetra-tion dropped from 220 per 1000 population to 154 between 1987 and 1992. Yet the UNESCO Australian figure for 1990 hardly records a blip. For reasons of both reliability and availability, the 2000 data in Table 13.2 is based on the market analysts Euromonitor.

All sources find a similar range of variations in newspaper circulation. The Japanese and three Scandinavian countries come at the top. The Italians are well behind all the other selected countries, with the French, Irish and Belgians next lowest. These relative standings have been broadly consistent over the three decades. The range between top and bottom became greater. Three of the top four countries – Japan, Norway and Finland – were the only ones in which circulation rates increased.

Between 1980 and 2000, Australia's daily newspaper circulation per 1000 population halved. This was a much sharper decline than in any of the other selected countries. This is mainly a consequence of so many newspapers closing, and of how demography and history have shaped Australia's newspaper market. It is also consistent with the comparatively low public approval of Australian newspapers recorded in Table 18.8.

It may or may not be related to Australia's distinctive pattern of press ownership. Table 13.3 gives the proportion of circulation accounted for by the two largest proprietors. As the number of newspaper titles has dwindled, the concentration of ownership has tended to increase. In Australia the two largest proprietors accounted for double the average of the selected countries.

Table 13.4 shows the average number of hours of television watched each week in the 1990s. The three Scandinavian countries, which come near the top of newspaper circulation, watch the least amount of television. The Italians and the French, near the bottom on newspaper circulation, come near the top, just behind the British and Americans on time spent watching television. Australia ranks in the middle, right on the mean of the 13 countries for which we have data.

Table 13.5: Television's institutional basis

Ownership of free-to-air terrestrial television broadcasting and number of channels (public + private) available in largest city

	1970		1999	
	System	Channels	System	Channels
Austria	Public	2	Public	2
Denmark	Public	3	Public	2
Netherlands	Public	2	Public	3
Switzerland	Public	3	Public	3
Belgium	Public	2	Mixed	2+2
France	Public	4	Mixed	2+3
Germany	Public	3	Mixed	3+3
Ireland	Public	2	Mixed	3+1
Italy	Public	2	Mixed	3+8
New Zealand	Public	1	Mixed	2+2
Norway	Public	2	Mixed	2+1
Sweden	Public	2	Mixed	2+1
Australia	**Mixed**	**1+3**	**Mixed**	**2+3**
Canada	Mixed	2+1	Mixed	2+2
Finland	Mixed	2+1	Mixed	3+2
Japan	Mixed	2+5	Mixed	2+5
United Kingdom	Mixed	2+1	Mixed	3+2
United States	Private	–	Mixed	–

Table 13.6: Sources of television revenue

Percentage of television revenue from following sources, 1999

	Advertising	Subscription	Public
Australia	**70**	**–**	**18**
Japan	67	14	19
Italy	59	11	23
United States	56	44	0
Belgium	55	12	34
United Kingdom	48	26	26
Austria	44	19	37
Netherlands	42	11	45
Germany	41	26	34
Ireland	41	43	16
New Zealand	41	34	6
Finland	39	14	47
France	39	37	24
Sweden	35	33	32
Canada	34	48	12
Switzerland	30	–	67
Norway	29	–	66
Denmark	27	26	47
Mean	44	26	31

Table 13.7: Television's share of advertising revenue, %

	1980	1999
Italy	26	53
Japan	–	43
Belgium	8	40
United States	–	37
Australia	**33**	**35**
France	14	34
United Kingdom	27	33
Ireland	29	26
Austria	30	24
Germany	10	23
Finland	15	21
Sweden	0	20
Denmark	0	19
Netherlands	7	17
Norway	0	13
Switzerland	8	–
Mean	15	29

No data on New Zealand or Canada. Australian figure is for 1994.

Television

In none of the selected countries did broadcasting (first radio and later television) develop as just another industry where market forces could reign. Partly this was because of technological necessity, but even more centrally it was because of the cultural peculiarities and political power of broadcasting. There was an almost universal belief that a free market could not operate in television, that it would produce rubbish – with no standards, no local content, no quality drama, no children's programs, no quality news or current affairs. And last but not least, no profits.

Whereas in none of the countries is there any government-owned newspaper, only in America was there no publicly owned television channel. Indeed Table 13.5 shows that in nearly every mainland European country a government monopoly prevailed. Everywhere television's development was subject to considerable regulation.

In five countries a mixed system of public and private prevailed. But their mix and traditions differed considerably. In Britain, television began as a BBC monopoly, and then the private Independent Television Network began in 1954. Later a second BBC channel was added, so that the public channels outnumbered the private 2:1. In addition, there was not one single owner for the private channel to be their fiefdom, but a complicated governance arrangement and stringent regulations about its operation and programming. In Australia, the private channels were able to be fully controlled by particular corporations, and initially outnumbered the public channel 2:1, which expanded to 3:1 less than a decade after television began in 1956.

Table 13.5 also records that despite the different beginnings, there was considerable convergence in the last decades of the 20th century, with nearly all countries moving towards a multi-channel environment and increased commercial participation. By 1999 terrestrial free-to-air television remained a public monopoly in only four countries, and as will be seen in Tables 13.11 to 13.13, these countries had moved considerably towards a multi-channel environment via other means

of delivering services (including from across national borders).

There are three possible means of financing television, and all have their disadvantages. The first, and most common in the English-speaking countries, is by advertising. The implicit equation is that viewers pay for the TV programming by buying the products advertised. This can occasionally produce subservience to advertisers, but the more fundamental objection is that depending on market structure, it produces no institutional incentives towards excellence or catering to minority audiences.

The second means of financing is through the government, either by licence fee or from consolidated revenue. Especially when there is a government monopoly, this method has the potential for political subservience. Its basic problem is the lack of relationship between the funding mechanism and the audience. There are no performance-based incentives for ensuring responsiveness to public taste.

The third means is by subscription. This is the most honest in the sense that there is a direct relationship between audience and product. For a long time it was not technically possible. When it became so, its key disadvantage was that viewers had become accustomed to thinking of television viewing as free.

Table 13.6 shows that there are considerable variations in how television is financed in the selected countries. In Switzerland and Norway, the public purse was still the principal means. In Canada and the United States, pay TV services were approaching half of total revenue. Australia topped the rankings in terms of the proportion of revenue coming from advertising, testimony also to its relative underdevelopment of pay TV and public funding.

In some countries where television began as a public monopoly financed by government, there was no television advertising. But television is now a major medium for advertising in most countries (Table 13.7), and its share of the advertising dollar has been increasing in most.

Table 13.8: Public broadcasting
Public broadcasters' revenue and audience shares, 1999, %

	Share total TV revenue	Share audience
Netherlands	93	36
Austria	80	65
Norway	71	40
Denmark	66	68
New Zealand	66	–
Finland	64	44
Belgium	60	40
Italy	49	48
Germany	47	42
United Kingdom	41	49
Ireland	41	51
Sweden	40	47
France	31	42
Australia	**24**	**16**
Japan	19	–
Canada	19	10
Switzerland	–	34
Mean	51	43

Table 13.9: Public broadcasters' funding levels
Public broadcasters' revenue, 1999, US$

	Revenue per capita	Public funding per capita
Denmark	117	76
Austria	96	47
Norway	86	80
United Kingdom	83	57
Switzerland	83	56
Finland	73	69
New Zealand	66	6
Ireland	66	28
Germany	64	49
Netherlands	58	39
Sweden	51	48
Belgium	47	31
Italy	47	22
Japan	44	44
France	43	23
Australia	**29**	**23**
Canada	25	16
Mean	63	42

Table 13.10: Sources of funds for public broadcasting
Percentage of public broadcasters' funds from following sources, 1999

	Public	Commercial	Other
Japan	100	0	0
Finland	95	0	5
Norway	93	0	7
Sweden	93	7	0
Australia	**80**	**0**	**20**
Germany	77	17	6
United Kingdom	69	30	0
Netherlands	67	23	11
Switzerland	67	30	3
Belgium	65	30	5
Denmark	65	28	7
Canada	64	31	5
France	54	46	0
Austria	49	50	1
Italy	47	41	11
Ireland	43	57	0
New Zealand	9	63	28
Mean	67	27	6

Public broadcasting

As we saw in Table 13.5, in all the selected countries except the United States, television began with a public broadcaster playing a central role, and indeed, in most of the countries, having a monopoly role. As Table 13.8 shows, taking television as a whole, none of them still enjoys a complete monopoly, though in seven countries they still command most of television revenue.

Public broadcasters are defined most simply as those owned by the government, though many of them, like the ABC and BBC, have independence built into their role and operations. But as Tables 13.9 and 13.10 show, this does not necessarily mean that government funding is their only source of finance. As Table 13.9 shows on average, two-thirds of their funding comes from the public purse ($42 out of an average of $63), and as Table 13.10 shows overall, these public broadcasters receive an average of a quarter of their income from commercial sources. For only two, Ireland and New Zealand, was advertising their major income source.

Australia's ABC is among a minority which receive negligible income from advertising. But the ABC's diversification is shown by its 20% coming from 'other' sources, which includes program sales, renting equipment, and such activities as ABC Books and ABC shops. There are problems in the construction of this table. Advertising is not allowed on domestic BBC services, so its 30% of revenue from that source seems anomalous, and must also include the sales and so on included in the ABC's 'other' column. Other aspects of the OECD data are also not as precise as they could be. Sometimes it seems that both ABC and SBS are counted as public broadcasters, and other times just the ABC. Similarly, in Table 13.8, for Australia and nine other countries the public broadcasters' share of television revenue includes money that goes to those organisations for radio and other services as well. This has the effect of inflating their apparent share of television revenue. The

ABC's share of such revenue would certainly drop to less than 20%, probably down to 16%, if only television's share of the total ABC budget were included.

Taken together, the tables show that the ABC has a more marginal role in Australian television than most of the other public broadcasters in their countries. In Table 13.8 it ranks third lowest and in Table 13.9 second last. In both cases it received less than half the average of the others. In terms of dollars per head of population, for example, the BBC's budget was about 2.5 times the ABC's.

This points to one problem in funding public broadcasters. There is no objective formula about what level they should be funded at. According to the ABC, in real terms its budget in 2003 was about 70% of what it had been in 1985, as successive governments cut it for macro-budgetary and political reasons. As the ABC has been forced to contract, the commercial media have been expanding. ANU economist Professor Glenn Withers has estimated that the average hour of ABC television costs 42% as much as the average hour on commercial television, while for radio the equivalent figure is 40%. In 1981, the two figures were 71% and 48% respectively.

Tables 13.8 to 13.10 do not address the distinctive mandate of public compared with commercial broadcasters. An international report by the consultancy firm McKinsey & Company for the BBC, found three patterns among public broadcasters. In some countries, such as Italy and New Zealand, where they relied mainly on advertising income, they commanded substantial audience share, but their programming mix was indistinguishable from commercial broadcasters. In others, such as the United Kingdom, Sweden and Germany, they successfully combined substantial audience share with distinctive programming. The ABC was in a third group which had maintained their distinctiveness in programming, but poorer funding meant they commanded smaller audience shares.

Table 13.11: Means of receiving television

Percentage of households receiving television via different delivery technologies, 1999

	Terrestrial only	Cable	Satellite
Belgium	0	96	4
Denmark	1	57	42
Switzerland	3	87	10
Netherlands	6	90	5
Germany	16	53	31
United States	21	67	12
Austria	25	35	40
Canada	25	69	6
Sweden	29	50	21
Norway	32	45	22
Japan	34	26	41
Finland	41	44	15
Ireland	41	50	9
United Kingdom	68	12	21
France	71	12	17
Australia	**78**	**16**	**6**
Italy	90	0	10
New Zealand	92	0	8
Mean	38	45	18

Table 13.12: Pay TV

Percentage of households subscribing to pay TV service, 1999, and % of subscribers for each means of delivery

	Pay TV	Cable	Satellite	Terrestrial
Belgium	118	92	0	8
Norway	102	64	36	0
Switzerland	97	100	0	0
Netherlands	90	99	1	0
United States	77	87	13	0
Canada	74	94	6	0
Denmark	72	80	20	0
Japan	65	40	60	0
Sweden	64	78	22	0
Ireland	60	82	18	0
Germany	55	96	4	0
Finland	49	91	10	0
France	44	26	25	48
Austria	35	100	0	0
United Kingdom	31	39	55	6
Australia	**22**	**75**	**25**	**0**
New Zealand	19	0	28	72
Italy	11	4	49	47
Mean	60	69	21	10

Percentage of pay TV can exceed 100% because one household can subscribe to more than one service.

Table 13.13: Cable TV subscribers

Cable TV subscribers per 1000 population

	1990	1995	2000
Netherlands	292	377	388
Belgium	338	358	373
Switzerland	271	329	358
Denmark	88	228	265
Canada	262	266	259
United States	220	239	252
Germany	111	193	247
Sweden	173	212	199
Finland	134	160	184
Norway	112	155	184
Ireland	111	133	177
Japan	55	88	147
Austria	60	93	123
Australia	**0**	**0**	**68**
United Kingdom	3	24	57
France	9	32	45
New Zealand	0	0	4
Italy	0	0	1
Mean	124	160	185

New media and pay television

Television can be received through three principal means of transmission. Everywhere in the developed world, it began as a terrestrial service. Transmitters sending out electromagnetic waves to antennas receiving the signals allowed viewers to watch the pictures in their own homes. Terrestrial services are received only over a limited area and the possible number of services is limited by the width of the radio spectrum.

Next came the development of cable, originating in America as a way of overcoming problems with terrestrial signals. As cable technology has developed further, the number of channels that can be carried is enormous, and consistent, high-quality reception is assured. Its great drawback is the initial cost of laying out the cable, and it is most suited to densely populated areas. It is the only one of the technologies that allows two-way communication.

Last came satellite. Geo-stationary satellites can transmit a television signal over a very wide footprint: the one satellite may allow a service to many countries. This taming of geography is the satellite's principal virtue, and with digitalisation, the one satellite can provide many channels (though not as many as cable). Installation of satellite dishes to receive the signal can sometimes be costly, and depending on topography, surrounding buildings and trees, may be difficult.

Although cable and satellite are associated with pay TV services, there is no necessary connection between means of transmission and sources of revenue. Now that the technology exists for encrypted terrestrial transmission, any means of delivery can in theory be associated with any means of financial support.

Tables 13.11 to 13.13 show great variations between the selected countries in the way television has developed. By 1999, in four countries – Belgium, Denmark, Switzerland and the Netherlands – only a very small proportion of households still received television, mainly via a terrestrial signal. In contrast, in Italy and New Zealand more than 90% of households still received television only in this way, and cable TV remained undeveloped. Australia had the third smallest proportion receiving television via cable and satellite.

In all three tables, the same five countries – Italy, New Zealand, Australia, the United Kingdom and France – ranked in the bottom third as the slowest to embrace the newer means of delivery. The reasons may vary between the countries. Possible factors include governmental or commercial reluctance to invest in the new infrastructure, policy decisions restricting the development of new services, or a lack of content offerings attractive to the public. In Italy and Australia at least, the main beneficiaries of the slowness of new television services to penetrate have been the commercial proprietors of free-to-air services. The political influence of media moguls such as Silvio Berlusconi and Kerry Packer was surely part of the reason for those countries' relative inertia regarding new media.

There are also differences in the relative importance of cable and satellite. As might have been predicted, cable has been most important in geographically small and densely populated countries such as the Netherlands, Belgium and Switzerland. These countries were also prompted to develop cable because of spectrum congestion in terrestrial television. On the other hand, similarly densely populated Japan and the United Kingdom gave priority to satellite. In Japan's case, the desire to reach the whole population in its mountainous terrain may have been the reason. But the decision of the Thatcher Government in the 1980s to allow the development of satellite (which came to be dominated by Rupert Murdoch's company), but not to invest in cable, slowed the development of new media there. Cable services developed early in the United States and Canada, but given their geographic size, satellite has been predicted to become more prominent in their future media landscapes.

Table 14.1: Age at first marriage

Mean age at first marriages, females and males, 1980 and 1999

	Females 1980	Females 1999*	Males 1980	Males 1999*
Sweden	26.0	30.4	28.6	32.9
Denmark	24.6	30.1	27.2	32.5
France	23.0	29.1	25.1	31.2
Australia	**23.1**	**28.6**	**25.4**	**30.6**
Norway	23.6	28.6	–	31.1
Finland	24.4	28.3	26.5	30.5
Netherlands	23.2	28.3	25.5	30.7
Germany	22.9	28.2	25.7	30.9
Ireland	24.7	28.2	27.1	30.0
Switzerland	25.0	28.2	–	30.8
Austria	23.2	27.9	25.9	30.3
United Kingdom	23.7	27.7	25.2	29.8
Canada	24.3	27.4	–	29.0
Japan	25.9	27.3	28.7	30.0
Italy	23.9	27.1	27.1	30.0
New Zealand	22.2	27.1	24.8	29.2
Belgium	22.3	26.6	24.3	28.9
United States	–	25.0	–	26.0
Mean	23.9	28.0	26.2	30.2

Ranked according to age of females at first marriage, 1999.

Table 14.2: Divorce

Number of divorces per 100 marriages

	1970	1980	1990	2000 *
Ireland	–	–	–	8
Italy	4	4	9	13
Switzerland	14	31	28	26
Japan	9	18	22	33
Denmark	26	51	44	38
Netherlands	8	29	30	39
Norway	12	30	46	40
France	10	24	37	41
Germany	18	28	30	44
Canada	16	33	42	45
Australia	**11**	**36**	**35**	**46**
New Zealand	12	27	39	47
Austria	20	29	36	50
United States	33	50	48	51
Finland	15	32	53	53
United Kingdom	13	38	44	53
Sweden	30	53	48	54
Belgium	9	22	32	60
Mean	16	31	37	41

Table 14.3: Duration of marriage at divorce

Mean number of years married when divorced, 1999

Germany	5.2
United States	7.2
Australia	**7.8**
United Kingdom	7.8
Denmark	9.8
Austria	10.1
Sweden	10.2
Japan	10.3
Norway	10.5
Belgium	11.2
France	11.6
Finland	11.7
Netherlands	11.7
New Zealand	12.2
Switzerland	12.2
Canada	13.7
Italy	13.7
Mean	10.4

No data for Ireland.

14   FAMILY
Marriage

Family life, and especially marriage, is undergoing rapid and profound changes, which are partly reflected in Tables 14.1 and 14.2.

Table 14.1 shows that young people are increasingly delaying marriage. Even in the years between 1980 and 1999, the mean age at first marriage rose by around four years. In every single country, and among both sexes, the mean age at the time of first marriage rose. In Australia, the age at first marriage edged steadily downward over the decades until reaching its youngest point in 1971 (23.8 years for men and 21.4 years for women), but has been climbing since then. Moreover, compared with the previous generations' glacial movement towards ever younger marriage, the trend towards older marriage has been very rapid.

It has not been possible to obtain good longitudinal comparative data on one reason for the increasing tendency to delay marriage: the growing trend towards cohabitation. In Australia, the proportion of all heterosexual couples who were cohabiting rose from 1% in 1971 to 6% in 1986 and 10% in 1996. Moreover, cohabiting before marriage has now become the norm. Of people getting married in 1975, only 16% had cohabited, while in 2000 71% said they had.

The other major change in the selected countries has been towards the more frequent dissolution of marriages. Divorce rates rose by more than 2.5 times in the last three decades of the 20th century. However, countries differed enormously in their divorce rates in 2000: Italy and Ireland had fewer than 20 divorces per 100 marriages, while six countries had divorce rates of 50 or greater. In addition, we find very different trajectories. In several countries – for example Belgium, the United Kingdom, Austria, New Zealand – the pattern is one of steadily rising divorce rates up to the year 2000. In others, which previously led in the frequency of divorce, rates have stabilised. In 1980, the United States, Sweden and Denmark

far exceeded the others in their divorce rates, and were the only three countries with rates higher than 50. Since then all three have stabilised or declined.

In Australia, there was little change between 1980 and 1990, but a substantial increase again in the 1990s. Like Germany, the United States and United Kingdom, Table 14.3 shows that Australian marriages tend to result in divorce relatively early, with a mean duration of less than eight years.

Many explanations have been given for rising divorce rates, but the starting point must be changes in the legal availability and ease of divorce. In Australia, for example, before the *Family Law Act* introduced 'no fault' divorce, one partner had to be guilty in order to secure a divorce. This was both an expensive and potentially very messy process. Once the new Act came in to operation in 1976, there was an immediate surge in the number of divorces.

Similarly, before the increase in women's employment gave them greater financial independence, divorce was not a practical prospect for many women even if the marital relationship was an unhappy or violent one.

Beyond the legal and financial changes, many have hypothesised about more emotional and moral changes in the meaning of marriage and intimacy. It is impossible to jump from the quantitative data in the tables to the personal meanings which might lie behind it. However, it should also be noted that divorcees in all these countries tend to have a relatively high rate of marrying again. For example, in 1911 in only one in ten Australian marriages had either partner been married before (and the majority of these had been widowed). By the year 2000, one in three marriages involve at least one of the partners being married for the second time, following a previous divorce. High re-marriage rates suggest that disillusion with one particular marriage does not mean disillusion with marriage as such.

Table 14.4: Mother's age at birth of first child
Mean age, years

	1970	1980	1990	2000*
United States	25.4	25.7	26.3	24.9
Austria	–	24.6	25.0	26.3
Canada	23.1	24.6	26.4	26.8
Norway	23.6	25.2	25.5	26.9
Finland	24.4	25.7	26.8	27.4
Australia	**23.2**	**25.3**	**27.6**	**27.5**
Belgium	24.3	24.5	26.5	27.5
Denmark	23.7	24.6	26.4	27.7
Ireland	25.3	24.9	26.3	27.8
Japan	25.6	26.4	27.0	27.9
Sweden	25.9	25.5	26.3	27.9
Germany	24.0	25.2	26.9	28.0
Italy	25.1	25.1	26.9	28.0
Netherlands	24.3	25.6	27.6	28.6
France	23.8	24.9	27.0	28.7
Switzerland	25.1	26.4	27.6	28.7
United Kingdom	23.9	25.1	27.3	29.1
New Zealand	23.4	24.9	27.6	29.9
Mean	24.4	25.2	26.7	27.8

Table 14.5: Births outside marriage
Percentage of births to unmarried mothers

	1970	1980	1990	2000*
Japan	1	1	1	1
Italy	2	4	7	9
Belgium	3	4	12	17
Switzerland	4	5	6	20
Germany	7	12	15	23
Netherlands	2	4	11	25
Canada	10	13	26	28
Australia	**8**	**12**	**22**	**29**
Austria	13	18	24	31
Ireland	3	5	14	32
United States	11	18	28	33
Finland	6	13	25	39
United Kingdom	8	12	28	40
France	7	11	30	41
New Zealand	14	22	34	42
Denmark	11	33	46	45
Norway	7	15	39	49
Sweden	19	40	47	55
Mean	7	13	23	33

Table 14.6: Abortions
Abortions per 100 live births, 1997

	1997
United States	38
Australia	**36**
Sweden	34
Japan	29
Canada	28
Finland	26
Austria	25
Denmark	25
Italy	25
New Zealand	24
United Kingdom	24
Norway	23
France	21
Germany	14
Netherlands	11
Belgium	10
Ireland	10
Mean	24

Table 14.7: Lone mothers and fathers
Lone mother and father families as % of all families with children, mid-1990s

	Lone mothers	Lone fathers
Italy	5.3	1.1
Switzerland	8.9	–
Ireland	9.5	1.1
Belgium	9.7	1.2
Japan	10.0	1.8
France	11.4	1.8
Austria	13.4	1.9
Netherlands	13.5	2.4
Finland	13.9	1.9
Canada	14.3	–
Sweden	15.3	2.7
Australia	**15.5**	**2.3**
Germany	16.0	3.0
Denmark	16.2	2.4
Norway	18.7	1.9
United Kingdom	19.1	1.8
New Zealand	20.5	4.0
United States	25.0	3.9
Mean	14.6	2.2

Children

Just as the selected countries are undergoing rapid change in the social norms surrounding marriage, so the changes to do with having children are just as dramatic. In the year 2000, as Table 1.8 showed, in 17 of the 18 countries each woman on average had less than two children, with an 18-nation mean of 1.6 children per woman.

Table 14.4 shows how women are delaying having children. Between 1970 and 2000 the 18-nation mean for mother's age at the time of her first birth rose by more than three years, from 24.4 to 27.8 years. Just as the United States was the only country where each woman has on average more than two children, so it was the only country where the mean age at first birth was under 25.

Australia fell very close to the mean in 2000, one of nine countries where the average was between 27.4 and 28.0 years. In contrast, in 1970 Australian women ranked second youngest at the birth of their first child, mean age 23.2, just behind Canada and ahead of New Zealand. But Australia (and even more so New Zealand and the United Kingdom) has seen a greater than average trend towards later childbirth.

Changes in social attitudes are also apparent in the way the proportion of births to unmarried mothers rose almost fivefold in the same 30 years (Table 14.5). In Sweden more than half of all births now occur outside marriage, and in Norway and Denmark the figure is almost half. The rise is substantial in all countries except Japan, while Italy is the only other country where the proportion of births outside marriage is still less than 10%. Especially when combined with the trend towards mothers having their first child at a later age, it is likely that for many women it is a deliberate choice to delay marriage until after the birth.

Table 14.7 shows that on average in these countries in the 1990s around one in six families with children had just one parent. There are substantial differences between the countries, ranging from 29% in the United States to 6% in Italy, with the Australian figure of 18% just above the mean. But in all of them, it is far more common for children in single-parent families to live with their mother than with their father, on average by a ratio of seven to one.

It would, however, be wrong to jump too directly from the figures in Table 14.5 to Table 14.7. British figures (likely to be repeated elsewhere) show that three-quarters of births outside marriage were jointly registered by both parents, and most of them were living together. Most single-parent families result from later marriage break-ups.

Explaining these trends involves many potential factors, but clearly one relevant consideration is the increased control women have over their own fertility. It was not possible to get systematic data on contraception. While there is data on the contemporary prevalence of legal abortion, comparative trend data is complicated because of variations and changes in its legal availability, and the impossibility of getting reliable data on the number of illegal abortions.

The data on abortions in Table 14.6 shows that the average across these 18 countries was around one abortion for every four live births in 1997. The United States and Australia had the highest rates. Abortion rates did not correlate strongly with any of the other tables about childbirth. To the extent that it was possible to get trend data for several European countries, it showed most of them having either stable or falling abortion rates between 1980 and 1999. Some countries, such as the Netherlands, showed a considerable decline, perhaps because of better contraceptive practices.

Table 14.8: Births to adolescent women

Births to 15 to 19-year-old women per 1000 women in age group per year

	1970	1998
Japan	4.4	4.6
Switzerland	22.6	5.5
Netherlands	22.6	6.3
Sweden	33.9	6.5
Italy	27.4	6.6
Denmark	32.4	8.1
Finland	32.2	9.2
France	36.8	9.3
Belgium	31.2	9.9
Norway	44.6	12.4
Germany	55.5	13.1
Austria	58.2	14.0
Australia	**50.9**	**18.4**
Ireland	16.9	18.7
Canada	42.1	20.2
New Zealand	64.3	29.8
United Kingdom	49.4	30.8
United States	69.2	52.1
Mean	38.6	15.3

Table 14.9: Proportion of adolescent women having a child

Percentage of 20-year-old women who had a child in their teens, 1990s

Japan	2
Switzerland	2
Italy	3
Netherlands	3
Sweden	3
Belgium	4
Denmark	4
Finland	4
France	4
Norway	5
Germany	6
Austria	7
Ireland	8
Australia	**9**
Canada	10
United Kingdom	13
New Zealand	14
United States	22
Mean	7

Table 14.10: Adolescent women and motherhood

Births to mothers aged 15–19 as % of all births

	1970	1980	1990	1994
United States	17.3	15.3	12.6	12.8
New Zealand	–	10.9	7.9	7.4
Canada	11.8	8.7	5.9	6.1
United Kingdom	–	7.0	6.2	5.0
Australia	**11.0**	**7.6**	**5.7**	**4.9**
Ireland	–	3.7	3.9	3.9
Austria	9.8	9.5	4.5	3.4
Germany	9.3	7.5	3.4	2.7
Italy	4.4	5.0	2.4	–
Norway	7.7	5.8	3.1	2.3
Belgium	5.7	4.7	2.2	–
France	6.5	4.7	2.5	1.9
Finland	7.7	4.2	1.9	1.7
Sweden	6.4	3.2	2.1	1.6
Denmark	6.3	3.9	2.6	1.6
Japan	1.0	0.9	1.4	1.4
Netherlands	3.9	2.3	1.6	1.2
Switzerland	3.6	2.4	1.2	0.9
Mean	7.5	6.0	4.0	3.7

Table 14.11: Adolescent mothers and marriage

Percentage of adolescent mothers married, 1990s

Switzerland	91
Japan	86
Italy	55
Belgium	42
Germany	39
Netherlands	35
Austria	31
Denmark	23
United States	21
Finland	18
Sweden	18
Canada	17
France	15
Norway	10
United Kingdom	10
Australia	**9**
New Zealand	6
Ireland	4
Mean	29

Ranked according to proportion in 1994, assuming Italy and Belgium stayed at their 1990 level.

Births to adolescent mothers

Tables 14.8 to 14.11 offer different perspectives on teenage women and motherhood. As Table 14.4 documented, the average age at which women first give birth increased in the last three decades of the 20th century. Parallel to that trend, Table 14.8 shows that the birth rate among adolescent women more than halved in the same period. Similarly, Table 14.10 shows that while births to teenage mothers were always a fairly low proportion of all births, they have become even lower: the 18-nation mean halved between 1970 and 1994.

Tables 14.8 and 14.9 both show that adolescent women are much more likely to become mothers in the English-speaking countries than in Europe or Japan. Table 14.8 gives the birth rate – the number of children born to adolescent women per 1000 adolescent women each year – while Table 14.9 gives the proportion of women who become mothers while still adolescents. The United States heads both tables, with an adolescent birth rate of 52 per 1000, while more than one in five American women became mothers by the age of 20. This is substantially higher than the other English-speaking countries, and more than three times higher than the average of the European countries in the table. Only one in 50 Japanese and Swiss women are mothers by the age of 20.

A major reason for America's contemporary pre-eminence was its relative lack of change between 1970 and 1998. Japan was consistently low, and Ireland remained roughly the same, but of the other countries the United States showed proportionately the least decline (down 17 percentage points). In contrast, the Austrian rate declined by 44 percentage points, the German by 42 and the Norwegian by 32. While Australian adolescent motherhood rates are still just above the 18-country mean, they have declined more strongly than the common trend, and much more strongly than the other English-speaking countries.

Table 14.5 shows (by transposition) that two-thirds of women were married when giving birth, while Table 14.11 shows that more than two-thirds of adolescent mothers were unmarried at the time of giving birth. Table 14.11 shows an extraordinary range: from 91% of Swiss teenage mothers being married to only 4% in Ireland. The marriage rates of teenage mothers show some relationship, though an imperfect one, to rates of teenage motherhood. The three countries with the lowest motherhood rate are the three with the highest marriage rate, while some but not all of the English-speaking countries have the highest rates of unmarried teenage mothers. In particular, New Zealand and Australia have respectively the second and third lowest marriage rates, with less than one in ten of teenage mothers being married.

As in all data on the family, it is dangerous to leap from quantitative patterns to qualitative meaning. Often of course births to adolescent women are part of a fulfilling and valuable life for both mother and child. But as the OECD has argued, 'teenage births are often seen as a problem because they tend to be strongly associated with a wide range of disadvantages for mothers, children and society in general.' In so far as teenage motherhood is associated with unintended pregnancy and unstable parenting relationships, it can be associated with future social problems. Moreover, it tends to be higher among disadvantaged groups, and if it is associated with young women giving up educational and occupational opportunities, it can be part of a syndrome of perpetuating disadvantage. According to UNICEF, across the countries of the European Union, women who gave birth as teenagers were twice as likely to be living in poverty.

Simply looking at teenage motherhood rates is too crude and generalised a means for examining such problems. However, if the reduction in teenage motherhood rates is associated with greater opportunity and autonomy for young women in their life choices, the trend in Table 14.8 is a heartening one.

Table 14.12: Income of different family types

Average disposable incomes of different family types as a % of overall average disposable income of working age population in each country, mid-1990s, where that average is set at 100

	Single adult with children	Single adult, no children	Two adults with children	Two adults, no children
Sweden	72	74	101	131
Australia	**57**	**92**	**93**	**129**
United Kingdom	51	92	93	127
United States	49	99	93	127
Belgium	69	126	85	125
Netherlands	55	80	93	123
Canada	57	85	94	120
Italy	52	93	91	118
Norway	67	73	99	117
Denmark	59	75	100	115
France	66	94	97	113
Finland	76	75	100	112
Germany	57	90	95	112
Austria	87	85	98	110
Mean	62	88	95	120

Ranked according to relative income of two adults, no children.
No data for Ireland, Japan, New Zealand, Switzerland.

Table 14.14: Mothers with young children and working

Percentage of mothers in employment and with at least one child under 6

	1989	2001
Sweden	85	76
Denmark	–	74
Norway	65	73
Austria	67	66
Belgium	70	66
Netherlands	61	66
New Zealand	32	61
United States	54	61
Finland	–	59
France	56	59
United Kingdom	56	56
Germany	51	53
Italy	46	47
Australia	**42**	**45**
Ireland	25	44
Japan	36	34
Mean	53	59

No data for Canada or Switzerland.

Table 14.13: Women's employment and motherhood

Percentage of women aged 25–54 in employment according to their number of children, 2000

	No children	One child	Two+ children
Sweden	82	81	82
Norway	83	83	78
Denmark	79	88	77
Finland	79	79	74
Belgium	66	72	69
Canada	77	75	68
Austria	76	76	66
Switzerland	84	76	66
United States	79	76	65
Netherlands	75	70	63
United Kingdom	80	73	62
France	74	74	59
New Zealand	81	67	59
Germany	77	70	56
Australia	**68**	**55**	**43**
Italy	53	52	42
Ireland	66	51	41
Mean	75	72	63

Ranked according to employment rate of mothers with two or more children.
No data on Japan.

Table 14.15: Mothers and part-time work

Percentage of employed women working part-time, 2000, according to their number of children

	None	One child	Two+ children
Netherlands	38	73	83
Switzerland	34	58	67
Australia	**41**	**54**	**63**
United Kingdom	24	47	63
Germany	24	45	60
New Zealand	21	38	51
Ireland	17	37	46
Belgium	29	35	46
Austria	17	34	44
Norway	25	34	41
Italy	20	27	34
France	20	24	32
Canada	17	23	31
United States	10	16	24
Sweden	15	17	22
Denmark	19	13	16
Finland	8	9	14
Mean	22	34	43

No data on Japan.

Mothers and work

It may be, as the romantic adage claims, that two can live as cheaply as one, but it is certainly not the case that four can live as cheaply as two. The National Centre for Social and Economic Modelling calculated that the total cost in 2003 dollars for the average Australian family to raise two children from birth to age 20 is $448 000.

Table 14.12 shows that the most affluent family type in all these societies is, not surprisingly, two adults with no children. On average, they have around a quarter more disposable income than families consisting of two adults with children. The gap between the two is actually largest in Australia. Similarly, in nearly all these countries single-parent families are the worst off financially.

The financial consequence of having children is doubtless a large part of explaining the decline in fertility in advanced industrial democracies. Based on an extensive survey of Australian families, demographer Peter McDonald concluded: 'A preference for two children remains dominant among men and women in their early twenties. This means that very low fertility is more the product of constraint than of preference.'

Because nearly all young women are employed when they first become pregnant, a decision about having a baby is inextricably tied also to decisions about future work. For both financial reasons and because of their own aspirations, a very large proportion of women continue to work after becoming mothers. Table 14.13 shows that the employment rate of women with one child is only very slightly less than that for women with no children, though the employment rate of women with two or more children drops more substantially. Moreover, as Table 14.14 shows, more than half of mothers return to work while their children are fairly young.

Table 14.13 shows the Scandinavian countries generally having the highest employment rates for women both with and without children, and motherhood makes almost no difference to their employment participation. At the other end of the scale, Ireland and Italy both have relatively low rates of employment for women without children, and experience a further drop in their workforce participation after having children. It may be surprising, but Australia ranks third lowest above only Italy and Ireland in the employment rate for mothers with two children, and only in these three countries is that rate less than 50%. If there were data on Japan, it would no doubt join these three, as it ranks lowest in Table 14.14.

Reconciling motherhood and work is one of the key challenges in contemporary society, and it has many dimensions. One is the availability of part-time work for parents who want it. Table 14.15 shows, as might be expected, that working mothers are more likely to be in part-time employment than women without children, and that the proportion of part-time work further increases with mothers having two or more children.

Table 14.15 shows a different pattern of national differences from Tables 14.13 and 14.14. Three of the four Scandinavian countries at the top on the overall employment rate for mothers are at the bottom for part-time work rates, while the United States and Canada also have low proportions of women working part-time. In contrast, the top six countries in Table 14.15, including Australia, have more than half of employed mothers with more than one child working part-time. On the other hand this means that the proportion of Australian mothers working full-time is comparatively even lower.

Table 14.16: Maternity leave

National statutory maternity leave provisions, latest available year, 1998–2003

	Paid leave?	Provider of coverage	Duration of leave (weeks)	Pay level %
Austria	Yes	Government	16	100
Belgium	Yes	Government	15	82
Canada	Yes	Insurance	17	55
Denmark	Yes	Government	28	90
Finland	Yes	Government	53	80
France	Yes	Government	21	100
Germany	Yes	Govt + employ	14	100
Ireland	Yes	Government	14	70
Italy	Yes	Government	22	80
Japan	Yes	Insurance	14	60
Netherlands	Yes	Government	16	100
New Zealand	Yes	–	–	–
Norway	Yes	Government	52	80
Sweden	Yes	Government	65	75
Switzerland	Yes	Employer	8	100
United Kingdom	Yes	Government	16	90
Australia	**No**	**NA**	**52**	**0**
United States	No	NA	14	0

Table 14.17: Financial support for families

Supplementary income (% extra) available to a one-earner, two-child family compared to a single worker (for those on average male wages in manufacturing). Supplementary income includes cash allowances and tax concessions

	1975	1990	2001
Germany	15.9	21.2	21.8
Belgium	21.1	39.1	20.2
Austria	23.0	23.6	19.8
Ireland	16.5	17.1	14.6
Italy	12.6	14.5	14.1
Switzerland	10.5	14.1	13.0
United Kingdom	14.4	12.7	13.0
Denmark	15.6	26.3	12.9
France	23.5	19.2	12.6
Netherlands	15.8	12.3	11.6
United States	13.6	9.7	11.4
Norway	14.8	25.7	11.1
Canada	12.5	15.0	10.4
Australia	**13.7**	**10.7**	**10.0**
Sweden	16.9	15.0	9.5
Finland	21.5	20.8	8.9
Japan	5.9	7.3	4.2
New Zealand	9.9	2.5	2.8
Mean	15.4	17.0	12.3

Table 14.18: Child support packages

Child support packages for 'representative' family cases after all taxes, costs and benefits; % of average earnings, July 2001

	%
Austria	17.2
Finland	13.9
France	10.9
Sweden	10.2
Norway	9.7
Belgium	9.0
Germany	8.3
Denmark	7.7
United Kingdom	7.5
Ireland	6.9
Australia	**6.7**
Canada	2.0
Italy	2.0
United States	1.6
New Zealand	−0.4
Japan	−1.5
Netherlands	−1.9
Mean	6.5

No data on Switzerland.

Table 14.19: Child care

Percentage of young children (0–6) who use day care facilities late 1990s. Final column = % of very young children (0–3) in publicly funded child care, early 1990s

	0 to 3-year-olds	3–6 years*	Publicly funded places
Denmark	64	91	50
United States	54	70	2
Sweden	48	80	33
Canada	45	50	5
New Zealand	45	90	–
Norway	40	80	20
Ireland	38	40	–
United Kingdom	34	60	2
Belgium	30	97	30
France	29	99	23
Finland	22	66	27
Australia	**15**	**60**	**5**
Japan	13	34	–
Germany	8	40	4
Italy	6	95	6
Netherlands	6	98	8
Austria	4	68	3
Mean	29	72	16

* Actually to mandatory school age, which is 6 in most countries.
No data for Switzerland.

Family policies

Democratic governments have been properly cautious about adopting population policies that smack of social engineering. But as fertility rates have fallen below natural replacement levels, and many countries face the likelihood of population decline in coming decades, there has been increasing willingness to talk about population targets. In the 1999 United Nations survey of population policies, 28 countries considered that their fertility rate was too low.

Governments' policy tools for encouraging fertility are fairly limited. They include legislative provisions, financial supports and the provision of facilities. The most basic legislative policy for encouraging childbirth is maternity leave. Maternity leave provisions were slow to develop in English-speaking countries, because the traditional view was that mothers did not or should not work. In contrast, Norwegian women had the right to maternity leave before they had the right to vote. As female labour force participation increased in nearly all the selected countries, the demands for maternity leave also increased. Over the decades, the right to return to the mother's previous position was guaranteed, while periods of unpaid and paid leave have gradually been increased in most countries.

Table 14.16 gives data on nationally legislated maternity leave provisions. Public policies regarding maternity leave defy simple summary, as the permutations of periods of full pay and reduced pay are so various. Mothers can often supplement the guaranteed period of paid leave with unpaid or lesser-paid leave. In some countries there are also provisions for paternal leave. In Scandinavian countries (and now New Zealand) a child's birth is followed by parental leave provisions, available to either parent.

Table 14.16 shows that although relatively generous in providing weeks of unpaid leave, Australia is one of two laggards among advanced democracies in failing to offer paid maternity leave as a right. The most common means is for governments (through social security) to pay the leave, though some use (compulsory) insurance schemes and only a few place any direct financial onus on employers.

Note, however, that the table refers to legislatively mandated entitlements. Some types of employers – particularly in the public sector, but also in larger private corporations – sometimes give other paid or unpaid leave. A 2002 estimate was that 39% of Australian female employees have access to some paid maternity leave, lasting on average about seven weeks.

No financially feasible public policy could cover the financial costs of having children, suggested by Table 14.12. However, giving families financial assistance, either through child allowances or through tax concessions, has been universal among these countries (Table 14.17), though the means and rationales have varied greatly over time and between countries. In many countries, including Australia, assistance is means-tested, but the level at which it cuts off is above the level of the average worker in manufacturing.

Bradshaw and Finch have provided far more embracing and sophisticated data than previously existed. They examined the total package of child benefits, the whole array of tax concessions, cash benefits, subsidised services and the charges associated with childrearing. Because benefits in all countries vary so much depending on family types and economic circumstances, they also take a large range of representative family types. The necessarily simplified summary of their results in Table 14.18 shows a very large range. In three countries the charges incurred outweigh all benefits to produce a negative value. At the other extreme, Austria is by far the most generous in its child support package. Australia's total is close to the average.

A final and centrally important policy is aimed at providing resources that help reconcile employment with parenthood. The use of child care (Table 14.19) shows considerable though not perfect correlation with mothers being in employment (Table 14.13). Australia is in the bottom third of both tables, and also low in the availability of publicly funded child care places shown in the final column.

Table 15.1: Gender Development Index

Range = from .000 (lowest) to 1.000 (highest), 2002

Australia	**.956**
Belgium	.943
Norway	.941
Sweden	.940
Canada	.938
United States	.937
Finland	.933
Netherlands	.933
United Kingdom	.932
Japan	.927
France	.926
Denmark	.925
Switzerland	.923
Austria	.921
Germany	.920
Ireland	.917
New Zealand	.915
Italy	.907
Mean	.930

Table 15.2: Gender Empowerment Measure

Range = from .000 (lowest) to 1.000 (highest), 2002

Norway	.837
Sweden	.824
Denmark	.821
Finland	.803
Netherlands	.781
Canada	.777
Germany	.765
New Zealand	.765
Australia	**.759**
United States	.757
Austria	.745
Switzerland	.718
Belgium	.706
United Kingdom	.684
Ireland	.675
Italy	.539
Japan	.527
Mean	.734

No data for France.

15 GENDER
Indices of gender inequality

The United Nations Development Programme has constructed two indices of women's position in society. The Gender Development Index is based on the Human Development Index, but then adjusted to reflect the degree of gender differences on its components.

Overall the GDI rankings are very close to the HDI rankings in Table 1.20. For example, the same five countries rank bottom, and in the same order, in both tables. The fact that the 18-country mean for the GDI is almost identical to the HDI shows that both measures reflect the general affluence and social development of these societies, and that in these aspects of development women are not strongly disadvantaged.

There are three dimensions to the GDI. On the first, longevity, women on average outlive men in all the selected countries. On the second, educational attainment, gender differences have broadly disappeared, and in some countries are now slightly reversed with females outperforming males. This leaves only the third component, differences in earned income, where women tend to score substantially lower.

It may surprise that Australia ranks top on the GDI (Table 15.1). Its premier ranking probably owes most to the increasing educational levels reached by younger Australian females.

The GDI gives scores considerably higher than the second index of women's position in society, the Gender Empowerment Measure. The GEM is designed to reveal women's opportunity to take an active part in economic and political life. It is composed of several dimensions: women's share of parliamentary seats, their share of senior management and decision-making roles, their proportion of professional and technical positions, and their power over economic resources, as measured by the relative earned income by each sex. (This component is the same as in the GDI.)

The GEM's 18-country mean of .734 trails well behind the GDI's .930, suggesting that inequality and discrimination are still much more pertinent in the exercise of social power. On the GEM the differences between countries reflect what most feminists would have suspected: the Scandinavian countries and the Netherlands fill the top five positions, and the range from top to bottom is much wider, with Italy and Japan particularly lagging behind in equal empowerment for women. Australia, like the United States and New Zealand, ranks around the middle.

Because of changing methodologies over time (and perhaps because of the difficulties of gaining reliable data on a global scale) the UNDP does not offer trends for these indices. However, in the tables in other sections on labour force participation and educational achievement, as well as in some tables on individual components in the next few pages, it can be seen that in most countries there have been tangible changes in women's roles and opportunities. But the much lower scores on the GEM than the GDI are a reminder that inequalities in power have been slower to change.

Table 15.3: Female and male earned income

Female earned income as % of male, 2000

	Total
Denmark	70
Finland	70
Australia	**69**
Sweden	68
New Zealand	67
Norway	64
Canada	62
United States	62
United Kingdom	61
Netherlands	52
Germany	50
Austria	50
Switzerland	50
Belgium	44
Italy	44
Japan	44
Ireland	40
Mean	57

No data for France.

Table 15.4: Gender wage ratio

Ratio of female to male hourly earnings, 1998
100 = equality

Australia	**91**
Belgium	91
Denmark	89
France	87
New Zealand	86
Sweden	86
Italy	85
Canada	82
Finland	82
Ireland	81
Germany	80
Netherlands	80
United Kingdom	80
Austria	79
United States	79
Switzerland	76
Mean	83

No data on Norway or Japan.

Table 15.5: Work time in market and non-market activities

Percentage of work time spent on market activities

	Total	Males	Females
Denmark	68	79	58
Canada	53	65	41
Finland	51	64	39
Norway	50	64	38
United States	50	63	37
France	46	60	33
New Zealand	46	60	32
United Kingdom	51	68	37
Germany	44	61	30
Australia	**46**	**62**	**30**
Austria	49	71	31
Netherlands	48	69	27
Japan	66	93	43
Italy	45	77	22
Mean	51	68	36

Ranked in ascending order according to the difference between sexes.
No data for Belgium, Ireland, Sweden and Switzerland.

Table 15.6: Division of housework

Gender Division of Labour Index, 1994
Range = 1.00 (female does all) through 2.50 (equality) to 5.00 (male does all)

Norway	2.26
United States	2.26
Canada	2.25
Sweden	2.25
New Zealand	2.13
United Kingdom	2.11
Germany	2.10
Netherlands	2.04
Australia	**2.03**
Austria	1.89
Ireland	1.83
Italy	1.74
Japan	1.50
Mean	2.03

No data on Belgium, Denmark, Finland, France and Switzerland.

Gender differences in paid and unpaid work

Table 15.3 on income disparity between the sexes aims to capture their relative access to a society's material resources, and the capacity for economic independence among men and women. The figure shows that in all these societies the earned income of women is considerably less than for men, averaging 57%. But there is a considerable range, with a group clustered near the top – between 67 and 70% – including Australia, New Zealand and the Scandinavian countries, and another group at the bottom – between 40 and 44%, consisting of Ireland, Japan, Italy and Belgium.

These scores are not a simple measure of occupational discrimination, but rather a much broader measure of access to a society's economic resources. They do not mean, for example, that men and women employed in the same job and working the same hours receive different amounts of pay. Rather they reflect a combination of factors: the relative labour force participation of women; the relative numbers working in full and part-time positions; as well as their relative access to better-paying jobs.

A more precise measure is found in Table 15.4, which compares the relative hourly earnings. (The most basic measure of income discrimination would be to compare the incomes of males and females in the same occupations with the same qualifications and so on.) Table 15.4 shows less difference between the sexes than Table 15.3, though it still paints a picture considerably less than equality, where the ratio would equal 100. Australia and Belgium rank first, while Switzerland shows the greatest disparity.

Women's increasing participation in the formal (i.e. paid) labour force has made more acute the difficulties of balancing work and home. Issues of equity arise also in the distribution of domestic labour tasks. Table 15.5 is an interesting but problematic exploration of gender differences in total work time. The study of time use is a growing and enlightening but difficult area of study. The figures here describe the total amount of work time devoted to market and non-market (domestic) activities. It does not give total figures for the amount of work time in different countries, or compare work with leisure time. Like Table 15.3, it makes no allowances for different labour force participation, part-time jobs and so on. Despite the lack of more penetrating data, the pattern of national differences is revealing. Gender equality was greatest in Denmark, where women spent 21% more of their work time on non-market activities than men. At the other end, Japanese men did almost no domestic work, while Italian women devoted the lowest proportion of their work time to market activities (with, more surprisingly, Dutch women only slightly ahead of them.) Australia is right on the mean in the difference between men and women.

One international comparative survey that probed such issues was the International Social Science Project study on the family in 1994. Only 13 of the selected countries participated, but Table 15.6 reports Batalova and Cohen's measure of the sharing of housework. Their gender division of labour is an index based on four traditionally female task variables: who usually does laundry; cares for sick family members; does shopping; and plans dinner. It assigns the value 1 when the wife always does the task to 5 when the husband always does the task. Then by combining the four tasks, they produce an index between 1 and 5. A higher score reflects a greater household contribution by the husband. No country reaches the point of equality (2.50), let alone has husbands doing most of the housework. However, a woman interested in an equitable division of housework tasks would be best advised to marry a Norwegian or American. Australia ranks in the bottom half, but there is a large gap between it and the four countries which score less than 2.00. As in the previous table, Japanese and Italian men rank at the bottom.

Table 15.7: Female doctors

Female doctors as % of the total

	1980	1990	2000
Finland	33.3	42.4	50.7
Sweden	22.0	34.0	39.2
Norway	17.2	23.7	37.2
Germany	21.6	29.0	37.1
Ireland	–	–	35.7
Netherlands	20.4	24.3	35.1
France	21.0	28.3	34.6
United Kingdom	19.5	27.7	34.5
Austria	20.8	25.9	33.1
New Zealand	16.4	23.9	32.6
Canada	15.0	23.8	31.1
Italy	17.1	24.8	30.2
Switzerland	16.5	21.9	29.1
Belgium	14.7	21.4	28.1
Australia	**18.9**	**23.8**	**27.8**
Denmark	20.3	24.4	27.0
United States	10.8	17.3	23.1
Japan	9.7	11.3	14.3
Mean	18.5	25.2	32.3

Table 15.8: Females in professional and technical occupations

Female professional and technical workers as % of total, 2000

Finland	56
New Zealand	54
United States	54
Canada	53
Belgium	50
Denmark	50
Germany	50
Ireland	50
Austria	49
Norway	49
Sweden	49
Australia	**48**
Netherlands	46
Japan	45
United Kingdom	45
Italy	44
Switzerland	42
Mean	49

Table 15.9: Women's employment rates and educational attainment

Employment rate of women aged 25–54, 2000, by level of education and difference from male rate

	Less than upper secondary, %	Secondary gap	Tertiary, %	Tertiary gap
Sweden	65.4	14.5	87.8	4.3
Denmark	68.2	9.2	88.7	4.5
Norway	63.8	14.6	87.3	4.9
Finland	69.5	8.3	84.8	8.0
United Kingdom	49.7	17.3	86.4	8.0
France	56.5	23.6	83.1	8.5
Belgium	47.4	32.3	86.7	8.6
Netherlands	53.4	32.8	86.6	8.8
Austria	61.6	17.6	86.5	9.2
Canada	52.0	20.8	79.8	9.2
Germany	55.4	20.9	83.4	10.5
New Zealand	54.8	21.2	78.7	10.7
Australia	**58.1**	**21.5**	**79.9**	**11.5**
United States	49.7	26.5	81.9	11.6
Switzerland	70.3	19.8	85.6	12.0
Italy	35.8	46.8	78.7	12.4
Ireland	33.7	39.5	79.9	13.3
Japan	62.6	25.7	62.7	33.5
Mean	56.0	22.9	82.7	10.5

Women and occupational inequalities

With women's increasing labour force participation, two issues have often been raised. One is sexual segregation in the division of labour, with some occupations female-dominated while others are male enclaves and difficult for women to break into. The other, encapsulated in the phrase 'glass ceiling', is used to describe barriers to women rising higher than certain levels in organisational hierarchies. Tables 15.7 to 15.9 chart some aspects of these issues.

The only table where we have good longitudinal data is 15.7, and it shows a considerable improvement in the number of female doctors between 1980 and 2000. In the selected countries in 1980, less than one in five doctors was a woman, but by 2000 the figure had risen to one in three. The data for earlier decades is too partial to tabulate, but the mean percentage for ten countries in 1960 was only 12% (just less than one doctor in eight).

This overall increase is far from uniform among the 18 countries. Only in Finland has the proportion of female doctors tipped 50%, more than double the rate for the two lowest countries, the United States and Japan. However, while these countries started from the lowest base in 1980, both are increasing their numbers fairly rapidly. In 2000 Australia ranked fourth bottom (a position very slightly affected by its latest available figure being from 1998). Australia ranked at the mean in 1980, but the number of female doctors grew less quickly in the next two decades than in many other countries.

Table 15.8 finds there was very close to gender equity overall in these 18 countries in professional and technical occupations. Most of the countries, including Australia, are clustered around 50%, with Switzerland bringing up the rear at 42%. Table 15.8 is based on a very generic grouping, perhaps too broad to give a penetrating picture of the gendered structuring of occupational opportunities.

One way of breaking through discriminatory barriers is to ensure one is fully qualified, and Table 15.9 suggests how important education has been as a pathway for increasing women's occupational opportunities. It shows that tertiary-educated women have a much higher employment rate than those finishing with secondary education – rising from 56% to 83% for the 18-country mean. The table also shows that at both secondary and tertiary education levels, women have a lower employment rate than men, but that among the tertiary-educated the average gap among the 18 countries halves, down to 10.5%.

The gap between men's and women's employment rate among the secondary educated shows much more variation than at tertiary level. The gap is least in Finland (8%) and greatest in Italy (47%). Secondary-educated Irish and Italian women have the lowest employment rates, both with only around a third being employed. The highest rate is in Switzerland at 70%. But most pertinently, the highest rate for those with secondary qualifications is below the tertiary employment rate for all but one country. Leaving aside the outlier Japan, all other 17 countries have between 79% and 89% employment rates for tertiary-educated females.

Perhaps more than any other table, this data highlights the obstacles facing Japanese women. Japan is the only country where tertiary education does not substantially boost the employment rate of women. Instead it is the same for both levels of education, meaning that the gender gap for employment in Japan among the tertiary-educated is 33 percentage points, compared to a mean of 9 for the other 17 countries.

These tables cannot give penetrating data on the extent of glass ceilings. Tables 15.7 and 15.9 suggest that women's representation still falls considerably short of equality but that their presence is substantial, and that where we can tell, that presence is increasing. So the glass ceiling may not have disappeared, but neither does it seem to be immovable.

Table 15.10: Women in parliament

Women members of lower houses of parliament as % of total

	1975	1987	1995	2003
Sweden	21	29	40	45
Denmark	16	29	33	38
Finland	23	32	34	38
Netherlands	9	20	31	37
Norway	16	34	39	36
Austria	8	12	23	34
Germany	6	15	26	32
New Zealand	5	14	21	28
Australia	**0**	**6**	**10**	**25**
Belgium	7	8	12	23
Switzerland	8	14	18	23
Canada	3	10	18	21
United Kingdom	4	6	10	18
United States	4	5	11	14
Ireland	3	8	13	13
France	2	6	6	12
Italy	4	13	15	12
Japan	1	1	3	7
Mean	8	15	20	25

Table 15.11: Women cabinet ministers

Women cabinet ministers as % of total

	1994	2000
Sweden	30	55
Denmark	29	45
Finland	39	44
New Zealand	8	44
Norway	35	42
France	7	38
Germany	16	36
United Kingdom	9	33
United States	14	32
Austria	16	31
Netherlands	31	31
Switzerland	17	29
Canada	14	24
Australia	**13**	**20**
Belgium	11	19
Ireland	16	19
Italy	12	18
Japan	6	6
Mean	18	31

Table 15.12: Women's attitudes to equal rights

Percentage of women (F) agreeing with these statements in 1999 poll

	F should have equal rights	F do have equal rights	F are in better position than grandmothers' time	F are happier than in grandmothers' time
Netherlands	80	20	92	25
Australia	**77**	**25**	**95**	**38**
United Kingdom	73	9	93	42
Belgium	70	12	90	41
Canada	70	8	93	33
Germany	70	7	94	29
United States	62	8	93	28
Switzerland	39	14	92	27
Japan	21	0	96	82
Mean	62	11	93	38

Women in public life

Table 15.10 shows both how women were marginalised in politics in previous decades and how rapidly their representation in parliament has grown, trebling in less than three decades. In 1975 less than one in twelve members of parliament was a woman. By 2003 it was up to a quarter, though in no country was the split 50–50.

As on many feminist issues, the leaders are the Scandinavian countries plus the Netherlands, and the laggards are Japan, Italy, France and Ireland. The four Scandinavian countries each had a higher representation of women in parliament in 1975 than Australia had reached by 1995.

The most common comparative indicators only give lower house figures as most countries are either uni-cameral or not strongly bicameral (Table 2.9). Australia is probably the only one of the selected countries where this can be misleading. Traditionally, there were more women in the Australian Senate than the House, though more recently the proportions are about equal.

It was widely accepted among electoral scholars that women (and other disadvantaged groups) were more likely to become members of parliament under a multi-member than single-member electoral system (Table 2.13). It can be seen from Table 15.10 that the English-speaking single-member electorate countries tend to rank in the bottom half. These countries were all very low on women's representation in the 1970s, though all have increased greatly since then. The highest is New Zealand, which changed its electoral system in the 1990s.

Moreover, women are not just becoming backbench members of parliament. Table 15.11 shows that their ministerial representation is slightly higher than their parliamentary numbers. Unfortunately we do not have such a long run of data here, but even between 1994 and 2000, women's ministerial representation increased substantially. Sweden is the only country with a majority of female ministers. Australia ranks in the bottom third and is one of the few countries that has a lower proportion of women ministers than of MPs.

The political impact of women's issues depends not only on the number of women directly in political life, but on the nature of the public opinion politicians are responding to. It is not often that we can get the same poll questions asked across all 18 countries, but an interesting poll in the *Economist* probed some basic attitudes on women's issues, though unfortunately including only nine of our countries.

In 1999 the *Economist* polled women about whether they should have the same rights as men. This principle gains majority but far from overwhelming support among these women (Table 15.12). Endorsement was highest in the Netherlands (80%) and second strongest in Australia (77%). But it did not command majority support among either Swiss or Japanese women. The idea that women actually enjoyed the same rights as men did not find majority agreement in any of the countries. A quarter of Australian women agreed, making it the highest of the nine.

Over 90% of women in all nine countries thought they were in a better position than their grandmothers' generation. This very general statement can encompass everything from material standards of living, educational and work opportunities, contraceptive control and improved health, to labour-saving technological advances such as the washing machine. But only a minority thought that women were happier than in their grandmothers' day. Interestingly, only in Japan did a strong majority (82%) of women endorse the idea.

Table 16.1: Home ownership

Home ownership as % of all households

	1960	1975	1990	2000
Ireland	60	71	81	83
Italy	45	50	67	78
New Zealand	69	68	71	–
United Kingdom	42	49	68	69
Australia	**63**	**67**	**70**	**69**
Canada	66	60	64	67
Finland	57	59	67	67
Belgium	50	55	62	65
United States	64	65	64	65
Japan	71	59	61	60
Sweden	36	35	42	60
Norway	53	53	59	–
Austria	38	41	55	–
France	41	45	54	54
Denmark	43	49	51	53
Netherlands	29	35	44	49
Germany	29	36	38	43
Switzerland	34	28	30	–
Mean	49	51	58	61

Ranked according to 2000 home ownership with missing countries ranked according to their 1990 level. Mean for 2000 includes these countries' 1990 figures.

Table 16.2: Cost of housing

Real change in house price indices 1995–2002, nationwide averages, %

Ireland	152
United Kingdom	89
Netherlands	83
Sweden	56
Australia	**53**
Belgium	39
France	31
United States	27
Italy	8
Canada	2
Germany	−13
Japan	−19
Mean	42

No data on Austria, Denmark, Finland, New Zealand, Norway or Switzerland.

Table 16.3: Household sizes

Percentage of households with one, two and five or more people, late 1990s

	One person	Two people	5+ people	Average size
Ireland	22	23	23	3.1
Japan	–	–	–	2.8
Italy	21	25	11	2.7
Australia	**20**	**31**	**13**	**2.6**
Canada	24	32	10	2.6
United States	26	32	10	2.6
Austria	30	29	9	2.5
Finland	28	32	9	2.5
France	28	32	9	2.5
Belgium	31	31	7	2.4
United Kingdom	27	34	8	2.4
Netherlands	33	35	6	2.3
Switzerland	32	32	7	2.3
Denmark	37	33	5	2.2
Germany	34	34	5	2.2
Norway	34	26	8	2.2
Sweden	40	31	5	2.1
Mean	29	31	9	2.5

No data on New Zealand.

Table 16.4: Size of houses

Proportion of houses with five or more rooms, 2002

Canada	75
New Zealand	74
United Kingdom	73
United States	72
Australia	**70**
Ireland	67
Norway	44
Netherlands	43
Germany	40
Italy	38
Belgium	36
France	36
Japan	31
Denmark	29
Switzerland	27
Sweden	23
Austria	19
Finland	14
Mean	45

16   LIFESTYLES AND CONSUMPTION
Housing and households

An Englishman's house may be his castle, but traditionally most of them were rented. Housing is one area where Australia's development differed sharply from its colonial founder's. As early as 1911 half of Australians owned their home, a figure that was reached in Britain only in the 1970s.

The selected countries show very different rates of home ownership (Table 16.1). They are lowest (just over half or less) in some European countries which for several generations have been highly urbanised and densely populated. Traditionally they were highest where land was relatively cheapest: in more rural societies and those with lower population density. The four New World countries, for example, had among the highest rates of home ownership in 1960. In that year Japan had the highest rate and its declining rate over the next 15 years reflects its rapidly increasing urbanisation. Many families owned their small village homes, but their children could not afford to buy real estate in Tokyo.

The countries show contrasting trajectories. The rate of home ownership is still increasing in countries such as Ireland, Italy, Sweden. But in most it seems to have reached a plateau. Australia, New Zealand, Canada and the United States – the traditional leaders in home ownership rates – saw almost no change between 1960 and 2000. This figure includes both those who own their home outright and those still paying off their mortgage. ABS figures show that in Australia what is probably a relatively high 38% of households have no mortgage, while around 32% still do. Most of the rest – around 25% – pay rent to a private landlord, and what is probably a relatively low 5% are in publicly subsidised rented housing. In several other countries, public provision and employer provision of housing is substantially higher.

Housing shows little sign of becoming more affordable. Table 16.2 shows that in ten of the 12 countries on which there was data, housing

costs rose faster than the general cost of living between 1995 and 2002, and substantially faster in five countries, including Australia.

In all 18 countries average household size is falling. The mean household size declined from 2.8 in 1981 to 2.5 in the late 1990s. Only in Ireland does the average household consist of more than three people, while in Sweden it is down to 2.1. The average size of households in Australia fell steadily through the 20th century. At the 1911 census, the average was 4.5 and 90 years later down to 2.6, and the trend is accelerating, down from 3.0 in 1980 to 2.6 20 years later.

The declining household size reflects rises in single-person and couple households. Between 1911 and 1961 the proportion of single-person households in Australia was roughly constant, fluctuating between 8% and 11%, but in the next 40 years it almost doubled. Around 40% of single-person households comprise people aged over 65. Apart from a larger aged population, other reasons for the declining size of households are declining numbers of children per family and more family break-ups.

Table 16.4 points indirectly to the extra spaciousness of homes in the English-speaking countries. Only in these six countries (including Ireland) do more than two-thirds of houses have five or more rooms. In all others it is less than half, with only 14% of Finnish homes having five or more rooms. We do not have extensive comparative data on the area of houses. A Japanese publication gave the late 1990s average area of houses in the United States as 158 square metres, France 106, the United Kingdom 98 and Japan 93. In Australia, the size of new houses (a different category) was 186 square metres. This figure was up by almost 30% since 1980. So while Australian households are becoming smaller, new houses are not, perhaps reflecting Australians' tendency to equate quality of housing with space.

Table 16.5: Total food consumption

Per capita daily calorie intake

	1961	1970	1980	1990	2000
United States	2 883	3 026	3 169	3 486	3 772
Austria	3 189	3 232	3 354	3 490	3 757
Belgium	2 975	3 095	3 300	3 532	3 701
Italy	2 914	3 422	3 590	3 591	3 661
Ireland	3 354	3 445	3 664	3 644	3 613
France	3 194	3 302	3 375	3 512	3 591
Germany	2 889	3 148	3 339	3 311	3 451
Norway	3 004	3 022	3 351	3 144	3 414
Denmark	3 187	3 158	3 127	3 162	3 396
United Kingdom	3 240	3 279	3 114	3 219	3 334
Netherlands	3 058	3 022	3 073	3 291	3 294
Switzerland	3 521	3 478	3 491	3 346	3 293
New Zealand	2 900	2 967	3 096	3 249	3 252
Finland	3 265	3 121	3 091	3 144	3 227
Australia	**3 086**	**3 237**	**3 055**	**3 218**	**3 176**
Canada	2 787	2 903	2 918	2 995	3 174
Sweden	2 836	2 877	2 992	2 975	3 109
Japan	2 468	2 716	2 721	2 822	2 762
Mean	3 042	3 136	3 212	3 285	3 388

Table 16.6: Consumption of fish

Kilograms per person per year

	1980	1990	2000
Japan	64.7	71.2	64.9
Norway	44.0	45.3	51.0
Finland	29.0	34.9	32.1
France	25.2	32.3	31.2
Sweden	31.5	30.8	30.8
New Zealand	15.8	20.9	28.9
Denmark	27.9	27.5	26.5
Italy	16.7	23.2	24.6
Canada	20.2	23.8	24.5
United States	16.0	21.5	22.0
Australia	**15.0**	**18.9**	**21.6**
Belgium	19.3	19.6	21.6
United Kingdom	16.5	20.5	21.6
Netherlands	10.0	10.9	20.6
Switzerland	11.0	16.7	18.8
Ireland	17.6	18.0	16.1
Austria	7.1	11.4	14.5
Germany	13.3	15.8	14.5
Mean	22.3	25.7	27.0

Table 16.7: Consumption of fruit and vegetables

Kilograms per capita per year

	1960*	1970	1980	1990	2000 *
Italy	226	299	282	302	313
Australia	**190**	**228**	**230**	**275**	**284**
Belgium	143	170	159	217	259
Norway	147	153	179	201	251
Canada	177	167	213	229	249
United States	171	183	211	233	243
Netherlands	139	179	175	215	223
France	204	219	178	203	214
Austria	201	182	211	215	209
Denmark	90	122	116	155	209
Switzerland	208	217	235	212	192
Germany	131	171	175	198	185
Sweden	96	125	128	163	185
New Zealand	110	128	147	156	171
Japan	124	180	177	165	165
United Kingdom	175	174	167	164	162
Ireland	82	100	142	150	142
Finland	–	49	71	92	105
Mean	154	169	177	197	209

Table 16.8: Consumption of sugar

Kilograms per capita per year

	1961	1970	1980	1990	2000
New Zealand	42	43	40	46	49
Belgium	28	35	32	37	44
Netherlands	43	45	41	51	42
Sweden	42	42	40	39	41
Austria	36	37	39	37	40
Norway	40	40	38	37	40
Switzerland	47	46	39	39	40
Ireland	49	50	42	39	37
Australia	**49**	**49**	**48**	**42**	**36**
Denmark	47	49	42	38	34
Finland	41	45	34	36	34
France	28	36	30	32	33
Germany	30	33	36	27	33
Canada	41	43	36	35	32
United Kingdom	48	45	40	38	31
United States	42	44	37	28	30
Italy	22	28	31	27	26
Japan	15	27	23	21	16
Mean	38	41	37	36	35

1960 or closest available year.

Food consumption

People in the selected countries vary considerably in how much food they eat. Table 16.5 reports the mean daily calorie intake per person between 1970 and 2000. It is based on OECD figures from the UN agency the Food and Agriculture Organisation.

According to Table 16.5, Americans eat the most calories daily and Japanese the least. In all the countries except Japan people consume on average more than 3000 calories a day. The four countries at the top of Table 16.5 all increased their average food intake substantially over the decades shown. Other countries showed much smaller increases, remained broadly stable or even decreased slightly. As a result the variation between selected countries was greater in 2000 than in the earlier decades.

The FAO's food balance sheets for individual nations are the main source of data for comparing food intake between countries, and are by far the best data available, though there will always be methodological issues in such an enterprise. In addition to total food intake, the FAO gives some data on apparent consumption of different food types. The phrase 'apparent consumption' must be noted because the data represents estimates based on the amounts of food entering households and restaurants. There is significant wastage, so actual food consumption by individuals will be considerably less.

The Japanese come bottom of Table 16.5 by a long way and top of Table 16.6 by an even greater margin, eating more fish than double the mean of the other nations. Norway is clearly in second place, while the Germanic diet of Germany, Austria and Switzerland is the least interested in sea food. Many of the countries with greatest consumption of fish are islands or have long coastlines. The most notable exception is Ireland. Perhaps for health reasons, the New World English-speaking countries increased their fish consumption considerably between 1980 and 2000.

While the increase in total food intake in Table 16.5 is almost certainly associated with an increase in weight problems in some of the selected countries, Tables 16.6 to 16.8 do not suggest that at least in these specific areas the composition of the diet has become less healthy. While consumption of fish showed a modest overall increase, Table 16.7 suggests a relatively large increase in consumption of fruit and vegetables. It shows both great variations in consumption in 2000, and also greatly varying trends over the previous four decades. Italy ranks top, ahead of Australia, and Italians eat roughly three times as much fruit and vegetables as the bottom-ranking Finns. Around half the countries, including the seven top-ranking countries plus Denmark and Sweden, increased their yearly per capita consumption by close to 100 kilograms or more. Others increased by less, and a few remained fairly constant (France, Austria, Switzerland and the United Kingdom).

Despite Australia's good comparative rating on Table 16.7, official surveys found an unexpected drop in Vitamin C intake among both children and adults between 1985 and 1995, mainly due to a decline in fruit consumption among adults and of fruit juice consumption among children. The 1995 National Nutrition Survey found that 42% of Australian adults had not eaten any fruit on the day of the survey, and only 17% had eaten the recommended 300 grams. It also found that 16% had not eaten any vegetables (including potatoes) on the survey day, and only 32% had eaten the recommended 300 grams.

Perhaps surprisingly, sugar intake did not increase over the 40 years between 1961 and 2000. But the slight decrease in the 18-country mean in Table 16.8 hides a fair degree of individual variation between countries. Several English-speaking countries – the United States, United Kingdom, Australia and Ireland – showed downward trends of at least 10 kilograms per person. Belgium showed a similar trend in the other direction, as did the already sweet-toothed New Zealanders.

Table 16.9: Obese females

Percentage of female population with Body Mass Index > 30

	1980	1990	2000
Japan	3	3	3
Norway	–	–	6
Switzerland	–	5	7
Italy	–	–	8
Austria	–	9	9
Denmark	–	–	9
France	–	6	9
Ireland	–	–	9
Sweden	5	6	9
Netherlands	6	7	10
Finland	8	9	11
Germany	–	–	11
Belgium	–	–	12
Canada	–	–	14
New Zealand	–	13	19
United Kingdom	8	16	21
Australia	**8**	**12**	**22**
United States	17	26	34
Mean	8	10	12

Table 16.10: Obese males

Percentage of male population with Body Mass Index > 30

	1980	1990	2000
Japan	1	2	2
Norway	–	–	7
Switzerland	–	6	7
Austria	–	8	9
France	–	6	9
Italy	–	–	9
Netherlands	4	5	9
Sweden	5	5	9
Denmark	–	8	10
Belgium	–	–	11
Finland	7	8	11
Germany	–	–	12
Ireland	–	–	12
New Zealand	–	10	15
Canada	–	–	16
Australia	**9**	**10**	**19**
United Kingdom	6	13	21
United States	12	21	28
Mean	7	9	12

Table 16.11: Overweight females

Percentage of female population with Body Mass Index 25–30

	1980	1990	2000 *
Japan	18	19	18
France	–	19	20
Austria	–	–	21
Denmark	–	–	25
Italy	–	–	25
Sweden	–	–	27
United States	–	25	28
Netherlands	23	24	30
New Zealand	–	25	30
Australia	**19**	**24**	**31**
United Kingdom	24	29	34
Mean	21	24	26

No data on Belgium, Canada, Finland, Germany, Ireland, Norway or Switzerland.

Table 16.12: Overweight males

Percentage of male population with Body Mass Index 25–30

	1980	1990	2000 *
Japan	17	21	25
France	–	29	34
Netherlands	33	34	39
Denmark	–	–	40
Italy	–	–	40
New Zealand	–	40	40
Sweden	–	–	40
United States	–	40	40
United Kingdom	33	40	45
Australia	**37**	**42**	**48**
Austria	–	–	54
Mean	30	35	41

No data on Belgium, Canada, Finland, Germany, Ireland, Norway or Switzerland.

Obesity

The English-speaking countries are facing an epidemic of obesity. Tables 16.9 and 16.10 show that America leads the world in obese women and men by a considerable distance. The next several places are taken by the other English-speaking countries. Australia ranks second among the selected countries among women and third among men. There were great differences between countries. While one in three American women was obese in 2000, only one in 33 Japanese women and one in 16 Norwegian women were.

Obesity is defined as a Body Mass Index of 30 or more. The BMI is the ratio of a person's weight (in kilograms) to the square of their height (in metres). A person six feet tall (1.83 metres) becomes defined as obese when they weigh 100 kilograms or more. The term over-weight is defined as having a BMI from 25 to less than 30.

The data in Tables 16.11 and 16.12 is annoyingly incomplete, but the English-speaking countries still rank highly. Altogether 62% of American women and 68% of American men were obese or overweight, again putting their country in the lead. But when the two categories are combined, Australia (53% of females and 67% of males) and Britain (55% and 66%) almost equal them.

In the United States rather more women than men are obese (34:28%), but elsewhere there is little difference between the sexes. However, males substantially outnumber females in the overweight category. Australia's 48:31% difference is considerable, but the most spectacular difference is in Austria: 54:21%.

Although obesity data from 1980 was available from only seven countries, among those countries only the United States, Britain and Australia showed hugely dramatic increases.

There has been great speculation about the causes of this rapid change. Australian data shows that the proportion of overweight or obese people increases with age, peaking with 74% of 55 to 74-year-old men and 71% of 65 to 74-year-old women in those categories. At the same time each age cohort has been heavier than its predecessors. In just ten years from 1985 to 1995, the proportion of obese girls aged 7–15 increased from 1.2% to 5.5% and of boys from 1.4% to 4.7%.

Overweight and obesity result when energy intake from diet continuously exceeds energy output through activity. While individual differences are due to a mix of genetic and environmental factors, the trend towards greater proportions of the population becoming obese must be found in behavioural changes, and they must be found by looking at patterns of both activity and diet. Table 16.5 can give us only very limited help in this, because it refers to the population mean, while these tables refer to a changing share of the population. It is true that the United States tops both Table 16.5 and Tables 16.9 and 16.10, and its mean calorie intake has increased very substantially. But the same is not true of the other English-speaking countries that rank so highly in the obesity tables, though a relatively stable mean can hide a changing distribution, with some people eating more and others less.

While there is doubt about all the causes of increasing obesity, there is none about the dramatic extent of the increase, and unfortunately neither is there any doubt about the negative health consequences that it brings. Excess body weight is associated with many health problems including coronary heart disease, Type 2 diabetes, respiratory disease and some cancers. The Australian Institute of Health and Welfare estimated that overweight and obesity accounted for over 4% of the total burden of disease in Australia in 1996.

Table 16.13: Consumption of hot drinks
Kilograms of coffee and tea consumed per person per year, 2002

	Coffee	Tea
Norway	10.7	0.4
Finland	10.1	0.3
Denmark	9.7	0.2
Sweden	7.8	0.4
Netherlands	7.1	0.8
Switzerland	7.0	0.4
Germany	5.7	0.7
Austria	5.5	0.3
Belgium	5.0	0.1
France	3.9	0.2
Italy	3.2	0.1
United States	3.0	0.2
Canada	2.4	0.2
Australia	**2.0**	**0.8**
Japan	1.4	0.9
United Kingdom	1.2	2.3
New Zealand	0.9	1.0
Ireland	0.7	1.5
Mean 2002	4.9	0.6
Mean 1997	4.6	0.6

Table 16.14: Consumption of cold drinks
Consumption of carbonated soft drinks, fruit and vegetable juices, and bottled water: Litres per person per year, 2002

	Soft drinks	Fruit juice	Bottled water
United States	216.0	42.8	46.8
Ireland	126.0	15.1	27.1
Canada	119.8	52.6	29.7
Norway	119.8	21.4	20.9
Belgium	102.9	22.5	117.1
Australia	**100.1**	**34.4**	**17.3**
United Kingdom	96.5	29.3	25.4
Netherlands	96.1	28.1	16.9
New Zealand	84.2	24.8	5.4
Sweden	82.4	35.5	19.1
Switzerland	81.4	22.8	111.2
Denmark	80.0	15.7	11.4
Austria	78.8	37.3	86.5
Germany	72.0	38.6	109.2
Finland	52.0	33.0	14.0
Italy	50.2	13.6	155.0
France	37.2	23.5	146.6
Japan	21.6	20.7	10.4
Mean 2002	89.8	28.4	53.9
Mean 1997	84.0	24.7	42.6

Hot and cold drinks

Coffee consumption across these 18 countries is around seven times as high as tea consumption. Tea drinking is largely the preserve of the English and some of those they colonised. Table 16.13 shows that only in the United Kingdom, Ireland and New Zealand do people consume more tea than coffee. Those three countries, followed by Japan and Australia, were the leading tea consumers, though of course the Japanese drink green rather than black tea. The Boston Tea Party, one of the key actions leading to the American War of Independence, must have had a lasting impact on North American tastes. Despite their English colonial experience, they share the coffee-drinking preferences of mainland Europe, coming near the bottom of the table on tea consumption.

In coffee consumption, the 11 mainland European countries all rank ahead of the seven other countries. Within mainland Europe, coffee consumption shows some correlation with the coldness of the climate. Table 16.13 shows the Scandinavians ahead, followed by the Swiss and Dutch. The world-famous coffee-makers of Italy are rightly celebrated, but Italians only consume about a third as much coffee as Norwegians and Finns.

It is not surprising (Table 16.14) that the United States, the home of Coca-Cola and mass advertising, is the leader in consuming carbonated soft drinks, but the scale of their lead is surprising. The gap between America and second-placed Ireland is as great as the gap between Ireland and 17th-placed France. These figures are per head of population including children and adults of all ages. As with all averages, they conceal great variations. On these figures, however, the average Australian consumes almost three-quarters of a 375 ml can a day.

Fruit juice consumption is on average around a third that of carbonated soft drinks (Table 16.14). The Canadians ranked highest, gaining their ascendancy because of a one-third increase in consumption between 1997 and 2002, while most other countries remained stable. Australia comes in a second group quite a bit behind Canada. Fruit juice seems particularly unpopular in Italy.

The only one of these beverages showing very rapid growth between 1997 and 2002 is bottled water (Table 16.14). The term includes 'sparkling' water, 'mineral' water and purified/table water. Some countries remain largely immune to its appeals, but in others its sales are increasing substantially. The French and Italians are clear leaders, clearly preferring bottled water to fruit juice and carbonated soft drinks, an order of preference also true of some other European countries. Australia remains relatively low in the rankings, but almost doubled its per capita consumption in the five years.

Reasons for the growth can only be speculated on, but may include suspicions about the main water supply, a greater health consciousness about the dangers of dehydration, and the reluctance of some food outlets to supply free water.

Table 16.15: Alcohol consumption

Litres of alcohol consumed per person (aged 15 years and over) per year

	1960	1970	1980	1990	2000
France	23.7	22.3	20.6	16.5	12.9
Ireland	7.1	10.6	13.8	10.5	12.3
Denmark	5.5	8.6	11.7	11.7	11.5
Austria	10.9	13.9	13.8	12.6	11.3
Switzerland	12.1	14.2	13.5	12.9	11.2
Germany	7.5	13.4	12.7	13.8	10.5
Belgium	8.9	12.3	14.0	12.1	10.2
United Kingdom	–	7.1	9.4	9.7	10.2
Netherlands	3.7	7.7	11.3	9.9	10.0
Australia	**9.4**	**11.6**	**12.9**	**10.5**	**9.8**
New Zealand	5.3	9.8	11.8	10.1	8.9
Italy	16.6	18.2	13.2	10.9	8.7
Finland	2.7	5.8	7.9	9.5	8.6
Japan	–	6.9	8.1	8.9	8.3
United States	7.8	9.5	10.5	9.3	8.3
Canada	7.2	8.7	11.1	9.2	7.7
Sweden	4.8	7.2	6.7	6.4	6.2
Norway	3.4	4.7	5.3	5.0	5.6
Mean	8.5	10.7	11.6	10.5	9.6

Table 16.16: Beer and wine consumption

Litres of beer and wine consumed per person per year

	Beer 1997	Beer 2002	Wine 1997	Wine 2002
Ireland	163	155	8	13
Germany	124	119	25	26
Austria	115	106	34	36
Belgium	101	98	28	30
Denmark	117	98	29	32
United Kingdom	100	97	16	20
Australia	**96**	**89**	**19**	**21**
United States	86	85	7	7
Netherlands	84	80	15	20
Finland	81	79	8	10
New Zealand	83	78	18	19
Canada	67	70	8	10
Switzerland	60	57	41	42
Norway	55	56	9	11
Sweden	57	56	12	16
Japan	56	55	11	10
France	43	41	51	47
Italy	26	29	61	54
Mean	84	81	22	24

Ranked according to 2002 beer consumption.

Table 16.17: Consumption of spirits and flavoured alcoholic drinks

Litres of spirits and flavoured alcoholic drinks consumed per person per year, 2000

	Flavoured alcoholic drinks 1997	Flavoured alcoholic drinks 2002	Spirits 1997	Spirits 2002
Australia	**3.6**	**9.8**	**2.9**	**2.6**
New Zealand	2.3	7.7	2.7	2.3
United Kingdom	0.6	4.4	3.7	3.9
Ireland	2.5	3.9	4.1	5.3
United States	1.4	3.8	4.6	4.8
Japan	1.5	3.5	7.5	8.2
Germany	1.5	3.2	6.1	5.3
Finland	4.7	2.8	5.1	5.7
Austria	1.3	2.6	3.4	3.2
Canada	1.2	2.1	4.0	4.3
Switzerland	0.1	1.5	2.2	2.4
Belgium	0.1	1.1	2.7	2.6
France	1.2	1.0	7.6	7.2
Italy	0.5	0.7	2.7	2.7
Netherlands	0.2	0.3	5.1	4.7
Norway	0.2	0.2	2.2	2.4
Sweden	0.3	0.1	2.7	2.9
Denmark	0.1	0.1	2.7	2.7
Mean	1.3	2.7	4.0	4.1

Ranked according to 2002 consumption of flavoured alcoholic drinks.

Alcohol

Alcohol consumption trended steadily upwards until 1980, but has been declining since. Table 16.15 shows that in the selected countries the mean amount of pure alcohol each person consumed each year peaked at 11.6 litres in 1980, and had declined to 9.6 litres by 2000.

Several countries, including Australia, show an overall trend to increase, and then a decrease. One can only speculate on the reasons for this, but it is plausible that in the decades of growing affluence following World War II, increasing alcohol consumption was part of the rewards people reaped. However from the 1970s and 1980s onwards, there has been a greater sense of the dangers of over-consumption that came with affluence. Perhaps a greater health consciousness has increasingly tempered alcohol intake.

The French top the list but have also shown the greatest decline: down from 23.7 litres in 1960 to just over half, 12.9 litres in 2000. At the abstemious end of the table are the Swedes and Norwegians, with the North American countries just above them. Contrary to some versions of the national self-image, Australia ranks exactly in the middle.

Although national differences are still substantial, there is also a notable trend towards convergence among the selected countries. The average French person still consumes twice as much alcohol as the average Norwegian, but there was far more variation in 1960 and 1970 than in 2000. Heavy-drinking countries such as France and Italy have declined the most, while several lower-rating countries – notably Denmark, the Netherlands and Finland – have increased the most.

Despite the general convergence in overall alcoholic intake, globalisation has not yet dissolved the contrasts between national taste buds. The other tables on the page show the different national tastes in the main alcoholic drinks. Note that this data, from the leading market analysts Euromonitor, shows per person consumption for the whole population, whereas the OECD figure in Table 16.15 is only for those aged 15 or more. Table 16.15 is for litres of pure alcohol, while 16.16 and 16.17

are for the volumes of each drink – with wine averaging around 12%, beer 5–7%, flavoured alcoholic drinks 5–9%, and spirits up to 40% in alcohol content.

The Irish have a large lead in beer consumption, ahead of the Germans and Austrians, with Australia ranked seventh. Overall the consumption of beer between 1997 and 2002 declined slightly, while wine consumption rose slightly across the selected countries. The two countries – Italy and France – which rank lowest on beer consumption rate highest on wine consumption. Wine drinking has not become as widespread in North America and Scandinavia.

Australian wine consumption is edging up, but still ranks below the mean. According to WHO figures, in terms of pure alcohol consumed, in 1961 beer formed 74% of Australia's alcohol intake, and wine 12%. In 1999 beer was 50% and wine 33%.

Japan and France are the very clear leaders in spirits consumption. Spirits include a diverse array of drinks – whisky, brandy, rum, gin, vodka, sake etc. – whose popularity varies considerably between countries.

In flavoured alcoholic beverages – drinks where an alcoholic base is mixed with soft drinks by the manufacturer – Australia and New Zealand have the highest consumption. This market shows much greater volatility, but overall is the only category growing substantially, doubling over the five years between 1997 and 2002.

The problems associated with alcohol are not revealed by figures on average per person intake. There is no good comparative data on alcohol's role in traffic accidents and violence. Serious health and social problems are often associated with binge drinking and/or long-term alcoholism. In Australia, surveys show that 10% of males and 9% of females are consuming alcohol at levels likely to cause long-term harm (more than 29 and 15 standard drinks a week respectively). Overall 48% of Australians (aged 14+) drink alcohol at least weekly, and another 35% consume it more occasionally.

Table 16.18: Tobacco consumption

Grams of tobacco consumed per person (aged 15 or more) per year

	1960	1970	1980	1990	2000
Finland	–	–	1 492	1 376	957
New Zealand	3 293	3 114	2 856	1 971	1 312
Australia	**3 576**	**3 309**	**2 843**	**1 972**	**1 349**
United Kingdom	3 080	2 680	2 954	2 285	1 398
Canada	4 640	3 267	2 940	1 913	1 506
Norway	1 735	2 104	2 169	1 956	1 509
Denmark	–	2 227	2 022	1 854	1 611
United States	4 720	4 170	3 460	2 218	1 633
Sweden	2 040	2 180	1 990	1 850	1 710
Ireland	2 653	3 015	3 381	1 770	1 834
France	2 180	2 130	2 262	2 255	1 912
Austria	1 969	2 509	2 691	2 329	2 157
Belgium	3 217	3 555	3 077	2 462	2 243
Germany	1 790	2 685	2 843	1 929	2 262
Netherlands	2 647	2 963	3 588	3 043	2 472
Italy	1 658	2 093	2 643	–	–
Switzerland	1 900	2 640	3 025	–	–
Japan	2 350	2 442	2 528	3 220	3 176
Mean	2 694	2 732	2 688	2 150	1 815

Ranked according to 2000 consumption, with Italy and Switzerland placed according to their 1980 figures.

Table 16.19: Female daily smokers

Percentage of females who smoke daily

	1970	1980	1990	2000
Japan	16	14	14	15
Italy	–	17	18	17
United States	31	29	23	17
Canada	30	29	27	18
Germany	–	21	22	19
Australia	**28**	**31**	**27**	**20**
Finland	–	17	20	20
France	–	16	19	21
Sweden	–	29	26	21
Belgium	–	28	26	22
Austria	–	17	20	23
New Zealand	–	29	27	25
United Kingdom	44	37	29	25
Ireland	43	34	29	27
Switzerland	–	28	29	27
Denmark	47	44	42	29
Netherlands	42	34	32	29
Norway	32	30	33	32
Mean	33	27	26	23

Table 16.20: Male daily smokers

Percentage of males who smoke daily

	1970	1980	1990	2000
Sweden	–	35	26	17
Canada	49	37	30	21
United States	44	38	28	21
Australia	**45**	**41**	**30**	**25**
New Zealand	–	40	27	25
Finland	–	35	32	27
Ireland	–	39	31	28
United Kingdom	55	42	31	29
Germany	–	48	38	31
Norway	51	42	36	31
Denmark	68	57	47	32
Italy	–	54	38	32
France	53	46	38	33
Belgium	45	41	38	34
Austria	45	41	36	36
Netherlands	75	52	43	36
Switzerland	–	45	39	38
Japan	78	70	61	52
Mean	56	45	36	30

Tobacco consumption

The first scientific articles drawing a link between smoking and health problems appeared around 1950. In the following decades an overwhelming array of evidence linked smoking to cancer and heart diseases and to a range of lesser medical problems, and this information gradually penetrated into the public consciousness. The Australian Institute of Health and Welfare reports that smoking is the largest single preventable cause of premature mortality.

Given the strength of the evidence and the magnitude of the problems, perhaps the amazing thing is how tobacco consumption has persisted. However, its downward trend is clear in Tables 16.18 to 16.20. Table 16.18 shows that the mean for tobacco consumption in the selected countries rose until 1970 but has declined sharply since. Nevertheless there are great variations between countries, both in current consumption levels and in the timing of changes in habits.

In 1960, the English-speaking New World countries had the highest per capita tobacco consumption. America and Canada led the way with over 4500 grams each year. In third and fourth places were Australia and New Zealand. But it is also in these countries that the decline started and has been greatest. All began to decline in the 1960s, and each now has a per capita tobacco consumption around a third of their 1960 levels.

All the other countries started with lower initial rates of tobacco consumption, but many started reducing their consumption much later. Japan was the last of the selected countries to start changing habits, with reductions only beginning (and then very slight ones) in the 1990s. But several European countries were also slow to adjust to the dangers of tobacco. The Netherlands, Belgium, Austria and France not only had rising consumption into the 1980s but have reduced much less than the English-speaking countries. (The German data is complicated by unification.)

It is sometimes claimed that in recent years men are smoking less but women are smoking more. Overall Tables 16.19 and 16.20 show that the proportions of daily smokers in both sexes are dropping, though in many countries the rate of decrease is greater among men. So the once substantial gap between men and women who are daily smokers has narrowed. In 1980 there was a difference of 18 percentage points, while in 2000 it was only 7 percentage points. In Australia (25:20%) and most other countries male daily smokers still outnumber females. Only in Norway and Sweden did the percentage of female daily smokers slightly outnumber males, while in Denmark and Ireland they were close to parity. A special note of sympathy should be sounded for Japanese women, who have the smallest proportion of smokers among these countries, while Japanese males rate most highly (52:15%).

The AIHW has noted how differences between the sexes in tobacco smoking were matched by trends in deaths from lung cancer. Mortality among men peaked almost a quarter of a century after the peak of tobacco consumption in 1960, but was still rising among women. Danish women for example had the highest percentage of daily smokers until 1990, and this correlated with Denmark having the lowest female life expectancy (Table 1.7) and highest number of premature deaths from cancer (Table 6.35).

The total reduction in tobacco consumption recorded in Table 16.18 is greater than suggested by the declining numbers of daily smokers recorded in Tables 16.19 and 16.20. The discrepancy suggests that those who are regular smokers today have reduced their smoking compared with those in the past. They still smoke daily but consume fewer cigarettes.

Discrepancies in the relative rankings of countries on the different tables can also be indicative of different smoking habits. The United States ranks second bottom in both male and female daily smokers, but on total tobacco consumption ranks in the middle, suggesting that those who do smoke are fairly heavy smokers. Similarly, Japanese men must be very heavy smokers.

Table 16.21: Working time to buy meat

Number of minutes worked by average manufacturing worker to buy one kilo of the following meats:

	Beef	Chicken	Fish
Australia	30	27	36
Germany	30	8	36
Finland	41	14	24
New Zealand	45	19	48
Canada	48	16	–
United States	50	12	58
United Kingdom	52	24	55
Norway	61	23	44
Austria	61	22	95
Italy	76	33	66
Ireland	77	64	78
Denmark	78	11	23
France	82	32	73
Belgium	82	21	84
Switzerland	102	22	64
Japan	137	41	62
Mean	66	24	56

No data on Netherlands or Sweden.

Table 16.22: Working time to buy everyday foods

Number of minutes worked by average manufacturing worker to buy the following:

	Coffee	Bread	Milk
Denmark	19	5	2
Finland	22	8	3
Norway	25	8	4
Germany	26	7	2
France	26	11	6
United States	30	14	3
Switzerland	32	7	3
Italy	33	12	9
Canada	36	7	5
Australia	45	8	6
Austria	45	13	5
Belgium	52	9	4
Ireland	60	11	4
New Zealand	62	8	5
United Kingdom	88	4	3
Japan	88	15	8
Mean	43	9	5

No data on Sweden or the Netherlands.

Table 16.23: Working time to buy consumer durables

Hours worked by average manufacturing worker to buy the following:

	Car	Refrigerator	Television
Switzerland	614	14	22
Germany	861	17	32
United Kingdom	956	45	28
Italy	989	33	44
New Zealand	1 175	37	20
Japan	1 182	60	15
Denmark	1 206	29	13
Australia	**1 244**	**60**	**50**
United States	1 459	29	15
Belgium	1 500	43	68
Norway	1 517	18	22
Canada	1 552	–	–
France	1 600	36	22
Austria	1 672	38	42
Finland	1 681	24	20
Ireland	1 823	45	32
Mean	1 314	35	29

Working time to purchase consumer items

The comparison of income levels only becomes meaningful if the cost of buying the necessities and luxuries of life is also considered. The International Metalworkers' Federation, based in Geneva, has for many years conducted surveys on the purchasing power of working time for manufacturing workers. The most recent survey included data on 68 countries across a wide variety of consumer goods. Even though having one single measure like this must oversimplify to some extent, the Federation has paid great care to problems of equivalence, for example specifying consumer goods of roughly equal quality or the middle of the market range.

The study illuminates how relatively well off workers are in their capacity to buy goods. Over the mix of goods reported in Tables 16.21 to 16.23, German workers seem to be in the best position overall. Perhaps more interesting is the way the survey throws light on how differently the same commodities are priced in different countries, reflecting local availability, cost structures and demand, as well as differing consumption taxes and levels of protection.

Table 16.21 confirms what many Australians travelling overseas have discovered, that the price of beef is lower in Australia than nearly everywhere else. A Japanese manufacturing worker needs to work 4.5 times as long as an Australian or German to purchase beef. (The basket of foods selected has a bias towards a Western diet, which partly accounts for the Japanese food bill seeming so high.) In every country beef is more expensive than chicken, which is particularly cheap in Germany and for some reason expensive in Ireland.

As might have been predicted, the traditional Scandinavian taste for fish and their seafaring traditions are reflected in cheaper prices, especially in Denmark and Finland, while landlocked Austria is the most expensive on seafood.

The figures on the price of coffee in Table 16.22 show a fairly high correlation with the amounts of coffee consumed, as reported in Table 16.13. Coffee is relatively more expensive in the traditional tea-drinking countries at the bottom of the table.

While food is relatively cheap for Australian workers, the picture is different for the consumer durables in Table 16.23. An Australian manufacturing worker has to work more than three times as long as workers from Denmark, the United States and Japan to purchase a television. Similarly Australians are equal last (puzzlingly with the Japanese, for whom televisions and cars are much cheaper) in the time they need to work to buy a refrigerator.

The time taken to purchase a car shows huge variation from the Swiss low of 614 hours of work up to the Irish 1823. Australia is ranked almost exactly in the middle.

Table 17.1: Total official crime rate
Crimes recorded by police per 100 population

	1990	2000
Ireland	2.5	1.9
Japan	1.3	1.9
Switzerland	5.3	3.8
Italy	4.4	3.9
United States	5.8	4.2
France	6.2	6.4
Austria	5.9	6.9
Norway	5.6	7.3
Finland	8.7	7.4
Netherlands	7.1	7.4
Australia	**6.5**	**7.5**
Canada	9.5	7.6
Germany	7.0	7.6
Belgium	3.5	8.2
Denmark	10.3	9.5
United Kingdom	8.9	9.6
New Zealand	12.1	11.2
Sweden	14.2	13.7
Mean	6.9	7.0

Table 17.2: Victims of crime
Proportion of population reporting they had been victims of crime in the previous twelve months

	1992	2000
Japan	8.5	15.2
Norway	16.4	–
Switzerland	15.6	18.2
Austria	–	18.8
Finland	21.2	19.1
United States	26.1	21.1
Belgium	19.3	21.4
France	19.4	21.4
Germany	21.9	–
Denmark	–	23.0
Canada	28.4	23.8
Italy	24.6	–
Sweden	21.5	24.7
Netherlands	31.3	25.2
United Kingdom	30.2	26.4
New Zealand	29.4	–
Australia	**28.6**	**30.0**
Mean	22.9	22.2

Ranked according to reported crime rate in 2000. Those with data lacking are placed at their 1992 rate. No data on Ireland.

17 CRIME AND SOCIAL PROBLEMS
Crime rates

Crime and Social Problems is one of the sections of this book where the capacity of statistics to capture reality is most problematic. In measuring overall crime rates, there are two main methods, reported respectively in Tables 17.1 and 17.2, but each has its own problems.

Table 17.1 reports crimes officially recorded by the police per 100 population. Official crime statistics are always haunted by the 'dark figure' – the gap between the official and the actual rates of crime. The dark figure has two main sources: either that crime is not reported to the police or that reported crime is not recorded. Neither is constant either over time or between countries. It used to be the case, for example, that very serious offences such as sexual assaults and child abuse were not reported because the victim felt powerless to achieve justice or feared the police process that would follow. One suspects that the proportion of such offences now reported has increased substantially.

Even after a report is made, police have some discretion about whether and how it is recorded. Sometimes ulterior bureaucratic-political motives may enter: either deflating the rate of unsolved crimes to make police look more effective or inflating it in order to plead for extra resources. More importantly, the recorded rate reflects levels and patterns of policing, especially in some categories such as drug offences and public order offences.

So the differences between countries in official crime rates reported in Table 17.1 may first of all reflect differences in the incidence of crime. But equally the data may be affected by differences in official definitions, levels of policing, routines of reporting, and victims' willingness to report offences to the police.

The other major method of gauging the rate of crime is through surveys of the public, asking them to report if and how they have been victims. The United Nations has coordinated four waves of the International Crime Victims Survey – 1989, 1992, 1996, 2000 – to collect systematic comparative data on the experience of crime.

The success of this exercise rests on several factors. The most fundamental is the willingness of countries to participate. Australia has taken part in three ICVS surveys, all except 1996. In contrast, Ireland has not participated in any. The next issue is whether the surveys are based on representative samples, especially pertinent because victims of crime are often concentrated among deprived groups – ethnic minorities or the very poor, who are often underrepresented in survey research. Finally it depends on the willingness of respondents to answer honestly in the survey situation, for example without any fear of retribution, and to bring the same interpretations to the same questions.

Table 17.1 shows that Sweden has the highest officially recorded crime rate, and Table 17.2 that Australia has the highest proportion saying they have been victims. In both cases Japan ranks lowest. But these cross-national differences must be interpreted cautiously.

Remembering all the reservations, Tables 17.1 and 17.2 are still revealing. First, by both measures crime rates remained broadly constant over the last decade of the 20th century. Second, all countries show a much higher rate for claimed experience of crime than is suggested by the official rate – on average by a factor of about three. It is notable, however, that the discrepancy is less in Sweden than in most other countries, suggesting that the high official rate in Sweden is at least partly because of its more comprehensive recording of crime. Sweden and Italy have almost identical proportions (25%) reporting they have been victims of crime, but there is a great difference in their official rates (13.7:3.9%).

Methodological issues may also contribute to Australia having the highest number reporting they have been victims of crime, but while these make minute comparisons hazardous, they are not sufficient to obliterate the reality that Australia does have a relatively high crime rate.

Table 17.3: Homicides

Number of homicides per 100 000 population

	1980	1985	1990	1995	1999
Japan	0.9	0.8	0.6	0.5	0.6
France	1.0	1.2	1.0	1.0	0.7
United Kingdom	1.2	0.8	0.7	1.0	0.8
Austria	1.2	1.4	1.6	1.0	0.9
Denmark	1.3	1.4	1.0	1.1	0.9
Germany	1.2	1.2	1.0	1.1	0.9
Ireland	0.8	0.7	0.7	0.8	1.0
Norway	1.1	1.0	1.1	1.0	1.0
Sweden	1.2	1.3	1.2	1.0	1.1
Italy	1.9	1.4	2.5	1.4	1.2
Netherlands	0.8	0.8	0.9	1.2	1.2
Canada	2.0	2.0	2.0	1.6	1.4
Switzerland	1.0	1.5	1.4	0.9	1.4
Australia	**1.9**	**2.0**	**2.1**	**1.6**	**1.5**
New Zealand	1.6	2.0	2.3	1.2	1.5
Belgium	1.5	2.0	1.3	1.5	1.7
Finland	3.3	2.7	3.0	2.8	2.4
United States	9.6	7.8	9.6	8.8	6.8
Mean	1.9	1.8	1.9	1.6	1.5

Table 17.4: Use of cannabis and amphetamines

Percentage of population aged 15+ responding they had used
these drugs in the previous twelve months, 1999

	Cannabis	Amphetamines
Japan	0.1	0.3
Sweden	1.0	0.2
Finland	2.5	0.2
Austria	3.0	0.5
Norway	3.8	0.4
Denmark	4.0	0.7
Germany	4.1	0.5
Italy	4.6	0.5
France	4.7	0.3
Belgium	5.0	0.7
Netherlands	5.2	0.4
Canada	7.4	0.2
Ireland	7.9	0.7
Switzerland	8.5	0.8
United Kingdom	9.0	3.0
United States	12.3	0.7
Australia	**17.9**	**3.6**
New Zealand	22.2	2.5
Mean	6.8	0.9

Homicide and drug-taking

Table 17.3 shows that murder rates very slightly trended downwards between 1980 and 1999, but also that there are stark differences between the selected countries. Although the American rate declined in the 1990s, it was still by far the highest, with a rate over four times the overall mean. In 1999 an American had a ten times greater chance of being a homicide victim than did a Japanese.

Finland had the next highest homicide rate. Every other country had a rate of less than two homicide victims per 100 000 per year. Australia was part of a group with a relatively high rate of 1.5 or greater, while most countries had 1.2 or less. (Homicide includes both murder and manslaughter, with murder comprising about 90% of the total figure.)

Many factors contribute to the total murder rate in a society, but it seems plausible that one factor contributing to the extraordinary American rate is the widespread possession of firearms. In America, 66% of the 15 517 murders in 2000 were committed with firearms. In contrast, in Australia in 2001, only 16% of murders were committed with a firearm. The proportion has trended down steadily since the 1996 figure of 32% (a peak because of the Port Arthur massacre). Knives were the most commonly used weapon, but in around half the cases no weapon was identified (with the killings being caused by bashing, strangulation, and so on).

Apart from homicide, where there are relatively few problems of classification, the complications caused by different national methods in recording crimes make the comparison of different types of crime unfruitful for our purposes. However, one relatively well-defined area is illicit drug-taking. Table 17.4 reports data based on surveys asking people about their drug-taking. Surveying offenders is likely to be much more problematic than surveying victims, and there are very few areas where accurate information is likely to be forthcoming. It is not likely to

elicit any self-confessed murderers. Similarly, drugs such as heroin are disproportionately concentrated in strata (homeless, imprisoned, hospitalised) that are not normally reached by household surveys, and heroin-users are also less likely to admit their behaviour, fearing arrest or ostracism. However, asking people about their consumption of less serious drugs may yield more valid results.

Table 17.4 has New Zealand and Australia topping the list of self-confessed cannabis-users, with the United States and United Kingdom somewhat back in third and fourth places. In the second column, Australia, the United Kingdom and New Zealand easily outstrip the other countries in confessed use of amphetamines.

Again, methodological issues confound drawing easy conclusions. It may be that the survey research is more inclusive in these English-speaking countries. There may also be subtle differences in how people respond to survey situations. There are three tables reported in this book based on survey research where Australia comes first when it would not necessarily be expected to. One is here in self-confessed drug-taking; another is Table 17.2 in reporting they had been victims of crime, and the third is Tables 18.9 and 18.10 on membership of voluntary organisations. Are these all areas where Australia really does rank first, or is there an unsuspected national syndrome of responding yes in surveys?

Probably the answer is somewhere in the middle, but in each case it is likely that Australia does rank very high, and possibly highest. Although it is difficult to know the reasons for these figures, it is also the case that the countries that are highest on self-professed drug-taking are among those where government social expenditure is least and social inequality greatest. It would be unwise to accept the Australian figures on self-confessed drug-taking uncritically. It would be equally unwise to simply dismiss them as an unreliable aberration.

Table 17.5: Police officers

Number of police officers per 100 000 population, 2000

	2000 *
Italy	559
Austria	367
Belgium	343
Ireland	307
Germany	292
Sweden	257
Norway	248
United States	244
United Kingdom	234
Australia	**219**
France	211
Switzerland	202
Netherlands	199
Denmark	195
Canada	182
Japan	182
New Zealand	181
Finland	158
Mean	254

Table 17.7: Perceptions of safety and risk

Proportions in International Crime Victims Survey 2000 reporting that they feel:

	Only small risk of burglary	Safe walking in dark
Finland	84	81
Austria	82	78
Sweden	79	85
United States	78	82
Denmark	75	81
Norway	68	–
Canada	66	82
Switzerland	64	77
Netherlands	62	81
United Kingdom	58	70
Australia	**57**	**64**
Belgium	48	77
Italy	46	65
Germany	45	–
Japan	43	78
France	43	77
New Zealand	42	62
Mean	61	76

No data on Ireland.

Table 17.6: Reporting of crime to police

Proportions in International Crime Victims Survey 2000

	Reporting crime to police	Giving problems with police as reason for not reporting	Saying police do a good job controlling crime in their area
New Zealand	60	–	79
Netherlands	58	20	52
Sweden	57	27	61
Denmark	56	24	71
Belgium	53	90	64
United Kingdom	53	30	72
Switzerland	52	24	67
United States	52	33	89
Australia	**50**	**17**	**76**
France	49	24	65
Canada	48	17	87
Germany	48	–	67
Austria	46	–	76
Norway	43	–	70
Finland	41	16	70
Italy	40	–	–
Japan	39	32	54
Mean	50	22	69

No data on Ireland.

Police and perceptions of crime

Responses to crime vary greatly among the selected countries: in the numbers of police employed (Table 17.5), in the proportion of offences that are reported to police by victims, in the satisfaction with police (Table 17.6) and in how safe people feel (Table 17.7). If anything, the responses to crime show even more variation than does the incidence of crime.

Italy has by far the largest number of police officers, more than twice the overall mean and 50% more than the second-ranking country, Austria. This seems partly because Italy includes as police several categories of regulatory and enforcement officials that other nations do not. The lack of relationship between numbers of police and official crime rates is readily apparent by comparing the three lowest-ranking countries in Table 17.5 with Table 17.1. Finland with the lowest number of police officers rates in the middle of the recorded crime rates; New Zealand with the second lowest ratio is second highest in the crime rates; while Japan, third lowest in police officers, has the lowest recorded rate.

That effective policing is not simply a matter of resources is also shown by the peculiar patterns of Italy. Ironically Italy, with by far the most police proportionately, has one of the lowest proportions of victims reporting crime to the police (Table 17.6) and Italians are among those who feel least safe walking in the dark and are also relatively fearful of burglary (Table 17.7). Moreover, as Table 18.8 shows, they have the second lowest level of confidence in the police. The other lowest country on confidence in police is Belgium, which has proportionally the third biggest police force among these countries.

Table 17.6 shows that victims reported the crime to the police only half the time. Reporting ranged from a high of 60% in New Zealand down to 39% in Japan, with Australia ranking exactly on the mean at 50%. The ICVS in 2000, from which this data comes, also probed the reasons for failing to report the crime. The overwhelming reasons were that victims felt the offence was too insignificant or unsuitable for reporting to the police. Respondents were also offered a range of reasons that reflected on their confidence in the police force, in particular its willingness or capacity to do anything about the crime. Column 2 sums the responses (people could give more than one) where victims gave problems with the police as their reason for not reporting the crime. Among those where data is available, by far the country with least confidence in their police is Belgium, where responses of this kind dwarf the numbers from any other country: 90 compared with the second highest, the United States, totalling 30. Australia, Canada and Finland have the lowest proportion giving problems with the police as their reason for failing to report the offence. Overall, however, as the final column shows, majorities of respondents in all countries thought the police were doing a good job controlling crime in their area.

The ICVS survey also probed feelings of risk and safety. Three-quarters of people said they felt safe walking in the dark, and there was only a moderate range of variation between the countries, from the mid-80s (Sweden) down to the low 60s – Australia, New Zealand and Italy. There is a much bigger range of variation in people's perception of the risk of burglary. In five countries – Finland, Austria, Sweden, the United States and Denmark – three-quarters or more felt the risk was small. But in six others less than half the respondents felt that way. Australia again ranked in the more fearful half. Perception of risk bears a problematic relationship to actual risk. This is most obvious with Japan where the objective risk of burglary is the lowest, but the Japanese still rank among those most fearful of it.

Table 17.8: Imprisonment rates

Prisoners per 100 000 population

	1982	1990	2000
Japan	46	38	45
Finland	99	65	50
Denmark	62	64	60
Norway	46	57	60
Sweden	55	58	65
France	59	80	80
Ireland	–	56	80
Austria	–	82	85
Belgium	64	65	85
Netherlands	32	44	85
Switzerland	–	77	90
Germany	80	78	95
Italy	62	52	95
Canada	107	109	105
Australia	**46**	**85**	**110**
United Kingdom	91	92	123
New Zealand	84	120	145
United States	301	457	700
Mean	82	85	120

Table 17.9: Capital punishment

Death penalty in abolitionist countries

	Does country retain death penalty?	Year abolished for ordinary crimes (all crimes)	Year of last execution
Australia	**No**	**1985**	**1967**
Austria	No	1950 (1968)	1950
Belgium	No	1996	1950
Canada	No	1976 (1998)	1962
Denmark	No	1933 (1978)	1950
Finland	No	1949 (1972)	1944
France	No	1981	1977
Germany*	No	1949	1949
Ireland	No	1990	1954
Italy	No	1947 (1994)	1947
Netherlands	No	1870 (1982)	1952
New Zealand	No	1989	–
Norway	No	1905 (1979)	1948
Sweden	No	1921 (1972)	1910
Switzerland	No	1942 (1992)	1944
United Kingdom	No	1973 (1998)	1964

* West Germany abolished the death penalty in 1949, East Germany in 1987.

Death penalty in retentionist countries

Country	Does country retain death penalty?	Number under death sentence in 2001	Number executed in 2000
Japan	Yes	110	3
United States	Yes	3700	85

Punishment

Imprisonment rates in the selected countries show enormous variation. The United States has a unique profile, with a rate four times higher than the second-ranking country and having more than doubled since 1982. Then come four other English-speaking countries, with a mean imprisonment rate of 121 per 100 000 population, while the mean for the other 13 countries is only around 60% of that, at 75 per 100 000. The Scandinavian countries and Japan have the lowest frequency of imprisonment, with rates varying between 45 and 65.

According to American scholar Marie Gottschalk, American incarceration practices were not exceptional for most of the 20th century. Until 1970 the United States had a rate higher, but not remarkably higher, than other Western countries. From then on, its imprisonment rates escalated far more sharply than any other country's. Australia and New Zealand, starting from a much lower base and somewhat later than the United States, have also shown dramatic increases.

Punishment practices seem to bear little relationship to the prevalence of crime. Although recorded crime rates remained fairly constant between 1990 and 2000, the mean imprisonment rate for the 18 countries went up by around 40% in the same decade. Twelve countries increased imprisonment rates. In some, officially recorded crime rates were down, and in others they were constant. The Netherlands, for example, increased its imprisonment rate from 45 to 85, while total crime remained essentially unchanged. Similarly the rankings of countries in their imprisonment rate seem to bear little relationship to crime rates. Japan has the lowest for both, but otherwise there is little correlation.

The two tables are too crude to draw more penetrating conclusions. The per capita imprisonment rate is determined by the rate at which people are arrested, the seriousness of their offences, the rate at which they are convicted, the proportion of those given a prison sentence, and the average length of the term imposed. It is not possible then to conclude definitively that the increased imprisonment rate reflects increasingly punitive attitudes, or to know how it may interact with the crime rate.

Neither can any conclusions be drawn supporting the deterrent effect of capital punishment. Table 17.9 shows that all but two of these countries have abolished capital punishment. Of the only two countries that retain the death penalty, the United States has the highest homicide rate and Japan the lowest. According to Amnesty International figures, Canada abolished capital punishment in 1976. The preceding year its homicide rate was 3.1 per 100 000. By 1999 it was down to 1.4.

None of the other 16 countries has executed anyone for over a quarter of a century, and some of them for the last half-century or longer. Ironically the last execution among them occurred in France in 1977, the year that the United States resumed exercising the death penalty. Between 1977 and 2000, there were 683 executions in the United States.

A somewhat bizarre aspect of the two countries that retain the death penalty is that they sentence far more people to death than they execute. At the end of 2000, 3700 Americans were on death row. If they continue to execute them at the rate of 85 a year, it will take 40 years for all those already sentenced to be executed.

Table 17.10: Suicides

Number of suicides per 100 000 population

	1960	1970	1980	1990	2000 *
Italy	6.2	5.6	6.7	6.5	6.3
United Kingdom	9.7	7.3	8.1	7.4	6.9
Netherlands	7.3	8.5	9.9	8.7	8.5
United States	11.4	12.3	11.6	11.9	10.7
Germany	17.5	20.2	18.5	13.1	11.2
Canada	8.8	12.4	13.9	12.0	11.4
Norway	6.2	8.1	12.7	14.4	11.8
Sweden	15.9	20.4	19.0	15.0	11.9
Denmark	19.7	20.4	29.2	20.5	12.1
Australia	**11.3**	**13.3**	**11.2**	**12.5**	**12.4**
Ireland	3.0	1.9	7.1	10.1	13.2
New Zealand	10.7	10.8	11.3	13.4	15.2
France	14.9	14.7	17.9	17.7	15.4
Austria	21.2	23.0	23.7	20.5	16.3
Switzerland	18.6	18.2	23.8	19.1	16.3
Belgium	13.3	15.1	20.1	16.6	18.5
Japan	25.1	17.1	17.8	14.5	19.9
Finland	21.6	21.4	25.2	27.8	21.2
Mean	13.5	13.9	16.0	14.5	13.0

Table 17.11: Female suicide rates

Number of suicides per 100 000 population among females

	1960	2000 *
Italy	3.7	2.8
United Kingdom	7.1	2.9
Ireland	1.8	3.8
United States	5.2	4.0
Canada	3.5	4.6
Australia	**6.4**	**4.9**
Germany	11.1	5.5
Netherlands	5.4	5.5
Norway	2.3	6.3
Denmark	12.8	6.5
Sweden	7.9	6.6
New Zealand	5.9	6.8
France	7.3	7.7
Austria	12.9	8.2
Switzerland	10.2	8.3
Finland	9.1	8.5
Belgium	7.0	9.8
Japan	20.7	10.8
Mean	7.8	6.3

Table 17.12: Male suicide rate

Number of suicides per 100 000 population among males

	1960	2000 *
Italy	9.2	10.4
United Kingdom	13.0	10.9
Netherlands	9.3	11.7
Norway	10.2	17.4
Sweden	24.3	17.4
Germany	25.1	17.6
United States	18.3	18.0
Denmark	27.0	18.2
Australia	**16.4**	**20.2**
Canada	14.0	20.3
Ireland	4.2	22.7
New Zealand	15.7	23.9
France	24.6	24.2
Switzerland	28.4	25.0
Austria	31.7	26.2
Belgium	20.8	28.2
Japan	29.9	29.6
Finland	36.7	34.7
Mean	19.9	20.9

Table 17.13: Suicides and age groups

Suicide rates per 100 000 by age group, late 1990s

	15–24	25–34	35–44	45–54	56–64	65–74	75+
Italy	4.3	7.3	7.7	9.1	12.0	14.3	21.8
Germany	4.7	9.4	15.8	28.8	32.6	34.4	45.9
United Kingdom	6.7	10.6	11.4	9.3	7.9	7.5	9.2
Netherlands	6.8	10.6	14.2	12.7	12.9	14.0	15.1
Japan	8.6	14.1	16.2	23.7	26.7	23.7	42.3
Ireland	8.8	14.0	15.2	11.0	15.7	10.8	6.5
Denmark	9.3	16.9	23.9	35.9	32.1	43.9	46.3
Sweden	9.4	13.8	21.0	23.0	20.9	19.4	27.0
France	10.3	21.3	28.5	28.4	26.8	31.2	48.0
Belgium	10.7	19.0	23.0	24.5	23.8	29.7	42.3
United States	13.7	15.3	15.3	14.3	13.3	15.3	22.0
Australia	**14.6**	**18.7**	**15.9**	**14.7**	**13.7**	**11.8**	**16.0**
Austria	15.0	20.8	25.2	27.9	28.9	33.2	57.1
Canada	15.0	18.0	19.2	18.5	15.1	12.1	12.2
Switzerland	17.9	18.8	21.8	27.8	27.4	30.7	50.6
Finland	22.8	33.0	44.0	43.4	43.8	28.1	23.3
New Zealand	26.7	25.1	14.8	14.7	13.3	17.0	13.6
Mean	12.1	16.9	19.6	21.6	21.6	22.2	29.4

Ranked according to suicide rate for 15 to 24-year-olds.
No data on Norway.

Suicide

Each year, suicide claims almost ten times as many victims in the selected countries as homicide does. In Table 17.10, the overall mean rate in 2000 was almost the same as it had been in 1960, rising in the first two decades but then falling again in the next two.

It is not clear what aspects of societies explain the variations in suicide rates, or why they change over time, but the differences are substantial. Finland has triple the rate of Italy. By 1990 Japan's rate had fallen to around 60% of its 1960 level but rose sharply again in the 1990s (perhaps because of increased economic stresses). Denmark's suicide rate rose sharply, until by 1980 it ranked highest, but then fell even more sharply so that by 2000 it had more than halved. Australia is almost exactly in the middle of the table, and has shown less fluctuation than several other countries, though it has trended slightly upwards.

None of the patterns which sometimes explain the clustering of countries on other phenomena correlates well with suicide. Catholic Italy has the lowest rate, but Catholic Belgium and Austria have among the highest, while Catholic Ireland is in the middle. Scandinavian Finland has the highest rate, but the other three Scandinavian countries are in the other half of the table. None of the English-speaking countries is in the worst third, but they are spread throughout the rest of the table, with Britain having the second lowest rate.

Tables 17.11 and 17.12 show that in all the countries, males are more likely to commit suicide than females. Over the 40 years the gap increased slightly, so that in 2000 males were three times as likely as females to die by suicide. In Australia, males were five times more likely to commit suicide than females.

There is an important difference between countries in the age distribution of suicides. Traditionally suicide was much higher among the oldest age groups. This is still the case in some countries. Italy, the lowest-ranking country in youth suicides in Table 17.13, for example, shows a steadily increasing suicide rate with age. Similar trends are apparent in other European countries, such as Austria, Switzerland and Belgium, Germany and Denmark. In these European countries, by far the highest suicide rate is found among those over 75, the second highest among 65 to 74-year-olds with steadily decreasing rates down through the age groups. Other countries show a broadly similar trend but not quite so neatly.

New Zealand is notable for having the reverse trend. Its suicide rate is much higher among younger people than older people. Although less dramatically, Australia to a large extent follows the New Zealand pattern. Its rate is higher than the 18-nation mean for those below 34 years of age, and lower for all the older age groups.

Although all suicide is tragic, youth suicide is particularly so, because it means people are being denied more years of life. The Australian and New Zealand distributions show that suicide is taking a heavy toll of young males in these countries.

Table 17.14: Childhood deaths from injury

Annual deaths from injury per 100 000 children (aged 1–14 years)

	1971–75	1991–95	Share of all child deaths 1990s %
Sweden	13.0	5.2	33
Italy	16.3	6.1	28
United Kingdom	14.3	6.1	29
Netherlands	20.1	6.6	30
Norway	21.6	7.6	37
Denmark	19.9	8.1	36
Finland	24.7	8.2	43
Germany	28.4	8.3	38
Ireland	17.2	8.3	39
Japan	22.4	8.4	36
France	19.4	9.1	41
Belgium	20.0	9.2	40
Austria	23.7	9.3	42
Australia	**22.3**	**9.5**	**42**
Switzerland	22.5	9.6	40
Canada	27.8	9.7	44
New Zealand	23.7	13.7	47
United States	24.8	14.1	49
Mean	21.2	8.8	39

Ranked according to mortality rate 1990s.

Table 17.15: Mortality among young adults

Average standardised mortality rates per 100 000 population, 15 to 35-year-olds, 1955–94

	Suicide	Homicide	Motor vehicle injury	Three causes combined
United Kingdom	6.72	1.19	15.77	23.68
Norway	10.47	0.95	13.18	24.60
Netherlands	6.60	0.95	17.13	24.68
Ireland	6.48	0.93	17.71	25.12
Italy	4.21	2.01	21.35	27.57
Sweden	15.02	1.22	15.17	31.41
Japan	18.26	1.20	13.94	33.40
Denmark	14.93	1.02	18.03	33.98
France	11.77	1.32	27.61	40.70
Belgium	10.86	1.26	28.74	40.86
Switzerland	18.88	1.04	22.48	42.40
Finland	23.91	2.88	17.00	43.79
Germany	14.82	1.31	29.08	45.21
Canada	13.81	2.65	29.91	46.37
New Zealand	12.26	1.94	33.49	47.69
Australia	**13.19**	**2.28**	**33.35**	**48.82**
Austria	18.65	1.41	34.43	54.49
United States	12.22	14.06	33.11	59.39
Mean	12.95	2.20	23.41	38.56

Young deaths from misadventure

The death of healthy young people with their whole lives before them is particularly tragic. Tables 17.14 and 17.15 report on the incidence of deaths among children and young adults. Table 17.14 reports a UNICEF study of child deaths from injury, while 17.15 comes from American scholar Patrick Heuvelink's examination of mortality rates from three main causes of death for young adults (aged 15–35) over a 40-year period.

Heuvelink's data shows that American youths are at greatest risk from these three causes of death overall, having more than twice the mortality rate of the five countries with the lowest rates. But if death from homicide is removed, American youth's greater vulnerability is substantially reduced. Thirteen countries have a death rate from homicide of less than two young adults per 100 000, compared to America's 14.

The United States is the only country where deaths from homicide outnumber deaths from suicide. Overall the mean death rate from suicide is six times as great as from homicide, while the contrasts between countries are just as great. Finland is the only country with a youth suicide mortality rate greater than 20, while four of the five countries at the top of the table – Britain, the Netherlands, Ireland and Italy – have figures of less than seven.

The biggest of these three killers of young adults was deaths from motor vehicle accidents. Its overall mean was almost twice that of suicides. In Japan and Finland, however, the figures were reversed. Both had relatively high fatality rates from suicide and low ones from car accidents.

Because motor vehicle deaths contribute the largest share, rankings on this cause of death correlate highly with the total. The bottom four countries on the table also have the worst death rates from car accidents. Austria is the worst, but New Zealand, Australia and the United States have almost identical rates.

While Heuvelink examines the period as a whole, the UNICEF study also looks at changes in child deaths from injury. Table 17.14 shows a heartening trend. Child deaths from injuries dropped by more than half between the early 1970s and early 1990s. But deaths from other causes declined even more quickly, so that the proportion of deaths from injury rose from 25% to 39% of all child deaths.

Traffic accidents accounted for 41% of child deaths from injury in the early 1990s – more often the child being killed while a pedestrian or on a bicycle than as a passenger in a car. The second highest group, comprising 15%, were deaths from drowning, while next most important (14%) were intentional causes: murder, manslaughter and suicide. Fire (7%) and falls (4%) were also relatively common.

In both sets of data males are far more likely to die than females. This difference is already present in very young children but becomes greater in the teenage years and greater still among young adults.

American children, like American young adults, are most at risk. The rankings are broadly similar in the two tables. The United Kingdom, Sweden, Italy, Norway and the Netherlands are near the safest end of the spectrum in both; the United States, New Zealand, Australia, Canada, Austria and Switzerland are at the dangerous end. The two results seem to point to fairly pervasive differences in these societies, especially regarding road safety, but also in degrees of violence. On a more optimistic note, these figures, as well as others in the book, show that in many ways these societies are becoming safer for their citizens and future citizens.

Table 17.16: Motor vehicle deaths
Fatalities per 100 000 population

	1960	1970	1980	1990	1999 *
Sweden	14.4	16.5	10.4	8.4	5.6
United Kingdom	14.7	14.2	11.7	9.4	5.6
Netherlands	17.6	24.8	13.1	8.3	7.2
Finland	18.1	23.8	11.7	12.8	8.6
Switzerland	23.1	26.1	18.5	13.3	8.6
Norway	8.6	15.0	8.7	7.6	8.7
Japan	15.9	22.4	10.5	11.3	8.8
Denmark	17.1	24.2	13.5	11.2	9.4
Canada	22.6	25.7	21.6	13.7	9.6
Germany	25.6	32.2	19.6	11.2	9.8
Australia	**28.0**	**32.8**	**23.9**	**13.8**	**10.0**
Austria	27.6	33.3	24.0	17.2	10.4
Ireland	9.3	17.0	17.1	13.4	11.6
Italy	17.8	24.3	18.7	14.6	12.9
France	18.1	23.2	20.0	17.2	13.7
New Zealand	16.5	24.2	19.0	21.7	14.0
Belgium	19.2	29.9	24.3	17.7	15.4
United States	23.2	27.6	22.0	18.2	15.5
Mean	18.7	24.3	17.1	13.4	10.3

Figure for Belgium = 1995.

Table 17.17: Injuries from road traffic accidents
Number per 100 000 population

	1960	1970	1980	1990	1999
Finland	219	348	177	256	175
Denmark	–	516	294	207	177
Australia	**600**	**732**	**218**	**233**	**184**
Sweden	288	276	232	263	248
Norway	173	303	251	280	257
France	405	633	619	398	286
Netherlands	421	528	400	348	330
Ireland	192	314	250	269	330
New Zealand	518	728	523	325	333
Switzerland	642	574	506	436	412
Italy	401	424	395	390	549
United Kingdom	674	668	585	604	555
Germany	819	877	813	709	635
Austria	924	943	830	786	679
Belgium	859	1 101	836	865	696
Canada	–	641	1 073	948	719
Japan	310	937	512	639	831
United States	–	975	1 251	1 295	1 187
Mean	496	640	542	514	477

Table 17.18: Cars
Cars per 1000 population

	1980	1990	1999 *
Italy	303	476	539
Germany	297	386	508
Austria	297	387	495
Switzerland	356	449	486
Australia	**401**	**450**	**485**
New Zealand	420	436	481
United States	536	573	478
France	355	405	469
Canada	417	468	459
Belgium	–	385	448
Sweden	347	426	437
Norway	302	380	407
Finland	256	386	403
Japan	203	283	395
Netherlands	322	368	383
United Kingdom	268	341	373
Denmark	271	320	353
Ireland	216	227	272
Mean	327	397	437

Deaths from car accidents

Table 17.16 shows that deaths from motor vehicle accidents remain a very acute social problem. Especially because of the age structure of its victims – with young males in particular disproportionately represented – it is probably still the most important cause of premature mortality in the selected countries. Despite this, Table 17.16 also shows a very considerable policy success. The death toll across all these societies in 1999 was only about 40% of the 1970 figure, a very substantial reduction. If the Australian rate had stayed at its disastrous 1970 peak, then about 4000 more Australians would have died on the roads in 2000 than did so.

As cars became more widely affordable in the decades after World War II, the death toll from car accidents rose enormously. But every single country had a substantially lower death toll in 1999 than in 1970, providing testimony to the capacity of well-directed policies to ameliorate the problem. To varying degrees in different countries, the arsenal of changes has included: improved car design; compulsory wearing of seat belts; improved road design, including the identification of 'black spots'; reductions in speed limits; a much stricter approach to driving under the influence of alcohol, including random breath testing; and improved driver education.

In the worst-ranking countries – Austria, Australia and Germany – the 1970 fatality rate had soared to over 30 per 100 000. Each of those countries then reduced its rate substantially so that by 1999 they figure in the middle of the table. However, they still have fatality rates almost double those of the safest countries, Sweden and Britain.

Table 17.18 is a reminder that this success in reducing the road toll occurred even though at the same time car ownership was still rising. Overall in these countries the number of cars per 1000 people rose by about a third in the last 20 years of the 20th century. Only the United States, the previous world leader in car penetration, showed a steady reduction through the 1990s.

The rise tended to be greatest in those countries where the rate of car ownership had been lowest. The less densely populated New World countries – the United States, New Zealand, Canada and Australia – were the only countries with more than four cars for every ten people in 1980. By 1999, 13 countries exceeded that rate. Four of the five countries falling below it were densely populated and highly urbanised. The exception was Ireland, which had not yet translated its growing affluence into high car ownership.

The data on injuries from road accidents in Table 17.17 is much less reliable. Differences in definition about how serious injuries are before they are included certainly account for some of the variations. The Australian injury rate, for example, trended down through the 1970s, to 640 in 1979, but then dropped precipitously to 218 in 1980. This is clearly because of a change in definition rather than a real change of that magnitude.

One would expect the rankings in Tables 17.16 and 17.17 to be broadly similar, and the United States suffers the heaviest toll in both. One possible reason for a discrepancy would be that if a country with dense traffic had a high number of crashes but at lower speeds, then there could be more injuries but fewer fatalities. This could explain Japan's jump to rank second in 17.17.

In very general terms, Table 17.17 shows a similar curve to Table 17.16, with the 18-nation mean peaking in 1970 and then trending down. But the data is so confounded by the possibility of different definitions that little confidence can be had in either the precise comparisons or trends. The most important lesson to be drawn from Table 17.18 is that the toll from road traffic smashes is not only in the fatalities. For every fatality there are on average almost a further 50 serious injuries.

Table 17.19: Gambling and gaming machines

Gaming machines: numbers and expenditure, 1999; all expenditure in $A

	Expenditure on gaming machines per adult ($)	Gaming machines per 10 000 adults	Expenditure per machine ($)	Maximum average loss per hour ($)	Total legal gaming machines (000s)
France	–	–	–	–	53
Germany	–	–	–	–	227
Canada	80	26	32 200	186	58
United Kingdom	90	59	14 500	130	266
United States	150	29	50 500	705	583
New Zealand	160	62	26 100	156	16
Japan	370	474	7 880	52	4 691
Australia	**420**	**133**	**32 000**	**720**	**185**

Gambling

It is commonly asserted that Australians are unusually, even uniquely, fond of gambling. Although good comparative data is not easily obtainable, to the extent that it exists, it tends to confirm the stereotype. There is certainly ample data to show that expenditure on gambling is increasing in Australia.

In 1998, the average Australian household lost around 3% of its disposable income on gambling. This is almost a doubling since 1973, when the equivalent figure was 1.6%. According to a Congressional study over almost exactly the same period (1974–97), American expenditure on gambling rose from 0.3% to 0.7% of personal income. In 2001, the average Australian adult's annual gambling losses totalled around $1000.

The increase in total gambling in Australia is overwhelmingly due to an increase in expenditure on gaming machines. Betting on racing rose only slightly in those 25 years, from around $1.3 billion to $1.7 billion (both in 1998$), but its share of total legal gambling expenditure dropped from 49% to 15%. In contrast, expenditure on gaming machines rose from $1 billion to $6 billion. Their share continued to increase in the following years. By 2000–01 they formed 63% of total gambling revenue, up from 57% just three years earlier.

The best comparative data on gaming machines that we have comes from a Productivity Commission report published in 1999. That report grouped machines into three types. High-intensity machines, the most common in Australia and the United States, have high spending per game with a high speed of play. Amusement with prizes machines involve both lower spending and a comparatively slower speed of play. Japanese-style pachinko machines and pinball-style machines elsewhere have the lowest stakes and slowest play. As Table 17.16 shows, a consistently losing player playing continuously at normal speed for an hour would lose $52 in Japan but $720 in Australia, and expenditure per machine is more than six times higher in the United States than Japan.

Thus although in Table 17.19 Japan has the highest proportionate number of gaming machines and the highest absolute total, it does not have the high-intensity machines that dominate in the United States and Australia. According to the Productivity Commission data, the United States has 64% of the world total of high-intensity gaming machines, while Australia, with around 0.3% of the world's population, has 20%.

Overall Australian expenditure on gaming machines, at $420 per year, is considerably higher than in the other countries in the table. Some would regard that figure as simply a waste, while others would think the accompanying enjoyment made it a worthwhile expenditure. But of course, the average figure is not uniformly distributed through the population. The human tragedy comes with those who become gambling addicts or problem gamblers, often with a devastating impact on their family and work lives. The US Congressional study estimated that at some stage of their lives, 3 million American adults had a pathological gambling problem. In Australia, the Productivity Commission estimated 2.1% of adults (293 000 people) were experiencing significant problems with their gambling, including 1% of adults having severe problems.

Although governments sometimes make pious noises about both the increases in gambling and the problems it causes, they also have a vested interest in its growth. In 1997, American governments raised $US34 billion in revenue from gambling. The same year Australian governments raised $3.8 billion, a fourfold increase in real terms on a quarter of a century earlier.

Table 18.1: Religious tradition

Self-described religious affiliation in the 1970s, %

	Roman Catholic	Protestant	Non-Christian	No religion
Ireland	96	4	0	0
Belgium	92	0	1	7
Austria	90	7	0	3
Italy	87	0	0	13
France	80	2	4	14
Switzerland	52	46	1	1
Canada	50	43	2	5
Germany	46	48	2	4
Netherlands	44	43	2	11
Australia	**32**	**57**	**1**	**10**
United States	31	58	5	6
New Zealand	18	75	1	6
United Kingdom	14	74	3	9
Sweden	2	71	0	27
Denmark	1	95	1	3
Finland	1	94	0	5
Japan	1	2	87	11
Norway	0	98	0	2

18   RELIGION, VALUES AND ATTITUDES
Religious tradition

Barrett's Encyclopaedia, from whose data Table 18.1 is drawn, documented religious practices in the 1970s. The religious affiliations in Table 18.1 are a guide to religious heritage rather than contemporary belief, and while in some countries the number describing themselves as having no religion was already substantial, it has almost certainly risen further since.

In terms of the broad historical influence of religious traditions, the 18 countries fall into five groups. First, and by itself, is Japan – the only country among our 18 with a predominantly non-Christian tradition. The predominant religions in Japan are Buddhism and Shinto, with many Japanese professing both.

The second group consists of those where Catholicism is dominant and where Protestantism never established itself very broadly in the population. It comprises the five countries at the top of table 18.1: Ireland, Belgium, Austria, Italy and France. In each, the Catholic Church has played an important role in the country's politics, and religious conflict has figured not as Catholic versus Protestant but rather clerical versus anti-clerical.

The four Scandinavian countries near the bottom of the table form a third group. Here Protestantism triumphed to become the dominant religion. Historically the eclipse of Catholicism was to some extent tied in with their development as nations and their national identity. Monarchs in Denmark, Norway and Sweden, for example, are obliged to be Protestant.

The final two groups comprise eight countries where Catholicism and Protestantism have had to learn to coexist, sometimes with histories of sharp sectarian conflict. Four countries – Switzerland, Canada, Germany and the Netherlands – have close to numerical equality, or a slight Catholic majority. There are considerable differences in their religious histories, depending on how politically mobilised the Catholic Church was, and on their histories of sectarian conflict. In the Netherlands, for example, the bitterness of the religious struggles and the prospect of eternal stalemate ushered in a political system based on consensus and mutual compromise. In Switzerland and Canada religious differences are also overlaid by linguistic ones and there was some degree of territorial segregation between them.

The final group comprises the four English-speaking countries where there is a clear Protestant majority and a Catholic minority. It must be remembered that the Protestants in these countries were far from unified. In Australia, for example, there was always a clear divide between the Anglicans and other Protestant churches, which were also divided among themselves. The proportion of Catholics is larger in Australia and the United States, where its membership has been boosted by waves of immigrants, especially the Irish and Italians. In Britain and New Zealand, Catholics are a smaller minority, and their political importance consequently less.

It is difficult to be definitive about how the content of the different religions has influenced contemporary national policies and outlooks. Certainly those countries with the most religious pluralism were the earliest and most emphatic in separating church and state.

The four predominantly Protestant Scandinavian countries have been the most secular, with the apparent decline of religious belief and practice greatest in them. They have also been world leaders in the development of the welfare state and manifest the strongest social conscience, being for example among the most generous in their overseas aid contributions. Where there has been a Catholic near-monopoly, that church's influence in areas like divorce, abortion and education has been more apparent. But again there has been considerable divergence between these countries in such matters. National traditions have many sources beyond religious denominations, and policies are rarely reducible to their country's religious heritage.

Table 18.2: Religious beliefs

Proportion in 1990s surveys who say they believe in:

Country	God	The soul	Sin	Life after death	Heaven	The devil	Hell
Ireland	98	88	87	83	90	55	53
United States	96	93	89	79	86	72	72
Italy	90	77	72	68	52	40	40
Canada	89	85	74	69	71	43	41
Austria	87	73	66	56	47	23	20
Switzerland	84	84	61	64	45	30	23
Australia	**80**	**85**	**74**	**64**	**63**	**47**	**41**
Finland	80	80	71	60	60	41	33
United Kingdom	79	71	72	53	61	33	29
Germany	77	79	60	52	39	19	15
Belgium	71	61	46	45	34	19	16
Norway	67	57	45	46	45	26	19
Netherlands	65	72	46	45	37	18	14
Denmark	64	47	24	34	19	10	8
France	62	55	43	44	32	20	17
Japan	60	69	28	50	40	18	28
Sweden	51	64	32	44	34	15	10
Mean	76	73	58	56	50	31	28

Table 18.3: Role of religion in an individual's life

Proportion in 1990s surveys who say they do or think the following:

Country	Attend church at least once a week	Find comfort in religion	Describe self as religious	Religion very or rather important	Often think of meaning of life	Importance of God
Ireland	81	83	72	84	34	7.9
United States	45	81	83	81	48	8.1
Italy	38	69	85	68	48	7.1
Canada	27	62	71	61	44	6.9
Belgium	26	48	69	47	29	5.3
Austria	25	61	81	59	28	5.3
Netherlands	20	45	61	44	31	4.9
Switzerland	20	55	66	50	45	7.6
Australia	**17**	**49**	**59**	**48**	**45**	**5.7**
Germany	14	48	58	34	36	5.8
United Kingdom	14	46	57	46	36	5.7
France	10	36	51	43	39	4.4
Norway	5	38	47	39	32	4.9
Finland	4	52	58	43	39	6.9
Sweden	4	30	32	28	26	4.6
Denmark	3	27	73	31	29	3.9
Japan	3	38	25	22	23	4.8
Mean	21	51	62	49	36	5.9

Religious beliefs and practices

Tables 18.2 and 18.3 portray a confusing array of beliefs, but the overall picture is one of societies that no longer fully accept and observe the religious traditions they inherited but are reluctant to reject all aspects of them.

The data comes from the World Values Survey project, initiated by Professor Ronald Inglehart. By administering the same survey to representative samples in different countries, and asking questions which concentrate more on enduring values than the most immediate political controversies, it has generated very valuable cross-national data. On very abstract questions like these ones about religious belief, there is no guarantee that any two individuals understand the same thing by soul or heaven or the devil, and the differences in interpretation on such questions between a Japanese and a Frenchman, for example, could be considerable. Moreover, survey research is a rather blunt instrument for exploring the subtleties of religious belief, but it is the only way to gain broadly representative data to show nationwide patterns of belief.

Table 18.2 shows that belief in God and the soul still command a majority in all these societies, while the capacity of the devil and hell to inspire fear has greatly diminished. Table 18.3, however, suggests that religion is more often professed than practised, and does not seem to be a central concern or comfort for most of the respondents to these surveys. While on average around three-quarters say they believe in God, only around half find comfort in religion or think that religion is very or rather important.

It would surprise few to find that Ireland is generally the most religious and Sweden and Denmark the most secular of these societies. The Irish, for example, top the list of those believing in God, life after death and heaven; are the most likely to say they find comfort in religion; the most likely to say religion is important; and (by a huge margin) are the most regular church attenders.

However, the patterns of belief and unbelief contain many surprises. Americans, for example, are in some respects more religious than the Irish. In both there is almost universal belief in God and the soul, and very large majorities describing themselves as religious and finding comfort in religion. Most surprisingly, America is – overwhelmingly – the country with most people saying they believe in the devil and in hell. The 18-nation mean is about three in ten people believing in the devil, but it ranges from 10% of Danes to 72% of Americans. A similar range is found in beliefs about hell.

On many items, the Scandinavian countries and Japan (with its very different religious heritage) come at the less religious end of the spectrum. At the more religious end, Canada is often fairly close to its American neighbour, while Italy sometimes rivals Ireland in its religiosity. Countries with a predominantly Catholic heritage do not all appear so religious, however. France is in the secular half on most questions, while Belgium and Austria show great variations. On most of these questions, Australia is fairly much in the middle, and on some aspects, for example belief in the soul and sin, somewhat above the mean.

In no country does a majority say that they often think about the meaning of life. Despite this, and despite the relative lack of church attendance, many seem reluctant to shed their religious self-image. For example, only 3% of Danes attend church weekly, but 73% of them still describe themselves as religious.

Perhaps the strangest question was one which asked respondents to rate the importance of God to them on a scale from one to ten. It is rather unclear what a rating of, say, four or seven on such a scale might mean. Overall, however, God rated 5.9.

Table 18.4: Happiness and life satisfaction scales

Means of national surveys on a ten-point scale, 1980s surveys

	Happiness	Life satisfaction
Ireland	7.82	7.58
Canada	7.76	7.60
Australia	**7.75**	**7.67**
United Kingdom	7.74	7.41
Denmark	7.67	7.92
Netherlands	7.63	7.46
Sweden	7.62	7.80
Belgium	7.57	7.07
United States	7.55	6.94
Norway	7.45	7.67
Finland	7.35	7.68
France	7.24	6.29
Switzerland	6.99	8.60
Germany	6.98	6.94
Japan	6.94	6.20
Austria	6.68	7.10
Italy	6.47	6.24
Mean	7.39	7.30

Table 18.5: Happiness

Percentage describing themselves as very happy and not very or not at all happy, 1990s surveys

	Very happy	Not very/not at all happy
Netherlands	46	7
Ireland	44	7
Australia	**43**	**6**
Denmark	43	6
United States	43	9
Belgium	40	7
Sweden	40	4
Switzerland	37	5
United Kingdom	34	9
Austria	30	9
Canada	30	21
Norway	30	6
Japan	26	13
France	25	8
Finland	23	9
Germany	17	14
Italy	16	14
Mean	33	9

Table 18.6: Life satisfaction

Mean of self-ratings on ten-point scale, 1990s surveys

Denmark	8.2
Switzerland	8.2
Canada	7.9
Ireland	7.9
Sweden	7.9
Netherlands	7.8
Finland	7.7
Norway	7.7
United States	7.7
Australia	**7.6**
Belgium	7.6
United Kingdom	7.5
Italy	7.3
Germany	7.1
France	6.8
Japan	6.6
Austria	6.5
Mean	7.5

Table 18.7: Financial satisfaction and freedom in decision-making

Mean of self-ratings on ten-point scale, 1990s surveys

	Financial satisfaction	Freedom in decisions
Switzerland	7.8	7.3
Netherlands	7.5	6.2
Belgium	7.2	6.6
Denmark	7.2	7.0
Canada	7.1	7.6
Italy	7.0	6.5
Ireland	6.8	7.1
Norway	6.7	7.2
USA	6.7	7.6
Finland	6.6	7.7
Sweden	6.6	7.4
Germany	6.5	6.9
United Kingdom	6.5	7.0
Australia	**6.4**	**7.6**
Austria	6.4	6.0
Japan	6.2	5.6
France	5.9	6.2
Mean	6.8	7.0

Happiness and life satisfaction

You may think that you can't quantify happiness, and of course you are right. However, Dutch sociologist Ruut Veenhoven has spent decades building up his World Database of Happiness. He has scoured the globe for survey research items gauging how happy and how satisfied with life different groups of people say they are. He has then correlated these subjective expressions with indicators of what he calls the livability of societies. These latter include wealth, equality, freedom and knowledge. He has also sought to correlate expressions of happiness with behaviours involving mental distress, such as suicide (with in that case very slight correlation.)

The first column of Table 18.4 reports the means of how happy national samples say they are on a ten-point scale, while the second column reports how satisfied they feel with life. The data is mainly from the 1980s, though there seems to be only slight variation over time in how national samples respond to this survey situation. On this necessarily superficial measure, the Irish top the list for happiness, but the most notable feature is how closely grouped the countries are: twelve countries have their means between 7.82 and 7.24 on the happiness scale. (Veenhoven's data shows more variation between rich and poor countries than among these rich countries.)

The data on life satisfaction shows a close correlation with that on happiness. It is impossible to know what different meanings respondents bring to the two terms, but life satisfaction evokes greater variation than the happiness questions. Although they are very much in the middle of the countries on happiness, the Swiss have a considerable lead in life satisfaction, with a mean national self-rating of 8.6, the only country with a mean over 8.0.

The World Values Survey probed these areas with four different questions. One asked respondents to rate their happiness on a four-point scale: very, quite, not very or not at all. Table 18.5 gives the proportions replying very happy and combines the not very and not at all happy.

The other three questions asked respondents to rate themselves on a ten-point scale: All things considered, how satisfied are you with your life as a whole these days? Please use this card to help you answer 1 (Dissatisfied) to 10 (Satisfied) (Table 18.6). A similarly structured question asked How satisfied are you with the financial situation of your household? (Table 18.7). A final one asked 'some people feel they have completely free choice and control over their lives, while other people feel that what they do has no real effect on what happens to them', with 1 meaning none at all and 10 a great deal (Table 18.7).

These tables suggest that people express greater satisfaction with their life overall and their happiness than they do with their financial satisfaction and decision-making freedom. Although on all the questions the countries are fairly closely grouped – none of the ten-point scales has a range greater than 1.9 – some interesting national differences emerge.

Probably overall the Swiss and the Danes profess the greatest satisfaction, but both are less satisfied with their decision-making freedom. Canadians were near the top on most of the measures but have a higher proportion expressing unhappiness than anywhere else. The Irish are high on general levels of happiness and satisfaction, but more near the middle of the field on financial satisfaction and decision-making freedom.

At the other end, the Austrians, Japanese and French rank consistently near the bottom on all three scales. While the Japanese and French have fewer people near the top and more in the middle, the Austrians are more polarised, with a larger rump expressing discontent.

Australians' ratings vary considerably – near the bottom on financial satisfaction, around the middle on life satisfaction, near the top on some measures of happiness, and also near the top on feelings of decision-making freedom.

Table 18.8: Confidence in social institutions

Proportion in 1990s surveys expressing confidence in each of the institutions

	Police	Legal system	Armed forces	Companies	Church
Norway	88 ++	72 ++	69 ++	56	49
Ireland	86 ++	47	61	52	72 ++
United States	73	48	65 ++	52	72 ++
Canada	84 ++	54	57	51	63 ++
Denmark	89 ++	79 ++	46	38 –	47
France	67	58	56	67 ++	49
Finland	82	68 ++	72 ++	47	47
Sweden	78	59	52	59	43
Switzerland	70	68 ++	49	46	42
Netherlands	73	63	31 –	48	32
United Kingdom	77	53	81 ++	47	45
Belgium	51 –	46 –	34 –	50	51
Australia	**76**	**35 –**	**68 ++**	**59**	**43**
Japan	69	61	44	38 –	12
Italy	55 –	32 –	46	62 ++	60 ++
Austria	67	58	29 –	42	50
Germany	66	56	38	35 –	38
Mean	74	56	53	50	48

	Civil service	Parliament	Trade unions	Press	National mean
Norway	47	64 ++	63 ++	38	61
Ireland	59 ++	50	42	36	56
United States	56 ++	38	34	44 ++	54
Canada	50	37	35	46 ++	53
Denmark	51	42	46	31	52
France	49	48	32	38	52
Finland	34 –	32 –	44	33	51
Sweden	45	46	42	31	51
Switzerland	50	47	38	26	48
Netherlands	46	53 ++	53 ++	36	48
United Kingdom	46	44	27 –	15 –	48
Belgium	42	42	37	43 ++	44
Australia	**38**	**31 –**	**26 –**	**16 –**	**44**
Japan	36	28 –	36	65 ++	43
Italy	25 –	31 –	33	40	43
Austria	42	41	35	18 –	42
Germany	37	39	35	27	41
Mean	44	42	39	34	49

Countries arranged in order of their overall confidence in institutions (see final column: national mean).
Columns arranged in order of institution with greatest mean confidence (the police) down to that with the least (the press).
++ country = 10 percentage points above mean; – country = 10 percentage points below mean.

Confidence in public institutions

Table 18.8 shows that Norwegians have the highest level of confidence in their social institutions and that the police are usually ranked first among the institutions by a considerable margin.

The final column shows each country's mean proportion expressing confidence across nine social institutions. With an overall mean of 61%, Norwegians are the most satisfied, ahead of the Irish and Americans. At the other end is a group of six countries where the overall mean is 44% or lower. This group includes Australia and Britain, along with the defeated powers of World War II: Germany, Austria, Italy and Japan.

The police are the only institution that gain clear majority approval in all countries, but three others – the legal system, armed forces and companies – have overall majority confidence. These differential patterns of confidence in public institutions are likely to be fairly enduring, though there can be short-term fluctuations depending on good or bad publicity. Italy and Belgium, the two countries with the lowest confidence in the police, had both had long-running scandals, for example, but in both the scandals derived from long-term problems of policing.

The same two countries, plus Australia, have the lowest levels of confidence in the legal system. This raises another issue in interpreting responses to broad survey questions. Each institution covers a variety of phenomena, and respondents may be evaluating different aspects of these. The administration of criminal justice may have been more problematic in the minds of Italians, for example, while Australians may be thinking of the legal system's expense and complications. Similarly, when the press is invoked some may think of quality newspapers, others of sensational tabloids. And when people are asked about their confidence in the armed forces, are they expressing their views about their integrity and competence or about militarism more generally?

Perhaps it is for this reason that the armed forces produce a greater spread of opinion than most other institutions. From a high of 81% (the British) the figures range down to a low of 29% (the Austrians). The military is the only institution on which Australians rank substantially (i.e. 10 percentage points or more) above the 17-nation mean.

Apart from the legal system, there were three other institutions – the bottom three on the list overall – where Australians are substantially (10 percentage points or more) lower than the 17-nation mean.

In only three countries – Norway, the Netherlands and Ireland – does parliament, the central democratic institution, receive a majority expressing confidence. In Australia, Japan and Italy only around three in ten express satisfaction. Italy and Japan had a record of political scandals and crises, so it is rather sobering that the Australian parliament has a similar level of public endorsement.

Trade unions are not very popular in any of these countries, but the Norwegian and Dutch publics give them majority approval. The two countries registering the lowest confidence are Britain and Australia.

The press provokes the lowest public rating among these nine institutions. But as with trade unions, the British and Australians express the least confidence in their newspapers. This is not something shared across the English-speaking countries, because Canada and the United States have relatively high confidence in their press. By far the highest approval comes from the Japanese. At 65%, four times as many Japanese express confidence in their press as do Australians.

All three of the lowest three rating institutions – parliament, trade unions and the press – have conflict built into their role. Perhaps this, or the way those conflicts are pursued, is the reason for their lowly ratings. It is not clear why Australians are particularly disapproving.

It is not easy to know what either the causes or consequences of such low confidence might be. But neither is there any room for complacency among these democracies about the apparently dissatisfied dispositions of their publics.

Table 18.9: Active members of voluntary organisations

Proportion saying they are active members of the following types of organisations, 1990s surveys

	Sport*	Church*	Education*	Charity	Professional	Unions	Parties	Environmental	Other*
Australia	37	21	25	18	20	12	3	7	16
United States	15	39	16	15	13	6	12	6	13
Norway	18	7	10	7	6	11	3	1	11
Sweden	22	5	8	5	4	10	4	2	14
Switzerland	34	8	8	3	5	3	3	2	7
Canada	13	15	9	6	5	4	4	4	9
Germany	19	10	7	5	3	5	3	2	6
Finland	14	8	8	5	4	6	4	2	8
Netherlands	9	9	10	9	2	2	2	3	4
Belgium	6	7	7	6	2	2	2	2	2
France	6	5	5	5	3	2	2	2	4
Denmark	11	2	5	2	3	3	2	1	4
Ireland	7	7	4	7	1	1	2	1	2
Italy	7	7	3	3	1	3	4	2	2
Japan	8	4	5	2	4	2	2	1	4
Austria	7	6	4	3	1	2	3	1	3
United Kingdom	0	6	3	5	2	1	2	2	0
Mean	14	10	8	6	5	4	3	2	6

Countries are ranked according to their total claimed active memberships.
Columns are ordered according to the size of their membership across all countries (except for the residual category of other).
* Actual categories offered were church or religious organisation; sport or recreation organisation; art, music or educational organisation; and any other voluntary organisation.

Table 18.10: Membership of voluntary organisations

Proportion saying they are either active or passive members of the following types of organisations, 1990s surveys

	Sports	Church	Unions	Education	Charity	Professional	Parties	Environmental	Other
Australia	52	47	23	37	30	30	10	17	22
United States	30	63	15	28	25	24	31	16	21
Sweden	39	20	61	18	15	14	13	12	27
Netherlands	44	36	20	37	20	14	10	25	11
Finland	29	58	45	21	14	12	12	7	17
Norway	36	21	44	17	19	21	15	5	25
Switzerland	49	26	11	18	15	18	13	15	12
Denmark	34	7	49	13	6	12	7	13	11
Germany	34	26	22	13	13	10	8	6	12
Canada	24	26	13	18	9	17	8	8	14
Belgium	20	13	14	16	12	7	6	7	5
United Kingdom	17	17	15	10	9	10	5	5	7
Austria	17	16	19	8	6	6	12	3	6
Ireland	24	15	9	11	9	5	4	2	3
Japan	15	10	11	9	4	10	5	2	7
France	16	6	5	9	7	6	3	3	6
Italy	12	8	6	5	5	4	5	4	3
Mean	29	24	22	17	13	13	10	9	12

Countries are ranked according to their total claimed active memberships.
Columns are ordered according to the size of their membership across all countries (except for the residual category of other).

Membership of voluntary organisations

It may be surprising to see that Australia tops the list for those professing membership of voluntary organisations in Tables 18.9 and 18.10. The United States comes second, and these two countries are well ahead of all the others, especially in the proportions saying they are active members, but also in the number of total memberships claimed.

As is always a possibility in survey research, the results may be to some extent a method-ological artefact. They may reflect not so much real differences in behaviour as differences in responses to the survey situation. Perhaps for some reason Australians and Americans are more likely to give positive responses when confronted by a pollster. More importantly, there may be subtle differences in understanding of words like 'active' and 'member'. For example, in the item on religion, despite the fact that the Irish are overwhelmingly the greatest church attenders (Table 18.3), only 7% say they are active members of a church or religious organisation. This seems to reflect different interpretations of what to be a member of a religious organisation is.

Similarly the phrase 'active' member may be subject to nuances of cultural understanding that bias the results. It is notable that the gap between Australia and the United States and nations such as Sweden, the Netherlands and Finland is much greater on active than on total memberships.

Such methodological complications mean we must interpret the results with caution, but it is also likely that the results in Tables 18.9 and 18.10 do reflect substantial differences between countries and between the types of organisations in which they participate. It is not surprising, for example, that sporting and recreational organisations are the most popular, or that Australia heads the list in membership of these. The fact that less than 1% of Britons say they are active members of a sporting club also seems to correlate with other manifestations of national performance!

Neither is it surprising that the greatest disproportion between active and total membership is found in trade unions. Only 4% claim to be active members of a union, but total membership runs at 22%. Moreover the rankings on union membership correlate broadly with the figures given in Table 4.28. However, the result of 12% of Australians claiming to be active union members is less supported by other observations. Similarly, the high figures on membership of political parties are dubious (cf. Table 2.26) and it should be remembered that the United States and Canada do not have the formal membership structures that the other democracies do.

The relatively high proportion of people saying they belong to an art, music or educational organisation, both overall and especially in Australia, is partly explained by the relative strength of parent and teacher organisations in that country.

In recent years there has been considerable commentary on the importance of social capital in explaining the vibrancy of communities and the resilience of societies and democratic politics. Participation in voluntary organisations, in so far as it reflects civic engagement and individuals' feelings of efficacy, is one indicator of social capital. It would be unwise to extrapolate too boldly from the results in Tables 18.9 and 18.10 to larger social phenomena. Nor do we have many reliable comparative historical yardsticks to measure if there has been a decline over time.

However, the results do paint an overall picture of what many would judge to be undesirably low rates of participation. They also suggest substantial differences in civic participation between countries. It is likely that the survey situation exaggerates the contrasts, and one should not attach too much weight to precise gradations down the table. But equally it is plausible that there is greater membership in voluntary associations, and perhaps social capital, in Australia and America than there is in low-ranking France and Italy.

Table 18.11: Political interest

Proportions in 1990s surveys responding that they:

	Discuss politics frequently	Are very or somewhat interested in politics	Hold politics very or rather important
Germany	29	74	48
Denmark	24	54	43
Norway	22	70	48
Austria	20	54	35
Canada	19	58	48
Sweden	18	49	46
Switzerland	18	54	38
Australia	**16**	**56**	**50**
United States	15	62	55
Netherlands	15	62	53
United Kingdom	13	47	42
Italy	13	29	31
France	12	38	33
Ireland	12	37	28
Belgium	9	30	25
Finland	8	42	22
Japan	6	57	60
Mean	16	51	41

Table 18.12: Political action

Proportion of respondents in 1990s surveys who have ever:

	Signed a petition	Joined a boycott	Attended a demonstration
Australia	**79**	**22**	**18**
Canada	77	24	22
Sweden	72	25	26
United States	72	19	16
United Kingdom	68	14	14
Switzerland	66	11	17
Norway	63	15	23
Germany	61	11	27
Japan	58	6	12
France	54	13	33
Denmark	51	11	27
Netherlands	51	9	25
Italy	48	11	36
Austria	48	5	10
Belgium	47	9	23
Ireland	42	7	17
Finland	40	13	13
Mean	61	14	22

Political interest and activity

Table 18.11 finds far more people professing to be interested in politics and thinking it is important than being willing to discuss it. This syndrome is most pronounced among the Japanese. They rank lowest on the first question 'When you get together with your friends, would you say you discuss political matters frequently, occasionally or never?' with only 6% replying that they discuss politics frequently. In contrast they rank highest on the last question, with 60% of them ranking politics very or rather important on a four-point scale. They also fall well above the mean in the middle column, with 57% saying they are very or somewhat interested in politics, when offered a four-point scale.

While the disproportion is starkest among the Japanese, it is evident in many other nations as well. The Americans and Dutch claim to be fairly reticent in discussing politics (15%), just below the 17-country mean, but both rank equal third (62%) in their professions of interest in politics (62%), and second and third respectively (55% and 53%) in thinking politics is important.

Australia shared the same pattern, though in more muted form. It was right on the mean (16%) in the proportion saying they discuss politics frequently, but substantially above the mean in interest in politics and thinking it important. Of course, democracy includes the freedom not to talk about politics, but the contrasts between the three columns are rather puzzling.

The Germans are the most consistently engaged with politics, topping the list in the first two columns and also ranking high in the third. This engagement was probably boosted by the recent reunification of Germany, no other countries experiencing political changes of such magnitude during the period. Norway also consistently ranked near the top in all three columns, perhaps related to the relative confidence they showed in their social institutions in Table 18.8.

At the other end of the table are several European countries that consistently rank in the bottom third on all three questions. Finland, Belgium, Ireland, France and Italy are five of the seven bottom-ranking countries in column 1, the five bottom-ranking countries in column 2 and the five bottom-ranking countries in column 3.

The same five countries are also the only ones in Table 18.12 where less than a majority say they have ever signed a petition. Table 18.12 is based on a series of questions asking respondents if they had ever engaged in various forms of political action.

Not surprisingly, far more claimed to have signed a petition than the other more confronting and contentious types of action. Claiming to have signed one petition does not by itself indicate high levels of political activism. However, Australia ranks highest on this dimension; with Canada and Sweden they are also the three countries which rank highest on joining a boycott, with in each case more than one in five saying they had done this.

Different democracies have contrasting political cultures and patterns of political action. While generally ranking low on political interest and signing petitions, the Italians and French head the rankings of those who have taken part in demonstrations. In both cases more than 30% of respondents claimed to have done this. So whereas in Australia the ratio of those having signed a petition to those having attended a demonstration was 4:1 (79% to18%), in Italy the ratio was 4:3 (48% to 36%).

The combination of tables paints a somewhat puzzling mix of attitudes in Australia. The figures in Tables 18.11 and 18.12, as well as those in 18.9 and 18.10, give the lie to any idea that Australians are peculiarly apathetic. On the other hand, their very low rate of membership in political parties (2.27) and cynicism about social institutions (18.8) paint a less rosy picture.

Table 18.13: National pride

Percentage responding in 1990s surveys that they were very proud or not proud of their nationality

	Very proud	Not proud
Ireland	77	2
United States	77	2
Australia	**70**	**3**
Canada	60	6
United Kingdom	53	11
Austria	53	7
Norway	48	14
Finland	44	13
Sweden	43	13
Denmark	42	13
Italy	40	12
France	35	13
Switzerland	34	20
Belgium	31	18
Japan	27	36
Netherlands	23	23
Germany	20	34
Mean	46	14

Table 18.14: Willingness to fight in a war

Percentage in 1990s surveys responding that they are willing to fight for their country

Norway	90
Sweden	90
Denmark	89
Finland	86
United States	78
Australia	**75**
United Kingdom	74
Switzerland	74
Netherlands	69
Canada	68
France	66
Austria	66
Ireland	61
Germany	47
Belgium	39
Italy	31
Japan	23
Mean	66

War and nation

Tables 18.13 and 18.14 reveal some curiosities: speaking English inspires patriotism, while the apparently peace-loving Scandinavians are the most willing to fight for their country.

Respondents were asked how proud they were to be (their nationality), and offered four possibilities: very, quite, not very or not at all. Table 18.13 reports those saying very in the first column and in the second column combines those saying not very and not at all proud. It omits those saying quite proud. It shows a great spread of responses, from 77% of Irish and Americans saying they are very proud of their nationality down to only 20% of Germans.

The top six expressing national pride are the English-speaking countries (including Ireland) plus Austria. All the other countries have less than 50% saying they are very proud. Six countries, from France down, have 35% or less expressing great pride. The second column amplifies this pattern. In Ireland, the United States and Australia, there are only 2–3% saying they are not proud.

Two of the defeated World War II powers, Germans and Japanese, are the most likely to say they are not proud of their nationality, and the only countries to have more saying not proud than very proud. Their Axis ally Italy has responses much closer to the 17-nation means.

Bitter war memories are doubtless also relevant to the numbers saying they would be willing to fight in a war. Of the four countries with fewer than 50% saying they would fight, Japan, Italy and Germany are three, with Belgium the fourth. There is a big gap between these four up to the next lowest, the Irish.

The relatively low ranking of the Irish on this question contrasts with their strong expression of national pride, and the relationship between the rankings on the two questions is an interesting mixture. Overall there is a rough correlation, but with some notable exceptions. Apart from the Irish, the Austrians rank high on pride and low on willingness to fight. In contrast, the Dutch and the Swiss are relatively low on national pride but above average in their professed willingness to fight.

The four Scandinavian countries that were in the middle of the list on national pride top the rankings in professed willingness to fight a war for their country. The United States, Australia and Britain form a coalition of the next most willing.

This is not a question about approval of any particular war, but rather a general statement of willingness to fight for their country. Perhaps this is why it bears no relationship at all to the propensity of countries to fight in wars. It is interesting that the four countries most willing to fight have barely been involved in any wars over the last half-century. Similarly the Swiss, with their long history of neutralism, profess greater willingness to go to war for their country than the French, with their strong militaristic tradition. Quite what sentiments this question taps is therefore open to conjecture, but it is not simply either militarism or patriotism.

Table 18.15: Political orientation

Self-placement on left–right scale (left = 1; 10 = right)
in 1990s surveys

	Mean score	Far left %	Far right %
Italy	4.8	28	10
France	4.9	26	12
Germany	5.1	19	9
United Kingdom	5.4	14	13
Netherlands	5.4	20	16
Australia	**5.4**	**13**	**13**
Sweden	5.5	21	20
Switzerland	5.5	15	18
Canada	5.6	9	13
Norway	5.6	13	18
Denmark	5.7	12	21
Belgium	5.7	14	21
USA	5.8	10	18
Finland	5.8	12	22
Japan	6.0	8	19
Ireland	6.1	7	23
Austria	6.3	6	21

Table 18.16: Attitudes to the environment

Percentage in 1990s surveys willing to pay more taxes to
prevent environmental damage

Sweden	80
Norway	74
Denmark	70
Australia	**69**
United Kingdom	68
Netherlands	68
Canada	64
United States	60
Japan	59
Germany	58
Italy	55
Finland	55
France	54
Austria	52
Ireland	51
Switzerland	43
Belgium	40
Mean	60

Orientations to politics and the environment

The World Values Survey asked few questions about current political issues, but it did ask people to place themselves in terms of left-wing and right-wing: 'In political matters, people talk of "the left" and "the right". How would you place your views on this scale, generally speaking?' It then offered them a ten-point scale with 1 as left and 10 as right.

The ten-point scale makes 5.5 the mid-point, and not surprisingly there is a rush to the middle. The outstanding feature of Table 18.15 is the clustering of 13 of the 17 countries, including Australia, with a mean between 5 and 6. Italy and France are placed at the left end just below 5, and Ireland and Austria at the right, just above 6. Most people think of themselves as moderate and place themselves in the middle of the spectrum, but this would seem to owe more to the psychology of perceptions than a positive ideological commitment.

Moreover, what people assume left and right mean would vary enormously between countries, and their judgements are no doubt anchored by the spectrum of debate in their own country, rather than by any more universal meaning. The countries that most often had left-wing governments and most often had right-wing governments (Table 2.24) both cluster in the middle. But how close is a Swedish 5.5 to an American 5.8, for example?

While the great majority of people place themselves around the middle of the spectrum, the self-placement near one or other of the extremes provides some interest. The final two columns of Table 18.15 present the proportions identifying themselves near one or other end. (Far left means they circled 1–3, and far right that they circled 8–10.)

The importance of looking at distribution as well as at the mean is shown by contrasting Sweden and Canada. The two countries differ by only 0.1% in their means, but while Canada has the lowest proportion (21%), labelling themselves towards the extremes, Sweden has

the highest (41%), equally split between left and right. The polarised responses attest to the relatively ideological nature of politics in Sweden. The different distributions are likely to reflect, and in turn result in, very different types of political contestation in the two countries. Australians, after the Canadians, are the second most inclined to see themselves in the middle. Only 26% put themselves near the extremes, and they are equally split, 13% on each side.

In the three countries at the top of the table – Italy, France and Germany – those identifying as far left outnumber those on the far right by at least 10 percentage points. In the four countries at the bottom of the table – Austria, Ireland, Japan and Finland – the reverse applies, with at least 10 percentage points more identifying themselves with the far right than the far left. But the social meaning of such figures, and the reasons for them, can only be guessed at.

In one of the few substantive policy areas where attitudes were probed, people were asked to respond to the statement 'I would agree to an increase in taxes if the extra money were used to prevent environmental damage'. They were offered four options: strongly agree, agree, disagree and strongly disagree.

The sentiment in favour of the environment commands a majority in all countries except two. But only in the top three – Sweden, Norway and Denmark – did more than 20% strongly agree. Australia ranked fourth in the proportion of respondents agreeing or strongly agreeing.

The question counterposes tax and environment, and it is perhaps notable that the three countries ranking highest in their willingness to pay more tax are already the most highly taxed countries. At the other end it is not clear if the Swiss or Belgians do not see the urgency of environmental issues or are reacting against a further tax impost.

Table 18.17: Can people be trusted?

Percentage in 1990s surveys agreeing that people can be trusted

Norway	65
Sweden	63
Denmark	58
Netherlands	54
Finland	54
Canada	53
Ireland	47
United States	44
Japan	42
Australia	**40**
Switzerland	39
United Kingdom	38
Germany	35
Italy	35
Belgium	34
Austria	32
France	23
Mean	44

Table 18.18: Favoured groups when jobs are scarce

Percentages in 1990s surveys agreeing with the following priorities:

	Men	Forced retirement	Own nationality
Austria	50	44	77
Italy	40	55	71
Ireland	36	47	69
Belgium	37	49	63
Switzerland	29	58	62
France	33	49	63
Germany	28	50	59
Finland	14	48	72
United Kingdom	31	43	53
Japan	33	8	63
Canada	19	31	53
Norway	15	36	50
Netherlands	25	42	33
Australia	**26**	**26**	**45**
USA	23	15	56
Denmark	11	24	53
Sweden	8	16	30
Mean	27	38	57

Ranked in descending order of total over the three categories endorsing favouring some over others.

Table 18.19: Undesirable neighbours

Percentage in 1990s surveys thinking the following groups were undesirable neighbours:

	Drug addicts	Heavy drinkers	Political extremists	Criminal record	People with AIDS	Emotionally unstable	Homo-sexuals	Immigrants	Different race
Japan	91	58	82	50	77	62	69	17	11
Austria	60	60	50	32	68	20	43	20	8
USA	80	61	36	54	24	47	34	10	8
Italy	59	51	38	48	42	34	37	13	12
Australia	**74**	**60**	**45**	**45**	**15**	**38**	**25**	**5**	**5**
Germany	56	56	71	27	19	27	26	13	8
Finland	75	54	23	39	24	30	28	10	17
UK	64	57	38	41	20	28	29	11	8
Ireland	64	34	33	52	35	30	33	5	6
Canada	63	55	33	43	21	30	30	6	5
Belgium	53	49	44	30	24	22	24	20	17
Netherlands	73	60	58	28	15	19	11	9	7
Norway	64	34	42	43	21	31	18	14	11
Switzerland	39	35	40	13	88	11	19	6	5
Sweden	68	41	44	35	13	21	15	7	5
France	44	50	37	20	15	17	24	13	9
Denmark	54	34	10	28	9	11	12	12	7
Mean	64	50	43	37	31	28	28	11	9

Ranked according to total number of groups thought undesirable.
Columns ordered according to perceived undesirability of groups.

Attitudes to others

The World Values Survey had three items probing general attitudes to others. The first simply asked 'Generally speaking, would you say that most people can be trusted or that you can't be too careful in dealing with people?' Countries from northern and western mainland Europe rank highest in saying people can be trusted, while (with rather less geographical neatness) countries from southern and eastern Europe rank lowest (Table 18.17). It cannot be deduced whether this response reflects respondents' differential experience of the trustworthiness of people. However, the Scandinavians and Dutch are the most trusting, and the French the least trusting. Australia is near the bottom of the middle group, slightly less trusting than the overall 17-nation mean.

The correlation is far from perfect, but the rankings in Table 18.17 overlap with Table 18.14, countries' professed willingness to fight in a war. The Scandinavians top both lists, while Belgium, Italy and Germany are near the bottom in both.

Another series of questions probed attitudes about whether some groups had more right to a job than others. The actual questions were 'Do you agree that when jobs are scarce, men should have more right to a job than women?', 'When jobs are scarce, older people should be forced to retire from work early', and 'When jobs are scarce, employers should give priority to (nationals) over immigrants'.

Austrians' social conservatism is evident in Table 18.18. They easily top the countries in saying both that men should be favoured over women and that Austrians deserve jobs more than immigrants. Several other countries with a strong Catholic tradition – Italy, Ireland and Belgium – rank behind Austria. Sweden is at the other end of the scale, by far the most reluctant to accord any group privileges over others. Sweden ranked bottom in columns one and three. Denmark was second lowest, with Norway and the Netherlands also in the bottom third.

There was most rejection of the proposition that men should be favoured for jobs (a 17-nation mean of 27%), and greatest endorsement of the idea that one's own nationality should be favoured over immigrants (mean 57%). While the responses for columns one and three overlap considerably, column two, on forcing older people out of the workforce, shows a different pattern. The idea is most emphatically rejected by the Japanese. This may reflect both different attitudes to the aged and concern about their financial well-being in retirement.

Australia, with the United States, is near the bottom on Table 18.18. Most notably, only three countries have majorities rejecting the idea that their own nationals have more right to jobs than immigrants. The proposition is strongly rejected by the Swedes and Dutch, and somewhat less emphatically, also rejected by Australians.

Finally respondents were presented with a list of 'various groups of people' and asked to indicate 'any that you would not like to have as neighbours'. Table 18.19 shows that the Japanese are the most fastidious about their neighbours and the Danes the least so.

In interpreting these results, as with several other questions, it is important to remember that the same label may conjure different images in different countries. The Japanese and Germans have by far the largest number not wanting political extremists as neighbours, and it may be that respondents in those countries are more likely to think of violent extremists because of their own national pasts.

It is not surprising that drug addicts are the most rejected category of potential neighbour. It is more surprising that heavy drinkers are less acceptable than those with a criminal record. The table shows, at least in this type of survey situation, a much greater readiness to accept different racial groups and immigrants, but the relatively high rates of rejecting people with AIDS (88% in Switzerland) and homosexuals may be surprising.

Table 18.20: Attitudes to changes in social values

Percentage in 1990s surveys agreeing that a change in the following directions would be a good thing:

	Greater respect for authority	Less emphasis on money	Decrease in importance of work	More emphasis on family life
Ireland	83	73	22	94
United States	77	70	25	94
United Kingdom	77	65	32	89
Australia	**73**	**69**	**33**	**95**
Canada	64	62	31	94
France	59	71	36	90
Netherlands	52	63	35	67
Belgium	49	66	44	85
Italy	47	72	25	92
Austria	47	55	23	92
Switzerland	40	76	44	90
Denmark	35	78	27	95
Norway	32	60	21	95
Germany	32	54	29	88
Finland	27	61	21	94
Sweden	21	70	33	86
Japan	6	42	6	87
Mean	48	65	29	90

Table 18.21: Attitudes to scientific and technological development

Percentage in 1990s surveys agreeing with the following propositions:

	Scientific advances are beneficial to mankind	More emphasis on technological development
United States	63	61
Australia	**57**	**58**
Canada	55	64
United Kingdom	47	67
Finland	47	53
Sweden	47	35
Germany	46	57
Denmark	43	59
France	42	76
Ireland	40	61
Switzerland	38	49
Norway	38	47
Netherlands	37	48
Italy	36	61
Belgium	34	56
Austria	31	42
Japan	26	65
Mean	43	56

Attitudes to changes in way of life

Respondents were shown a list of possible changes in our way of life and asked to indicate if they thought such a change would be a good thing, a bad thing or one they didn't mind. By far the most popular change in Table 18.20 was more emphasis on family life. Only the Dutch seemed a little reluctant to give greater priority to their relatives. Everywhere else it attracted 85% or more endorsement. Fully seven countries, including Australia, had 94% or 95% endorsing the idea.

The middle two columns provide an interesting contrast, and suggest that the nexus between work and money is far from automatic. Decreasing the importance of work received only minority support, while having less emphasis on money was supported by twice as many.

Decreasing the emphasis on work did not receive majority endorsement in any of the countries. The Belgians and Swiss were keenest on the idea, with 44% saying it would be a good thing. By far the most opposed were the Japanese, with only 6% endorsing the idea. In contrast, decreasing the emphasis on money received majority support in all countries except Japan. The Danes and the Swiss were most receptive. On both items, Australia fell just within the top half of countries endorsing the ideas, close to the 17-nation mean.

By far the greatest diversity among the responses to the suggested changes was the idea of greater respect for authority. Here responses ranged from 83% endorsement in Ireland down to 6% in Japan. As with pride in nationality (Table 18.13), the five English-speaking countries were the ones most wanting greater respect in authority. In ten of the 17 countries it did not receive majority support, and in many countries, especially Japan, was viewed with considerable distaste.

These responses provide an interesting guide to national sentiments but are not a guide to what is likely to happen. The Japanese are not about to become rebellious against

authority, for example. Again, we also need to be aware that different countries bring their own experiences in interpreting such questions. Some may be reacting against the danger of authoritarianism, for example, others expressing their approval or disapproval of rowdy minorities.

Four of the same five English-speaking countries (now minus Ireland) that wanted more respect for authority also ranked highest in their belief in the efficacy of science. Table 18.21 shows that the idea that scientific advances are beneficial to mankind only received majority support in America, Australia and Canada. Double the proportion of Americans as of Japanese and Austrians supported the idea.

Although the question formats were different, the idea of more emphasis on technological development received considerably more endorsement, and the ordering of countries was quite different. Only 42% of the French think scientific advances are beneficial, but 76% of them approve greater emphasis on technology. Similarly, the Japanese proportion of 26% on scientific advances jumps to 65% on technology. One country, Sweden, moved considerably in the other direction: down from 47% on science to 35% on technology. Australia is essentially the same on both (57–58%), but that means it drops from second highest endorsement of science to the middle of the field on technology.

Again we can only guess at the meanings different respondents attach to these questions. For some science may conjure ideas of genetic meddling, while technology seems benign and useful. For others, perhaps many Swedes, technology may conjure ideas of dehumanisation. Nevertheless the general scepticism towards science and to a lesser extent technology – and the majority wanting less emphasis on money – find considerable proportions of these publics somewhat at odds with the driving forces within their societies.

SOURCES AND REFERENCES

Note: All OECD documents are published by the OECD in Paris, so these publication details are not given. Sometimes "OECD" and/or a date are part of the document's title, sometimes not.

1 People

Table 1.1: Figures for 1900 are from B. R. Mitchell, *International Historical Statistics: Africa, Asia and Oceania 1750–1993* (3rd edn, Stockton Press, NY, 1998) and the *United Nations Statistical Yearbook 1955* (UN, NY, 1957). Figures for 1950 and 2000 are from US Census Bureau International Data Base at www.census.gov/cgi-bin/ipc. Quotes about Australia's population needs are from Doug Cocks, *People Policy: Australia's Population Choices* (Sydney, University of New South Wales Press, 1996).

Note: In 1900 Austria was still part of the Austro-Hungarian empire and Ireland was united as a British colony. The table gives estimates for the 1900 population of the territories comprising the contemporary nation-states. Similarly, in 1950 Germany was divided into East and West, but the table figure is for a united Germany.

Table 1.2: *OECD in Figures 2000.*

Table 1.3: Calculated from figures in Table 1.1.

Table 1.4: US Census Bureau International Data Base at www.census.gov/cgi-bin/ipc.

Table 1.5: Figures for 1900 are from the *United Nations Statistical Yearbook 1955* (UN, NY, 1957); for the Netherlands, the figure is for 1910. Figures for 1950 are from UN, *World Population Prospects: The 1996 Revision* (UN, NY, 1996), Table A26, p. 318f. Figures for 2000 are from US Census Bureau International Data Base at www.census.gov/cgi-bin/ipc. See also James C. Riley, *Rising Life Expectancy: A Global History* (Cambridge University Press, 2001), p. 1; Hugo, Graeme, *A Century of Population Change in Australia* (Year Book Australia, 2001, available at http://www.abs.gov.au/ausstats); OECD,

Health at a Glance (2002); ABS, *Measuring Australia's Progress* (ABS, Canberra, 2002), p. 18.

Tables 1.6 and 1.7: *OECD Health Data 2002* (CD ROM).

Table 1.8: 1900 and 1950 data are from Jean-Claude Chesnais, *The Demographic Transition. Stages, Patterns and Economic Implications: A Longitudinal Study of Sixty-Seven Countries Covering the Period 1720–1984* (Oxford University Press, Oxford, 1992), Appendix 1, p. 517ff. Note that the nearest available year to 1900 given for Canada is 1921, United States 1909, Australia 1901. The UK figure for 1900 and 1950 is England and Wales only. In both years Scotland was somewhat higher. The 2000 data are from US Bureau of the Census, International Data Base at www.census.gov/cgi-bin.ipc/idbsprd.

Table 1.9: Data for 1900 and 1950 is from Chesnais, *The Demographic Transition;* 1975 and 2000 figures from *OECD Health Data 2002.*

Tables 1.10 and 1.11: Calculated from *OECD Health Data 2001* (CD ROM).

Table 1.12: Columns 1 and 2 are taken from the OECD database on immigration found at SourceOECD at www.oecd.org. That database only gives figures for the years 1980–94. Columns 3 and 4 are taken from the Migration Information Source at http://migrationinformation.org and come originally from UN figures.

Table 1.13: The figures for around 1980 and 1990 can be found in OECD, *Trends in International Migration* (1993), pp. 29, 187. The figure for 2000 is taken from *OECD in Figures 2002.*

Table 1.14: Calculated from OECD, *Trends in International Migration* (2000), p. 307.

The estimate for the global number of migrants is from Philip Martin and Jonas Widgren, 'International Migration: Facing the Challenge', *Population Bulletin* (Population Reference Bureau, Washington DC), V57, N1, March 2002.

Table 1.15: UNHCR, *Refugees and Others of Concern to UNHCR 1999 Statistical Overview* (Geneva, July 2000). See Tables V.2 and V.18 at http://www.unhcr.ch. The quote about asylum-seekers in Europe and estimate for illegal immigrants in the United States are from Martin and Widgren, 'International Migration'.

Table 1.16: UNHCR, *Refugees and Others of Concern*, Table I.2. In that table the number of refugees is calculated for the New World countries as the total accepted from 1995–99, while for several European countries it is 1990–99. No reason is given for the discrepancy, so Table 1.16 consistently gives the number accepted for the whole decade.

Table 1.17: Jonathan Coppel et al., 'Trends in Immigration and Economic Consequences', OECD Economics Department Working Paper 284, June 2001, p. 19.

The category 'other' mainly applies to people from countries with automatic rights of entry, such as New Zealanders into Australia, and EU countries into Denmark and Switzerland.

Table 1.18: Data for 1975 and 2000 are from UNDP, *Human Development Report 2002* at www.undp.org. The proportion living in cities of over 750 000 is taken from UNDP, *Human Development Report 1998* (UN, NY, 1998), p. 199.

Table 1.19: City populations and proportion of national population are taken from UN, *Statistical Yearbook 44th* edition, 1997 (UN, NY, 2000), p. 47ff. The figures on population density are from John Tepper Marlin et al., *Book of World City Rankings* (NY, Free Press, 1986), pp. 528–9. See also: Jan-Erik Lane, David McKay and Kenneth Newton, *Political Data Handbook OECD Countries* (2nd edn, Oxford University Press, Oxford, 1997), p. 17.

Table 1.20: UNDP, *Human Development Report 2002*, pp. 34–5, 149, 153. The quote is from *Human Development Report 1993*, p. 104.

2 Government and Politics

Table 2.1: The dates for the beginning of continuous elections come from Robert Dahl, *Polyarchy: Participation and Opposition* (Yale University Press, New Haven, 1971, pp. 42, 249). The table does not includes interruptions due to external occupation, for example of some European countries during the Nazi occupation in World War II. The dates for independence and current constitution come from Jan-Erik Lane, David McKay and Kenneth Newton, *Political Data Handbook: OECD Countries* (Oxford University Press, Oxford, 1991), p. 112. See also: Arend Lijphart, *Democracies: Patterns of Majoritarian and Consensus Government in Twenty-One Countries* (Yale University Press, New Haven, 1984).

Tables 2.2 and 2.3: Lane, McKay and Newton, *Political Data Handbook*, p. 111, and Inter-Parliamentary Union at www.ipu.org.

Table 2.4: Lijphart, *Democracies*.

Table 2.5: Sources include Lijphart, *Democracies* and CIA, *World Fact Book*.

Table 2.6: *OECD Revenue Statistics 1965–2000* (2001), p. 200. Often figures for Central Government's tax share excludes social security on the grounds that 'Social security funds may be distinguished by the fact that they are separately organised from the other activities of government units and hold their assets and liabilities separately from the latter. They are separate institutional units . . .' (p. 277). On the other hand, social security in all other ways looks just like a central government tax, and we have included it that way in the table.

Table 2.7: Cols 2 and 3 are from Lijphart, *Democracies*; col. 4 is from Jaap Woldendorp, Hans Keman and Ian Budge, *Party Government* *in 48 Democracies (1945–1998). Composition – Duration – Personnel* (Kluwer Academic Publishers, Dordrecht, 2000).

Table 2.8: Lawrence Le Duc, Richard G. Niemi and Pippa Norris, 'Introduction: The Present and Future of Democratic Elections', in Le Duc, Niemi and Norris (eds), *Comparing Democracies: Elections and Voting in Global Perspective* (Sage, London, 1996), pp. 13–15.

Table 2.9: Lijphart, *Democracies*. Other information is drawn from George Tsebelis and Jeanette Money, *Bi-Cameralism* (Cambridge University Press, 1997).

Table 2.10: Woldendorp, Keman and Budge, *Party Government in 48 Democracies*.

Table 2.11: G. Bingham Powell Jr, *Elections as Instruments of Democracy. Majoritarian and Proportional Visions* (Yale University Press, New Haven, 2000), pp. 34, 39.

Table 2.12: Shaun Bowler, 'Parties in Legislature: Two Competing Explanations', in Russell J. Dalton and Martin P. Wattenberg (eds), *Parties without Partisans: Political Change in Advanced Industrial Democracies* (Oxford University Press, 2000), p. 170, citing data from the Inter-Parliamentary Union.

Table 2.13: Le Duc, Niemi and Norris, 'Introduction', pp. 13–15.

Tables 2.14 and 2.15: Lijphart, *Patterns of Democracy*, p. 313. The Gallagher Index of Disproportionality is explained on pp. 157–8. For Table 2.15 the number of elections is compiled from several sources, including the IDEA website http://www.idea.int/vt/country_view.cfm and http://www.electionworld.org, plus Thomas T. Mackie and Richard Rose, *The International Almanac of Electoral History* (3rd edn, Macmillan, London, 1991)

Table 2.16: Le Duc, Niemi and Norris, 'Introduction', pp. 45–8. See also David M. Farrell and Paul Webb, 'Political Parties as Campaign Organisations', in Dalton and Wattenberg (eds), *Parties without Partisans*, p. 107; Anthony Smith, 'Mass Communications', in D. Butler et al. (eds), *Democracy at the Polls*

(American Enterprise Institute, Washington DC, 1981).

Table 2.17: Le Duc, Niemi and Norris, 'Introduction'. See also Farrell and Webb, 'Political Parties as Campaign Organisations', p. 107.

Table 2.18: Lijphart, *Patterns of Democracy*, p. 312.

Table 2.19: G. Bingham Powell Jr, *Elections as Instruments of Democracy: Majoritarian and Proportional Visions* (Yale University Press, New Haven, 2000), pp. 74, 78.

Table 2.20: Adapted from Woldendorp, Keman and Budge, *Party Government in 48 Democracies*. Note that this is the proportion of governments formed in the various ways, not the length of time each country had such governments. Their category of caretaker government – by nature usually very short-lived – has been eliminated, and the proportions recalculated, in order to give a more accurate comparative picture. This most substantially affected the figures for the Netherlands and Germany, for which, respectively, fully 20% and 16% of governments were listed as caretaker.

Table 2.21: Woldendorp, Keman and Budge, *Party Government in 48 Democracies*.

Table 2.22: Kaare Strom, 'Parties at the Core of Government', in Dalton and Wattenberg (eds), *Parties without Partisans*, pp. 198–9.

Table 2.23: Calculated using data from several sources, including Woldendorp, Keman and Budge, *Party Government in 48 Democracies*; Thomas T. Mackie and Richard Rose, *The International Almanac of Electoral History* (3rd edn, Macmillan, London, 1991); Ian Gorvin (ed.), *Elections since 1945: A Worldwide Reference Compendium* (Longman, Essex, 1989); plus http://www.terra.es and http://www.parties-and-elections.de.

This table involved making several judgements and decisions. The United States only allows a president two terms, so if the candidate from the same party as the retiring president won, this was considered continuity. In the semi-presidential countries, the results are for parliamentary elections, but the dual executive creates problems of interpretation, especially in periods of divided government. President Mitterrand, for example, twice used his power to appoint a prime minister with only minority support, who then won the election. These have been included as continuity. Similarly, sometimes the composition of the government changed between elections because of changing support in the parliament; the results report the result for the incumbent government contesting the election.

Table 2.24: Manfred G. Schmidt, 'The impact of Political Parties, Constitutional Structures and Veto Players on Public Policy', in Hans Keman (ed.) *Comparative Democratic Politics* (Sage, London, 2002), p. 169.

Table 2.25: Compiled from data at the International Institute for Democracy and Electoral Assistance found at http://www.idea.int/vt/country_view.cfm. Data for nearly all countries goes back to the first election after World War II. US presidential voting turnout data (as proportion of registered voters) only dates back to 1964, but as proportion of the voting-age population, it goes back to 1946. In countries with voluntary voting, there is differential turnout for different types of elections. The national elections chosen for the table are included on the basis that they are the crucial ones in the formation of the national government. For the United States that is presidential elections. The mean voting turnout for congressional elections was 58%. Conversely, parliamentary elections were used in the semi-presidential systems of Finland and France. In those countries, however, voting turnout tends to be somewhat higher for presidential elections.

Table 2.26: Susan Scarrow, 'Parties without Members? Party Organisation in a Changing Electoral Environment', in Dalton and Wattenberg (eds), *Parties without Partisans*, p. 90.

Tables 2.27 and 2.28: Transparency International at www.transparency.org.

3 Economy

Table 3.1: Angus Maddison, *The World Economy: A Millennial Perspective* (Development Centre of the OECD, Paris, 2001), pp. 185, 215.

Table 3.2: Annex to *OECD Society at a Glance: OECD Social Indicators Edition 2002* (2003). See data at Table GE1.1 at www.oecd.org/els/social/indicators.

Table 3.3: Maddison, *The World Economy*, pp. 186, 216.

Table 3.4: This table has been calculated from data in Angus Maddison, *Monitoring the World Economy 1820–1992* (Development Centre of the OECD, Paris, 1995). In his 2001 work, Maddison revised some of these figures, but all by small amounts. The figures for Ireland and Switzerland are incomplete in the earlier years. In order to calculate mean growth rates for the entire half-century, we have substituted the 1890 figure as the 1889 figure for Ireland. More problematically, we have interpolated a Swiss figure for 1889 from the data for 1870 and 1900.

Tables 3.5 and 3.6: *OECD Historical Statistics* (CD ROM, 2001). For Table 3.6 see also OECD, *Historical Statistics 1960–1995* (1997). When the OECD updated its historical statistics (and issued them in CD ROM form), it made the earliest year 1970 rather than 1960. The first reason for this was probably that with several new members there was not always reliable harmonised data going back to 1960. The second reason is that several of the measures have been revised to take account of changed definitions, or more authoritative data. Thus where the data has been consistent throughout we have used both sources and made 1960 the base year, but when the revisions have been substantial we have started from 1970. This is why Table 3.4 begins at 1970 but 3.5 goes back to 1960; it also explains the different starting years of some other tables in this section.

Tables 3.7–3.11: *OECD Historical Statistics.*

Table 3.12: *Economist*, 27 April 2002.

Tables 3.13–3.15: *OECD Historical Statistics*; OECD, *Historical Statistics 1960–1995*. To explain different starting years please see note to reference for Table 3.5. Sectors are sometimes described as primary, secondary and tertiary, which are slightly different from these categories. Primary includes mining as well as agriculture. Similarly secondary (or industry) is more inclusive than manufacturing, also including construction for example.

Table 3.16: FAO, *Compendium of Food and Agriculture Indicators 2001* at http://www.fao.org.

Table 3.17: Figure for 2001 from *OECD in Figures 2002*/Supplement 1 at www.oecd.org; 1986 figure from *OECD Economic Outlook 2001*, p. 181.

Table 3.18: World Bank, *World Development Indicators* (CD ROM).

Table 3.19: *OECD Statistics on International Trade in Services* (2001); *OECD Trade in Services* (2001); Balance of trade for Switzerland and New Zealand = 1999; for Sweden, the Netherlands, Finland and Belgium, 1990 figures are for 1991 or 1992.

Table 3.20: OECD, *Economic Outlook 2002*, Annex Table 26.

Table 3.21: *OECD Historical Statistics.*

Table 3.22: Reserve Bank of Australia.

Table 3.23: *OECD Bank Profitability: Financial Statements of Banks 2002* (2002).

Table 3.24: World Bank, *Bank Concentration Data*. Accessed from http://econ.worldbank.org.

Table 3.25: Calculated from *OECD Bank Profitability*. Note that data on branch numbers for Canada and the United States comes from the Bank for International Settlements Committee on Payment and Settlement System, *Statistics on Payment and Settlement Systems in Selected Countries* (Basle, July 2002), and may not be directly comparable with the other countries.

Table 3.26: Bank for International Settlements Committee and Bank for International Settlements, *Payment Systems in Australia* (1999), plus national sources. Data available at www.bis.org.

Table 3.27 and 3.28: OECD, *Foreign Direct Investment Statistics* (2002).

Table 3.29: OECD, *Economic Outlook 2002*, Annex Table 13.

Table 3.30: OECD, *The Sources of Economic Growth in the OECD Countries* (OECD, Paris, 2003), pp. 174–5.

4 Work and the Labour Force

Table 4.1: *OECD Historical Statistics.*

Table 4.2: Annex to *OECD Society at a Glance: OECD Social Indicators* (2nd edn, 2003). See Table GE3.2, at www.oecd.org/els/social/indicators.

Tables 4.3 and 4.4: *OECD Historical Statistics.* For Table 4.3, note that male labour force participation can equal over 100 (Swiss figure for 1960–73) because it includes males younger than 15 or over 64 who are participating in the labour force.

Table 4.5: World Bank, *World Development Indicators 2002* (CD ROM).

Tables 4.6 and 4.7: ILO, *Key Indicators of the Labour Market 2001–2002* (CD ROM). Figure for 2000 is from OECD, *Employment Outlook 2003*. Sources are harmonised with each other.

Tables 4.8 and 4.9: ILO, *Key Indicators.*

Table 4.10 and 4.11: Peter Scherer, 'Socio-economic change and social policy', in *OECD Family, Market and Community: Equity and Efficiency in Social Policy* (Social Policy Studies 21, 1997), pp. 35, 36.

Table 4.12: *OECD Historical Statistics.*

Tables 4.13 and 4.14: OECD, *Labour Force Statistics 1980–2000* (2001).

Table 4.15: ILO, *Key Indicators*. Figure for 2000 is from *OECD Employment Outlook 2003*. Sources are harmonised with each other.

Table 4.16: ILO, *Key Indicators*.

Table 4.17: OECD, *Trends in International Migration* (2000 edn), p. 49. The same data is also available at *OECD Employment Outlook 2001*, p. 173. In Australia, Canada and the United States, 'foreign' is defined by country of birth, in other countries by citizenship (see commentary on Table 1.13).

Table 4.18: OECD, *Employment Outlook 2002* (OECD, Paris, 2002), p. 316ff.

Table 4.19: *OECD Labour Force Statistics 1980–2000* (2001); OECD, *Labour Market Statistics Indicators* at www.oecd.org/scripts/cde; and *OECD Employment Outlook 2002*, Statistical Annex. Unfortunately, before 1985 there was not a harmonised definition of part-time work and the variety of national definitions makes meaningful comparison impossible.

Table 4.20: *OECD Labour Force Statistics*.

Table 4.21: OECD Labour Market Statistics Database. Median hourly earnings of part-time compared to full-time workers is from John M. Evans et al., 'Trends in Working Hours in OECD Countries', OECD Labour Market and Social Policy Occasional Paper 45, March 2001. ABS figure cited in Richard Denniss, 'Annual leave in Australia: An analysis of entitlements, usage and preferences' (Australia Institute, Canberra, Discussion Paper 56, July 2003).

Table 4.22: *OECD Employment Outlook 1996*. See also Iain Campbell and John Burgess, 'Casual employment in Australia and temporary work in Europe: developing a cross-national comparison', *Work, Employment and Society* 15(1) 2001, pp. 171–84.

Table 4.23: *OECD Employment Outlook 1995*, pp. 138, 139.

Table 4.24: OECD Labour Market Statistics Database.

Table 4.25: ILO, *Key Indicators* for 1980 and 1990; OECD, *Employment Outlook 2002*, Statistical Annex for 2000. (The two sets of data correlate almost perfectly: OECD figures for Belgium, Denmark and Ireland were used in earlier years to fill gaps in the ILO data.) Australian data is from Iain Campbell, 'Extended Working Hours in Australia', *Labour and Industry*, 13(1) August 2002, p. 95. See also Ian Watson, John Buchanan, Iain Campbell and Chris Briggs, *Fragmented Futures: New Challenges in Working Life* (Sydney, Federation Press, 2003).

Table 4.26: ILO, *Key Indicators*.

Table 4.27: For 13 countries, the source is European Industrial Relations Observatory, 'On-line Industrial relations in the EU, Japan and USA, 2000' at www.eiro.eurofound.ie/2001/11/feature/tn0111148f.html; and Richard Denniss, 'Annual leave in Australia'. Public holidays vary by state in Australia. The table figure is for New South Wales. Some states have an extra day per year.

Table 4.28: Figures are from the OECD at www.oecd.org/scripts/cde/members/LFSDATAAuthenticate.asp. The 2000 figures are from EIRO for France, Ireland and Italy, and are 1995 figures for Belgium, Denmark and Norway.

Table 4.29: These rates of annual days lost per 1000 employees are the authors' compilations based on two sources: the *ILO Yearbook of Labour Statistics 2002* (ILO, Geneva, 60th edn), plus several earlier editions for total days lost; and the OECD's figures for total employment for various years from *OECD Labour Force Statistics 1980–2000*. There were several gaps in the data for industrial disputes, which have been averaged out (a less than perfect procedure given the volatility of annual rates of industrial disputation).

Table 4.30: The sources for the first two columns are Tables 4.28 and 4.29. The principal source for the other columns is Franz Traxler, Sabine Blaschke and Bernhard Kittel, *National Labour Relations in Internationalised Markets: A Comparative Study of Institutions, Change and Performance* (Oxford University Press, Oxford, 2001), especially pp. 41, 184, 196. The wage-setting arrangements are abstracted from the more elaborate measures in this work and especially in Lane Kenworthy's

'Corporatism and Unemployment in the 1980s and 1990s', *American Sociological Review* V67, June 2002, pp. 367–88 and 'Wage-Setting Measures: A Survey and Assessment', *World Politics* 54, October 2001, pp. 57–98. See 'Wage-Setting Coordination Scores' at http://www.emory.edu/SOC/lkenworthy.

See also the very extensive data set compiled by Golden, Lange and Wallerstein at http://www.shelley.polisci.ucla.edu/data and Greg Bamber, Russell Lansbury and Nick Wailes (eds), *International and Comparative Employment Relations* (4th edn, Allen & Unwin, Sydney, 2004).

5 Government Taxes and Spending

Table 5.1: *OECD Historical Statistics 1960–1995* (1997) and *OECD Historical Statistics 1970–1999* (CD ROM, 2000).

Table 5.2: *OECD Revenue Statistics 1965–2001* (2002), pp. 73–4.

Table 5.3: Calculated from ibid.

Tables 5.4 and 5.5: ibid., pp. 78–85. In Table 5.5, means for 1970 from *OECD Revenue Statistics 1965–2000* (2001).

Tables 5.6 and 5.7: Statistical Annex to *OECD Economic Outlook 2002*.

Table 5.8: *OECD Historical Statistics 1970–1999* and *OECD Historical Statistics 1960–1995* (1997), plus Statistical Annex to *OECD Economic Outlook 2002*.

Table 5.9: Rauf Gonenc, Maria Maher and Giuseppe Nicoletti, 'The Implementation and the Effects of Regulatory Reform: Past Experience and Current Issues', *OECD Economic Studies* 32, 2001/1, p. 56.

Table 5.10: OECD, *Employment Outlook 2002*, p. 293.

Table 5.11: Figures calculated from *OECD in Figures 2002*, p. 58.

Table 5.12: Faye Steiner, 'Regulation, Industry Structure and Performance in the Electricity Supply Industry', *OECD Economic Studies* 32, 2001/1, pp. 155–6.

Tables 5.13, 5.14 and 5.15: Source for all tables for earlier periods is *OECD Historical Statistics 1970–1999* and *OECD Historical Statistics 1960–1995*. For unemployment and budget deficits, source for latest years is Statistical Annex to *OECD Economic Outlook 2002*; for per capita economic growth it is OECD, *The Sources of Economic Growth in OECD Countries* (2003); and for inflation *OECD in Figures 2002*.

6 Health

Table 6.1: *OECD Health Data 2003* (Source: OECD at www.oecd.org); 1960 data for Denmark, Germany, the Netherlands and Denmark 1970 from Howard Oxley and MacFarlan, *OECD Economic Studies* 24, 1995. On health spending on older people, see also Julia Lynch, 'The Age Orientation of Social Policy Regimes in OECD Countries' (LIS Working Paper 308, September 2001 at www.lisproject.org).

Table 6.2: Uwe Reinhardt, Peter S. Hussey and Gerard F. Anderson, 'Cross-National Comparisons of Health Systems using OECD Data, 1999', *Health Affairs* V21 N3, May 2002, p. 170. The data on doctors' incomes comes from p. 175. For 1990–2000, see Gerard F. Anderson et al., 'It's the Prices, Stupid: Why the United States is so different from other countries', *Health Affairs* V22, N3, May 2003.

Table 6.3: Annex to *OECD Society at a Glance. OECD Social Indicators Edition 2002* (OECD, Paris, 2003), Table HE5.1.

Tables 6.4 and 6.5: *OECD Health Data 2003* plus *OECD Health Data 2002*.

Table 6.6: WHO, *The World Health Report 2002*.

Table 6.7: ibid. See discussion in Chapter 2, and *OECD Health at a Glance* (2001), p. 44.

Tables 6.8–6.9: *OECD Health Data 2003* plus *OECD Health Data 2002*.

Tables 6.10 and 6.11: *OECD Health Data 2003*.

Tables 6.12–6.19: *OECD Health Data 2003* plus *OECD Health Data 2002*. For Table 6.15, discussion also draws on *OECD Health at a Glance 2001*, p. 34.

Table 6.20: 1900, 1925, 1950 and 1975 data are from Jean-Claude Chesnais, *The Demographic Transition. Stages, Patterns and Economic Implications: A Longitudinal Study of Sixty-Seven Countries Covering the Period 1720–1984* (Oxford University Press, Oxford, 1992), Appendix 4, p. 582ff. For 2000, the source is *OECD Health Data 2003*.

Table 6.21: *OECD Health Data 2003* and *OECD Health Data 2002*.

Table 6.22: UNDP, *Human Development Report 2002* at www.undp.org.

Table 6.23: Annex to OECD, *Society at a Glance*. See data at Table HE3.1 at www.oecd.org/els/social/indicators.

Tables 6.24–6.35: *OECD Health Data 2003* and *Health Data 2002*. Belgium LAY = 1995. For Tables 6.28–6.31, see also Australian Institute of Health and Welfare, *Australia's Health 2002* (AIHW, Canberra, 2002), p. 38. *Note:* In Tables 6.32–6.35, 2003 Health data for Belgium and France gave radical reduction in cancer PYLL rates.

Table 6.36: *OECD Health Data 2002*.

Table 6.37: *OECD Health Data 2003*.

Table 6.38: *OECD Health Data 2002*. Data on incidence of AIDS in Africa is from UNDP, *Human Development Report 2003* (UN, NY, 2003), pp. 41–2, 261. Data on deaths from AIDS in 2002 from UNAIDS, reported in *Economist*, 30 November 2002.

7 Education

Tables 7.1–7.4: *OECD Education at a Glance: OECD Indicators 2003*.

Table 7.5: Figure for 2000 is from ibid., Annex Table B2.1; 1994 figure is from *OECD Education at a Glance 1997*, p. 62; 1987 figure is from OECD, *Education in OECD Countries 1987–88. 1990 Special Edition*, p. 115. Note that 1994 figures for Belgium, United Kingdom, Switzerland and Norway are estimates, based on the assumption that private share was the same as in 1999; 1987 figures for Austria, Belgium, United Kingdom and Sweden are based on private share being the same as in 1994 or 1999. See Simon Marginson, *Educating Australia: Government, Economy and Citizen since 1960* (Cambridge University Press, 1997), p. 26.

Table 7.6: Figures for 1975 and 1985 are from *OECD Education at a Glance 1997*, p. 66; for 1995 and 2000, from *OECD Education at a Glance 2003*, Annex Table B4.1.

Tables 7.7–7.10: *OECD Education at a Glance 2003*.

Tables 7.11 and 7.12: *OECD Education at a Glance 2002*, Annex Tables D2.2 and D6 respectively.

Tables 7.13–7.15: *OECD Education at a Glance 2003*.

Table 7.16: *OECD Education at a Glance 2002*, Annex Table A2.2. See also Mark Considine et al., *The Comparative Performance of Australia as a Knowledge Nation*. Report to the Chifley Research Centre, June 2001, especially pp. 17, 25 and Data Appendix.

Table 7.17: OECD, *Starting Strong: Early Childhood Education and Care* (2001), p. 188.

Tables 7.18 and 7.19: OECD, *Society at a Glance 2001*, Statistical Annex A9.

Table 7.20: OECD, *Education at a Glance 2002*, Annex Table B2.1. See also OECD, *Starting*

Strong: Early Childhood Education and Care (2001), p. 189 for data on public expenditure on pre-primary education. See also UNICEF, *A League Table of Educational Disadvantage in Rich Nations* (Innocenti Report Card, 4, Florence, November 2002). See www.unicef-icdc.org.

Tables 7.21–7.24: *Literacy in the Information Age: Final Report of the International Adult Literacy Survey* (OECD and Statistics Canada, 2000).

Tables 7.25–7.27: *Literacy Skills for the World of Tomorrow: Further Results from PISA 2000*

(OECD and UNESCO, 2003) and *Knowledge and Skills for Life: First Results from PISA 2000* (OECD, 2001). Summary data also available in *OECD Education at a Glance 2002*.

Table 7.28: *OECD Society at a Glance 2002*, Statistical Annex Table and/or *OECD Education at a Glance 2002*, Table A9.

Tables 7.29–7.31: *Literacy Skills for the World of Tomorrow: Further Results from PISA 2000* (OECD and UNESCO, 2003) and/or *OECD Education at a Glance 2002*.

8 Social Welfare

Tables 8.1 and 8.2: Luxembourg Income Study at http://www.lisproject.org/keyfigures/ineqtable.htm. This study is the most extensive and long-running attempt to generate comparative data on income and inequality. Its principal research tool has been household survey data, and so the availability of data varies with the years in which surveys were conducted in different countries. Some of the data dates back to the 1970s, and some runs up to 2000, but for most countries it is more limited and sporadic, especially before the 1990s. The latest Australian data is from 1994. The Japanese figure is from the OECD. The LIS data is based on surveys of households and the data then converted to estimates for the population, based on an equivalence scale. For details, see http://www.lisproject.org/keyfigures/methods.htm. All their measures of inequality are based on disposable income.

Table 8.3: Timothy M. Smeeding and Lee Rainwater, 'Comparing Living Standards across Nations: Real incomes at the top, the bottom and the middle' (Social Policy Research Centre, University of New South Wales, Discussion Paper 120, December 2002), p. 18. The last column is from page 17.

Tables 8.4–8.6: Michael F. Forster, 'Trends and Driving Factors in Income Distribution and Poverty in the OECD Area', *OECD Labour Market and Social Policy Occasional Paper 42,*

August 2000, pp. 83–4. General government transfers include all public cash transfer benefits. Taxes include all direct income taxes, including employee social security contributions. Income groups were built on the basis of final disposable adjusted income.

Table 8.7: Howard Oxley et al., 'Income Distribution and Poverty in 13 OECD Countries', *OECD Economic Studies* 29, 1997, p. 94; and Roman Arjona et al., 'Growth, inequality and social protection', *OECD Labour Market and Social Policy Occasional Paper* 51, June 2001, p. 63. Note this table gives the OECD estimates of the Gini for final disposable income, which for some countries differ slightly from the LIS data given in Table 8.1.

Table 8.8: Timothy M. Smeeding, 'Globalisation, Inequality and the Rich Countries of the G-20: Evidence from the Luxembourg Income Study' (Social Policy Research Centre, University of New South Wales, Discussion Paper 122, December 2002), p. 22. See also Michael Forster and Mark Pearson, 'Income Distribution and Poverty in the OECD Area: Trends and Driving Forces', *OECD Economic Studies* 34, 2002/1, p. 12.

Table 8.9: LIS at http://www.lisproject.org/keyfigures/ineqtable.htm.

Table 8.10: UNDP, *Human Development Report 2002* at www.undp.org, pp. 35, 160. For a discussion of measures of poverty, see David

Brady, 'Rethinking the Sociological Measurement of Poverty', LIS Working Paper 264, August 2002. See http://www.lisproject.org. See also Adam Kuper and Jessica Kuper (eds), *The Social Science Encyclopaedia* (2nd edn, Routledge, London, 1996) and Peter Saunders, 'Poverty and deprivation in Australia', in *Year Book Australia 1996* (ABS, Canberra).

Table 8.11: UNDP, *Human Development Report 2002*, p. 160.

Table 8.12: Annex to *OECD Society at a Glance. OECD Social Indicators Edition 2002*. See data at Table EQ3.2 at www.oecd.org/els/social/indicators.

Table 8.13: *OECD Historical Statistics* (CD ROM).

Table 8.14: Willem Adema, *Net Social Expenditure* (2nd edn, OECD Labour Market and Social Policy Occasional Paper 52, 2001) Note that this includes public health spending. Data also available in Annex to *OECD Society at a Glance . . . 2002*, Table EQ4.1, www.oecd.org/els/social/indicators.

Table 8.15: Annex to *OECD Society at a Glance 2002*. See data at Table EQ3.2 at www.oecd.org/els/social/indicators.

Table 8.16: LIS at http://www.lisproject.org/keyfigures/ineqtable.htm.

Table 8.17: Annex to *OECD Society at a Glance 2002*. See data at Table EQ1.1 at www.oecd.org/els/social/indicators.

Table 8.18: ibid., Statistical Annex Table C6. Source for old people living with their children is Richard Disney and Edward Whitehouse, 'The Economic Well-Being of Older People in International Perspective: A Critical Review' (LIS Working Paper 306, June 2002), p. 7; see p. 30 for figure on home ownership among aged pensioners.

Table 8.19: Annex to *OECD Society at a Glance 2002*. See data at Table EQ3.2 at www.oecd.org/els/social/indicators.

Table 8.20: ibid. See data at Table SS10.1 at www.oecd.org/els/social/indicators.

Table 8.21: Julia Lynch, 'The Age Orientation of Social Policy Regimes in OECD Countries', LIS Working Paper 308, September 2001 at http://www.lisproject.org.

Table 8.22: OECD, *Employment Outlook 2002*, p. 325ff.

Table 8.23: UNICEF, *A League Table of Child Poverty in Rich Nations* (Innocenti Research Centre, Florence, Issue 1, June 2000); and Roderick Beaujot and Jianye Liu, 'Children, Social Assistance and Outcomes: Cross National Comparisons', LIS Working Paper 304, June 2002.

Table 8.24: LIS at http://www.lisproject.org/keyfigures/ineqtable.htm.

Table 8.25: Forster, 'Trends and Driving Factors', pp. 101–2. See also Jonathan Bradshaw et al., *The Employment of Lone Parents: A Comparison of Policy in 20 Countries* (Family Policy Studies Centre, London, 1996), p. 46.

Table 8.26: Annex to *OECD Society at a Glance 2002*. See data at Table SS9.1 at www.oecd.org/els/social/indicators.

Table 8.27: ibid., Table SS5.1.

Table 8.28: ibid., Table EQ6.

9 International Relations

Table 9.1: SIPRI data for 2000 is taken from UNDP, *Human Development Report 2002* (Oxford University Press, NY, 2002), p. 216. Figures for 1970, 1980 and 1990 are from SIPRI as found in the Comparative Welfare States Data Set, assembled by Evelyne Huber, Charles Ragin and John D. Stephens at http://www.lisproject.org. Because of revisions over time in estimating size of GDP and in reassessing data, there may be small discrepancies in the estimates of military expenditure as a proportion of GDP in earlier years. The comparison of US with other countries' 2001 military expenditure was found at http://projects.sipri.se.

Table 9.2: SIPRI data for 1970 and 2000 in the same places as for Table 9.1.

Table 9.3: SIPRI, *Yearbook 2001* (Oxford University Press, Oxford, 2001), pp. 353–8. Share of exports data is taken from UNDP, *Human Development Report 2002*, p. 216.

Table 9.4: *OECD Development Assistance* (2002), pp. 201, 207. Further figures on Australian aid are taken from AusAid, *Statistical Summary 2000–2001: Australia's Overseas Aid Program* (Commonwealth of Australia, Canberra, May 2002).

Table 9.5: *OECD Development Assistance*, p. 253.

Table 9.6: UNDP, *Human Development Report 1998* (Oxford University Press, Oxford 1998).

10 Environment

Tables 10.1–10.4: *World Resources: A Report by the World Resources Institute and the International Institute for Environment and Development* (Basic Books, NY, 2001).

Table 10.5: Hal Turton and Clive Hamilton, 'Updating per capita emissions for industrialised countries' (Australia Institute, Canberra, 2002) at www.tai.org.au.

Table 10.6: *OECD Environmental Indicators* (2001), p. 17.

Table 10.7: International Energy Agency, CO_2 *Emissions from Fuel Combustion* (IEA, Paris, 2002). See also the information sheets on global warming issued by the UN Framework Convention on Climate Change at http://unfccc.int. The quote in the first paragraph is from IEA, *Beyond Kyoto: Energy Dynamics and Climate Stabilisation* (IEA, Paris, 2001), p. 12. In addition, this commentary, like nearly all the other commentaries in this chapter, draws on two excellent Australian publications: *Measuring Australia's Progress* (ABS, Canberra, 2002) and *Australia: State of the Environment 2001. Independent Report to the Commonwealth Minister for the Environment and Heritage* (Department of Environment and Heritage and CSIRO Publishing, Melbourne, 2001).

Table 10.8: IEA, *Energy Balances of OECD Countries 1999–2000* (IEA, Paris, 2001), Annex Table A3, p. 332.

Table 10.9: ibid., Annex Table A2, p. 331.

Table 10.10: ibid., Annex Table A14, p. 345; IEA, *Electricity Information* (IEA, Paris, 2003), p. I.72.

Table 10.11: IEA, *Energy Balances of OECD Countries*, Annex Table A13, p. 344.

Tables 10.12 and 10.13: Data for 1998 is from *OECD Environmental Indicators*, pp. 27, 29; 1980 and 1990 data is from *OECD Health Data 2002* (CD ROM). Data on concentrations in air is from *Environmental Sustainability Index* (Global Leaders of Tomorrow Environment Task Force, World Economic Forum, Annual Meeting 2002), pp. 267, 277.

Table 10.14: *World Resources: A Report by the World Resources Institute and the International Institute for Environment and Development* (Basic Books, NY, 2001).

Table 10.15: Source for prices: Gerhard P. Metschies, *Prices and Vehicle Taxation* (2nd edn, October 2001, Deutsche Gesellschaft für Technische Zusammenarbeit GmbH); source for tax levels: IEA, *Energy Balances of OECD Countries*, Annex Table A17, p. 349. Discussion also draws on *OECD Economic Surveys: Australia* (2001), Ch. IV 'Enhancing environmentally sustainable growth'.

Table 10.16: *OECD Environmental Indicators*, p. 104. See also Myriam Linster and Frederique Zegel, 'Pollution Abatement and Control in OECD Countries', OECD Working Group on Environmental Information and Outlooks (July 2003), at www.oecd.org.

Table 10.17: *OECD Environmental Data Compendium: 2002 Electronic Update*, Chapter 5, p. 11, at www.oecd.org.

Table 10.18: ibid., p. 46.

Table 10.19: ibid.

Table 10.20: Mathis Wackemagel, Chad Monfreda and Diana Deumling, *Ecological Footprint of Nations. November 2002 Update*, at http://www.redefiningprogress.org/ publications. Information on OECD consumption totals is from *OECD Environmental Outlook*, p. 68.

Table 10.21: *OECD Environmental Indicators*, p. 50.

Table 10.22: *OECD Environmental Data Compendium.*

11 Science and Technology

Table 11.1: OECD, *Science and Technology and Industry Scoreboard 2001*, Annex Table 1.1

Table 11.2: ibid., Annex Table 2.1.

Table 11.3: ibid., Annex Table 9.2.1.

Table 11.4: ibid., Annex Table 3.2.

Table 11.5: ibid., Annex Table 3.2.

Table 11.6: ibid., Annex Table 4.4.

Table 11.7: OECD, *Measuring the Information Economy 2002* (2002). Data files available at www.oecd.org.

12 Telecommunications and Computing

Tables 12.1 and 12.2: For later years: *Yearbook of Statistics. Telecommunication Services 1992–2001* (International Telecommunications Union, Geneva, 2003); for earlier years: Telecommunications Indicators Handbook Stars Database (International Telecommunications Union, 2000).

Table 12.3: OECD, *Communications Outlook 2003*, Table 3.2.

Table 12.4: ibid., Table 5.1.

Table 12.5: *OECD Science and Technology Indicators 2001*, Table B4.2.

Table 12.6: OECD, *Communications Outlook 2003*, Table 5.6.

Table 12.7: ibid., Table 5.7. See also National Office for the Information Economy, *The Current State of Play: Australia's Scorecard, April 2002* at http://www.noie.gov.au.

Table 12.8: OECD, *Communications Outlook 2003*, Table 6.9.

Table 12.9: ibid., Table 6.5.

Table 12.10: ibid., Table 2.4, 2.5. See also OECD, *Communications Outlook 2001*, pp. 13, 24.

Table 12.11: OECD, *Communications Outlook 2003*, Table 2.7.

Table 12.12: ibid., Table 8.3; 1980 data calculation based on Telecommunications Indicators Handbook Stars Database (International Telecommunications Union, 2000).

Table 12.13: OECD, *Communications Outlook 2003*, Table 8.5.

Table 12.14: ibid., Table 3.12.

Table 12.15: *OECD Science and Technology Indicators 2001*. See also *Economist Technology Quarterly* 14 December 2002.

13 Media

Table 13.1: World Bank, *World Development Indicators 2002* (CD ROM).

Table 13.2: For 1970, 1980 and 1990, *UNESCO Statistical Yearbook 1999* (UNESCO Publishing, Paris, 1999), pp. IV–114ff. Source for 2000 data is Euromonitor, except for Italy, where it is a 1995 figure taken from Euromedia Research Group, *The Media in Western Europe: The Euromedia Handbook* (2nd edn, Sage, London, 1997). Italian circulation figures are very unreliable but this figure is probably more consistent with those for earlier decades. On Australia, see also Rodney Tiffen, 'Media Policy', in Judith Brett, James Gillespie and Murray Goot (eds), *Developments in Australian Politics* (Macmillan, Melbourne, 1994), p. 333.

Table 13.3: Alfonso Sanchez-Tabernero, *Media Concentration in Europe: Commercial Enterprise and the Public Interest* (European Institute for the Media, Media Monograph 16, 1993). The Australian figure is from Tiffen, 'Media Policy' and the American figure is from Benjamin Compaine and Douglas Gomery, *Who Owns the Media? Competition and Concentration in the Mass Media Industry* (3rd edn, Lawrence Erlbaum Associates, Publishers, London, 2000), p. 12.

Table 13.4: Figures for European countries are from Andries van den Broek, 'Leisure across Europe. Comparing 14 populations, conveying 1 pattern' (Paper to International Association for Time Use Research, Annual Conference, Lisbon, 2002). The American figure is from Sanchez-Tabernero, *Media Concentration in Europe*. The Australian figure is from *Australian Commercial Television 1986–1995* (Bureau of Transport and Communication Economics, AGPS, Canberra, 1996).

Table 13.5: The columns on the 1970s come from Sanchez-Tabernero, *Media Concentration in Europe* for the European countries, and for 1999, data for all countries comes from *OECD Communications Outlook 2001*.

Table 13.6: ibid. In 2003 the *OECD Communications Outlook* concentrated entirely on telecommunications and dropped broadcasting, so unfortunately much of the data in this section is from 1999.

Tables 13.7–13.9: *OECD Communications Outlook 2001*.

Table 13.10: ibid. Discussion also draws on: ABC Triennial Funding Submission Summary 2003–2006, p. 3, available at http://www.abc.net.au. See also Glenn Withers, 'Funding Public Service broadcasters', *Southern Review* 35(1) 2002, pp. 107–19; McKinsey & Company, *Public Service Broadcasters Around the World* (1999).

Note: The most difficult issue of classification was to exclude the American PBS – an innovative and exemplary broadcaster – from this definition of public broadcasters. It began much later than American commercial TV, starting only in 1969 as a coalition of educational broadcasters in different cities. On air, it advertises itself as a private corporation. Compared with public broadcasters in other countries, it is a much more minor presence in the total media structure, and its sources of funding are much more decentralised. According to the OECD, in 1999 it received $250 million in public funding, which comprised 34% of its income and 0.3% of total American television revenue. PBS's total budget comprised 2.0% of total TV revenue, and it had less than 0.5% of the audience.

Tables 13.11 and 13.12: *OECD Communications Outlook 2001*.

Table 13.13: World Bank, *World Development Indicators 2002*.

Tables 13.14 and 13.15: *OECD Communications Outlook 2001*.

14 Family

Table 14.1: 1980 figures and 1999 figures for EU countries are from *European Social Statistics Demography 2001* at http://europa.eu.int. Australian figures are from ABS, *Year Book Australia 2003 – Population. Marriages and Divorces* at http://www.abs.gov.au/Ausstats, and the latest figure is for 2001. Figures for other European and North American countries come from UN Economic Commission for Europe, *Trends in Europe and North America 2001* (UN, NY, 2001). New Zealand figures from Maureen Baker, *Families, Labour and Love* (Allen & Unwin, Sydney, 2001). Japanese figures from *Japan Almanac 1998* (Asahi Shimbun, Tokyo). Figures for other countries from UN Statistics Division, *The World's Women 2000: Trends and Statistics* at http://unstats.un.org/unsd/demographic/ww2000/table2a.htm. Other Australian data comes from ABS, *Year Book Australia 2003* and Ruth Weston et al., 'Families in Transition', *Family Matters 60*, Spring/Summer 2001 (Australian Institute of Family Studies).

Table 14.2: Annex to *OECD Society at a Glance*. OECD *Social Indicators Edition 2002*. See data at Table GE5.1 at www.oecd.org/els/social/indicators. Data for Ireland from Economic Commission for Europe, *Trends in Europe and North America 2001* (UN, Geneva, 2001).

Table 14.3: OECD, *Society at a Glance*, Table GE5.1.

Table 14.4: ibid., Table GE4.2, supplemented by R. Lesthaeghe and G. Moors, 'Recent trends in fertility and household formation in the industrialised world', *Review of Population and Social Policy*, 9, 2000.

Table 14.5: 2000 figures for EU countries from European Social Statistics Demography 2001 edn at http://europa.eu.int and from Innocenti Report Card, *A League Table of Teenage Births in Rich Nations* (UNICEF, Florence, 2001) at www.unicef-icdc.org. Figures for 1970, 1980, 1990 are from Jean-Paul Sardon, 'The Demographic Situation of Europe and the Developed Countries Overseas: An Annual Report', *Population: An* *English Selection* Vol. 12, 2000, pp. 293–328. See also UK Government, *Social Trends 2003 edition* (HMSO, London, p. 41).

Table 14.6: Lesthaeghe and Moors, 'Recent trends'. See also 'The Demographic Situation of Europe'.

Table 14.7: Jonathan Bradshaw et al., *The Employment of Lone Parents: A Comparison of Policy in 20 Countries* (Family Policy Studies Centre, London, 1996). Data on single mothers in Canada and Switzerland from Luxembourg Income Study at http://www.lisproject.org/keyfigures/ineqtable.htm

Tables 14.8 and 14.9: Others from Innocenti Report Card, *A League Table of Teenage Births*.

Table 14.10: Peter Scherer, 'Socio-economic change and social policy', in OECD, *Family, Market and Community: Equity and Efficiency in Social Policy, Social Policy Studies*, 21, 1997.

Table 14.11: Others from Innocenti Report Card, *A League Table of Teenage Births*. OECD quote is from *Society at a Glance 2003*, p. 80.

Table 14.12: Michael Forster and Mark Pearson, 'Income Distribution and Poverty in the OECD Area: Trends and Driving Forces', *OECD Economic Studies*, 34, 2002/1. See also R. Percival and A. Harding, 'The Costs of Children in Australia Today' (February 2003) available at NATSEM website: http://www.natsem.canberra.edu.au.

Tables 14.13 and 14.14: Annex to *OECD Society at a Glance 2002*. See data at Tables SS4.2 and SS4.1 respectively, at www.oecd.org/els/social/indicators.

Table 14.15: *OECD Employment Outlook 2002*, p. 78.

Table 14.16: Sex Discrimination Unit, HREOC, *Valuing Parenthood – Options for Paid Maternity Leave: Interim Paper 2002* at http://www.hreoc.gov.au/sex_discrimination/pml/valuing_parenthood.pdf; Anne Helene Gauthier, *The State and the Family: A Comparative Analysis of Family Policies in Industrialised*

Countries (Clarendon Press, Oxford, 1996), p. 170; *Economist*, 28(2) 1998; David W. Kalisch, Tetsuya Aman and Libbie A. Buchele, *Social and Health Policies in OECD Countries* (OECD Labour Market and Social Policy Occasional Papers 33, July 1998); Steve O'Neill and Bronwen Shepherd, 'Paid Maternity Leave' (Parliament of Australia, Department of the Parliamentary Library, September 2002). Available at http://www.aph.gov.au/library. Since these were published, New Zealand has adopted paid maternity leave.

Table 14.17: Gauthier, *The State and the Family*, p. 170. Source for 2001 figures is OECD, *Taxing Wages 2000–2001* (OECD, Paris, 2002), p. 98. See also Peter McDonald, 'The "toolbox" of

public policies to impact on fertility – a global view' (ANU, Demography Program, 2000).

Table 14.18: Jonathan Bradshaw and Naomi Finch, *A Comparison of Child Benefit Packages in 22 Countries* (Department for Work and Pensions Research Report 174, Leeds, 2002) at http://www.york.ac.uk/inst/spru/research/summs/chilben22.htm.

Table 14.19: *OECD Society at a Glance 2001*, Statistical Annex A9. Source for Publicly Funded Child Care data: Becky Pettit and Jennifer Hook, 'The Structure of Women's Employment in Comparative Perspective' (LIS Working Paper 330, September 2002), p. 18.

15 Gender

Tables 15.1–15.3: UNDP, *Human Development Report 2002* (Oxford University Press, NY, 2002); for Table 15.2 see especially p. 35.

Table 15.4: *OECD Employment Outlook 2002*, p. 97.

Table 15.5: UNDP, *Human Development Report 2002*.

Table 15.6: Jeanne A. Batalova and Philip N. Cohen, 'Premarital Cohabitation and Housework: Couples in Cross-National Perspective', *Journal of Marriage and Family* 64, August 2002, p. 748.

Table 15.7: *OECD Health Data 2002* (CD ROM) available year for Australia, Japan = 1998; Denmark = 1995; 1980 figures for Canada and France are interpolated.

Table 15.8: UNDP, *Human Development Report 2002*.

Table 15.9: *OECD Employment Outlook 2002*, p. 74.

Table 15.10: Figures for 2003 from the Inter-Parliamentary Union, found at http://www.ipu.org; for 1991, UNDP, *Human Development Report 1993*; for 1975 and 1987, Jan-Erik Lane, David McKay and Kenneth Newton, *Political Data Handbook. OECD Countries* (2nd edn, Oxford University Press, Oxford, 1995), p. 134.

Table 15.11: Figures for 2000 from UNDP, *Human Development Report 2002*; 1994 figures from UN Statistics Division at http://www.un.org/Depts/unsd/ww2000/table6a.htm.

Table 15.12: *Economist* 9 October 1999.

16 Lifestyle

Table 16.1: Francis G. Castles, *Comparative Public Policy: Patterns of Post-War Transformation* (Edward Elgar, Cheltenham, UK, 1998), p. 251. Figures for 2000 come from *Economist*, 30 March 2002, and Euromonitor accessed

at http://www.euromonitor.com. Historical comparison between Australia and the United Kingdom comes from Lois Bryson, 'Australia: The transformation of the Wage-Earners' Welfare State', in Pete Alcock and Gary

Craig (eds), *International Social Policy: Welfare Regimes in the Developed World* (Palgrave, NY, 2001), p. 71.

Other Australian data is from the ABS reports accessed at http://www.abs.gov.au and Peter Saunders, 'Household Income and its Distribution', *Australian Economic Indicators*, June 2001 (ABS, Canberra).

Table 16.2: *Economist*, 31 May 2003.

Table 16.3: Economic Commission for Europe Statistical Division, *Trends in Europe and North America 2001* (UN Economic Commission for Europe, NY, 2001), p. 74. Household sizes for 1981 come from *Eurostat Yearbook 1996* (2nd edn, Office for Official Publications of the European Communities, Luxembourg, 1996).

Table 16.4: Figures are all from the market analysts Euromonitor, accessed at http://www.euromonitor.com. See also *Japan Almanac 1998* (Asahi Shimbun, Tokyo, 1998).

Table 16.5: *OECD Health Data 2003* (Source: OECD at www.oecd.org). Based on FAO data.

Table 16.6: *OECD Environmental Data Compendium: 2002 Wildlife* at www.oecd.org, p. 15. Based on FAO data.

Tables 16.7 and 16.8: *OECD Health Data 2003*. Based on FAO data. See also AIHW, *Australia's Health 2002* (AIHW, Canberra, 2002), p. 140.

Tables 16.9–16.12: *OECD Health Data 2003*. See also AIHW, *Australia's Health 2002*, p. 121ff.

Tables 16.13 and 16.14: Global Market Information Database, published by Euromonitor, accessed at http://www.euromonitor.com.

Table 16.15: *OECD Health Data 2002* (CD ROM).

Tables 16.16 and 16.17: Global Market Information Database. See also WHO data at http://www3.who.int/whosis/alcohol. Other Australian data is from AIHW, *Australia's Health 2002*, pp. 142–3.

Tables 16.18–16.20: *OECD Health Data 2003*. Michael de Looper and Kuldeep Bhatia, *International Health: How Australia Compares* (AIHW, Canberra, 1998), p. 141.

Tables 16.21–16.23: International Metalworkers' Federation, *The Purchasing Power of Working Time 2002: An International Comparison of Average Net Hourly Earnings 2001* (International Metalworkers' Federation, Geneva, 2002). Available at http://www.imfmetal.org.

17 Social Problems

Table 17.1: Gordon Barclay and Cynthia Tavares, 'International comparisons of criminal justice statistics 2000' at http://www.homeoffice.gov.uk/rds/.

Table 17.2: UN International Victims of Crime Survey at http://ruljis.leidenuniv.nl/group/jfcr/www/icvs/Index.htm; also available at www.unicri.it/icvs/it. There have been four waves of surveys: in 1989, 1992, 1996 and 2000. Not all countries participated in all waves. The final column reports 2000 data where available (1996 data Austria). The first column reports the 1992 data, and uses 1989 if not available (Norway, West Germany, Japan). Although crime rates for 1992, 1996 and 2000 are fairly consistent, in several countries there was a jump between 1989 and 1992, probably

for methodological rather than substantive reasons.

Table 17.3: *OECD Health Data 2002*. The Australian rate for firearms use can be found at http://www.abs.gov.au, while the American figure is taken from http://www.ojp.usdoj.gov/bjs/guns.htm. See also *Australian Crime. Facts and Figures 2002* (Australian Institute of Crime, available at http://www.aic.gov.au) and *Crime and Justice Bulletin* (NSW Bureau of Crime Statistics and Research 57, May 2001).

Table 17.4: UN International Drug Control Programme figures, reported in *OECD Society at a Glance 2002*. See data at Table CO7.2 at www.oecd.org/els/social/indicators.

Table 17.5: Seventh UN Survey of Crime Trends and Operations of Criminal Justice Systems, covering the period 1998–2000. Available at http://www.odccp.org/odccp/crime_cicp_surveys.html.

Tables 17.6 and 17.7: UN International Crime Victims' Survey, at http://ruljis.leidenuniv.nl/group/jfcr/www/icvs/Index.htm.

Table 17.8: Figures for 1982, 1990 from OECD, *Society at a Glance*, Statistical Annex; and Economic Commission for Europe Statistical Division, *Trends in Europe and North America 2001: The Statistical Yearbook of the Economic Commission for Europe* (UN, Geneva, 2001). Irish figure for 1990 = 1994. Figures for 2000 are from Roy Walmsley, *World Prison Population List* (3rd edn). (Findings 166; UK Home Office, London, 2002). See also Marie Gottschalk, 'Black Flower: Prisons and the Future of Incarceration', *Annals of the American Academy of Political and Social Sciences* 582, July 2002, p. 206.

Table 17.9: Economic Commission for Europe Statistical Division, *Trends in Europe and North America 2001*, p. 229 plus Amnesty International at http://www.web.amnesty.org.

Table 17.10–17.12: *OECD Health Data 2002* (CD ROM).

Table 17.13: *OECD Society at a Glance 2001*, Statistical Annex Table D3.

Table 17.14: UNICEF Innocenti Research Centre, *A League Table of Child Deaths by Injury in Rich Nations* (UNICEF, Florence, 2001) available at http://www.unicef-icdc.org.

Table 17.15: Patrick Heuvelink, 'An international comparison of adolescent and young adult mortality', *Annals of the American Academy of Political and Social Sciences* 580, March 2002.

Tables 17.16 and 17.17: *OECD Health Data 2002*.

Table 17.18: World Bank, *World Development Indicators 2002* (CD ROM).

Table 17.19: Productivity Commission. Table data is from Appendix N, Gaming Machines and some international comparisons, while the text draws on several chapters, and in addition ABS, *Gambling Industries, Australia* (18 July 2002) at http://www.abs.gov.au/ausstats. The US congressional report information comes from *Economist* 26 June 1999.

18 Values and Attitudes

Table 18.1: D. B. Barrett (ed.), *World Christian Encylopaedia* (Oxford University Press, Oxford, 1982), reproduced in Jan-Erik Lane, David McKay and Kenneth Newton, *Political Data Handbook: OECD Countries* (Oxford University Press, Oxford, 1991), p. 21.

Table 18.2: Ronald Inglehart et al., *World Values Surveys* (Computer file from Inter-University Consortium for Political and Social Research, Institute for Social Research, Ann Arbor, Michigan.) There have been three waves of the World Values Survey. The first was carried out in the years 1981–84, the second between 1990 and 1993 and the third from 1995 to 1997. Each wave has used a different survey questionnaire, though many items have been used in all three. Altogether over 50 countries have participated in one or more of the world values surveys. Australian researchers took part in the first and third but not the second waves. New Zealand has not participated in any of the surveys, and so is not included in the tables in this section. The other 16 countries all participated in the second wave, and eight of them (plus Australia), participated in the third. The analysis in the tables combines second and third wave data (i.e. all 1990s) for the 17 countries. Hereafter referred to as World Values Survey.

Table 18.3: World Values Survey.

Table 18.4: Ruut Veenhoven, *Happiness in Nations: Subjective appreciation of life in 56 nations 1946–1992* (Studies in Socio-Cultural Transformation, Erasmus University of Rotterdam, 1993).

Tables 18.5–18.7: World Values Survey.

Table 18.8: ibid. In evaluating confidence in each institution, respondents were offered a four-point scale: A great deal; Quite a lot; Not very much; None at all. The table combines those responding a great deal and quite a lot.

Table 18.9–18.21: World Values Survey.

TABLES

1 People

2 Government and Politics

3 Economy

4   Work and the Labour Force

5   Government Taxes and Spending

6   Health

7   Education

8   Inequality and Social Welfare

9 International Relations

10 Environment

11 Science and Technology

12 Telecommunications and Computing

13 Media

14 Family

15 Gender

16 Lifestyles and Consumption

17   Crime and Social Problems

18   Religion, Values and Attitudes